Matthew

Westminster Bible Companion

Series Editors

Patrick D. Miller
David L. Bartlett

Matthew

THOMAS G. LONG

Westminster John Knox Press
LOUISVILLE • LONDON

For David, Susie, Melanie, Paul, Carly,
Rebekah, Nathan, and Daniel

"Your children will be like olive shoots around your table. . .
May you see your children's children."
(Psalm 128:3, 6)

Book design by Publisher's WorkGroup
Cover design by Drew Stevens

First edition
Published by Westminster John Knox Press
Louisville, Kentucky

This book is printed on acid-free paper that meets the American National Standards Institute Z39.48 standard. ♾

PRINTED IN THE UNITED STATES OF AMERICA

06 07 08 09 — 10 9 8 7 6

Library of Congress Cataloging-in-Publication Data
Long, Thomas G., date.
  Matthew / Thomas G. Long. — 1st ed.
     p.   cm.—(Westminster Bible companion)
  Includes bibliographical references.
  ISBN-13: 978-0-664-25257-1 (alk. paper)
  ISBN-10: 0-664-25257-5 (alk. paper)
  1. Bible. N.T. Matthew—Commentaries. I. Title. II. Series.
BS2575.3.3L66   1997
226.2'077—dc21   97-16942

Contents

Series Foreword

This series of study guides to the Bible is offered to the church and more specifically to the laity. In daily devotions, in church school classes, and in listening to the preached word, individual Christians turn to the Bible for a sustaining word, a challenging word, and a sense of direction. The word that scripture brings may be highly personal as one deals with the demands and surprises, the joys and sorrows, of daily life. It also may have broader dimensions as people wrestle with moral and theological issues that involve us all. In every congregation and denomination, controversies arise that send ministry and laity alike back to the Word of God to find direction for dealing with difficult matters that confront us.

A significant number of lay women and men in the church also find themselves called to the service of teaching. Most of the time they will be teaching the Bible. In many churches, the primary sustained attention to the Bible and the discovery of its riches for our lives have come from the ongoing teaching of the Bible by persons who have not engaged in formal theological education. They have been willing, and often eager, to study the Bible in order to help others drink from its living water.

This volume is part of a series of books, the Westminster Bible Companion, intended to help the laity of the church read the Bible more clearly and intelligently. Whether such reading is for personal direction or for the teaching of others, the reader cannot avoid the difficulties of trying to understand these words from long ago. The scriptures are clear and clearly available to everyone as they call us to faith in the God who is revealed in Jesus Christ and as they offer to every human being the word of salvation. No companion volumes are necessary in order to hear such words truly. Yet every reader of scripture who pauses to ponder and think further about any text has questions that are not immediately answerable simply by reading the text of scripture. Such questions may be about historical and geographical details or about words that are obscure or so loaded with meaning that one cannot tell at a glance what is at stake. They may be about

the fundamental meaning of a passage or about what connection a particular text might have to our contemporary world. Or a teacher preparing
for a church school class may simply want to know: What should I say
about this biblical passage when I have to teach it next Sunday? It is our
hope that these volumes, written by teachers and pastors with long experience studying and teaching the Bible in the church, will help members of
the church who want and need to study the Bible with their questions.

The New Revised Standard Version of the Bible is the basis for the in-
terpretive comments that each author provides. The NRSV text is presented at the beginning of the discussion so that the reader may have at
hand in a single volume both the scripture passage and the exposition of
its meaning. In some instances, where inclusion of the entire passage is not
necessary for understanding either the text or the interpreter's discussion,
the presentation of the NRSV text may be abbreviated. Usually, the whole
of the biblical text is given.

We hope this series will serve the community of faith, opening the
Word of God to all the people, so that they may be sustained and guided
by it.

Introduction

The Gospel of Matthew was not originally written to be a book in the Bible. It was intended instead to be a resource for a particular congregation—a group of worshiping, serving, praying, striving Christians. Eventually, of course, what became "The Gospel of Saint Matthew" was included in the Bible and became the first book in what we now call the New Testament; but the author of this book, who wrote many decades before there was a fixed New Testament, would surely have been surprised by this. He never imagined that his Gospel would be clasped between the black leather covers of something called "The Holy Bible" and read by countless people down through the centuries. He wrote his Gospel to speak to a very immediate and urgent congregational crisis. His original readers were wrestling with how to be faithful to Jesus Christ in a changing world and in difficult circumstances, and the Gospel of Matthew was a first-aid manual for this church in the midst of a struggle.

THE FIRST READERS OF MATTHEW

Often, the first question we ask about a biblical book is, Who wrote it? However, the place to start with Matthew is, Who *read* it? The original recipients, the first readers, of this Gospel can be called "Matthew's church," and when we understand something about his church, who they were and what concerned them, much else about the Gospel falls into place. Unfortunately, Matthew does not provide a handy thumbnail description of his church, and there is very little evidence about Matthew's church outside of the New Testament. So, we have to build a portrait of them out of small clues and threads of evidence found here and there in the Gospel itself. We cannot know everything with certainty, but we can make some good and educated guesses.

Perhaps most strikingly, it appears that Matthew's church was a congregation of Jews who had become Christians. In fact, some scholars think
that Matthew wrote to a small group of "Jesus believers" who were still active members of a Jewish synagogue, but in all probability Matthew's
church had already left the synagogue to form a separate Christian group.
Indeed, the angry verbal arrows aimed at the Jewish authorities all
through Matthew, combined with the fact that Matthew consistently
refers to the Jewish houses of prayer as "*their* synagogues," reinforces the
view that Matthew's church had only recently walked out of—or been
thrown out of—the local synagogue and that the relationship between
Matthew's church and "the synagogue across the street" was antagonistic.
Indeed, much of the angry rhetoric against Jews in Matthew's Gospel
must be understood not in the modern context of Christians versus Jews
(in which case it could well be taken as anti-Semitic) but as a family dispute among loyal and devout Jews—those who held that Jesus of Nazareth
was the Messiah and those who did not.

Because the members of Matthew's church had a Jewish heritage, their
scriptures were what is now called the Old Testament, and their traditions
of worship and devotion were firmly shaped in the cradle of the synagogue. Thus, now that they had ventured into the uncharted waters of
Christianity, the major question facing them was the relationship between
the old and the new, between the cherished traditions and commandments
of their Jewish legacy and the new demands of Christian discipleship.

At first, Matthew's church probably posed the question this way: "How
do we add our new faith in Jesus to our Jewish heritage?" Gradually, however, as they actually split from the synagogue and as they began to be
seen—and to see themselves—as a Christian church apart from the synagogue, the question was almost surely reversed. Now they wondered,
"How do we incorporate our Jewish customs and legacy into the new reality of the Christian faith?"

Matthew addresses this question over and over in his Gospel, and his
answer remains consistent: Christians do not throw out either their Jewish birthright or the Old Testament law. To the contrary, Jesus Christ fulfills rather than abolishes the Law and the Prophets.

Another factor affecting Matthew's church was that it was almost certainly located in an urban, cosmopolitan, and prosperous environment.
There were Gentiles in town, as well as Jews. There were ideas and
philosophies of all kinds being hawked in the public arena. The marketplace flourished with commerce. Matthew's church was not in some backwater village where everybody looked the same, believed the same, and
belonged to the same clan. Matthew's setting was one where people had

to carve out an identity among many competing possibilities, and much about the Gospel is aimed at helping Matthew's church define its distinct Christian character in a confusing world of rival claims.

Some have suggested that Matthew's church may have been in the great city of Alexandria; others have proposed the Palestinian port city of Caesarea Maritima. However, the most frequent suggestion is that Matthew's church was located in Antioch of Syria, a sizable metropolis with a large, mixed population. The fact that Ignatius, the Bishop of Antioch, seems to know the Gospel of Matthew and to quote from it as early as A.D. 110 favors this view.

Also, Matthew's church was facing what may politely be called "the Gentile question." As Jews, they were schooled to avoid Gentiles, to think of Gentiles as pagans, and to preserve their religious and ethnic identity by firmly maintaining the barriers between themselves and the seething Gentile masses. They believed that God's promises to Israel were pledges made to a select and favored people. But Matthew's church also believed and trusted Jesus, and the gospel Jesus taught has centrifugal force; like the prophetic tradition in the Old Testament, the gospel kept pushing them out into the larger world.

WHO WROTE THE GOSPEL OF MATTHEW? WHEN? WHAT WERE THE SOURCES?

Although we now call this gospel "The Gospel according to Matthew," actually we do not know the name of its author. The title was added at a later date and was not a part of the original text. The idea that it was written by Matthew the tax collector, who was one of Jesus' disciples and who appears in the pages of the Gospel (Matt. 9:9; 10:3), has been around since the second century; but most scholars seriously question this claim for a number of reasons, including the crucial fact that the author of Matthew depends heavily upon the Gospel of Mark as a source for his material and does not seem to have the kind of eyewitness perspective that one of Jesus' disciples would have.

Even though we cannot identify the author by name, we can infer some things about him from his style and from the content of his book. In all likelihood, the author of Matthew was male, Jewish, steeped in the Hebrew scriptures, and an accomplished writer in Greek. It may be that he has left at least one "fingerprint" in his Gospel when he records that "every scribe who has been trained for the kingdom of heaven is like the master of a household who brings out of his treasure what is new and what is old"

(Matt. 13:52). The author of Matthew writes and thinks like a "scribe," a scholar of the commandments, and, although he honors the old commandments, he is also "trained for the kingdom," and he understands the ancient law to take on new life and direction in Jesus.

Most scholars agree that Matthew was written sometime about A.D. 80–85, or about half a century after the crucifixion of Jesus. The author of Matthew appears to have employed several sources for his material. His main source is the Gospel of Mark, which was written a decade or more earlier. Though Matthew does not copy Mark exactly and freely amends much of the Markan material, he still incorporates approximately 90 percent of Mark into his Gospel.

However, the Gospel of Mark was not Matthew's only source. Some of the material we find in Matthew also appears in very similar form in the Gospel of Luke, and scholars have conjectured that the authors of these two Gospels must have had access to a common collection of the sayings of Jesus. Even though no copy of this document is extant (and, in fact, some suggest that it was an oral source rather than a written one), scholars have nonetheless given it a name: Q (the first letter in the German word for "source"). Beyond Mark and Q, the rest of the material in Matthew comes from either some special written sources that Matthew had or the stories that circulated orally in Matthew's community.

THE STRUCTURE OF THE GOSPEL OF MATTHEW

People who like neat outlines are troubled by the Gospel of Matthew. It is notoriously difficult to discern the organizational pattern of this Gospel, and no one has ever been able to propose a structure that satisfactorily explains the whole of Matthew's plan. The likely reason for this is not that Matthew is disorganized, but that the structure of Matthew is richer and more complex than any single outline can embody.

At least two major organizational principles seem to have governed the writer of Matthew. First, he follows the basic plot design of the Gospel of Mark and, as such, presents the life and ministry of Jesus in three large segments: (1) the identity of Jesus the Messiah (Matt. 1:1–4:11); (2) the message and ministry of Jesus (Matt. 4:12–16:20); and (3) the death and resurrection of Jesus (Matt. 16:21–28:20).

Second, Matthew gathers many of the teachings of Jesus into five rather long discourses, and these punctuate the action of the Gospel as follows:

Narrative Action—Matthew 1—4
   First Discourse: The Sermon on the Mount—Matthew 5—7
Narrative Action—Matthew 8—9
   Second Discourse: A Manual for Missionaries—Matthew 10
Narrative Action—Matthew 11—12
   Third Discourse: The Parables—Matthew 13
Narrative Action—Matthew 14—17
   Fourth Discourse: Living Together as the Church—Matthew 18
Narrative Action—Matthew 19—23
   Fifth Discourse: Jesus Teaches about the Future Judgment—Matthew 24—25
Narrative Action—Matthew 26—28

MATTHEW'S THEOLOGICAL PURPOSE

The Gospel of Matthew ends with the eleven disciples gathered around the risen Christ and hearing a startling word: "All authority in heaven and on earth has been given to me. Go therefore and make disciples of all nations" (Matt. 28:18–19). This is the climactic moment in the Gospel, and the whole of Matthew can be seen as an attempt to answer the questions raised by this scene: Who is Jesus? How did he obtain "all authority in heaven and on earth," and what kind of authority is this? Why is this tiny band of half-believing people being sent into the maelstrom of the world, to "all nations," and what is it that they are supposed to say and do when they get there?

In this final scene, everything is there. Jesus, who from the very beginning of Matthew's Gospel is the Messiah, is now seen to be the Lord of all peoples, and the disciples are in the position of learners, students clustered around the risen Christ. "For Matthew, to be a Christian is to be a pupil of Jesus" (Luz, *The Theology of the Gospel of Matthew*, 142), and the mission of the church is to go out into the world and to enable all human beings to become students of the living Christ. They do not go alone, however, for Jesus himself is present in their midst, giving life and peace, mercy and hope. "I am with you always, to the end of the age" (Matt. 28:20).

1. The Identity
of Jesus the Christ
Matthew 1:1–3:12

JESUS' FAMILY TREE
Matthew 1:1–17

1:1 An account of the genealogy of Jesus the Messiah, the son of David, the son of Abraham.

² Abraham was the father of Isaac, and Isaac the father of Jacob, and Jacob the father of Judah and his brothers, ³ and Judah the father of Perez and Zerah by Tamar, and Perez the father of Hezron, and Hezron the father of Aram, ⁴ and Aram the father of Aminadab, and Aminadab the father of Nahshon, and Nahshon the father of Salmon, ⁵ and Salmon the father of Boaz by Rahab, and Boaz the father of Obed by Ruth, and Obed the father of Jesse, ⁶ and Jesse the father of King David.

And David was the father of Solomon by the wife of Uriah, ⁷ and Solomon the father of Rehoboam, and Rehoboam the father of Abijah, and Abijah the father of Asaph, ⁸ and Asaph the father of Jehoshaphat, and Jehoshaphat the father of Joram, and Joram the father of Uzziah, ⁹ and Uzziah the father of Jotham, and Jotham the father of Ahaz, and Ahaz the father of Hezekiah, ¹⁰ and Hezekiah the father of Manasseh, and Manasseh the father of Amos, and Amos the father of Josiah, ¹¹ and Josiah the father of Jechoniah and his brothers, at the time of the deportation to Babylon.

¹² And after the deportation to Babylon: Jechoniah was the father of Salathiel, and Salathiel the father of Zerubbabel, ¹³ and Zerubbabel the father of Abiud, and Abiud the father of Eliakim, and Eliakim the father of Azor, ¹⁴ and Azor the father of Zadok, and Zadok the father of Achim, and Achim the father of Eliud, ¹⁵ and Eliud the father of Eleazar, and Eleazar the father of Matthan, and Matthan the father of Jacob, ¹⁶ and Jacob the father of Joseph the husband of Mary, of whom Jesus was born, who is called the Messiah.

¹⁷ So all the generations from Abraham to David are fourteen Sgenerations; and from David to the deportation to Babylon, fourteen generations; and from the deportation to Babylon to the Messiah, fourteen generations.

The Gospel of Matthew begins in a strange fashion, with a genealogy, a family tree, a lengthy recital of the names of the ancestors of Jesus. "Abraham was the father of Isaac," Matthew tells us, "and Isaac was the father of Jacob, and Jacob. . . . " On Matthew chants: So-and-so was the father of so-and-so, and he was, in turn, the father of so-and-so, the drumbeat of his voice tapping out over forty generations worth of Jesus' kinfolk.

To contemporary readers, this is certainly a curious and seemingly tedious way for Matthew to inaugurate his Gospel. After all, Matthew's account of the story of Jesus is a narrative of great suspense and emotional depth; and, as every skillful storyteller knows, a good story needs a gripping beginning. No alert novelist of today would dare risk numbing the readers at the novel's beginning by droning out a genealogical lesson.

But Matthew does. Why?

As it turns out, Matthew has excellent and strategic reasons for beginning his Gospel with a genealogy of Jesus. He wants to present his central character—Jesus—in a way that arouses the interest and touches the key concerns of his first readers. Matthew knows his readers. Jewish by heritage and Christian by conviction, they are no longer in the synagogue, but they are not yet sure how to be the "church." Their community is built on the foundation of Israel, but the doors and windows are increasingly being opened to the non-Jew, to the Gentile. They are, then, betwixt and between, the product of two cultures, attempting to balance the demands of the old with the dramatic challenges of the new.

In the early days of these Christian converts, their main question was no doubt how to weave their new trust in Jesus as Messiah into the well-worn cloth of their Judaism. Now, with the passage of time and separation from the synagogue, the question has reversed: How do we weave the strands of our Jewish heritage into the new fabric of Christian faith? In the light of our experience of Jesus Christ, what are we to make of the Torah, the law, the patriarchs, the prophets, the priests, and the kings of Israel? These are among the burning questions, Matthew knows, on the minds of his readers, and, by beginning with the genealogy of Jesus, he immediately addresses these concerns in a most engaging and pertinent manner.

Matthew's readers, unlike modern ones, would not have found this genealogy of Jesus to be dull reading at all. To the contrary, they would surely have been quite engaged by and interested in this family tree of Jesus. Encountering this genealogy, full of familiar names from the Jewish scriptures, would be much like our discovering an old family Bible in the attic and finding in it a record of our own ancestors' births, marriages, and deaths. Matthew's congregation would be familiar with the genealogical form, recognizing it as a literary pattern in their own scriptures (what we now call the Old Testament; see Ruth 4:18–22 and 1 Chronicles 2, for example).

They would not read the genealogy as a mere list, but rather as an anthology of stories, each name triggering an outpouring of memories. "Abraham was the father of Isaac," Matthew records, and the very mention of those two persons compels the readers to recall the story of that day when Abraham heard the chilling command, "Abraham, take your son, your only son Isaac, whom you love . . . and offer him as a burnt offering" (Genesis 22). "Solomon was the father of Rehoboam," states the genealogy, and the readers remember Solomon—his wealth, his wisdom, the day he determined which of two women was truly the mother of a disputed-over child. And they remember Rehoboam—his military ambitions, his stubbornness, his troubled kingly reign. On and on continues the list of names, some famous, some not as well known, but many of them—Jacob and Boaz and Jesse and David—calling forth well-loved and often-told stories. In contrast to the modern reader, who is apt to skim biblical genealogies, viewing them as tedious "filler," Matthew's readers would probably have read this section slowly, pausing to relish and remember at many places along the way.

However, Matthew opens his Gospel with a genealogy not only to intrigue his readers by triggering their memory of the tradition, but also to introduce his central character, Jesus, as the ultimate goal of that tradition. By sounding the roll call of Jesus' ancestors, Matthew presents Jesus' true *identity* as the essence of all that Israel meant. In the same way that we would say of a baby born to musical parents, "How could she not be a musician? She's got it in her blood, you know," so Matthew describes the streams of previous generations of Jewish history blending into a great and flowing heritage coursing toward Jesus. Jesus embodies the heart and soul of Israel; "he's got it in his blood."

Notice that before Matthew begins mustering the generations, he provides a brief preamble, a sort of headline at the beginning: "An account of the genealogy of Jesus the Messiah, the son of David, the son of Abraham" (Matt. 1:1). This heading serves to guide our reading of the genealogy and gives us an important clue about Matthew's purpose. If we were to say about a particular little girl, "Janice is certainly her grandmother's child," we would not literally mean, of course, that Janice was the biological child of her grandmother. We would mean that there is something about Janice that especially reminds us of her grandmother. Perhaps she looks much like her, or maybe they share similar personalities. What we would mean is, if you really want to know the essence of Janice as a person, look at her grandmother.

Just so, Matthew's headline gives us insight into the core of Jesus' identity. In effect, Matthew tells us, "I am going to enumerate the whole list of the generations of Jesus' ancestors, but the real key to knowing Jesus is to keep this in mind: He is especially the child of David and of Abraham and, by virtue of that, the Messiah."

In order to grasp the full import of this, we need to explore more deeply three marks of identification—Messiah, son of David, and son of Abraham:

1. *Messiah.* This term, also translated "Christ," technically means "anointed one." It has deep roots in the Old Testament, where kings and priests and others were anointed as a sign that they were appointed by God and set apart for their sacred tasks. Gradually the term "messiah" began to be associated most strongly with kingly leadership, and not with just any king, but with the hope that God would produce an *ideal* king for Israel, a king who would fulfill every hope of the nation for well-being. This king would be of the lineage of David (see, for example, Jer. 33:15 and Ezek. 37:24–25) and would bring peace, wisdom, righteousness, and prosperity to Israel. When Matthew identifies Jesus as the "Messiah," he means that the longed-for "King of kings" has now come, and all of the deepest messianic hopes of Israel have come to fulfillment in Jesus.

2. *Son of David.* Matthew's description of Jesus as "son of David" has two related meanings, one larger, one smaller. First, in the smaller sense, David was considered the most impressive, powerful, and able of Israel's kings, the high-water mark in Israel's national leadership. To be called a "son of David" was like describing an American politician as "Washingtonian," "Lincolnesque," and "Truman-like" in the same breath.

In the larger sense, the prophets had promised that the Messiah would spring out of a "branch from David"; that is, would be a lineal descendant of David and an heir to God's promises to preserve David's line forever (see 2 Sam. 7:11–17). But is Jesus a "son of David" in this way, too? Technically, no, because his unusual birth separates him from the Davidic line, biologically speaking. So, how can Matthew claim, on the one hand, that Jesus is "son of David" and, on the other hand, tell his readers that Jesus is, strictly considered in terms of human ancestors, exclusively the "son of Mary." Matthew recognizes this dilemma, of course; and the account of Joseph, which immediately follows the genealogy, is presented, in part, to address this question.

3. *Son of Abraham.* When Matthew calls Jesus the "son of Abraham," he recalls the stories of Abraham in Genesis, almost surely pointing to two aspects of Abraham's life. First, Abraham was a pioneer of faith in God, and, second, he was the one to whom God promised, "I will make of you

a great nation . . . and in you all the families of the earth shall be blessed" (Gen. 12:1–3). Jesus is a "son of Abraham" because he, too, is a pioneer in trusting God, and through him all the nations are called to a new identity as disciples (Matt. 28:19).

There are, however, some odd features to be found in this family tree of Jesus. First, the list of Jesus' forebears is tidily divided into three equal sets of generations, each set punctuated by a major figure or event of Jewish history: fourteen generations from Abraham to David, fourteen generations from David to the Babylonian exile, and fourteen generations from the exile to Jesus (Matt. 1:17).

It seems here that Matthew is more interested in making a theological point than in being genealogically precise. Almost every commentator has noted that this pattern of sets of uniformly numbered generations is an artificial creation, for each of these three time periods covers too many years to be spanned by only fourteen generations.

So why does Matthew insist on such neat math? The strongest explanation for the pattern of fourteens in the genealogy is that Matthew is following a Jewish literary technique of dividing epochs into equal parts, thereby making the theological claim that history is not haphazard, but under the control of God. Jesus' appearance in history, Matthew wants us to know, was no mere accident, no random birth. Other human births may be the result of a spin of the biological wheel of fortune, but not Jesus' birth. It was orderly, arranged, the result of God's careful plan and providence. What might appear to be the uncontrolled flood of the generations can now, in retrospect, be seen for what it truly is—a mighty river whose channel was carved out by the guiding and arranging hand of God, causing all of Israel's history to flow in orderly fashion toward this critical moment and person.

A second unusual feature of Matthew's presentation of the family tree of Jesus is the unconventional appearance of the names of five women in the list: Tamar, Rahab, Ruth, "the wife of Uriah" (Bathsheba), and, finally, Mary. The presence of these names would surprise, perhaps even shock, Matthew's first readers, because genealogies of that time usually listed only the male descendants. Imagine looking through the 1949 yearbook of West Point or some other traditionally all-male school and finding, here and there among the hundreds of photographs of young men, the pictures of five women. These exceptions to the rule would catch our attention and make us wonder about the circumstances that caused them to be included. Why, we would ask, are they there? Why, indeed? It is plain that Matthew has a point to make here, but what is it? Several explanations of what these five women have in common have been suggested, but most of these are not very persuasive. The best explanation for the presence of the names of these five women is that they represent, each in a unique way, a surprising interruption, an unexpected turn in the path of Israel's history. Read the story of how Tamar, refusing to allow her father-in-law, Judah, to throw her on society's rubbish heap, took the initiative to secure her rightful place by cleverly tricking Judah into admitting his fault (Genesis 38). Or read about Rahab's courageous collaboration with Hebrew spies (Joshua 2), about how Bathsheba moved from being the victim of David's lust to become the mother of the wise king Solomon (2 Samuel 11–12), or about how Ruth, a Moabite, restored the fortunes of her mother-in-law and, indeed, of all Israel through her determination (Ruth 1–4). In each account, these women stand surprisingly in the stream of Israel's history, causing unexpected ripples and crosscurrents. Taking the stories together, we begin to see that God does not write history only in straight lines, but also with dashes, swirls, and loops. Jesus' birth is yet another curved line of holy history, and Mary's name appears in the genealogy marking another spot where the sacred river flows in ways that human design could never have anticipated.

So, Matthew opens his Gospel with a genealogy and, by doing so, discloses the true identity of Jesus. To his Jewish-Christian readers, Matthew's message is unmistakable: Jesus is the culmination of all of Israel's history, the goal of their messianic hopes, the embodiment of their hunger for a true and perfect king, and the fulfillment of the promise to become a blessing to the whole human race. Jesus is Messiah; he is son of David; and he is son of Abraham. For Matthew's first readers, to belong to Jesus is not to leave their Jewish heritage behind, but rather to have discovered the One toward whom it was always leading.

But Matthew's first readers would almost surely have come to the end of the genealogy with an abrupt and uneasy sensation, a gnawing anxiety that something was amiss. Matthew traced the lineage of Jesus from Abraham on down, counting off the generations like steel links of a chain, but the chain suddenly breaks at the very last link: "Joseph the husband of Mary, of whom Jesus was born, who is called the Messiah" (Matt. 1:16). If Jesus is to be the Messiah, he must be the descendant of David, but it is *Joseph* who is David's descendant, and Jesus, we are told, is the biological child of Mary, not Joseph. After struggling mightily to show that Jesus has all of Israel's heritage in his blood, Matthew now seems to acknowledge that he doesn't actually have it in his blood at all. Matthew has marched, step by step, through the generations of the house of David, only to step sideways at the last moment. How can Jesus claim to be the "son of David"? Matthew is aware of this perplexity, and he responds by telling the astounding story of Joseph.

AN AMAZING BIRTH
AND A NEW RIGHTEOUSNESS
Matthew 1:18–25

1:18 Now the birth of Jesus the Messiah took place in this way. When his mother Mary had been engaged to Joseph, but before they lived together, she was found to be with child from the Holy Spirit. [19] Her husband Joseph, being a righteous man and unwilling to expose her to public disgrace, planned to dismiss her quietly. [20] But just when he had resolved to do this, an angel of the Lord appeared to him in a dream and said, "Joseph, son of David, do not be afraid to take Mary as your wife, for the child conceived in her is from the Holy Spirit. [21] She will bear a son, and you are to name him Jesus, for he will save his people from their sins." [22] All this took place to fulfill what had been spoken by the Lord through the prophet:

[23] "Look, the virgin shall conceive and bear a son,
and they shall name him Emmanuel,"

which means, "God is with us." [24] When Joseph awoke from sleep, he did as the angel of the Lord commanded him; he took her as his wife, [25] but had no marital relations with her until she had borne a son; and he named him Jesus.

When beginning students in science are studying an eclipse or some other solar event, they are told never to look directly at the sun but only indirectly. Similarly, Matthew shows us the miraculous birth of Jesus mainly indirectly, reflected in the life of Joseph. We perceive how this holy event transforms Joseph, and we see in Joseph the model for our response.

What does Matthew tell us about Joseph? First, he records his marital situation. Joseph and Mary are "engaged," but not yet living together. According to the customs of their time, Joseph and Mary would have been involved in a two-stage process of marriage. The first stage was betrothal, or "engagement," but in a much stronger sense than that word conveys in our time. When a woman was "engaged" to a man in ancient Palestine, she was bound to him through formal words of consent. Betrothal would often occur when the woman was quite young, twelve or thirteen years old. At this point, she was already viewed by society as the man's wife, waiting a period of time, usually about a year, for the second stage of the process, which was moving out of her family's home and into the home of her husband. Joseph and Mary are between these two stages.

Next, Matthew tells us Joseph's moral situation. Joseph is "a righteous man," which means that he is scrupulous about keeping the commandments of God, the Old Testament law, striving to live his life in harmony with the will of God, to follow to the letter all of the provisions of the Mosaic law.

But because Joseph is a righteous man, he is also a man in profound ethical crisis. Mary has been found to be pregnant, and Joseph knows that he is not the father. To Joseph's mind, then, Mary has been unfaithful to him. What does the law say about this? The commandments are clear: The woman is to be cast aside, perhaps even put to death (see Deut. 22:13–30). Joseph is a compassionate man, so he intends to dismiss Mary quietly; but he is a righteous man, and he will not swerve from the law. Mary is to be dismissed. The law commands it; the righteous Joseph will do it.

But just at this point, the story takes one of those surprising turns, one of those unexpected "sideways moves" of God's providence hinted at in the genealogy. An angel appears to Joseph in a dream and reveals to Joseph that what appears to him to be a moral outrage is, in fact, a holy disruption. The child in Mary's womb is not a violation of God's will, but an expression of it, a gift from the Holy Spirit.

The opening words of the angel are, "Joseph, son of David, do not be afraid to take Mary as your wife," and they are significant in two main ways. First, Joseph's identity as a descendant of the royal line of David is underscored. He is to become, in a sense, the "adoptive father" of Jesus, thereby bridging the break in the genealogical chain. Jesus will indeed be "the son of David," but by divine intervention and not in the customary biological manner. Second, Joseph is told not to be *afraid*. Joseph was *afraid* to keep Mary, *afraid* to violate the Mosaic law. Here at the beginning of the Gospel of Matthew, an angel says what another angel will say at the end of the Gospel, "Fear not, God is doing a new thing in the world" (see Matt. 28:5).

In the light of this new thing that God is doing in Jesus, Joseph is given a new commandment, a new and higher law, and urged to a new and higher righteousness: "Take Mary as your wife and give to the son she is about to bear the name Jesus." In other words, the angel tells Joseph to shatter the confines of the old law in order to keep the new law. Will Joseph remain "a righteous man" in the old sense, or will he respond to God's new act and become a genuinely righteous man walking God's new path of obedience? Joseph's dilemma mirrors, then, the predicament of Matthew's readers, pulled in different directions by their Jewish roots and their Christian experiences. How shall they be righteous? In the old way or in the new? Matthew's answer is clear: "Unless your righteousness exceeds that of the scribes and Pharisees, you will never enter the kingdom of heaven" (Matt. 5:20).

Joseph is transformed by the announcement of the angel; he is astoundingly responsive to this new and strange deed of God. He followed not the old commandment, but the new: He took Mary as his wife, and he named the child Jesus. He stands, therefore, at the beginning of Matthew's Gospel as the prototype for true righteousness and faithful discipleship. He has moved, as Matthew hopes all of his readers will move, from his own understanding of righteousness to God's.

Joseph becomes, therefore, a model for the Christian life. He learns that being truly righteous does not mean looking up a rule in a book and then doing the "right thing"; it means wrestling with the complexities of a problem, listening for the voice of God and then doing God's thing. To be a faithful disciple means prayerfully seeking to discover what God is doing in the difficult situations we face. How is God at work here to show mercy and saving power? Being righteous is never simply being pure and good in the abstract; genuine righteousness is always joining with God to do God's work in the world.

As Matthew completes the story of Jesus' birth, he seems less interested in the actual occurrence of the birth than about what the baby was named. Only in a minor clause are we informed that the birth of a son took place (Matt. 1:25); the emphasis falls upon the fact that Joseph named him "Jesus," the Greek form of the Hebrew name Joshua (Matt. 1:25). The reason for this is that Matthew wants to underscore two truths: (1) the mission of Jesus is to put God's salvation into action, and (2) Jesus is, by being named by Joseph, grafted into the lineage of David. The angel, who commanded Joseph to call the child Jesus "for he will save his people from their sins" (Matt. 1:21), was making a pun by connecting Jesus' name and his ministry of salvation ("Jesus" is derived from the Old Testament name "Joshua," which means "God helps" or "God saves").

Of course, only God can save people from sins, and that theological fact prompts Matthew to provide a second name for Jesus—"Emmanuel," a name that Matthew helpfully translates as "God is with us" (Matt. 1:23). Jesus saves people from their sins because in him "God is with us"; that is, through Jesus God's saving power is made present for sinful humanity.

Where does Matthew get the name Emmanuel? He draws it from a verse in Isaiah (Isa. 7:14) and states that the birth of Jesus "took place in order to fulfill" this word of the prophet (Matt. 1:22). Readers of Matthew will soon discover, as they make their way through the Gospel, that this strategy of quoting Old Testament prophecy and announcing its fulfillment in the life of Jesus is a favorite of Matthew's. Nearly a dozen times Matthew explicitly connects something about Jesus to a passage from one of the prophets (see Matt. 1:22–23; 2:15, 17–18, 23; 4:14–16; 8:17; 12:17–21; 13:14–15, 35; 21:4–5; 27:9–10).

To say that Jesus' birth "fulfills" Isaiah 7:14 does not mean that the prophet Isaiah had Jesus in mind when these words were first produced.

Indeed, Isaiah originally spoke this prophecy to a political and military crisis in his own time (see Isaiah 7), but Matthew hears the words of Isaiah pointing to more than this original moment in history.

Careful readers will notice that Matthew's quotation of Isaiah 7:14 is not exact. In fact, Matthew's version differs from the original in two important ways. First, Matthew identifies the woman who will bear a son as "the virgin," whereas Isaiah simply calls her "the young woman." The reason for this is that Matthew is quoting the Septuagint (the Greek version of the Old Testament), in which Isaiah's Hebrew word for "young woman" has been translated as "virgin." This translation is a happy one from Matthew's point of view, because he describes Mary as a virgin until Jesus' birth (Matt. 1:25).

The second difference between Isaiah and Matthew is that Isaiah's version indicates that it is the woman who names the child Emmanuel, but Matthew changes this to read "*they* shall name him Emmanuel" (Matt. 1:23). This alteration is to allow for the fact that Joseph gives Jesus his name—to clear the way for Joseph to claim this child he did not father, to name him, and to bring him into the household of David.

THE VISIT OF THE WISE MEN
Matthew 2:1–12

2:1 **In the time of King Herod, after Jesus was born in Bethlehem of Judea, wise men from the East came to Jerusalem,** [2] **asking, "Where is the child who has been born king of the Jews? For we observed his star at its rising, and have come to pay him homage."** [3] **When King Herod heard this, he was frightened, and all Jerusalem with him;** [4] **and calling together all the chief priests and scribes of the people, he inquired of them where the Messiah was to be born.** [5] **They told him, "In Bethlehem of Judea; for so it has been written by the prophet:**
[6]**'And you, Bethlehem, in the land of Judah,**
   are by no means least among the rulers of Judah;
  for from you shall come a ruler
    who is to shepherd my people Israel.'"
[7] **Then Herod secretly called for the wise men and learned from them the exact time when the star had appeared.** [8] **Then he sent them to Bethlehem, saying, "Go and search diligently for the child; and when you have found him, bring me word so that I may also go and pay him homage."** [9] **When they had heard the king, they set out; and there, ahead of them, went the star that they had seen at its rising, until it stopped over the place where the child was.** [10] **When they saw that the star had stopped, they were overwhelmed with joy.** [11] **On entering the house, they saw the child with Mary**

his mother; and they knelt down and paid him homage. Then, opening their treasure chests, they offered him gifts of gold, frankincense, and myrrh. 12 And having been warned in a dream not to return to Herod, they left for their own country by another road.

In telling the story of the visit of the star-gazing wise men from the East to worship the child Jesus, Matthew immediately captures the imagination of his readers. Like the exotic perfumes brought as gifts by the mysterious travelers, this narrative lingers enticingly in the senses. Indeed, almost any church Christmas pageant and many Christmas cards will disclose the power of this narrative to invite imaginative embellishment. Where the Gospel of Matthew is silent or spare, carols and artists and preachers and prayerful believers have filled in the blanks with vivid pictures. Over the years, the wise men have been transformed into kings, clothed in lavish royal robes and impressive turbans. Though Matthew does not tell us how many visitors there were, we have supplied this detail and almost always count them as three, the carol "We Three Kings" now fixed in our minds. Some even provide names for the wise men—Gaspar, Melchior, and Balthasar—and identify them as representing different races.

In summary, every generation of Christians has added to Matthew's story details taken from its own time and place. All of this speculation and embellishment may seem way beyond the strict bounds of Matthew's text, but it may not be outside of Matthew's overall aim. "[T]his imaginative reflection on the magi is not too far from Matthew's own intent," comments Raymond Brown. "In the persons of the magi Matthew was anticipating the Gentile Christians of his own community" (Brown, *The Birth of the Messiah*, 199).

In other words, Matthew himself was seeing in the wise men symbols of the Gentile Christians of his own day. Just as the wise men began by following a star, Gentile Christians started with nature alone as a source of God's revelation. It was only later that they were introduced to the scriptures. Also, just as the wise men from the East came to the child Jesus and worshiped him, so Gentile Christians had come to the point of worshiping Jesus Christ, the "king of the Jews." Thus, for Matthew the wise men were not only characters in the story of the birth of Jesus; they were also representative of people in his own community, Gentiles who adored Christ. So, when we dress the neighborhood children in yellow bathrobes and send them traipsing down the church aisle toward the manger, carrying foil-wrapped boxes of simulated gold, frankincense, and myrrh, we are, in a real sense, doing what Matthew himself did, seeing the characters of this ancient story in the light of the faithful people around us.

The story of the wise men is dramatically intricate, full of political intrigue. It primarily involves interplay among the following powerful characters:

King Herod (Matthew 2:1)

"Herod" is not the name of a particular individual but of a family, members of which governed Palestine and some of the surrounding areas, under Roman authority, for a century and a half starting in 55 B.C. Six of the "Herods" are mentioned or alluded to in the New Testament: Herod the Great (the Herod in this passage); three of his sons, Herod Archelaus (see Matt. 2:22), Herod Philip, who gave his name to the rebuilt town, Caesarea Philippi (see Matt. 16:13), and Herod Antipas, the Herod most often mentioned in the New Testament and the one who cast a shadow over Jesus' ministry (see Matt. 14:1); a grandson, Herod Agrippa I (Acts 12:1); and a great-grandson, Herod Agrippa II (Acts 25:13).

The principal villain of this story of the wise men is Herod the Great, the ruler of Palestine from about 37 B.C. to his death, which scholarship reckons to have been in 4 B.C. He was known as a strict Roman loyalist and one who mounted large-scale building projects to signal to his Roman superiors the importance of his Jewish kingdom. In terms of personality, he was known as a moody, cruel, and sometimes violent ruler, one who often imprisoned or executed even members of his own family.

Wise Men from the East (Matthew 2:1)

The wise men, or Magi, have been variously described as magicians, astrologers, Persian priests, or as a combination of all three. Matthew does not identify them with precision, although the fact that they followed a star surely adds weight to the idea that they were astrologers. Although we cannot say for certain who these wise men were or where they were from, beyond the vague "from the East," it is more important for Matthew's purposes to see them as startling symbols of the Gentile world suddenly arrived in the heartland of Judaism.

Chief Priests and Scribes (Matthew 2:4)

When Matthew lumps together the chief priests and the scribes, he means to gather in a single phrase all of the top leaders of the religious establishment in Jerusalem, something like saying "the Fortune 500 CEOs and all their corporate accountants." Technically, there was only one "chief priest," or high priest, but the plural "chief priests" evidently refers to the current high priest and former high priests, together with their families. The "scribes" were religious scholars, learned men who were experts in the Mosaic, or Old Testament, law.

This story shows how these characters—Herod, the chief priests and scribes, and the wise men—relate to the birth of Jesus. What happens is that the wise men, complete outsiders to the laws and prophecies of Israel, arrive in Jerusalem seeking the "king of the Jews" because they have observed a phenomenon in nature, the rising of a star. Their arrival produces two responses, both of them theologically important to Matthew.

The first response is that Herod "and all Jerusalem with him" (Matt. 2:3) are frightened. If the wise men are seeking a child who is "king of the Jews," this obviously calls into question the standing and stability of Herod himself, who is currently the political, Roman-authorized king of the Jews. The birth of the true Messiah undermines all pretenders to the throne. Indeed, the gospel exposes all human pretense and threatens all who would dominate others. Whenever the true nature of the gospel is understood by the powers-that-be, all swaggering despots turn fearful.

Each Christmas the Metropolitan Museum of Art in New York City has a nativity scene on display. In many ways, the elements are familiar— the shepherds, the cattle, the holy family. What is unusual, however, is that the manger is placed, not in the rustic setting of Bethlehem, but amid the fallen and ruined columns of a once-proud Roman building. The theological claim of this nativity scene is clear, and it is the same as that of Matthew: The humble birth of the Christ child shakes the foundations of the world and announces the fall of the mighty.

The second response to the inquiry of the wise men is that Herod calls together the religious officials for some Bible study to determine where the Messiah would be born. Putting their heads together, and combining Micah 5:2 and 2 Samuel 5:2, the authorities inform Herod that the Messiah, the "ruler who is to shepherd my people Israel" is to be born in "Bethlehem, in the land of Judah" (Matt. 2:6). Jesus, the great shepherd-king, is to be born in the village of David, the shepherd-king. The deceitful Herod then passes this information on to the wise men who head to Bethlehem, following the star to the house where the child Jesus and his mother are.

Note the interplay here between scripture and nature. Through nature (the star), the wise men know *that* the Christ has been born, but they need the scripture to tell them *where*, that is, take them to the place where they can worship him. In other words, they learn something of God from nature, but their knowledge is still incomplete. Behind this is Matthew's theological conviction that, even as the Gentiles stream into the Christian faith, they come to a faith defined and grounded in the Law and the Prophets. "Do not think that I have come to abolish the Law or the prophets," Jesus states. "I have come not to abolish but to fulfill" (Matt. 5:17). The wise men, as precursors of all the Gentile faithful, come to worship the Christ, but, like all Gentiles, they need the scripture to do so fully.

On the other hand, simply knowing the scripture is not enough to bring one to authentic Christian worship. The chief priests and scribes know the Bible, but they miss the Messiah. They understand the prophecies, but they do not come to the place of worship. Herod is taught the scripture, but his stated intention to "go and pay him homage" is a sinister, finally murderous, lie.

In terms of contemporary religious experience, the world is full of "stars in the East"—events in nature, personal experience, and history that point toward the mystery of God. The seemingly permanent Berlin Wall comes swiftly down in a sudden political storm, a daffodil opens in all its spring beauty and glory, a troubled relationship is healed, a child is born— all these experiences and countless others draw our attention to the divine mystery that pervades and pushes through human events. Without the defining and clarifying word of scripture, however, we could not recognize these holy moments for what they are; we would not be able to see God's face clearly in them. Like the wise men, we would be aware that something had happened, but we would not, without the revelation of God in scripture, know where or how to worship.

It is also true, though, that mastering the Bible is no guarantee of true worship. One can, like the chief priests and the scribes, know the biblical facts but completely miss the deeper biblical truth. One can memorize verses, but forget the gospel. One can recite the kings of Israel and overlook the King of Creation. One can, like Herod, be in favor of studying the scripture and still be on the wrong side of God's will.

The irony of the story of the wise men is that the religious insiders, those who knew the Law and the Prophets and who ought to have rejoiced at the Messiah's birth, were either indifferent to what they knew or, worse, were entangled in a plot against the Christ; whereas the outsiders, those who were about as distant as could be, theologically and geographically, from concern about the Jewish Messiah, end up joyfully lavishing gifts upon him and kneeling before him in worship.

The story of the wise men ends with their being warned in a dream not to go back to Herod, but to go directly to their own country (2:12). God spoke to Joseph, a true son of David, through a dream, and now God speaks to these Gentiles, sons of another family, in the same manner. As they head over the horizon, this is the last we see or hear of the wise men. They have entered the scene for a brief, but theologically significant, moment in the story of Jesus. But, even though we do not meet the wise men again, we will remember them at the end of Matthew's Gospel, when the disciples, like the wise men, pay homage to Jesus and, then, are told: "Go . . . and make disciples of all nations" (Matt. 28:19). Once visitors from the Gentile world came to the center of Israel to worship the king of the Jews; now the flow is to be reversed. The disciples, under the command of that king, are to venture out from their worship into the lands of the Gentiles, calling all nations to obey the Christ.

THE ESCAPE TO EGYPT
Matthew 2:13–15

> 2:13 **Now after they had left, an angel of the Lord appeared to Joseph in a dream and said, "Get up, take the child and his mother, and flee to Egypt, and remain there until I tell you; for Herod is about to search for the child, to destroy him."** [14] **Then Joseph got up, took the child and his mother by night, and went to Egypt,** [15] **and remained there until the death of Herod. This was to fulfill what had been spoken by the Lord through the prophet, "Out of Egypt I have called my son."**

This passage describes how Joseph, warned by God in a dream, fled with Mary and the boy Jesus away from the murderous Herod to the safety of Egypt. Once again, Joseph demonstrates that he is an example of the "higher righteousness" sought by Jesus (see comment on Matt. 1:18–25). Joseph's faith is not just a "book religion"; he is alert to the presence of God in the moment, ready to obey God's unpredictable Spirit. He listens to the voice of God's messenger and, without hesitation, leaves behind his familiar surroundings to enter the strange land of Egypt.

For the third time, Matthew tells a story about Jesus and, as is his custom, connects it to a specific Old Testament prophetic text. In this case, the flight into Egypt is linked to Hosea 11:1: "Out of Egypt I called my son." Some commentators have thought it curious that Matthew cites a verse about coming *out* of Egypt to underscore a narrative about Jesus and his family going *into* Egypt. Probably the best rendering of Matthew's thought is that it was clearly necessary for Jesus to be taken into Egypt in order for the prophecy about his coming out of Egypt to be fulfilled.

The larger theme, of course, is that Jesus is traveling the same path as did the people of Israel. The quoted passage in Hosea ("out of Egypt I called my son") refers to the exodus, to Israel being brought out of Egypt. Matthew is emphasizing the truth that Jesus is the embodiment and fulfillment of the mission and the identity of Israel. Everything that God called Israel to be, Jesus is.

We begin to see here the faint outlines of a theological theme that will become ever more prominent in Matthew—the hidden hand of God ruling human history. Viewed from the surface, we have in this story of Herod's deadly intrigue a sad bit of human history, one that is replayed almost every day in the newspapers. A political tyrant, quaking in his boots, is on the edge of engaging in a reign of terror to preserve his grip on the population. An innocent family is caught in the power play and must flee for their lives. Events seem out of control; one wonders if history is "a tale told by an idiot," full of suffering but impoverished in meaning. Matthew, however, sees beneath the surface. Although the course of human affairs seems to be scribbled at random, another story, this one a confident narrative of grace and redemption, is being firmly written by the hidden hand of God.

THE MURDER OF BETHLEHEM'S CHILDREN
Matthew 2:16–18

2:16 **When Herod saw that he had been tricked by the wise men, he was infuriated, and he sent and killed all the children in and around Bethlehem who were two years old or under, according to the time that he had learned from the wise men.** [17] **Then was fulfilled what had been spoken through the prophet Jeremiah:**
   [18] **"A voice was heard in Ramah,**
      wailing and loud lamentation,
   Rachel weeping for her children;
      she refused to be consoled, because they are no more."

Here the fury of a threatened Herod finds its most tragic expression. Figuring, on the basis of information obtained from the wise men, that Jesus was two years old or younger, Herod decides on a "permanent solution" to this threat from a new king of the Jews. He sends his militia to Bethlehem and murders all the male children up to two years of age.

Just as Jesus' birth in Bethlehem and his flight into Egypt were anticipated in scripture, even this horrific deed of Herod was, in its own way, a fulfillment of scripture, too. But here, in describing Herod's act of un-mitigated evil, Matthew changes his usual formula for introducing Old Testament prophecy. Instead of using language that implies that God caused this event to happen, such as "this was done in order to fulfill what was spoken by the prophet," Matthew, in this case, simply informs the reader that the crushing blow of Herod "fulfilled what had been spoken through the prophet Jeremiah." The subtle change in wording is impor-tant, for it stops firmly short of claiming that the murder of the children was God's will. The message is not that God summons evil to accomplish divine purposes, but that the scripture knows the tragic human destruc-tion woven into the fabric of history and that not even evil in its most cat-astrophic form, evil as cold and merciless as the murder of innocent chil-dren, can destroy God's ability to save.

As we gaze into the brutal face of Herod, we realize that we have seen this face before. Centuries before, another tyrant, Pharaoh, also at-tempted to eradicate God's purposes by killing all male children (Exod. 1:15–22). In that story, the infant Moses was spared in order to become the agent of God's salvation, just as in this story Jesus, the "new Moses," is spared in order to become a savior.

If we have seen Herod's hatred before in Pharaoh, we know that we will see it again and again. Pharaoh, Herod, Hitler, Stalin—the chroni-cles of human history are full of dictators who believe they can secure their power through murder and genocide. This text stands as a confi-dent word that the despots of this world come and go, but that God's will outlasts and overrules them all. This theological conviction can be seen in terse form in Matthew 2:19: "When Herod died, an angel of the Lord suddenly appeared. . . . " Herod is dead, but the Word of the Lord con-tinues. Herod is dead, but the messenger of the Lord is still appearing, speaking, guiding, protecting. Herod is dead, but the mercy of God is everlasting.

Herod's massacre, Matthew tells us, is a fulfillment of Jeremiah 31:15, in which Rachel, representing all Hebrew mothers, weeps over her sons' being taken into exile. Matthew may have selected this text for two rea-sons. First, the Old Testament figure Rachel, one of the wives of Jacob, was associated in Jewish lore with the village of Bethlehem. A popular leg-end, perhaps known to Matthew, placed Rachel's tomb there. Second, the Jeremiah passage refers to the Exile, and this extends the concept of Jesus' walking through the history of Israel. The story of the child Jesus has now been connected to the three major places in Israel's history: Bethlehem of Judea, the city of David; Egypt, the place from which the exodus occurred; and Ramah, the place of mourning for the Exile.

FROM EGYPT TO NAZARETH
Matthew 2:19–23

2:19 **When Herod died, an angel of the Lord suddenly appeared in a dream to Joseph in Egypt and said,** [20] **"Get up, take the child and his mother, and go to the land of Israel, for those who were seeking the child's life are dead."** [21] **Then Joseph got up, took the child and his mother, and went to the land of Israel.** [22] **But when he heard that Archelaus was ruling over Judea in place of his father Herod, he was afraid to go there. And after being warned in a dream, he went away to the district of Galilee.** [23] **There he made his home in a town called Nazareth, so that what had been spoken through the prophets might be fulfilled, "He will be called a Nazorean."**

Matthew wants to accomplish two purposes in this passage. First, because it was well known among early Christians that Jesus was from Nazareth, Matthew needed to account for how Jesus got from his birthplace, Bethlehem, to his hometown, Nazareth. So this passage recounts that when Herod died, Joseph returned to Israel from Egypt with his family. Upon discovering, however, that Herod's son Archelaus, every bit the cruel vulture that his father was, ruled over Judea, Joseph sought safety in the relatively more secure region of Galilee, settling down in the town of Nazareth.

Matthew's second purpose was more difficult to achieve. He wants to elaborate the theme of Jesus' geographical movements, including this move to Nazareth, as reenactments of Israel's pilgrimage and as fulfillments of scripture. So far, this has worked out nicely. Jesus was born in Bethlehem, and that city is clearly mentioned in Old Testament prophecy. Jesus fled to Egypt, and Egypt is, of course, the place of Israel's captivity. But now Jesus goes to Nazareth, and the problem is that Nazareth is never mentioned in the Old Testament. How can Matthew manage to connect Nazareth and the Old Testament?

He does so with a pun (like the one the angel made about Jesus' name in Matthew 1:21). The place name Nazareth is not in the Old Testament, and there is no Old Testament verse that reads "He will be called a Nazorean." The word *Nazareth* is, however, similar in spelling and sound to two words that are in the Old Testament: "nazarite," which refers to a person set apart as holy (see Numbers 6 and Judg. 13:5, 7); and the Hebrew word for branch, *neser*, which in Isaiah 11:1 is used to refer to the messiah. So, when Matthew tells us that Jesus made his home in Nazareth in order to fulfill "what had been spoken through the prophets," he uses the less precise plural form ("the prophets"), perhaps to indicate the more general character of this connection, and he probably means to evoke one or both of these plays on words: Jesus was indeed consecrated as holy, like a nazarite, and he was surely the messianic "branch" from the line of David.

The message of the angel that "those who were seeking the child's life are dead" (Matt. 2:20) is also theologically significant. It is obviously a crucial detail of the story being told, but it is an allusion as well—both backward to Moses (to whom similar words were spoken; see Exod. 4:19) and forward to the crucifixion. Indeed, the whole of Matthew 2 contains a number of foreshadowings of the crucifixion. For example, here, at the beginning of Jesus' life, the wise men call him "the King of the Jews," a title that will reappear when Pilate and his cohorts use it for him at the end (Matt. 27:11, 29, 37). The "chief priests and scribes of the people" are involved here at the outset, and they will reappear in threatening roles at the conclusion as well (Matt. 26:47, 57; 27:1). But most of all, a sinister pall of death is cast over the story of the Christ-child, reminding the reader that the birth of Jesus is already marked by his death, that Christmas stands in the shadow of Good Friday.

JOHN THE BAPTIST
Matthew 3:1–12

> 3:1 **In those days John the Baptist appeared in the wilderness of Judea, proclaiming,** 2 **"Repent, for the kingdom of heaven has come near."** 3 **This is the one of whom the prophet Isaiah spoke when he said,**
>> **"The voice of one crying out in the wilderness:**
>> **'Prepare the way of the Lord,**
>>> **make his paths straight.'"**
> 4 **Now John wore clothing of camel's hair with a leather belt around his waist, and his food was locusts and wild honey.** 5 **Then the people of Jerusalem and all Judea were going out to him, and all the region along the Jordan,** 6 **and they were baptized by him in the river Jordan, confessing their sins.**
> 7 **But when he saw many Pharisees and Sadducees coming for baptism, he said to them, "You brood of vipers! Who warned you to flee from the wrath to come?** 8 **Bear fruit worthy of repentance.** 9 **Do not presume to say to yourselves, 'We have Abraham as our ancestor'; for I tell you, God is able from these stones to raise up children to Abraham.** 10 **Even now the ax is lying at the root of the trees; every tree therefore that does not bear good fruit is cut down and thrown into the fire.**
> 11 **"I baptize you with water for repentance, but one who is more powerful than I is coming after me; I am not worthy to carry his sandals. He will baptize you with the Holy Spirit and fire.** 12 **His winnowing fork is in his**

hand, and he will clear his threshing floor and will gather his wheat into the granary; but the chaff he will burn with unquenchable fire."

Matthew adds to the *who* and the *where* of Jesus a word about the *when* of Jesus' ministry. In the very first verse of his Gospel, Matthew made a rich and complex theological claim about the *who* of Jesus, that Jesus is "the Messiah, the son of David, the son of Abraham" (Matt. 1:1). From that point on, Matthew has employed a variety of means to spell out this identity of Jesus. In order to save the world, God laid out a way of obedience and called Israel to journey along that road of promise and mission to places like Canaan, Egypt, and into exile. Matthew tells us that Jesus is the *where* of salvation because, even in his infancy, he traveled that pathway. Now, in chapter 3, Matthew expands the *who* and the *where* by announcing the *when* of Jesus' identity. Jesus is not only the climax of Israel's generations and the one who retraced Israel's path of obedience; he is also the one whose coming into the world brought down the curtain on the old era and raised the curtain on the new. Here, Matthew wants us to know that the turning of the epochs is in the hand of God; that, when Jesus was born, all of human history swung on its hinges, the massive plates of cosmic time shifted under the surface, and the Day of God's Salvation dawned.

As the door to a new era swings open, John the Baptist is the ideal hinge. He is dressed like the old age, but he points to the new. His preaching style is vintage Old Israel; his message paves the way for the New Israel. He appears to have wandered out of some retirement home for old prophets, but he announces the arrival of one who is even greater than the prophets. He baptizes with the water of the ancient Jordan River; he promises the coming of one who will baptize with the Holy Spirit and fire. Everything is about to change. The old is passing away; the new presses in. The long, lost night of hopelessness is coming to an end, and John the Baptist is the rooster who awakens the sleeping world with dawn's excited cry.

Who was John the Baptist? Most of what we know of him comes from the New Testament, although there is some mention of him outside the Bible. What is more important to our understanding of the Gospel of Matthew, however, is not the limited and speculative picture history presents of John the Baptist, but Matthew's own, very specific portrait of him. In Matthew, John is depicted in three ways:

1. *As an embodiment of Old Testament prophecy.* In Matthew's Gospel (and in the New Testament generally), John the Baptist speaks not as an isolated preacher but, rather, as the voice of the great Old Testament prophetic tradition.

One of the ways Matthew makes this point is by adapting Isaiah 40:3 to refer to John (Matthew follows the lead of the Gospel of Mark in doing this; see Mark 1:2–3). The original Isaiah text reads, "A voice cries out: 'In the wilderness prepare the way of the LORD, make straight in the desert a highway for our God.'" In its setting in Isaiah, this verse refers to the Jews' return to Jerusalem from the exile in Babylon in the sixth century B.C. In other words, the prophet is calling for the building of a road leading toward home and restoration ("the way of the LORD"); this highway is to be constructed "in the wilderness" stretching between Babylon and Jerusalem.

In Matthew, however, the verse now reads, "The voice of one crying out in the wilderness" (Matt. 3:3). In short, it is now the *voice* that is in the wilderness, not the highway, and this very clearly allows the verse to be connected to the desert preacher, John the Baptist, whose voice cried out from the Judean wilderness.

John is presented as an expression of the classical prophetic tradition also by what he wears. John is dressed like the great Old Testament prophet Elijah. In 2 Kings 1:8, Elijah is said to be "a hairy man, with a leather belt around his waist," and John the Baptist's garb, "clothing of camel's hair with a leather belt around his waist" (Matt. 3:4), is designed to call Elijah to mind. In the popular Judaism of Jesus' day, there was an expectation that one day God would bring in the messianic age, setting all things right, restoring the fortunes of Israel, and placing an ideal king on David's throne. A sign that this was about to happen is that Elijah would reappear. Symbolically, then, John the Baptist is old Elijah returned from the past (see Matt. 11:11–15), and his appearance in the wilderness stands as a sign of the nearness of the messianic age.

Theologically, the fact that John the Baptist invokes the memory and presence of Elijah and the old prophets means that all that Israel has been living toward, the best of Israel's faith and tradition, the deepest hope of the Jewish people, is about to come to fruition. It would be as if Abraham Lincoln should suddenly reappear to speak to the U.S. Congress, or if Martin Luther King, Jr. should return to lead a civil rights march, or if John Wesley should suddenly show up to preach at the Methodist annual conference. When one who represents the very spirit of a movement appears, the air bristles with the possibility for renewal. As the symbolic presence of Elijah, John the Baptist becomes more than a countryside preacher; he is the heart and soul of the Old Testament prophetic faith charging the atmosphere with the electricity of revival and change.

2. *As a preacher of repentance.* John's basic message is summed up by Matthew in a single sentence: "Repent, for the kingdom of heaven has come near" (Matt. 3:2).

The first part of John's message, the call to repent, is clearly dependent upon the second part, the nearness of the kingdom; but what does John have in mind when he proclaims that "the kingdom of heaven has come near"? The kingdom of heaven—the phrase is equivalent to "the kingdom of God" and is used in Matthew in accordance with a Jewish custom of avoiding writing or uttering the word *God*—describes that time in the future when everything that opposes God's good purposes for the world and for human life will be destroyed and all that expresses those purposes will be lifted up. This is "the kingdom of heaven," and John the Baptist stands in his wilderness pulpit, thundering the astounding good news that this kingdom, this dream for a world of peace and restoration, is very near.

How can this be true? How can John say that the promised kingdom of heaven, full of mercy and peace, has come near in human history? Or, more pointedly, how can we, centuries later, afford John's message any credibility? Many years have passed, and there are still wars and broken hearts and deep sorrow. When God's promises of peace and justice still seem so far away, how can we believe John when he says that "the kingdom of heaven has come near"?

The Gospel of Matthew connects John the Baptist's claim that "the kingdom has come near" firmly to Jesus. It is in Jesus that the kingdom has drawn near. In Jesus, what will finally be true in the future for the whole creation is a present reality. Jesus embodied and expressed the peace, love, and mercy that God wills for all people. Jesus took on all that opposes God, even death. His life was the place where God waged the decisive struggle against all the powers of evil, and his resurrection is the sign that "the strife is o'er, the battle done, the victory of life is won." Christian faith is the confident trust that what we have seen and heard and experienced in Jesus Christ is to be relied upon more than all else we see and hear and experience. It is the bold claim that though suffering, warfare, injustice, and death still savage and sting the creation, these forces have already been rendered impotent.

Because the kingdom of heaven has drawn near, John the Baptist urges his wilderness congregation to "repent." Repentance does not mean feeling sorry about the things one has done wrong or guilty about one's past. Repentance is a basic reorientation of one's life. In repentance, one turns from one framework of meaning to another, from one way of thinking about self, others, God, and life to another competing and compelling vision.

The people of Jerusalem and Judea who were baptized by John did so "confessing their sins." This means something much deeper than listing all the bad things one has done. This means coming to the recognition that one has been basing one's life on a lie, on a flawed view of what is true and of lasting value. Racism, for example, is a sin that infects us all. Confessing the sin of racism is much more than admitting that one has shown prejudice toward others or told jokes at the expense of another race. It means admitting that the entire framework of racism—the view that another race is somehow inferior or basically flawed—is wrong and evil. Repentance means turning away from that worldview and toward a basic vision of all races as cherished and valued in the eyes of God.

Repentance, then, is impossible unless one is given a new way of perceiving what is true and real. If John the Baptist had only cried, "Repent!" he would have been wasting his breath. People do not simply turn away from one way of life; they do so when they turn toward something deeper and truer. John gives, then, the reason for repenting when he also cries, "For the kingdom of heaven has come near." The nearness of the kingdom in Jesus is the gift of total healing for the world. John is preaching the message that, by the power of God, the kingdom has drawn near, that the long-sought salvation and peace that people have yearned for is now a reality. John tells his hearers that they can live in the power of this kingdom, and, thus, they can go home now and live as well persons.

So, John the Baptist is not merely appealing to people's desire to be better, to "be all you can be." Real moral change does not happen through inner resolve; it occurs when people realize that the world has changed around them. John, therefore, is calling upon people to recognize that the old world has passed away and the new has come. He wants them to redefine the way they see reality, to embrace the radical vision that God—not money, power, status, fear, disease, death, or any other power—rules the world. His words for this are "the kingdom of heaven has drawn near."

At this point in the Gospel of Matthew, we have only a hint of information about what the kingdom life involves. John announces that the kingdom is near, but he does not specify what a sufficient response to the kingdom would be. A full description awaits Jesus' Sermon on the Mount and his parables. Even so, Matthew's readers are not entirely in the dark about what is demanded, for they have already learned that the kingdom of heaven is the breaking in of something new and unpredictable. It demands a readiness to leave behind predictable, frozen-in-stone religious rules and patterns in favor of attentiveness to the Spirit of God in the immediate situation—the kind of obedience that we have already seen in Joseph, for example (Matt. 1:18–25; 2:13–15).

Indeed, Christians are always finding themselves in situations they could never have predicted, uncharted circumstances where the old maps cannot give all the direction needed. Parents who discover that their teenage son is addicted to alcohol, a school-board member who faces the issue of racial unrest in the local schools, a judge who must decide the fate of a defendant, a citizen presented a choice between voting "yes" for much-needed improvements in community roads and sewers or voting "no" to keep taxes from rising—none of these people can simply open the Bible to a verse that will tell them precisely what a Christian should do. Scripture provides guidance, of course, but Christians must also pray, study, engage in dialogue, and learn; Christians must listen for the voice of God, be prepared to throw away the old maps, remain open to God's Spirit, be ready to discern God's surprising will.

This theme of a newly formed obedience to God's will is underscored in John the Baptist's denunciation of the religious leaders, "You brood of vipers! Who warned you to flee from the wrath to come?" Matthew tells us that John is speaking to the Pharisees and the Sadducees, which is equivalent to saying that he is speaking to the Democrats and the Republicans, the fundamentalists and the liberals. Pharisees and Sadducees represented opposite ends of the political and religious spectrums in Judaism, but Matthew depicts them as united in their opposition to the kingdom of heaven. They will show up together again in Matthew, linked arm-in-arm against Jesus (see Matt. 16:1, 6, 11, 12). The kingdom of heaven, come near in Jesus, is so threatening to the powers-that-be that even natural enemies become allies to combat it. John charges the religious leaders with presumption, with the arrogance of assuming that faithfulness is a matter of inheritance. The religious leaders are proud of the fact that they are descendants of Abraham, but John warns them not to rely upon their status as "Abraham's children." Whenever God wants to do so, John taunts, God can make children of Abraham out of ordinary rocks.

What truly matters in the kingdom of heaven, John proclaims, is not one's blood line or party line but the ethical production line. Produce "fruit worthy of repentance," John cries, adding, "Every tree therefore that does not bear good fruit is cut down and thrown into the fire" (Matt. 3:8, 10). Neither John nor Matthew is teaching that one must do good works to enter the kingdom of heaven. Rather, the reverse is true. When one genuinely perceives that the kingdom of heaven has drawn near, one shows that awareness by doing good works. When an army of liberation sets free a prisoner-of-war camp, the prisoners respond by fleeing their cells and embracing their liberators. It would be very strange, indeed, if a prisoner remained in his cell and continued to act like a prisoner. Liberated prisoners act like free people. Just so, when God liberates the world, to act like slaves is a denial of that liberation. To say "I am a child of Abraham" or "I am a lifelong member of the church, just like my ancestors before me" badly misses the point. If you are free, you act free—period. If one sees that the kingdom has drawn near, then one acts like a person who belongs to the kingdom.

3. *As one who points to Jesus.* The mission of John the Baptist is not only to announce the arrival of the kingdom but also to point to the one who, in his person, has brought the kingdom near—Jesus.

John baptized people in the Jordan River, almost surely as a ritual sign of cleansing and repentance in the light of the approaching kingdom. He makes it clear, though, that his baptism is merely preparatory to, a fore-taste of, the baptism of Jesus. John's baptism is with water; Jesus' baptism is "with the Holy Spirit and fire."

What is this talk of a baptism of "Holy Spirit and fire"? The idea is complex, but crucial. Matthew understands that, at the end of time, God will judge the world; that is, God will bring in justice and set everything right. For the moment, the greedy and the cruel and the indifferent and the powerful seem to have history in their grasp. They call the shots; they decide how human society will go. But this is a temporary illusion. The final judgment is God's gracious "No" to the petty schemes of human evil and oppression and God's "Yes" to all that is good and righteous. Tyrants and those who prey upon the innocent may appear strong today, but no one and no thing that opposes God's righteousness will be allowed to stand forever; all that works against the kingdom of heaven will be "burned with unquenchable fire" (Matt. 3:12).

Matthew also understands that those who belong to Jesus Christ have already begun to experience the freedom and confidence of those who belong to the kingdom of heaven. They can live in a world of people all around them climbing over each other's backs to grasp a little more cash and know, nonetheless, that true treasure lies elsewhere. They discern that an anonymous life teaching children in an inner-city school is of more value, in the kingdom sense, than being famous enough to appear on the cover of a glitter magazine. They realize that dishing out meals in a soup kitchen for the homeless will stand eternally, long after the satisfaction of pulling down a six-figure income cutting corporate deals has been burned away. They can even stand at gravesides, peering into the terrible face of the final foe, and affirm, "If we have died with Christ, we shall surely be raised with him."

The truth of the matter is that even Christians do not live this way all of the time. Even Christians waver in their faith, fall down on their commitments. But here and there, now and then, they shine with a light that does not come from this world. How can Christians do this, even occasionally? It is not because they are stronger and more virtuous than other mortals; it is, rather, because they have been given a gift—the Holy Spirit.

The Holy Spirit is God, who gives the divine self to us as a gift. The Holy Spirit is given to us to teach wisdom, to guide us in the ways of mercy, to encourage our faith in a world where faith's vision seems foolish, to assure us that no matter how powerful evil may appear there is no lost good, and to confirm in our present ambiguous circumstances the bold promises of the gospel.

When John the Baptist says that his baptism is only of water, he means that he is simply a "preview of coming attractions." He is not the Christ; he announces the coming of the Christ. John is not the one who will set all things right; he points to the one who establishes justice.

Like John, Jesus Christ will also baptize, but not with water. Instead, Christ will baptize the faithful with the gift of the Holy Spirit. And at the end of time, Christ will baptize the whole creation with fire, burning away the rubbish of evil and purifying as gold all deeds of mercy, humility, peace, hope, and love.

2. Jesus' Identity Is Confirmed and Tested
Matthew 3:13–4:11

THE BAPTISM OF JESUS
Matthew 3:13–17

> 3:13 **Then Jesus came from Galilee to John at the Jordan, to be baptized by him.** [14] **John would have prevented him, saying, "I need to be baptized by you, and do you come to me?"** [15] **But Jesus answered him, "Let it be so now; for it is proper for us in this way to fulfill all righteousness." Then he consented.** [16] **And when Jesus had been baptized, just as he came up from the water, suddenly the heavens were opened to him and he saw the Spirit of God descending like a dove and alighting on him.** [17] **And a voice from heaven said, "This is my Son, the Beloved, with whom I am well pleased."**

In this passage Matthew recounts how Jesus was baptized in the Jordan River by John the Baptist. Matthew not only tells the basic details of the baptism, but he also conveys at least three major theological meanings of this event:

1. *Jesus is superior to John.* Matthew is the only Gospel to record the conversation between John and Jesus prior to the baptism. John, who has proclaimed that one more powerful than he is coming, immediately recognizes Jesus as this very one and, therefore, resists baptizing him, saying, "I need to be baptized by you." This reemphasizes the point, already made in Matthew 3:11–12, that John recognizes and acknowledges Jesus' superiority.

Why does Matthew include this material? Evidently, the popularity of John the Baptist remained strong among early Christians, and there may even have been a group, rivaling the church of Jesus, that continued to follow John's teachings. Some scholars point to this tension between the followers of Jesus and the followers of John as the reason that Matthew may have underscored the inferiority of John to Jesus.

Beyond the particular historical circumstances, however, the text stands as a reminder and a warning to all who would seek to magnify themselves while proclaiming the gospel. A glance at the church advertisements in a typical Saturday newspaper will often disclose large photographs of preachers, line sketches of lovely church buildings, lofty comments about the excellencies of choirs, and exaggerated claims about friendly congregations. One can make a good case for any or all of these ad strategies, but they run perilously close to lifting up the messengers over the message. John the Baptist forms the model for all subsequent witnesses to Christ when he confesses in humility, "I need to be baptized by you and not the other way around."

But, if Jesus is superior to John, then another question arises: Why does Jesus submit to John's baptism? If John baptizes "for repentance," why does Jesus, who was without sin, need to be baptized at all? John's question to Jesus seems to imply something of this puzzlement, and the meaning of the answer Jesus gives—"It is proper for us in this way to fulfill all righteousness"—is not immediately clear.

Scholars are divided over how Jesus' answer is to be interpreted. There are two main ways to understand it; each depends upon a different application of the word "righteousness," and both of them have merit. The first possibility is that "righteousness" in this passage refers to *human* righteousness, to the possibility that people can live in right relationship with God and others. For Matthew, of course, righteousness is possible only because of the saving work of Jesus Christ, and people can be righteous only by being joined to Christ. So, when Jesus indicates that his baptism will "fulfill all righteousness," he may mean that it is the will of God for him to save the world, to make righteousness a reality for humanity through joining himself to sinners, and his baptism signifies this identification with all humanity. Taken in this light, Jesus' baptism is a symbol of his total involvement in the human condition, his sharing in the fullness of human experience, in order that humanity may be forgiven, saved, and made righteous.

A second, and equally compelling, interpretation of Jesus' statement is that "righteousness" in this passage refers not primarily to human righteousness but, rather, to the righteousness of *God*, that is, to the way God works in the world to set things right. In Isaiah 63:15–64:2, the prophet cries out for redemption and salvation; he yearns for God to act swiftly, mightily, and compassionately to restore the faithful community. In other words, the prophet is calling to the heavens for the righteousness of God. "Look down from heaven and see . . . ," the prophet begs; "O that you would tear open the heavens and come down . . . to make your name known" (Isa. 63:15; 64:2).

Now, in the baptism of Jesus, this prophetic call for righteousness is being fulfilled. The heavens are torn open, and God is made known as the voice of God reveals the true and full identity of Jesus, "This is my Son." Thus, when Jesus says to John that the baptism is to "fulfill all righteousness," he means that the promise that God will tear open the skies and act mightily to save humanity is now being fulfilled through his own life.

2. *Jesus is the beloved Son.* The central purpose of the story of Jesus' baptism is to draw together the threads of Jesus' identity that have been woven into the fabric of Matthew's Gospel thus far. We have learned that Jesus is the Messiah, the son of David, the son of Abraham, the light to the Gentiles, the Nazorean, and the judge at the end of time. Now these elements are fused and shown to be even more than the sum of their parts: Finally and ultimately, Jesus is greater than any one of these descriptions; he is the beloved Son of God, with whom God is well pleased.

It is no less than the voice of God that declares Jesus to be "my Son, the Beloved, with whom I am well pleased" (Matt. 3:17). This phrase is a combination of Psalm 2:7 and Isaiah 42:1, and these verses together point to the identity of Jesus both as God's beloved Son and as the Suffering Servant, the one who will be "wounded for our transgressions" (Isa. 53:5). Matthew's version of what is said by the heavenly voice is slightly, but significantly, different from Mark's and Luke's. In Mark and Luke, the voice seems to speak to Jesus alone, "*You* are my Son." In Matthew, however, the heavenly voice declares Jesus' identity publicly, "*This* is my Son." In Matthew, therefore, the emphasis falls on Jesus' identity being declared openly to the whole world. The curtains have been pulled back, and now all can see who this Jesus truly is.

3. *Jesus' baptism is the prototype for our baptisms.* In this story of Jesus' baptism we find an anticipation of all subsequent Christian baptisms done in the name of the Trinity. Though it would be a mistake to think of Matthew teaching elaborate trinitarian theology (the doctrine of the Trinity was fully developed only after the New Testament period), we do see in the story of Jesus' baptism a depiction of all three persons of the Trinity in relationship. At the close of the Gospel of Matthew, Jesus sends his disciples out to the nations to baptize "in the name of the Father and of the Son and of the Holy Spirit" (Matt. 28:19), and here, at the beginning of Matthew, we see the prototype of that baptism: Father, Son, and Spirit gathered together in the event of baptism.

JESUS IS PUT TO THE TEST
Matthew 4:1–11

4:1 **Then Jesus was led up by the Spirit into the wilderness to be tempted by the devil.** [2] **He fasted forty days and forty nights, and afterwards he was famished.** [3] **The tempter came and said to him, "If you are the Son of God, command these stones to become loaves of bread."** [4] **But he answered, "It is written,**

> **'One does not live by bread alone,**
>   **but by every word that comes from the mouth of God.'"**

[5] **Then the devil took him to the holy city and placed him on the pinnacle of the temple,** [6] **saying to him, "If you are the Son of God, throw yourself down; for it is written,**

> **'He will command his angels concerning you,'**
> **and 'On their hands they will bear you up,**
> **so that you will not dash your foot against a stone.'"**

[7] **Jesus said to him, "Again it is written, 'Do not put the Lord your God to the test.'"**

[8] **Again, the devil took him to a very high mountain and showed him all the kingdoms of the world and their splendor;** [9] **and he said to him, "All these I will give you, if you will fall down and worship me."** [10] **Jesus said to him, "Away with you, Satan! for it is written,**

> **'Worship the Lord your God,**
>   **and serve only him.'"**

[11] **Then the devil left him, and suddenly angels came and waited on him.**

As soon as Jesus' identity is announced, this identity is immediately put to the test. Here, in the opening verses of chapter 4, Matthew recounts the story of how Jesus, newly announced as the Son of God, has his call and mission subjected to a series of three tests, or temptations, by the devil in the wilderness. Each of these temptations is of interest in its own right, but before we explore them in some detail, a prior question must be addressed: Whose temptations are these? Are they only Jesus' temptations, or are they ours, too? Are these the sort of temptations that all human beings face, or are these temptations unique to Jesus because of his extraordinary messianic role?

We can start to answer this question by recognizing that, long before these temptations were Jesus' temptations—or ours—they were Israel's temptations. The way this story is told in Matthew underscores the fact that Jesus in the wilderness is undergoing precisely the same tests, and in precisely the same sequence, as Israel did in the wilderness. Notice that Jesus is tempted first regarding hunger (Matt. 4:1–4), second regarding putting God to the test (Matt. 4:5–7), and third regarding false worship

(Matt. 4:8–10). These were the very temptations—and in the same order—experienced by the Israelites in the wilderness after the exodus from
slavery in Egypt (see Exodus 16; 17; and 19–32). If, as we noted in the
comments on chapter 2, the child Jesus follows the journey of Israel into
Egypt, now the adult Jesus retraces Israel's adventures in the wilderness.

Because the temptations Jesus faced are echoes of Israel's temptations,
the first readers of Matthew, with their ready knowledge of what we now
call the Old Testament, would realize that Jesus is on familiar ground
here, reenacting the story of the trials of God's people. Jesus has inherited
the legacy of Israel, and now he goes where they went—into the wilderness—to experience what they experienced—a time of testing. Where
they failed, he is faithful. Where they stumbled, he walks surely and un-
waveringly along the path of God's calling. All that God willed to create
in Israel has now come to fruition in this beloved son, Jesus.

What this means is that the temptations Jesus encountered are not his
alone; they are his, of course, but they are also the temptations of all God's
people. Israel faced them; Jesus faced them; and—what is also important
for us today—the church continues to face them. The ways in which
Jesus was tested symbolize all of the possibilities for doubt, misdirection,
faithless choices, and unholy distractions to which God's people are ever
at risk. What is extraordinary about this story is not the substance of the
temptations, for God's people have always been tempted this way. What
is extraordinary is the character of the one who was tempted. Unlike others, Jesus resisted the temptations and remained faithful to his calling. His
role as God's Son was placed in the crucible of temptation, and he
emerged obedient and true to his identity.

By telling this story as he does, Matthew wanted both to warn and to encourage his readers. Matthew warned his readers by reminding them of Israel's story, bringing to the surface the reality that God's people can buckle
under the pressure of testing and become, like their ancestors in the faith,
disobedient, "stiffnecked people" (Exod. 32:9). On the other hand, the
church, as God's people, can be encouraged, too, because the same Jesus
who remained true to his calling is the Christ who is present with the
church "always, to the end of the age" (Matt. 28:20), giving strength and
supporting the church in its own times of testing. So, Jesus' temptations
are the church's temptations, too. However, it is also important to note that
the temptations Jesus endured are not merely the routine sort of wiles and
seductions that everybody faces in life; they are the particular temptations
of those who are called to live as God's faithful people in the world.

This story is about the kind of trials and testings that happen to people—to Israel, to Jesus, and to the church—when they are called to be

God's people and to do God's work in the world. The testing of Jesus, the testings of Israel before him, and the testing of the church today are not primarily temptations to *do* what we would really like to do, but know we should not; they are temptations to *be* someone other than who God calls us to be, to deny that we are God's children.

Jesus' First Temptation
(Matthew 4:1–4)

In the New Testament, Satan is a figure representing the power of evil, all that opposes the will of God. Whenever we encounter a biblical reference to Satan, we should not allow ourselves to be distracted by Halloween images of a fiendish devil or by newspaper accounts of bloodthirsty Satanists. Satan personifies all adversaries of God, all those who obstruct and resist what God intends for human life. A community that turns its back on needy people can be at least as "Satanic" as a cult of devil worshipers. Even the very closest followers of Jesus can push against the will of God and thus assume the form of Satan (see Matt. 16:21–23).

Jesus' time of testing begins when this adversary, this tempter, the devil, challenges Jesus: "*If* you are the Son of God, command these stones to become loaves of bread" (Matt. 4:3). This little word *if* is yet another signal that this is to be a test of Jesus' identity and may be designed to create self-doubt in Jesus ("if you are . . ." being a much more subtle and effective assault on Jesus' self-understanding than the more direct "you are not the Son of God"). In any case, it is clear that this first temptation (as well as the others) will force to the surface just what sort of understanding of "Son of God" Jesus has and chooses to live.

The challenge to turn stones into bread is connected, of course, to the fact that Jesus is "famished" after his long fast, and this is the key to understanding this temptation. The devil is attempting to beguile Jesus into making the nature of his work too small—satisfying hunger—and the recipients of his work too few—only one, himself.

As Messiah, Jesus is called to a ministry of great size. As the Son of God, Jesus is called to a sweeping ministry, encompassing the whole of humanity; but the tempter places before him another idea—make it narrow. Don't meet all the needs, only the one you feel most urgently now. Don't pour out your life for all people; serve yourself first. Jesus' ministry as the Son is to be as vast as the heavens and as deep as the ocean; the devil alluringly holds out a thimble and suggests, "Why not merely fill this up?"

Jesus' answer to this temptation does not imply that providing bread to feed human hunger is a bad thing; it is just not the *only* thing. The faithful don't live by one word, one need, one issue, one passion, one conviction, and they don't live exclusively for themselves. They live, as Jesus reminded the tempter, by "every word that comes from the mouth of God" (Matt. 4:4—a quotation of Deut. 8:3).

The church experiences this form of temptation whenever it risks losing sight of the breadth of its calling or when we measure the effectiveness of the church according to how quickly it responds to our personal ideas and needs, our demand to be fed. "I'm bored; give me some excitement in worship." "I'm a parent; take my children and give them religion." "I don't like the way the church spends its money; change it now."

The good news of this temptation is that Jesus remained obedient to the God who speaks many words, not just one; who feeds the hungers of the whole world, and not just the voracious ministers, the demanding and ravenous church, or even the famished Messiah himself. Jesus is hungry, very hungry, but he will not allow the devil to restrict his diet, or ours. We are like people standing at the longest and most lavish buffet table in creation, the gospel banquet, but who, starving and distrustful, are tempted quickly to fill our plates with crusts of bread. We are given *every* word of God; we can trust every promise of the gospel to nourish and sustain us. Jesus resisted the temptation to make the gospel too small; and by doing so, he embodies, for all of humanity and for every hunger in creation, the whole Word of God, which gives life.

Jesus' Second Temptation
(Matthew 4:5–7)

In the second temptation, the devil plays cleverly on the first one. He takes Jesus to Jerusalem, the Holy City, places him high atop the temple, and says, in effect: "So, you want to quote Scripture at me to say that you trust every word that comes from the mouth of God? Well, I can quote Scripture, too. Here is a word from the mouth of God: 'God's angels will bear you up [a portion of Psalm 91:11–12].' Why don't you try that word out? Jump off the temple and see if God's word is trustworthy."

So, why does Jesus refuse this temptation? Giving the devil his due, doesn't the devil have a good point here? If Jesus, as the Son of God, lives by every word that comes from God's mouth, then why doesn't he demonstrate that confidence by taking a deep breath, bending his knees, and springing off the temple roof into the feathery protection of angels' wings, the sure promises of Psalm 91, the safety net of God's care, and the amazed admiration of the crowd below?

The answer, of course, is that such testing of God comes not from trust, but from the lack of it. Trying out the promises of God to "see if they really work" is a sign not of sure faith but of fundamental doubt. It implies that *we* are in God's position; we not only know God's promises, but we also know *how*, *when*, and *where* God is supposed to fulfill these divine promises. If God doesn't perform in just that prescribed way, either God must be a liar or there is no God. Putting God to the test dramatically reverses our relationship to God; *we* are in charge, and God is treated as our servant.

Jesus' Third Temptation (Matthew 4:8–11)

The third temptation involves both the lure of false worship and the empty, lying promise of "all the kingdoms of the world" (Matt. 4:8). Jesus will become Lord of all the kingdoms of the world, not by falling down before the devil, but by being nailed upon a cross. Indeed, this temptation may best be understood as the enticement to achieve the destination of his ministry without undergoing the sacrificial journey, to claim the victory without enduring the struggle. The ministry of Jesus will be hard and messy. It will involve teaching slow-learning disciples the secrets of the kingdom, touching the broken and diseased skin of lepers, facing the opposition of the religious leaders, being blown about in the treacherous winds of crowd opinion, having one of his own disciples betray him, and being forsaken by the rest of them. It will mean being handed over to the authorities like a common criminal, spit upon and mocked, finally being cruelly executed on a cross.

In other words, here we are early in Matthew's Gospel, and Jesus has many miles of toil and suffering to travel before the victory of resurrection. "Why not abbreviate the story?" entices the devil. "Why not cut out the suffering and the painful parts and get right on to the victory? Just bow down and worship me, and you can have what you seek on the spot, today."

The church faces the same temptation today when it attempts to find some easier and quicker road to travel than the way of the cross. Whenever the "power of positive thinking" gets substituted for the power of sacrificial love and costly grace, then the tempter smiles. Whenever we bow down to that which is not God—to nation, or race, or family, or social standing—hoping that this will fill our hearts, we succumb to this temptation. Whenever we attempt to soften the cost of discipleship and pretend that the work of Christ does not involve suffering, then we not only fall to this temptation, we take on, as Peter did later in Matthew's Gospel (Matt. 16:23), the role of the tempter. The good news of this episode is that Jesus does not waver from his calling, does not step off the way of suffering lured by the illusion of a shortcut, does not bypass the cross.

3. Jesus' Ministry Begins
Matthew 4:12–25

4:12 Now when Jesus heard that John had been arrested, he withdrew to Galilee. [13] He left Nazareth and made his home in Capernaum by the sea, in the territory of Zebulun and Naphtali, [14] so that what had been spoken through the prophet Isaiah might be fulfilled:
> [15] "Land of Zebulun, land of Naphtali,
>> on the road by the sea, across the Jordan, Galilee of the Gen
>> tiles—
> [16] the people who sat in darkness
>> have seen a great light,
> and for those who sat in the region and shadow of death
>> light has dawned."
>> [17] From that time Jesus began to proclaim, "Repent, for the kingdom of heaven has come near."

[18] As he walked by the Sea of Galilee, he saw two brothers, Simon, who is called Peter, and Andrew his brother, casting a net into the sea—for they were fishermen. [19] And he said to them, "Follow me, and I will make you fish for people." [20] Immediately they left their nets and followed him. [21] As he went from there, he saw two other brothers, James son of Zebedee and his brother John, in the boat with their father Zebedee, mending their nets, and he called them. [22] Immediately they left the boat and their father, and followed him.

[23] Jesus went throughout Galilee, teaching in their synagogues and proclaiming the good news of the kingdom and curing every disease and every sickness among the people. [24] So his fame spread throughout all Syria, and they brought to him all the sick, those who were afflicted with various diseases and pains, demoniacs, epileptics, and paralytics, and he cured them. [25] And great crowds followed him from Galilee, the Decapolis, Jerusalem, Judea, and from beyond the Jordan.

In the remainder of the fourth chapter, Matthew describes the inaugural events of the ministry of Jesus. This section is skillfully constructed to contain, in microcosm, the major themes that will be elaborated in the rest of the Gospel. Just as the first few weeks or the "first hundred days" of the terms of presidents and prime ministers are often closely watched for clues to the nature of things to come, so Matthew invites us to inspect closely these opening events of Jesus' public ministry. Everything to follow is found in embryonic form here. Let us examine the major facets of the debut of Jesus' work as the Son of God.

The Time (Matthew 4:12a)

Jesus' ministry begins when John the Baptist is arrested (the Greek word translated as "arrested" is used later in Matthew to describe Jesus' betrayal and arrest, thus linking the fate of John with that of Jesus). This seemingly offhand detail, that John was placed into custody, is actually quite significant. Matthew considered John the Baptist to be a pivotal figure, a sort of hinge on which the ages shifted. Before John, there was the time of the Law and the Prophets; after John, there is the messianic age of Jesus. John himself faces both directions; he is the last of the old prophets and the first of the gospel preachers (see also Matt. 11:7–15).

So, when John is arrested and removed from the scene, it is a theological cue that the time has come, that the tectonic plates have shifted and the earthquake of the promised messianic age has begun to shake the foundations of the world. The moment has arrived for Jesus, the Messiah, to stir into action.

The Place (Matthew 4:12b–16)

Jesus begins his ministry in Galilee, working out of the town of Capernaum as a home base. We have seen how Matthew often treats geographical movements as symbolic of theological truths (see, for example, the commentary on Matt. 2:13–15), and this is no exception. Capernaum is a town on the northwest shore of the Sea of Galilee, near the mouth of the Jordan River. Capernaum is in the vicinity of the regions occupied by the tribes of Zebulun and Naphtali (see Gen. 49:13; Deut. 33:23).

Matthew connects Jesus' move to Capernaum to Isaiah 9:1–2, which refers to the "land of Zebulun, land of Naphtali, on the road by the sea, across the Jordan, Galilee of the Gentiles" (Matt. 4:15). This linkage works two ways. First, like the other Old Testament prophecies cited by Matthew, it expresses Matthew's conviction that Jesus' life is unfolding not according to random chance but according to God's plan. Second, the mention of "Gentiles" anticipates the spread of the gospel beyond the boundaries of Judaism to "all nations" (Matt. 28:19).

The Message (Matthew 4:17)

Jesus begins his ministry by preaching, "Repent, for the kingdom of heaven has come near." Note that Jesus is preaching exactly the same message that John the Baptist preached (Matt. 3:2). The message of the kingdom has not changed; the messenger has, and that is a crucial difference. When John said the kingdom had come near, it was like a person pointing to a rain cloud on the horizon and saying that refreshing showers would soon come. When Jesus says the kingdom had drawn near, it means that the hoped-for kingdom was beginning to happen in and through him. In the inauguration of his ministry, in his words and deeds, the cloudburst of the kingdom has begun.

What does Jesus' message mean? What is encompassed by the words "the kingdom of heaven has come near"? We need not be too perplexed if we do not have a full understanding of Jesus' words at this point. One of the distinctive features of the Gospel of Matthew is that it includes large sections of Jesus' teaching. In the Gospel of Mark, we are told that Jesus was a teacher, but in Matthew we actually get to "go into the classroom" and hear many of his teachings about the kingdom. Here, Matthew gives us only a summary of Jesus' message, but the rest of Matthew's Gospel will unfold an increasingly complete picture of the character of the "kingdom of heaven." At this point, much about the kingdom of heaven as defined by Jesus remains hidden from view. What we *are* told now is that this kingdom will change everything, that its coming is a cause for repentance. The drawing near of God's reign calls for a basic reorientation, a moral turnaround, a reversal of direction.

The Disciples (Matthew 4:18–22)

With the exception of a brief mention of the calling of Matthew the tax collector (Matt. 9:9), these two adjoining stories describing the calling of four of Jesus' disciples—Peter, Andrew, James, and John—are the only accounts in the Gospel of Matthew that describe how Jesus acquired his twelve disciples. The names of the other disciples simply appear, somewhat abruptly, in Matthew 10:1–4. This narrative of the calling of the four fishermen, then, is no doubt intended to be a representative story, bringing into the light the basic dynamics of the calling of all the disciples.

As Matthew presents what happened by the Sea of Galilee, three factors are highlighted. First, he emphasizes the family relationships of the people involved. Peter and Andrew are specified as brothers, as are James and John. Indeed, Matthew is so eager to underscore the brotherly relationship of Peter and Andrew, he mentions it twice in the same sentence, and he does the same for James and John (Matt. 4:18 and 4:21)! That Zebedee is the father of James and John is similarly underscored.

Second, Matthew emphasizes their occupation, stressing the fact that all of these people were fishermen. We see them in action doing their jobs—sailing in a boat, mending nets, and casting nets. And Jesus' words, "Follow me, and I will make you fish for people" (Matt. 4:19), obviously connect to their roles as fishermen.

Third, Matthew emphasizes the swiftness of their reaction to Jesus. In the case of each pair of brothers, the response to Jesus is immediate. Instantly they left their nets; they left their boat; they left their father; and they followed Jesus.

Taken as a whole, then, these twin stories of the calling of four disciples make it clear that Jesus summons people from the fabric of family relationships—brother, sister, daughter, son, father, mother—and from the midst of the workaday world—fishing, teaching, clerking, cooking, building—into a new set of relationships and to a new vocation.

Does this mean that Jesus calls into question our family ties and creates conflict with our occupations? In a sense, yes. The kingdom of heaven doesn't exist to serve the family; the family exists to serve the kingdom of heaven (see Matt. 10:34–39 and 12:46–50). The goal of the kingdom is not to serve us in being more effective and productive in our jobs. Our work is truly effective when it serves to express the will of God. The patterns of our lives are not made secure by the kingdom of heaven; the kingdom of heaven rearranges them into the new design of God's own making.

In these stories of the calling of the disciples, then, Jesus disrupts family structures and disturbs patterns of working and living. He does so, however, not to destroy but to renew. Peter and Andrew do not cease being brothers; they are now brothers who do the will of God (Matt. 12:50). James and John do not cease being sons; they are now not only the children of Zebedee but also the children of God. All four of these disciples leave their fishing nets, but they do not stop fishing. They are now, in the nearness of the kingdom of heaven, fishers for people. Their past has not been obliterated; it has been transformed by Jesus' call to follow.

The Ministry (Matthew 4:23–25)

What is the shape of Jesus' ministry? What is the work of the kingdom of heaven? Here we have it in summary form: teaching, preaching, and healing (Matt. 4:23). In these three words, we have a comprehensive picture of Jesus' work; it is a ministry of word and of deed. It is an announcement of what God is doing, and it is instruction about what human beings are to do in response. It involves the body, the mind, and the spirit. It makes claims on the totality of human life.

The response to Jesus' ministry is dramatic. Jesus' reputation spreads like wildfire; people with all manners of sickness are brought to him; huge crowds from all points of the compass follow him. We catch a glimpse of the future, of where Jesus' ministry is going. Matthew tells this story with his eye both on the present and on the future. In the present tense, Matthew is describing Jesus' vast popularity with people from all over the region. In the future tense, however, Matthew is showing, symbolically, what will happen on history's horizon: The whole world, with every human need imaginable, will stream to Jesus, and all humanity will follow him, becoming his disciples.

How can Matthew think this way about the future? Did not these same crowds, at the end of Jesus' life, far from being his disciples, demand his death? The answer, of course, is that, in the power of the resurrection, the work of Jesus continues through the church. At the end of the Gospel of Matthew, the risen Christ sends the disciples into the whole world to perpetuate this ministry (Matt. 28:16–20). At the beginning of Jesus' ministry, all the world symbolically comes to Jesus; now, we are given the hopeful task of going into all the world with the gospel.

4. The Sermon on the Mount
Matthew 5:1–7:29

THE SETTING OF THE SERMON
Matthew 5:1

> 5:1 **When Jesus saw the crowds, he went up the mountain; and after he sat down, his disciples came to him.**

From the beginning, Jesus' ministry drew great crowds of people from many directions (Matt. 4:25). Matthew now indicates that Jesus, seeing these crowds, climbs a mountain in order to teach. This section of Matthew is popularly called "The Sermon on the Mount," but Matthew himself does not term it a sermon. More precisely, "The Sermon on the Mount" should be viewed less as a crafted sermon and more as a collection of various teachings of Jesus. Perhaps it should even be called "The Instruction on the Mount."

Indeed, it is a characteristic of the Gospel of Matthew to group Jesus' teachings into clusters (see Introduction), and this section of Matthew (chapters 5–7) constitutes the first and the longest of five such summaries of Jesus' words. Luke records a much shorter variation of the Sermon (Luke 6:20–49), and Matthew seems to have shaped the final form of this longer version by putting together sayings of Jesus drawn from several sources.

The unnamed mountain serves as a symbol for a place of momentous encounter, a place of revelation. Throughout the Gospel of Matthew, significant events in Jesus' life happen on mountains (for example, the third temptation, Matt. 4:1–8; the Transfiguration, Matt. 17:1–8; the commissioning of the disciples, Matt. 28:16–20), so Jesus' ascent at this moment signals that a crucial event is about to unfold. Also, the fact that Jesus proclaims the new law in the Sermon seems to indicate that the mountain signifies Mount Sinai, where Moses received the holy law (see Exodus 19).

That Jesus sits down is also symbolic; this classic posture of a Jewish teacher conveys solemn authority. Thus, Matthew pictures Jesus as an authoritative teacher atop a new Mount Sinai teaching the new law of the kingdom of heaven. We know that the audience included not only the disciples but also the crowds, because the crowds are specifically described at the end of the Sermon as being "astounded" (Matt. 7:28). Matthew invites us, then, to imagine that Jesus spoke to an audience arranged in two groups: first, the disciples, who have come near, and then the crowds behind them. Jesus, therefore, is symbolically speaking through the disciples to the world, anticipating the mission of the church to teach all the nations "to obey everything that I have commanded you" (Matt. 28:20).

THE BEATITUDES
Matthew 5:2–12

5:2 **Then he began to speak, and taught them, saying:**
    [3] **"Blessed are the poor in spirit, for theirs is the kingdom of heaven.**
    [4] **"Blessed are those who mourn, for they will be comforted.**
    [5] **"Blessed are the meek, for they will inherit the earth.**
    [6] **"Blessed are those who hunger and thirst for righteousness, for they will be filled.**
    [7] **"Blessed are the merciful, for they will receive mercy.**
    [8] **"Blessed are the pure in heart, for they will see God.**
    [9] **"Blessed are the peacemakers, for they will be called children of God.**
    [10] **"Blessed are those who are persecuted for righteousness' sake, for theirs is the kingdom of heaven.**
    [11] **"Blessed are you when people revile you and persecute you and utter all kinds of evil against you falsely on my account.** [12] **Rejoice and be glad, for your reward is great in heaven, for in the same way they persecuted the prophets who were before you.**

The preamble to the U.S. Constitution states: "We, the people of the United States, in order to form a more perfect union, establish justice, insure domestic tranquillity, provide for the common defense, promote the general welfare, and secure the blessings of liberty to ourselves and our posterity, do ordain and establish this Constitution for the United States of America."

This introductory statement defines the essence of the nation's vision of itself and expresses the sort of citizenry it hopes to embody. In a similar manner, the Sermon on the Mount is the "constitution" of the church of Jesus Christ, and the Beatitudes are its "preamble." The Beatitudes proclaim what is, in the light of the kingdom of heaven, unassailably true.

They describe the purpose of every holy law, the foundation of every custom, the aim of every practice of this new society, this colony of the kingdom, the church called and instructed by Jesus.

It becomes quickly apparent that the Beatitudes turn the world's values upside down. What is true for those who live in the power of the kingdom of heaven is a flat reversal of what is considered to be true in the culture at large. The Beatitudes declare that the poor in spirit, the meek, the peacemakers are the ones who are truly blessed. We live in a world, however, that pronounces the benediction over the self-sufficient, the assertive, and the power brokers. The people whom the world would see as pitiful—the mournful, the persecuted—are the very people Jesus claims are truly joyful.

Jesus speaks nine beatitudes in all, and taken together, they describe the traits of the citizenry of the kingdom of heaven. The first eight beatitudes are all constructed according to the same pattern:

1. An introductory phrase, "blessed are . . . ," which could also be rendered "joyful are . . ." or "deeply happy are . . . "
2. A statement specifying who these blessed ones are by naming some virtue or character trait.
3. A reason why they are joyful, namely, the promise of a specific reward, usually expressed in the future tense.

The use of verb tenses in the initial eight beatitudes is quite subtle and theologically important. Each beatitude begins in the present tense: "Blessed *are*. . . . " In other words, those who are blessed are joyful *now*, in the present. In six of the beatitudes, however, the specific reason why they are blessed lies not in the present, but in the future ("they will . . . "). What this indicates is that the church, the community of Christ, is a joyful people, but the source of their joy is not that they live easy lives in a happy world or that things are getting better every day, but that their trust is in God's coming kingdom.

The church of Jesus Christ sees its life in two frames of reference. First, it sees what everyone else sees, too—the world of human history, a world of struggle in which the church works and serves and lives out its mission. Based on the evidence from this world alone, there is little reason for hope or joy. War follows upon war, might makes right, and the innocent suffer every day.

But the church also possesses a second frame of reference. It sees what others do not see, that God is at work in this world even today and will surely bring all creation to a time of peace and rejoicing. This hoped-for time is the kingdom of heaven. For the world, the kingdom is a sure future; for the faithful, the kingdom is a present reality, giving strength and encouragement to its work.

If God's promise of the kingdom of heaven is an empty promise, then a life of seeking justice and showing mercy is a fool's illusion. Only the promised kingdom validates a life of hopeful service. But the promise of the kingdom is sure; therefore, joyful, blessed, happy are those who put their lives on the line, trusting that promise.

The first and the eighth beatitudes seem to be exceptions to this pattern of moving from the present to the future tense, for they maintain the present tense all the way to the conclusion: "for theirs *is* the kingdom of heaven." In fact, they are not exceptions, because they actually make the same theological point. What the Christian community possesses in the present is the promise of the coming kingdom of heaven. What *will be* for the whole of creation in the future is theirs *now* in the present.

Each of the nine beatitudes expresses an aspect of what it means to be "blessed" in the light of the kingdom of heaven:

In the *first beatitude* (Matt. 5:3), the blessed are the "poor in spirit," which could be paraphrased "spiritual beggars." This beatitude indicates that those who have come to the end of their own resources, who know that they cannot sustain hope and purpose out of their own strength, and who have thrown themselves on the mercy of God will not be abandoned. They have already been given, through the continuing presence of Christ, the kingdom of heaven.

The "poor in spirit" are those who experience poverty in many forms. It includes those who are pushed to the edges of society, who are trampled down economically. They are often forgotten by society, but they are not abandoned by God. It also includes people who are threatened by disease, whose minds are devoured by mental illness, whose lives have come apart. Those who cannot make meaning for themselves and fall down as beggars before the mercy of God will find themselves treated as royalty in the kingdom of heaven. Moreover, it includes those who have actively chosen, in the name of the Spirit, not to pander to their own desires but to become "poor" by assuming the disciplines of humility and obedience.

The *second beatitude* names as blessed "those who mourn" (Matt. 5:4). The kind of mourning referred to here is not so much mere sadness or weeping but prayers of lament over the hurt in the world. This mourning grows out of an awareness of the difference between the world as it is and the world as God wills it to be. In a television commercial of some years ago, the scene opens with a view of a typical American highway. As the camera panned across the roadway, we see everywhere the litter, carelessly cast-off garbage, and windblown refuse of a throwaway society. Finally, the camera comes to rest on the rugged face of a Native American. As he looks solemnly upon the spoiled landscape, a tear falls from his eye, his grief marking the distance between the world as it is and the world as it should be.

In similar fashion, God's people grieve over the spoiling of creation and the deep pains of human society. On a freezing night, a homeless woman dies alone in an abandoned building. A family dispute erupts into violence. Children become the prey of drug dealers. A man gradually loses confidence and dignity as he desperately seeks work in vain. A manufacturing firm pollutes the earth with lethal chemicals. The creation is out of joint. Human life is broken in many places. Things are not the way they are supposed to be, and the people of God lament, "O God, do not let your world hurt this way forever." The promise of the kingdom is that such lamenting prayers will surely be answered and such mourners will be comforted.

Both the *third beatitude,* "Blessed are the meek" (Matt. 5:5), and the *fourth,* "Blessed are those who hunger and thirst for righteousness" (Matt. 5:6), are based on images drawn from the psalms, probably Psalm 37 in the main, which indicate that "the meek shall inherit the land" (Psalm 37:11) and that the righteous will "in the days of famine . . . have abundance" (Psalm 37:19). What are "meekness" and "righteousness"? Psalm 37 itself gives us the best descriptions. "Righteousness" is the way of life of people who are generous with what they have, who speak for justice whenever possible, and who seek to do good in behalf of others (Psalm 37:26–27, 30). "Meekness" is not timidity or passivity but rather a patient trusting that God will act in due time, an insistence on being nonviolent even in the midst of a violent society, a contentment with the basic necessities of life even in a possession-hungry world, and taking delight in the gifts of God and the many comforts of faith (Psalm 37:3–5, 7–8, 14–17).

"Blessed are the merciful" states the *fifth beatitude* (Matt. 5:7). The "merciful" are people who show kindness to others, people who are more eager to forgive than to punish, more ready to show compassion than to exact their due. True mercy grows not out of intrinsic human goodness, but from the grateful awareness that God is merciful; those who discern that God is merciful are freed themselves to be merciful.

The *sixth beatitude,* "Blessed are the pure in heart" (Matt. 5:8), grows out of Psalm 24, which describes what is required of those who can enter the temple in Jerusalem to worship God: "Those who have clean hands and pure hearts, who do not lift up their souls to what is false, and do not swear deceitfully" (Psalm 24:4). The "heart" describes the inner person, that is, what a person truly is in contrast to what that person may appear to be outwardly. The "pure in heart," then, are those whose faith is genuine, people of integrity whose words are backed up by convictions, whose outward deeds match their inner commitments. In the psalm, the pure in heart were allowed into the presence of God in the temple sanctuary. In the beatitude, the pure in heart will "see God," that is, will be in communion with God, in the kingdom.

The *seventh beatitude* pronounces the benediction upon those who work to make peace: "Blessed are the peacemakers" (Matt. 5:9). In the background is the Old Testament word *shalom*, which means the well-being of the whole created order—in short, peace in every corner of creation. The term *peacemakers*, then, embraces those who work to halt wars among nations as well as those who seek harmony in personal relationships. It gathers up efforts to still the storms of human rage and all endeavors to bring serenity to distraught minds.

Sometimes peacemakers are seen to be troublemakers or unrealistic dreamers; this beatitude promises that, when the curtain is raised on the kingdom of heaven, they will be seen in a true light, as "the children of God."

Speaking of troublemakers, the *eighth beatitude* (Matt. 5:10) recognizes that those who seek righteousness are often rewarded for their efforts by being hassled, hounded, and intimidated. Righteousness is not a sweet virtue that everybody in the world desires. Those who take advantage of others for their own gain do not want the world to be fair and just. Those who benefit from the weakness of others do not want the world to be compassionate. Much money and power are invested in maintaining injustice. If every wage were fair, if every person were honored as a child of God, if every human being were safe from exploitation, many would lose their grip on status, self-gratification, and affluence. Seeking the right does not win universal approval; it stirs up the snakes, and this beatitude is realistic enough to admit it. But the world of injustice is obsolete, and those who work for God's new and just order already possess the kingdom of heaven.

The *ninth and final beatitude* (Matt. 5:11) continues the previous beatitude's theme of persecution of God's people, but it breaks the pattern of the other beatitudes. Instead of the now familiar refrain "Blessed are those . . . ," this beatitude becomes more pointed and personal: "Blessed are *you*. . . . "

The reason for this probably has to do with the circumstances of Matthew's community. For them, religious persecution was not a hypothetical possibility; it was a daily reality. As we noted in the Introduction, the church to which Matthew wrote was almost surely a group of Jewish Christians involved in a bitter and painful dispute with other

Jews. They saw themselves as the victims of rumors, false charges, and vicious distortions. The eighth and ninth beatitudes work together, then, as a word from Jesus particularly addressed to Matthew's community: "Blessed are my people when the world persecutes them. Indeed, blessed are you, readers of this Gospel, for I know that people are ridiculing you in public and muttering evil reports about you. Remember, they did the same to the prophets. So rejoice, your heavenly reward is great indeed."

WHAT GOOD IS THE CHURCH?
Matthew 5:13–16

5:13 "You are the salt of the earth; but if salt has lost its taste, how can its saltiness be restored? It is no longer good for anything, but is thrown out and trampled under foot.
    14 "You are the light of the world. A city built on a hill cannot be hid. 15 No one after lighting a lamp puts it under the bushel basket, but on the lampstand, and it gives light to all in the house. 16 In the same way, let your light shine before others, so that they may see your good works and give glory to your Father in heaven.

The church that lives according to the vision expressed in the Beatitudes is a colony of the kingdom of heaven placed in the midst of an alien culture. In a bellicose world, they are peacemakers. In a world that turns its head away from unpleasant sights, they mourn for the homeless, for the refugee, for the lost, for the brokenhearted.

But what good is that? The church, for all of its vision, is overpowered, outnumbered, and often overlooked. The ordeal of Matthew's church is representative of the experience of the church in many times and places—a small group trying with mixed results to live out an alternative life, set down in the midst of a teeming, fast-changing culture that neither appreciates nor understands them. The hardest part is not in being Christian for a day, but being faithful day after day, maintaining confidence in what, for all the world, appears to be a losing cause.

In the middle of these concerns, Jesus provides two astounding images of the church. First, the church is "the salt of the earth" (Matt. 5:13). The witness of kingdom people, seemingly drowned out by the noise of the world, works like salt; though it is only a little bit, it flavors the whole, sometimes in ways that cannot be seen. Second, the church is "the light of the world" (Matt. 5:14). One lamp, lifted up on a lampstand, can banish the gloom from a whole house; the flickering lights of a hilltop village can be seen for miles around.

In other words, Jesus is saying that what the people of God do in the world really counts. A pot of soup in the church basement for hungry people, a missionary physician giving a shot of penicillin, a team of Christians working for improved conditions in a refugee squatters camp, a word of tender comfort spoken in the name of Christ—all these deeds of mercy, and others like them, are the works of a church that flavors the world like salt and illumines the world like a candle held high in a cave.

Some have been perplexed that Jesus warned about salt losing its taste (5:13), for, technically speaking, salt does not ever lose its saltiness. The image should not be pressed too hard. The point is that the church, like salt, has one purpose—to live the kingdom life in the world. Whenever the church loses sight of that mission and becomes something else—a social club or a theological debating society, for example—it becomes as worthless as salt would be if it weren't salty.

Sometimes, like a light on a lampstand, like a city set on a hill, the church bursts forth into view, and the world looks to the church for guidance and illumination.

IS THE LAW OBSOLETE?
Matthew 5:17–20

> 5:17 **"Do not think that I have come to abolish the law or the prophets; I have come not to abolish but to fulfill. [18] For truly I tell you, until heaven and earth pass away, not one letter, not one stroke of a letter, will pass from the law until all is accomplished. [19] Therefore, whoever breaks one of the least of these commandments, and teaches others to do the same, will be called least in the kingdom of heaven; but whoever does them and teaches them will be called great in the kingdom of heaven. [20] For I tell you, unless your righteousness exceeds that of the scribes and Pharisees, you will never enter the kingdom of heaven.**

Matthew wrote his Gospel to a community of Jewish Christians, people who had been raised on the law of Moses as the embodiment of the will of God for human life. In family worship, Jewish children were taught to ask their parents, "What is the meaning of the decrees and the statutes and the ordinances that the LORD our God has commanded you?" (Deut. 6:20), and the adults were ready earnestly to answer, "The LORD commanded us to observe all these statutes, to fear the LORD our God, for our lasting good, so as to keep us alive" (Deut. 6:24).

In Judaism, the law is a blessing, a good gift, a source of life. But what about the Jewish law for Christians? What is the force of these ancient commandments now that the new event of Jesus Christ has occurred? This was an important and hotly debated question in many places in the early church (see, as examples, the argument over this problem in Acts 15, and also Paul's wrestling with the matter in Galatians).

There are two obvious, and diametrically opposed, resolutions to this question: one, that what we now call the Old Testament law remains in full effect for Christians; and, two, that the new freedom in Christ cancels and abolishes the requirements of the law. So, to put it simply, either Christ leaves the law intact or Christ replaces the law with something new. Which shall it be?

In the Sermon on the Mount, Jesus rejects both, offering instead a third alternative. The law neither remains as it is nor is it done away with; rather, it is fulfilled and transformed in Jesus Christ. Everything about "the law and the prophets" (that is, the Old Testament) was pointing prophetically toward its fulfillment in Jesus Christ (Matt. 5:17; see also Matt. 11:13). Therefore, every aspect of the Law and the Prophets must be seen, interpreted, and lived out in the light of Jesus Christ.

This means that the Christian community can discern in the commandments their true intent; they can pass through the literal requirements of the law into the heart of the law. Think of a powerful searchlight scanning over the night sky. The way this beacon works is that a relatively small source of light is passed through a great lens, which magnifies it into a powerful radiance that spreads over the sky. Now, think of a laser beam. Here the energy source is concentrated, its power transformed into a light of razor-sharp intensity. In Christ, the law becomes both a searchlight and a laser. When the law passes through the person and the event of Christ, it is both focused and enlarged, its potential to illumine and to guide human life both amplified and intensified.

Thus, Jesus begins this portion of the Sermon, a section that deals with the law of Moses, by cautioning, "Do not think that I have come to abolish the law or the prophets" (Matt. 5:17). No, even the smallest commandment stands (Matt. 5:18–19). But now, each and every commandment is seen through the eyes of the new thing that has happened in and through Jesus Christ.

What does this mean, in practical terms, for Christians? How do we view the commandments in the light of the Christian faith? It means that the church is to ask of every piece of the law, "What is the will of God that stands behind this commandment, and how may we be obedient to that will?" We can see examples of this in the Gospel of Matthew itself. Take the sabbath commandment, for instance. Later in Matthew, Jesus and his disciples will get into trouble with the religious officials, because, on the sabbath day, the disciples eat grain and Jesus heals a man, both technical violations of the commandment. Behind the sabbath commandment, however, stands a God who wills that human society be just and merciful, that human life be nourished and restored. This is the heart of the sabbath commandment. Jesus argues with the officials that, by violating the commandment's surface requirements, he and his disciples have, in fact, fulfilled its depths (see Matt. 12:1–14).

In the Sermon, Jesus expresses this move to the depths of the law by saying, "Unless your righteousness exceeds that of the scribes and Pharisees, you will never enter the kingdom of heaven" (Matt. 5:20). The word "exceeds," in this case, refers to the quality of righteousness rather than to the quantity. In other words, Jesus is not calling his hearers to determine how righteous the scribes and Pharisees are and then to do them one better ("they offer one lamb in sacrifice, so we'll offer two; they fast for three days, so we'll fast for four"). No, the followers of Jesus are called to a different *kind* of righteousness, a righteousness that seeks to be ever expressive of the merciful, forgiving, reconciling will of God that lies at the center of the law.

SIX EXAMPLES
OF GREATER RIGHTEOUSNESS
Matthew 5:21–48

> 5:21 "You have heard that it was said to those of ancient times, 'You shall not murder'; and 'whoever murders shall be liable to judgment.' [22] But I say to you that if you are angry with a brother or sister, you will be liable to judgment; and if you insult a brother or sister, you will be liable to the council; and if you say, 'You fool,' you will be liable to the hell of fire. [23] So when you are offering your gift at the altar, if you remember that your brother or sister has something against you, [24] leave your gift there before the altar and go; first be reconciled to your brother or sister, and then come and offer your gift. [25] Come to terms quickly with your accuser while you are on the way to court with him, or your accuser may hand you over to the judge, and the judge to the guard, and you will be thrown into prison. [26] Truly I tell you, you will never get out until you have paid the last penny.
>
> [27] "You have heard that it was said, 'You shall not commit adultery.' [28] But I say to you that everyone who looks at a woman with lust has already committed adultery with her in his heart. [29] If your right eye causes you to sin, tear it out and throw it away; it is better for you to lose one of your mem-

bers than for your whole body to be thrown into hell. ³⁰ And if your right hand causes you to sin, cut it off and throw it away; it is better for you to lose one of your members than for your whole body to go into hell.

³¹ "It was also said, 'Whoever divorces his wife, let him give her a certificate of divorce.' ³² But I say to you that anyone who divorces his wife, except on the ground of unchastity, causes her to commit adultery; and whoever marries a divorced woman commits adultery.

³³ "Again, you have heard that it was said to those of ancient times, 'You shall not swear falsely, but carry out the vows you have made to the Lord.' ³⁴ But I say to you, Do not swear at all, either by heaven, for it is the throne of God, ³⁵ or by the earth, for it is his footstool, or by Jerusalem, for it is the city of the great King. ³⁶ And do not swear by your head, for you cannot make one hair white or black. ³⁷ Let your word be 'Yes, Yes' or 'No, No'; anything more than this comes from the evil one.

³⁸ "You have heard that it was said, 'An eye for an eye and a tooth for a tooth.' ³⁹ But I say to you, Do not resist an evildoer. But if anyone strikes you on the right cheek, turn the other also; ⁴⁰ and if anyone wants to sue you and take your coat, give your cloak as well; ⁴¹ and if anyone forces you to go one mile, go also the second mile. ⁴² Give to everyone who begs from you, and do not refuse anyone who wants to borrow from you.

⁴³ "You have heard that it was said, 'You shall love your neighbor and hate your enemy.' ⁴⁴ But I say to you, Love your enemies and pray for those who persecute you, ⁴⁵ so that you may be children of your Father in heaven; for he makes his sun rise on the evil and on the good, and sends rain on the righteous and on the unrighteous. ⁴⁶ For if you love those who love you, what reward do you have? Do not even the tax collectors do the same? ⁴⁷ And if you greet only your brothers and sisters, what more are you doing than others? Do not even the Gentiles do the same? ⁴⁸ Be perfect, therefore, as your heavenly Father is perfect.

Having stated the way in which the deep intent of the law is still in force for the church, Jesus illustrates this with six examples of practical ethical issues where the heart of the law leads to a new and greater righteousness. Because each of these examples is introduced by the formula "it was said . . . but I say to you," they are often called the "six antitheses" or the "six oppositions," but these can be misleading labels. Jesus is not saying, "Now, this is what the old law said, but I'm going to cast that aside and give you a new and completely opposite law to replace it." Rather, he is saying, "Here is what the law says, and I am going to the heart of that law to show how children of the kingdom of heaven live out its deepest meaning."

Each of these six examples in the Sermon on the Mount almost surely addresses some concrete situation or problem, such as anger, divorce, sexual mores, that was undoubtedly a matter of concern and debate in

Matthew's church. Thus, we can best understand these if we think about what may have been happening in Matthew's congregation and how these six statements of Jesus would have been put to use.

Anger (Matthew 5:21–26)

Like every other congregation in the history of Christianity, Matthew's congregation undoubtedly had its share of squabbles, head-knocking disputes, bruised feelings, and church fights. Christians are saints, but their behavior is not always saintly. This was true even in the early church. Thus, this first example of how to live the kingdom law addresses the matter of angry words and broken relationships. It focuses on anger and spite within the Christian community, but it speaks wisdom applicable beyond the bounds of the church as well.

The Old Testament law condemned murder (Exod. 20:13; Deut. 5:18), but at the heart of this law lies a respect for the life of another, regard for the right of another to be, reverence for another as the creation of God. Jesus indicates that to level a brutal curse at a brother or sister is, at least in the moment of fury, to say, "I wish you were dead."

To boil over with rage and to sling poisonous words that seek to destroy another person renders one, Jesus says, "liable to judgment . . . to the hell of fire" (Matt. 5:21–22). Those are frightening words. Does Jesus mean that if you lose your temper at a church committee meeting and unload a piece of your mind on some poor soul across the table, that you stand a good chance of—as a sulfur and brimstone preacher might say—burning in everlasting fires of hell?

No, we can quickly say that this is not what Jesus means. Such an interpretation takes the language of this passage more literally than it means to be taken, and it is out of phase with the overall redemptive intent of Jesus' message (see, for example, Matt. 11:28–30 and Matt. 18:14). On the other hand, the language of this warning *is* intentionally tough, and it will not do for us to simply wave it off with the wishful hope that Jesus does not mean what he says.

What, then, does Jesus mean? In order to get at a better sense of this passage, we can begin with the concept of "judgment." Though we tend to hear the term as a finger-wagging, guilt-inducing product of a disciplinarian God, that is not what it intends. In the biblical sense, judgment is God's exercise of *good* judgment, repairing all that is harmful to humanity. Judgment is God's repairing of the broken creation. Judgment is God's scalpel carefully removing the malignant tissue that threatens life. Judgment is God's burning away of all that is cruel and spirit killing in order that we may breathe the air of compassion. Judgment is good news; it is God setting things right.

When God sets things right, there is no room, of course, for murder, but there is also no room for murderous words or vicious deeds. So, Jesus goes on to say, if you come to worship (literally, "offer your gift at the altar," Matt. 5:23) and remember that someone "has something against you," it should become a matter of immediate concern to do whatever is in your power to heal it. Worship depends upon a congregation of worshipers who seek to be reconciled with each other and with their neighbors. Therefore, Jesus urges us, before you open your mouth to sing "Peace Like a River," do what you humanly can to make peace with those around you. In order to underscore the urgency of this, Jesus uses a practical example: If you are sued by someone and he or she has a good case, you'd better settle out of court and as quickly as you can. If you delay too long and the case goes to court, you could find yourself in prison doing hard time (5:25–26). In other words, don't wait until it is too late—till tomorrow, till next year, or till kingdom come—to make peace with your brothers and sisters.

Jealousy and Strife (Matthew 5:27–30)

Matthew's congregation not only experienced the divisions caused by resentment; it also faced the jealousies and strife generated by sexual seductions. If raw anger toward a neighbor moves toward saying "I wish you were dead," lust toward another's spouse moves toward saying "I wish you were mine."

Marriages in the Christian community should strive, through the faithfulness between husband and wife, to be expressions of the faithfulness God demonstrates toward the world. Adultery, obviously, breaks the bond of faithfulness. Covetous desire contemplates such a break, and, thus, is the first step in that direction. The law of Moses forbids adultery (see Exod. 20:14; Deut. 5:18), not because it involves sexual intercourse but because it invades and destroys the marriage covenant, which forms the context for trusting and joyful sexuality. Jesus, therefore, again goes to the heart of the law by his word against lust. In our erotically charged society, constantly titillated by provocative sexual images in the popular media, this passage reminds us that sexual playfulness is not always harmless. Sexual urges are powerful, creative, and energizing; they can also divide, disrupt, and destroy.

However, there is one aspect of this passage that needs an extra measure of interpretation in our day, lest we misunderstand it—Jesus' statement that it would be better to cut off your hand or tear out your eye than to allow sight or touch to entice you to lust (Matt. 5:29–30). The language here is, of course, hyperbole, designed to make the point that the kingdom of heaven is so precious, so much of a treasure, that absolutely nothing should be allowed to interfere with our participation in it. We must be careful, though, not to put too much of a psychological spin on this text. In terms of contemporary psychology, we know that sexual energy and attraction are enduring parts of the human psyche. We are constantly "on" as sexual beings. It is not a matter of choice; it's a matter of being human. If, therefore, we interpret this text too subjectively and put our motives under the microscope, we would have to confess that sexual desire is always at work, to some degree or another. If that is the lust that Jesus opposes, then we would have to remove not only our eyes and our hands, but our brains as well.

Jesus speaks, however, not of psychological introspection, but of people's basic attitudes, the choices that we make about what we allow to take root in our imaginations, to shape our thoughts, to govern our actions, and to mold our relationships. For Jesus, lust is a covetousness at the heart of a person, a distortion of the human will, in other words, an intention to break a sacred covenant poised just this side of action. The notion of sexual feeling constantly bubbling up from a spring in the unconscious mind is a modern idea, unknown to people in Matthew's day. The notion of possessive sexual desire being fed, petted, nurtured, and trained until it is straining at the leash ready to spring into destructive action is as old as humanity itself—and obsolete, claims Jesus, in the kingdom of heaven.

Divorce (Matthew 5:31–32)

Because Matthew's congregation included marriages, it also included the possibility of divorce, and it inevitably had to struggle with that question. Indeed, the problem of divorce may have been a particularly pressing question in Matthew's church, because Matthew includes two sayings of Jesus regarding this issue in the Gospel (this text, Matt. 5:31–32, and Matt. 19:3–9).

The law of Moses specified a divorce procedure: If a man found something about his wife objectionable, he could write a certificate of divorce and send her out of the house (Deut. 24:1). Notice that this law assumes a male-dominated world, one where men are in charge and make the decisions about whether or not their wives are welcome in the home. The law, as it stands in Deuteronomy, does not directly challenge—indeed it protects—this male control, but it does put some constraints on it. The requirement to write a certificate of divorce gave at least a small measure of protection to the woman, for it certified that she had been divorced by her husband and allowed her to be remarried without the suspicion of adultery.

So, we must see this Old Testament divorce law in its own social context in the ancient world, namely, a patriarchal world in which a wife was seen as the legal property of the husband. The law moves, then, in two opposite directions at the same time; it both upholds this patriarchal society and works to change it to some degree. The Old Testament divorce law reflects the prevailing social customs and simply outlines the process for powerful husbands properly to dispose of their powerless wifely property, but it also modifies this absolute power of men over women by saying, in effect, "You must protect her by providing a certificate of divorce."

But the question for Jesus is, What is the heart of this divorce law? Is it on the side of the law that endorses the male prerogative to rid himself, without any ethical qualm, of his wife whenever he feels like it, so long as he fills out the proper papers? Or is it on the side of the protection for the woman and the valuing of her person reflected in the requirement to provide a certificate?

Jesus' statement leaves no doubt. There is no divorce procedure a man can follow that will leave him with clean hands. To abandon his wife, with or without a certificate, is, in essence, to treat her as worthless (that is the effect of the phrase "causes her to commit adultery," Matt. 5:32) and to be guilty of destroying her person. Even to participate in a secondary way in such a custom ("whoever marries a divorced woman," Matt. 5:32) is to support its evil effects. Jesus' statement in the Sermon on the Mount about divorce still assumes that divorce is always initiated by men. Note, however, the parallel statement of Jesus in Mark 10:2–12, which, evidently reflecting different social conditions than those reflected in Matthew, adds the possibility of a woman divorcing her husband.

Thus, Jesus clearly speaks to forbid divorce. The only exception to this rule is "unchastity" (Matt. 5:32), a word that is a translation of a Greek term (*porneia*), the meaning of which is unclear. It could refer to almost any form of sexual aberration but, in this context, probably means either adultery or incest.

The main point, however, is that Jesus allows no room for the practice of divorce in a culture where divorce is an assault on the value of persons, an abuse of power, and a trivializing of faithful commitments. How shall we receive Jesus' words today? Divorce is common in our society; hardly any family is untouched by it. Is divorce outside the bounds of the Christian faith? Is remarriage forbidden by the Sermon on the Mount?

In an environment where commitments are frivolous, where marriage covenants are taken lightly, and where divorce is easy, it is not difficult to apply Jesus' words. However, even in our divorce-saturated culture, this is rarely the case. In most instances, marriage is taken quite seriously, and divorce is a grave—sometimes even tragic—matter. Even though today approximately half of all marriages end in divorce, not many of them end easily, but rather with great cost, much pain, and deep wounds. Some people, to be sure, casually leave their marriages. Most divorced people, however, have left their marriages because, to the best of their ability to see, they had to. What do the words of Jesus mean for these people?

We need, first, to acknowledge that the word "divorce" in the Sermon on the Mount does not mean exactly what the word "divorce" means today. In the first-century world, divorce was similar to what we would call "abandonment"—someone simply walked out (or, more likely, threw the woman out) with little ceremony. In societies where the church has been a major factor, divorce laws have been changed to make abandonment illegal. In other words, most contemporary divorce laws have been affected, to some degree, by the Sermon on the Mount.

The most important need, though, is to discern what lies at the heart of Jesus' words, just as Jesus discerned what lay at the heart of the Mosaic law. Marriage is intended to be a communion between two people that expresses, in their mutual fidelity, the faithfulness of God. It is intended to be a place of safety, nurture, and honor for persons. In Jesus' day, the customs and practices of divorce were a direct assault on those values.

Today, ironically, a hopelessly broken marriage can itself sometimes be such an assault. A marriage can become distorted. It can betray its intended purposes and become a place where people are in physical or mental danger, where they are tragically dishonest and mutually destructive. Jesus' word about divorce was spoken to preserve the value of the people involved in marriages. When a marriage becomes the very arena where people are destroying each other, we should ask how can the safety, nurture, and honor of the marriage partners best be preserved? This will mean viewing with compassion the people and their relationship, not merely defending the institution of marriage as such. Marriage was made for humanity, not humanity for marriage.

Oaths (Matthew 5:33–37)

The fourth example of the greater righteousness has to do with the ancient custom of taking oaths. People in the ancient world would, in order to make a vow or promise more solemn, invoke the name of God—something like, "As God is my witness, I swear to you that. . . . " Remnants of this old practice remain today when witnesses in courts of law are pledged to "tell the truth, the whole truth, and nothing but the truth, so help me God" or when people mutter, "By God, I'm not going to let them get away with that!"

The Old Testament law condemned *false* oaths, that is, promising in the name of God to do something and, then, not doing it (Lev. 19:12). But Jesus sweeps away oaths of every kind, declaring, "Do not swear at all" (Matt. 5:34). Why? What is wrong with pledging to do something in the name of God, so long as you are true to your word? Some have argued that what Jesus is against here is the use of "swear words." Although this idea is not entirely beside the point (some of our modern "curse words" originated in religious oaths and curses), common profanity is not the main subject of this text.

The real issue has to do with what it means to utter the name of God. In the ancient world, names were bound up with the identity of a person. To know a person's name was to know something of the essence of that person; to say a person's name was, in a way, to call forth the presence of that person. This is true as well for the name of God. When Moses asked God, "What is your name?" Moses was not asking for information, but for a more intimate relationship. God replied with a name that is impossible to capture in translation; something like "I AM WHO I AM" is the best we can do (Exod. 3:13–14). And that seems to be the point about God's name. Something about the name of God slips from our linguistic grasp. We know the name of God; God gave it to Moses and, thus, to us. We can use God's name to call upon God and to find ourselves in the presence of God. But even when we name God, we name mystery; we name One whom we do not fully know: I AM WHO I AM. The person of God cannot be captured in human categories; God enters into relationship with us, but ever remains beyond our control.

What was happening in Matthew's community about oath taking that made this word of Jesus particularly relevant? Probably there was the casual use of oaths. Perhaps people were attaching "in the name of God" or "as God is my witness" to the common transactions of life, to everyday promises—the pledge to buy a cow, the vow to visit a relative, the commitment to pay a debt—hoping to summon the divine power to bolster them in life's routines.

This constituted a reversal of the proper divine-human relationship. Instead of human beings calling upon the mysterious name of God and being drawn up into the power of God's holy presence, people were using the name of God, arrogantly assuming that God could be controlled, domesticated, harnessed to pull whatever wagon they wanted to ride.

Jesus' word erases this practice: "You do not control God, so do not swear at all." As we read this passage, we can almost hear the familiar sounds of children trying to bargain with a parent.

> Jesus says, "Do not swear at all."
>
> "OK," the children reply, "we won't swear in God's name, but what about vowing, 'In heaven's name'?"
>
> "No, heaven is God's throne."
>
> "Well, then, what about swearing 'in the name of the earth'?"
>
> "No, don't swear that way either. The earth is God's footstool."
>
> "But surely we can at least swear by Jerusalem!"
>
> "No, indeed. Jerusalem is God's city. Indeed, everything is God's, and you cannot escape God's holy presence. You do not control God; you do not control the world. In fact, you do not even control the color of your own hair, so do not swear by that either!"
>
> "But, what can we say then?"
>
> "Tell the truth. You are given power over your own words, so when you say 'yes,' mean it, and when you say 'no,' mean that as well."

So, this example of the greater righteousness is about attempting to control God. Children of the kingdom of heaven do not practice magic; they practice ministry. They walk out the front door into the world and say what they mean—"yes, yes" and "no, no"—without trying to conjure God up with pious formulas. They do this not because they think they don't need God's help out in the world to live through the day. They do this because they know the whole world belongs to God and that God was already at work out there long before daybreak.

Retaliation (Matthew 5:38–42)

In a society based on raw power, the one with the strongest fists or the most guns wins. Instead of the Golden Rule, the ethic in such a world is "Do unto others first before they do unto you" or, at least, "If they do anything bad to you at all, finish them off before they do anything worse."

In such a "survival of the fittest" environment, the law of Moses was a mitigating, moderating force. "No," it said, "don't retaliate against other people with every ounce of destruction you can muster. Let the response be measured by the offense: an eye for an eye, and *only* an eye; a tooth for a tooth, but *only* a tooth" (see Exod. 21:24; Lev. 24:20; Deut. 19:21).

Thus, the Old Testament law set human society on a trajectory of moderation and restraint, and, now, Jesus brings that curve to its logical destination: "Do not resist an evildoer at all." Jesus provides some practical examples to illustrate this principle: If someone hits you on one cheek, offer the other one; if someone sues you in court, give them what they want, and even more; if someone forces you to go one mile, go two; and give to every beggar and borrower who asks.

It boggles the mind, of course, to think about living out this example literally in contemporary society. Imagine a Christian in New York City who got up one morning and decided to do what Jesus says here: to turn the other cheek, to give to every beggar, and to respond to every lawsuit by settling out of court for double the amount. This person would be broke, homeless, and in the emergency room of Bellevue Hospital before noon!

There are two main ways to think about this saying. First, Jesus provides something of a strategy for robbing violent and oppressive people of their cruel power. If a corrupt police officer hits an innocent man in the face with a billy club and the man retaliates by trying to hit back, then the officer has won, for he has established violence as the agenda. But, what if the man, struck on one cheek, should stand there firmly and thrust forward the other cheek, as if to say, "You may like violence but you are not in total control. I choose another way"? The turning of the other cheek discloses that cruel people may do violence, but they do not have the power to take away the dignity and humanity of other people.

That leads to the second way to understand Jesus' word—as good news that in God's new creation there will be no violence. No one will have to stockpile weapons or carry a can of chemical mace. People will not have to put deadbolts on their doors and set the alarms on their security systems to protect their possessions. Indeed, people will not want to lock up their belongings at all; they will want to share them with others. Lawyers and judges and suing people will be obsolete (as well as preachers and church committee meetings!). No one will resist a neighbor because no one will need to do so. This is the way it will be in the kingdom of heaven.

So, how can we live today in the light of that kingdom? Christians need to move past the idea of justice as fair play ("You do this to me; I deserve to do an equal amount back") and ask instead, "If someone does something evil to me, how may I respond with only good in return?" The idea here is not to be a victim ("You hit me once; here, please, hit me again"), but to be a human being created in God's image and, ultimately, to be a blessing, even to those who would do violence.

In Jesus' day, this meant opening up one's purse to the village beggar. In our day of homeless people thronging city streets, it may mean working for programs to provide jobs for those who need work, safe shelters for those in need of housing, food for the hungry, and community mental health services for those whose minds are diseased. In Jesus' day, living the kingdom ethic meant not swinging back when you were slapped, and showing that you refrained out of love rather than cowardice ("turn the other cheek"). In our day, it may mean working to see that police do not escalate violence in our communities, that words of anger spoken in our homes are met with words of compassion and not blows of aggression.

Love (Matthew 5:43–48)

Jesus' final example of the greater righteousness of the kingdom of heaven is, perhaps, the most radical and demanding example of all. The Old Testament law commanded, "Love your neighbor as yourself" (Lev. 19:18). The Old Testament says nothing about hating one's enemies, but many religious people interpreted the law to allow such. "It says 'love your neighbor,' " they would say to themselves. "That means I must love my neighbor, but I am free to act however I desire to my non-neighbors. So, I am obliged to love the family next door, but those blasphemous Samaritans and those unclean Gentiles—well, that's another matter."

The heart of the law, as Jesus interpreted it, was to love even your enemies and pray even for those who persecute you (Matt. 5:44). The reason that one ought to do this is because God is like this, and we are God's children. God does not hate the enemy; indeed, the good gifts of life—the sun and the rain—are lavished on everyone. If we love only those who love us, we are simply imitating the world (even scoundrels such as "tax collectors" love those who love them) rather than imitating God.

It is this call to be like God that best interprets the saying "Be perfect, therefore, as your heavenly Father is perfect" (Matt. 5:48). "Perfection" here is not making an A+ on every test; perfection is wholeness, consumed by love, holiness. To be "perfect" is to respond to other people—even our enemies—with the kind of compassion and desire for the good that expresses the way God responds to the world.

THREE PRACTICES
OF THE CHRISTIAN FAITH
Matthew 6:1–18

6:1 **"Beware of practicing your piety before others in order to be seen by them; for then you have no reward from your Father in heaven.**

2 "So whenever you give alms, do not sound a trumpet before you, as the hypocrites do in the synagogues and in the streets, so that they may be praised by others. Truly I tell you, they have received their reward. 3 But when you give alms, do not let your left hand know what your right hand is doing, 4 so that your alms may be done in secret; and your Father who sees in secret will reward you.

5 "And whenever you pray, do not be like the hypocrites; for they love to stand and pray in the synagogues and at the street corners, so that they may be seen by others. Truly I tell you, they have received their reward. 6 But whenever you pray, go into your room and shut the door and pray to your Father who is in secret; and your Father who sees in secret will reward you.

7 "When you are praying, do not heap up empty phrases as the Gentiles do; for they think that they will be heard because of their many words. 8 Do not be like them, for your Father knows what you need before you ask him.

9."Pray then in this way:
    Our Father in heaven,
        hallowed be your name.
10 Your kingdom come.
    Your will be done,
        on earth as it is in heaven.
11 Give us this day our daily bread.
12 And forgive us our debts,
        as we also have forgiven our debtors.
13 And do not bring us to the time of trial,
        but rescue us from the evil one.

14 For if you forgive others their trespasses, your heavenly Father will also forgive you; 15 but if you do not forgive others, neither will your Father forgive your trespasses.

16 "And whenever you fast, do not look dismal, like the hypocrites, for they disfigure their faces so as to show others that they are fasting. Truly I tell you, they have received their reward. 17 But when you fast, put oil on your head and wash your face, 18 so that your fasting may be seen not by others but by your Father who is in secret; and your Father who sees in secret will reward you.

According to an old joke, it was once said that many people would be equally shocked to hear Christianity doubted or to see it practiced. The Christian faith, of course, is not just a collection of ideas to be believed; it is also a set of deeds to be performed. There are things that Christians believe because they are Christians, but there are also things that Christians *do* because they are Christians. Some of these practices vary from place to place and tradition to tradition, but others—like worship, prayer, gathering for fellowship, studying scripture, and performing deeds of charity—are common to all Christians.

Here in this section of the Sermon on the Mount, Jesus addresses this matter of Christian practice, teaching about the proper way to observe three of the basic practices of the Christian community: giving money for the poor, prayer, and fasting. Why these three and not others? The answer is that these are representative practices, examples drawn from the world of Matthew's congregation. They are not the only important disciplines of the Christian faith, but ones that Matthew's readers, with their Jewish roots, would immediately recognize as significant, since almsgiving, prayer, and fasting were among the main outward marks of Judaism.

So, Jesus takes up these three familiar practices in order to illustrate that followers of Jesus, too, practice their faith, but with a difference. They continue the practices learned in Judaism of giving alms, praying, and fasting, but each of these practices is redefined in the light of the kingdom of heaven. If a practice is faith put into action, faith that can be *seen*, Jesus' main shift has to do with who does the seeing. Jesus teaches that practices are not performed for the benefit of other people, but only for God—for "your Father who sees in secret" (Matt. 6:4, 6, 18). Money is given to the poor, prayers are prayed, and fasting is performed not so that human eyes can see and be impressed, but before God alone.

But how does this fit in with Jesus' teaching in the previous chapter that Christians should be shining lights so that others can see their good works (Matt. 5:16)? If Christians practice the faith in secret, how can they let their light shine? This seeming contradiction clears up when we recognize that Jesus is speaking about two different types of action. There are some deeds that the church performs out in the world and in behalf of the world. For example, when Christians join with a local housing group to help construct needed shelter in a community, they do this because they believe they are doing the will of God, a God who cares for the world. They hope both to provide adequate housing for people who do not have it and to provide a witness to the society about the ways of God. In other words, when the church performs this sort of action, Christians let their light shine, not so the world will look up and say, "What a wonderful organization the church is!" but, instead, "What a merciful God they serve!"

There is, however, another kind of Christian action, what can be called the "interior disciplines" of the faith: prayer, worship, acts of personal devotion. These disciplines grow out of a relationship with God, and, indeed, they work to express, maintain, and deepen that relationship. These disciplines are performed before God alone—before "the Father who sees in secret," in the language of the Sermon on the Mount.

Almsgiving (Matthew 6:1–4)

Almsgiving, making offerings in behalf of the poor, was a regular part of the religious life among Jews and the early Christians. Just as is done today, some of these people gave earnestly, out of a sincere faith, and others gave so they could wear a tither's badge to the civic club. Jesus uses a joke to attack the behavior of hypocrites (literally, people who perform behind a mask, that is, people who appear one way but are really another way inside). He humorously pictures them blowing a trumpet to attract attention as they carry their offerings to the synagogue. When they give alms, what they really want is to be noticed. The sad reality is that they get what they want, but only that. "Truly I tell you," Jesus says, "they have received their reward" (Matt. 6:2).

Those who belong to the kingdom of heaven are called to engage in another practice. They give their offerings in secret. Jesus employs another bit of exaggeration to describe this: If the hypocrites play "Look at Me" on the trumpet when they toss their coins in the poor box, followers of Jesus should be so private that the left hand doesn't know what the right hand is doing (Matt. 6:3). Because the offerings are made in secret, there will be no fanfare. No one will exclaim, "Look at that impressive display of generosity!" but, even though such offerings are not seen in the public eye, they do count in the kingdom of heaven.

The phrase "your Father . . . will reward you" (Matt. 6:4) is literally "your Father . . . will pay you back." This is not to be taken in the sense that, when we are generous in giving to others, God owes us some kind of debt; we cannot put God in our debt. Rather, it points to a more radical and hopeful idea, the claim that human life—our life, the life of others—depends entirely upon the constant and infinite mercy of God. We float in an ocean of God's generosity. All that we have, all that we are comes by the mercy of God. So, when we are generous toward others, we are not writing checks on a limited account. We are drawing from an inexhaustible flow of divine grace; works of mercy never deplete the supply.

Prayer (Matthew 6:5–7)

The second discipline that Jesus names is prayer, and, again, the emphasis is on the contrast between the genuine and the hypocritical. Jesus protests against prayers that are showy and pompously verbose (Matt. 6:5, 7) and calls for authentic prayer to be done simply and in the privacy of one's own room.

At first glance, it would seem that Jesus is speaking out against two kinds of prayers: (1) lengthy prayers and (2) public prayers, that is, the kind of praying done in corporate worship and in prayer groups. To understand Jesus' word this way, however, would be to take this passage out of context. Jesus himself sometimes prayed for a long time (perhaps even all night! See Matthew 14:23–25). Moreover, he prayed in the presence of others, at the synagogue and with his disciples. Indeed, the language of Jesus' own model prayer (the "Lord's Prayer") assumes that more than one voice is praying (*"Our* Father . . .").

The real targets of Jesus' warning are not long prayers or public prayers, but ones in which we attempt to flatter ourselves and prayers that attempt to flatter God. Matthew's church was familiar with self-flattering prayer; they had seen it in the synagogue and perhaps even in their own congregation. Some worshipers would make a lavish show of being prayerful, firing off prayers uttered to be heard not primarily by God but by other people. When Jesus suggests entering your own room and shutting the door, he is using a figure of speech not to attack corporate prayer or to say that all praying should be done in a locked closet, but rather to make an emphatic point about the true audience of all prayer. It would be as if he had said, "When you pray, go into the deepest part of the loneliest swamp you know and hide behind the tallest tree where not even the birds and the squirrels can see you. Then, in that secluded and unseen place, you will know that all true prayer—whether it occurs in the quietness of your bedtime, in the middle of rush-hour traffic, or in unison in a vast congregation—is spoken only to the secret depths of God."

Some prayers are designed to flatter ourselves, but others are vain attempts to flatter God. In the popular religions of the first-century world, getting the gods to respond to one's needs was a bit like a person today attempting to get some service from a government bureaucracy. There were so many gods and so many subdivisions of the divine infrastructure, one was never sure from which god to request a certain service. Once one did locate the right godly contact, a little verbal bribery would often grease the skids. So, the prayers of pagans ("Gentiles" in Matt. 6:7) were piled up with divine names in hopes of hitting on the right one and filled with ingratiating compliments to curry the god's favor. So, when Jesus criticizes piling up "empty phrases" (Matt. 6:7), the target is not lengthy prayers per se, but what could be called "safecracker" prayers; that is, windy and fawning prayers that attempt to use flowery charm to pick the lock on the favor of the gods, to manipulate the gods into action by uttering the right combination of words.

But God is no stranger to us, and that is the point of Jesus' word about prayer. Jesus reassures us that we can pray, not as outsiders, but as God's children, tenderly, honestly, and confidently. In our secret, whispered prayers, we are known so well that God, like a mother listening with her heart to her children, can finish our sentences.

Interlude:
The Lord's Prayer (Matthew 6:8–15)

In the middle of his discussion of prayer, Jesus provides a model prayer, what we have come to call "The Lord's Prayer." There is evidence that the church, from the very beginning, used this prayer as an example, adding phrases to it as time went by. This process of development can actually be seen in the New Testament itself. A briefer, and perhaps earlier, version of the Lord's Prayer is found in Luke 11:1–4. Matthew's variation of the Lord's Prayer is longer and more rhythmic than Luke's. In other words, Matthew's version is easier to say aloud and probably reflects a shaping of the prayer for use in corporate worship. The familiar ending phrase "for the kingdom and the power and the glory are yours forever" seems to have been added at a later time, and therefore the New Revised Standard Version places this phrase in a footnote.

The prayer is divided into three sections:

1. *The Address to God: "Our Father in heaven."* To whom do we pray? These opening words appeal to a God who is as close to us as a parent—a "father" who knows everything we need before we ask; one who, at the same time, is a majestic, heavenly God, providing for the whole of creation.

As such, this opening phrase continues to guide prayer today, keeping it on course between distance and intimacy. We can be too careful about prayer, of course, trying to maintain proper balance, seeking to ensure that our prayer words are always considered and temperate. Real prayer is mostly not like that. Outside of the measured cadences of high liturgy, most Christian praying is urgently, and perhaps even joyfully, more reckless; it is an untamed cry from the needful heart.

So, we can pray boldly. When our words are too small, we are nonetheless taken into the very presence of the God who embraces the whole of creation. When our words are too formal and remote, we are nonetheless met in the middle of the road by the God who will not stay far away. The twin channel markers, the intimate "our Father" and the surpassing "in heaven," are visible in rough water, firmly directing us into the harbor of mercy.

2. *Petitions for the Victory of God.* In three short phrases, the Lord's Prayer next pleads with God to set things right, to push back all that harms and destroys, and to come in power to save all creation. The first of these

phrases, "hallowed be your name," is, in effect, a daring cry to "show the world who you are." When we refer to someone of good reputation, we sometimes say that they have a good name. This petition—"make your name holy"—appeals to God to act in the world in ways that will make every nation on the earth exult, "Now there's a God who has a good name!"

The second phrase, "your kingdom come," simply underscores the first by imploring God to make salvation visible in the world. If "hallowed be your name" seeks the holiness of God's name, then "your kingdom come" wants to put a face with the name. It entreats God to come and to roll back all the forces that enslave us; it is a message flashed from a captive people to the divine force of liberation out at sea, "Come ashore and free your people."

If "your kingdom come" asks God to occupy the beachhead and to overthrow the tyranny that crushes us, the third phrase, "your will be done, on earth as it is in heaven," anticipates the reign of peace, the time when heaven and earth are united in harmony. This phrase also constitutes a major transition in the Lord's Prayer, a turn from "heaven" to "earth," a move from "your will be done" to "give us this day," a shift from focusing upon the holiness of God to the needs of God's holy people.

The words "your will be done on earth" recognize that only God can save the world. No revolution, no reformation, no program for social improvement can fully heal the wounds of a hurting world; only God can do that, and so we cry, "Your will be done on earth!" But, as soon as we have uttered those words "on earth," we become aware of ourselves, our earth-bound selves. We are "on earth," and the prayer, which ascended to the holy heights of heaven, has now brought us firmly back to where we live, to the pew where we sit, to the shop where we work, to the relationships where we struggle to be responsible, to the place where we try to serve. It is God's heavenly will that is to be done, but it is on earth that it is to be accomplished. Built into the language of the prayer is the intrinsic connection between God's work and ours; a cry to the God of salvation leads us in God's name to our neighbor in need; a plea for the heavenly God to save empowers us to be earthly agents of reconciliation.

3. *Petitions for God's People.* At midpoint, the Lord's Prayer shifts its focus from God alone to the needs of God's people. The three phrases that were directed toward aspects of God's character ("your name . . . your kingdom . . . your will") are now matched by three phrases that ask God for help ("give us bread . . . forgive us . . . rescue us").

The first petition asks God to "give us this day our daily bread," and it basically asks God for the food necessary to make it through the day. What is most important about this request is what lies beneath it—an awareness that human life depends upon daily gifts from the hand of God. Full pantries and freezers cannot conceal the fact that were God to cease to provide for our needs, all life would perish. Like Israel in the wilderness receiving enough "manna" each day, Jesus' followers are to trust God for each day's nourishment (see Exodus 16).

The second of these petitions asks God to "forgive us our debts." This is, of course, a plea to God to forgive our sins ("debts" is a synonym for "sins"), but the very next phrase, "as we also have forgiven our debtors," seems to imply that we get from God only as much forgiveness as we can give to others. This is reinforced in Matthew 6:14–15, where Jesus says that "if you do not forgive others, neither will your Father forgive your trespasses." In other words, it would appear that God waits to see how forgiving we are and, then, matches our level. That interpretation, however, is theologically nearsighted. Our behavior does not somehow transform an unmerciful God into a merciful one. God is forgiving even when we are not. God is generous and merciful because God is God.

What, then, does it mean when Jesus says that "if you do not forgive others, neither will your Father forgive your trespasses" (Matt. 6:15)? In order to understand this, we must first remember that this is a word addressed to the church, to believers, to the followers of Jesus. In other words, Jesus is speaking to people who have already been forgiven, people whose sinful debts of enormous proportions have already been wiped off the books (see Matt. 18:23–35), people who have been trained in the school of forgiveness, people who have, through no merit of their own, been given passports in the kingdom of heaven. Being a citizen of God's kingdom, like being a citizen of a nation, is not just an idea; it is an identity, a way of life. To be a citizen of the kingdom of heaven is to see the world in kingdom ways and to practice the customs of that kingdom, such as forgiveness.

Thus, placed in the context of his larger message, Jesus' word on forgiveness is this: "You who follow me are citizens of the kingdom of heaven. In the kingdom all that is harmful is absent, all that is evil is destroyed, all that is sick is healed, and all that is sinful is forgiven. You are called to be faithful citizens of that kingdom, serving others and forgiving them over and over again, so that the whole world will know that God is a forgiving God. If you do not practice forgiveness, you are rejecting your own identity and saying, 'I no longer want to be a citizen of the kingdom.'"

Forgiveness is not a matter of bookkeeping; it is part of a living relationship with God and others. Forgiveness is not a matter of some distant divine accountant burning the note on our sinful debts and saying, "Well, that's that." Forgiveness is to the Christian life like breathing; constant and life-giving. What we breathe in from God's mercy we express to others. Inhale. Exhale. Forgive us, as we forgive; as we forgive, forgive us.

The third of these petitions is "do not bring us to the time of trial" (Matt. 6:13). The language is ambiguous, and scholars are not certain what "time of trial" Jesus had in mind. Does he refer to the daily temptations of the Christian life or to the final judgment, the great time of testing envisioned at the end of time? The answer, perhaps, is both. The language of the prayer catches up in a single stitch all the forms of temptation and testing that threaten to divide and defeat the followers of Jesus.

It would be a mistake to press too hard the question "Does God *cause* us to be tempted?" The Lord's Prayer is not a philosophical meditation on the origins of evil and temptation. It is, instead, the fervent prayer of the church pleading with God to hold them together and to give them strength to accomplish their mission in a difficult world. The best way to understand the petition "do not bring us to the time of trial" is to envision the congregation heading out the front door of the church to do God's work in a storm-tossed world and whispering the prayer "Keep us safe out there, O God. Let the forces of evil tremble to see us coming, rather than the other way around, and bring us home at the end of this day even stronger in faith than when we go out."

Fasting (Matthew 6:16–18)

The third of the three practices Jesus addresses in the sermon is fasting, a discipline that is frequently mentioned in scripture but infrequently observed in the church today. Richard J. Foster has observed: "In a culture where the landscape is dotted with shrines to the Golden Arches and an assortment of Pizza Temples, fasting seems out of place, out of step with the times" (Foster, *Celebration of Discipline: The Path to Spiritual Growth*, 47).

Fasting is, of course, the discipline of refraining from eating for a period of time, but what is the purpose of a fast? A fast is a form of worship; it is prayer in action. Some prayers are joyful and thankful, but fasting is most often an acted prayer of lament and submission. In the Bible, fasting is done in periods of national crisis (for example, 2 Chronicles 1—4), in times of repentance and renewal (see Jer. 36:9–20), and on occasions of humbling encounters with God (see Acts 9:9). The prophet Isaiah called Israel to a righteous fast, hungering for justice in the land (Isa. 58:1–12).

Jesus contrasts true fasting with that of the hypocrites, who contort their faces to show how sad and hungry they are. They seem to say, "Look at my piety. I am fasting." The hypocrites are like some politicians who ride in helicopters over natural disasters. Their faces are grim and mournful, but it is only a "photo opportunity." Being seen with a sad face is the point, and they have their reward. Hypocritical fasting is doleful on the outside but empty on the inside. True fasting, by contrast, is hungry for God and justice on the inside but, ironically, wears a joyful face ("put oil on your head and wash your face," Matt. 6:17).

THE DISTRACTION OF WEALTH
Matthew 6:19–34

6:19 "Do not store up for yourselves treasures on earth, where moth and rust consume and where thieves break in and steal; 20 but store up for yourselves treasures in heaven, where neither moth nor rust consumes and where thieves do not break in and steal. 21 For where your treasure is, there your heart will be also.

22 "The eye is the lamp of the body. So, if your eye is healthy, your whole body will be full of light; 23 but if your eye is unhealthy, your whole body will be full of darkness. If then the light in you is darkness, how great is the darkness!

24 "No one can serve two masters; for a slave will either hate the one and love the other, or be devoted to the one and despise the other. You cannot serve God and wealth.

25 "Therefore I tell you, do not worry about your life, what you will eat or what you will drink, or about your body, what you will wear. Is not life more than food, and the body more than clothing? 26 Look at the birds of the air; they neither sow nor reap nor gather into barns, and yet your heavenly Father feeds them. Are you not of more value than they? 27 And can any of you by worrying add a single hour to your span of life? 28 And why do you worry about clothing? Consider the lilies of the field, how they grow; they neither toil nor spin, 29 yet I tell you, even Solomon in all his glory was not clothed like one of these. 30 But if God so clothes the grass of the field, which is alive today and tomorrow is thrown into the oven, will he not much more clothe you—you of little faith? 31 Therefore do not worry, saying, 'What will we eat?' or 'What will we drink?' or 'What will we wear?' 32 For it is the Gentiles who strive for all these things; and indeed your heavenly Father knows that you need all these things. 33 But strive first for the kingdom of God and his righteousness, and all these things will be given to you as well.

34 "So do not worry about tomorrow, for tomorrow will bring worries of its own. Today's trouble is enough for today.

This section of the Sermon on the Mount begins a collection of teachings of Jesus on assorted matters. The contents of this portion of the Sermon are more varied, and the structure is looser than the earlier material, but one can still trace a common thread running throughout—namely, the urgency of seeking the kingdom of heaven above all earthly distractions.

In this passage, Jesus warns against the perennial human tendency to stockpile wealth as a hedge against insecurity. The problem with investing our sense of worth in cash and possessions is that such an investment is always at peril. It is never safe. Cash can be stolen; Porsches and Cadillacs rust; corporations collapse; moths eat dinner jackets. The "lifestyles of the rich and famous" are lifestyles of the always vulnerable and ever fearful. Moreover, there is always someone around who has more than we do, and the quest to keep up is an endless burden. Deadbolts, safety-deposit boxes, tax shelters—none of them finally protect what we really desire; none of them make secure a treasure worthy of our hearts.

What our hearts really desire, of course, is to count—to count *for something* and to count *to someone.* To come to the end of a day—or the end of a life—with the satisfaction of having stood for what is good, with the joy of having been loved and having loved well in return, with the memory of having shown mercy, and with the peace of having walked with God— these are the true treasures, the treasures of the kingdom, a fortune no thief can plunder.

The decision whether to store up treasures on earth or treasures in heaven is not one of mere financial planning; it is one of basic orientation. The call to "store up for yourselves treasures in heaven" (Matt. 6:20) is not a question of prudence. It is more radical than that; it is a question of vision and freedom—what a person sees and what holds a person captive. If a person sees life as a gift from God, a bountiful outpouring of God's providence, then that person is free to hold possessions with a light grasp and to be generous toward others. On the other hand, if life is seen as a competitive struggle between winners and losers over limited resources, then one is a slave to this struggle, and the only viable creed is "Where's Mine?"

It is this matter of basic orientation to which Jesus is intimating with the two images of the eye (Matt. 6:22–23) and the slave master (Matt. 6:24). First, he compares the human spirit to the eye, which is "the lamp of the body." Today, we think of the human eye as a receiver of light, but in the ancient world the eye was considered to be a *source* of light that illumined reality. So, the crucial issue is what one sees. If one's eye is healthy—that is, if one essentially has a generous spirit and sees the world in a benevolent light—then one's total life will be abounding. On the other hand, if one basically sees the world in a pinched and selfish way, then one's whole existence, even acts of apparent charity, will be begrudging.

Next, Jesus reminds his hearers that God and wealth are two demanding and competing masters. If a slave had two masters, what was to be done if these masters gave conflicting commands? The slave must choose, must turn toward one in loyalty and away from the other. God and wealth have different tasks in mind for their slaves. Wealth says, "Because of your superb credit, you are among the elite chosen to receive a Gold Card." God says, "Blessed are the poor in spirit, for theirs is the kingdom of heaven." Wealth says, "Indulge yourself, you've earned it." God says, "Blessed are the merciful, for they will receive mercy." There are two masters, but only one servant. Living *the* good life and living *a* good life pull in opposite directions. One cannot serve both God and wealth.

This section of Jesus' Sermon seems at first to be a loose collection of sayings about the distraction of wealth and possessions, but the "therefore" of verse 25 discloses that these passages are connected and indeed are moving to a climax. As we have seen, this section begins with a word about behavior ("Do not store up for yourselves treasures on earth"). But behavior is not a matter of sheer grit and determination but, rather, of what one sees about life ("if your eye is healthy"), and what one sees is, in turn, governed by who one serves ("You cannot serve God and wealth").

Ultimately, whether one serves God or wealth depends upon trust. The appeal to trust God is the goal of Jesus' picture of the birds of the air, who are fed by God even though they neither fret nor plan, and the lilies of the field, gloriously and colorfully clothed even though they have never touched a needle and thread. If God takes care of the birds and the wild flowers, Jesus promises, then surely God will take care of us. So, not only are we freed from compulsive anxiety about vain luxuries, we do not even need to worry about the basics, about food or clothing, because our God knows we need all these things (Matt. 6:31–32) and will provide.

At first, Jesus' words about the birds and the lilies, lovely as they are, are not very compelling. Sure, birds and lilies don't worry about life, but they also don't have mortgages, car payments, grocery bills, and college tuitions to keep them awake at night. All of us would like to be relieved of worry and anxiety, but Jesus appears to be suggesting an unrealistic strategy—"look at the birds, look at the lilies"—to which one is tempted to reply, "Yes, but look at the bills!"

Jesus, however, is not suggesting that human beings can be like birds or lilies. Indeed, he means to emphasize the difference between birds and lilies, on the one hand, and human beings, on the other. Compared with human beings, birds are insignificant creatures and lilies are trifling weeds ("the grass of the field"). If God cares so lavishly for inconsequential creatures, how much more will God provide for human beings.

Also, the verbs *look* at the birds of the air and *consider* the lilies of the field are, in Greek, very strong verbs. They mean to suggest more than a casual glance; they invite us to study and to scrutinize the carefree world of nature. Jesus commands us to look, *really* look, at a world where God provides freely and lavishly, a world where anxiety plays no part, where worry is not a reality. Jesus invites us to allow our imaginations to enter such a world, to compare this world with the world in which we must live out our lives.

The rent is still due, of course, and the department store still expects payment for jeans and coats, but we have seen this other world, this world of God's gracious and tender care, and it promises to overthrow the power of anxiety. We will still wonder if we can make the checkbook balance this month, but there is nothing in this world that can take away what God provides—dignity, a sense of worth, the confidence of being treasured in the heart of God.

It is fascinating that this section of the Sermon on wealth closes with a statement not about wealth at all, but about worry: "So do not worry about tomorrow" (Matt. 6:34). The hunger to acquire wealth, the temptation to serve possessions as our master rather than the living God, grows out of greed, but at its profoundest level it has to do with anxiety about the status, security, and survival of the self. "Our hearts are restless," said Augustine, "until they rest in Thee," and restless anxiety over what tomorrow may hold is a sign that our hearts have not found their true home.

There is a kind of worry about the coming day that is normal, even healthy. Tomorrow's chemistry test or job interview is bound to provoke concern, and this command "do not worry about tomorrow" is not an invitation to finesse the exam or to waltz into the interview unprepared. Rather, it speaks to the deeper, more basic fear that something is out there in the future that can destroy our basic worth as a human being, something finally stronger than God's care, some silent killer shark swimming toward us from the future.

The statement that "today's trouble is enough for today" (Matt. 6:34) was probably a popular saying that becomes, in the context of Jesus' sermon, a kingdom saying. Those who know that God summons the sun to rise are confident that, whatever tomorrow brings, it will also bring God with it. So, they are content to leave tomorrow's trouble to tomorrow, to roll up their sleeves, and as children of the kingdom face the problems that walk through the door today.

THE DISTRACTION
OF SELF-RIGHTEOUSNESS
Matthew 7:1–5

7:1 **"Do not judge, so that you may not be judged. 2 For with the judgment you make you will be judged, and the measure you give will be the measure**

you get. ³ Why do you see the speck in your neighbor's eye, but do not notice the log in your own eye? ⁴ Or how can you say to your neighbor, 'Let me take the speck out of your eye,' while the log is in your own eye? ⁵ You hypocrite, first take the log out of your own eye, and then you will see clearly to take the speck out of your neighbor's eye.

Love of money can obviously distract one from the kingdom of heaven, but so, ironically, can love of one's own moral rectitude. In every congregation there are the moral watchdogs, the faultfinders, those who are ready to point the finger of judgment at others. To this, Jesus says, "Do not judge, so that you may not be judged" (Matt. 7:1).

But what does Jesus mean? Can he mean that, literally, Christians are never to make moral judgments about the behavior and values of others? Are we never to raise an eyebrow in concern, a voice in protest? If someone is stealing money from the offering plates or abusing children selling drugs on the street or spreading vicious rumors in the community, are we to look the other way, throw up our hands, and say, "It's not my business to judge others"? Absolutely not. In fact, later in the Gospel of Matthew Jesus describes a procedure for the church to follow in confronting wrongdoing (see Matt. 18:15–20). The words "do not judge . . . " in context are not a prohibition against moral discernment but an invitation to participate in a process of moral growth. Many people would love to be moral judges, demanding change in others. Jesus requires that before we call for the transformation of someone else, we be transformed ourselves. The words "Do not judge," when we consider the whole passage, become "In the kingdom of heaven, your standards of judgment must be transformed; therefore do not judge *until*. . . . "

Until what? Following the flow of the passage, the process unfolds this way: If a member of the faith community sees a moral flaw in another person ("the speck in your neighbor's eye," Matt. 7:3) and is tempted to come down on the neighbor in moral judgment, that person is not to do so until engaging in deep self-examination ("take the log out of your own eye," Matt. 7:5). Then, and only then, can the neighbor's wrong be addressed.

Note that this process involves two kinds of transformation. First, finding the wrong in oneself before turning the moral searchlight upon anyone else causes one to move from self-righteousness to compassion. When we recognize that we, too, are broken and flawed, that we do not stand on unspoiled moral ground, then we move from harsh judgment to a tender concern to help the neighbor ("you will see clearly to take the speck out of your neighbor's eye," Matt. 7:5). Instead of a finger poked in the neighbor's face, we reach out mercifully to wipe the neighbor's eye.

Second, Jesus cracks something of a joke when he pictures people concerned about a fly speck in the neighbor's eye while remaining oblivious to a two-by-four in their own moral vision. Beneath the joke, however, lies a serious point: Only when we have stared into the abyss of our own moral failure can we be of genuine strength to others in their struggles. It will not do to say condescendingly to others, "Yes, yes, I feel so much compassion for you in your moral predicament because I've struggled a bit with that myself." Only those who realize the immensity of their moral struggle, those who have felt the full weight of the "log in their own eye," those who see the truth that they have been fighting a losing battle were it not for the mercy of God, only these are able to be a resource to others. This is a lesson that groups like Alcoholics Anonymous have learned well. Those who are fighting addiction are helped most not by people who scold and judge, but by those who have admitted their own powerlessness, those who confess that the springs of moral refreshment come only from God.

THE DISTRACTION OF HARD CASES
Matthew 7:6

> 7:6 **"Do not give what is holy to dogs; and do not throw your pearls before swine, or they will trample them under foot and turn and maul you.**

This strange verse about not giving what is holy to dogs and not throwing pearls before swine is notoriously difficult to interpret. Matthew's readers probably knew what "pearls" symbolized and what the "dogs" and "swine" stood for, but we can only guess about these images. We are guided, however, in our attempts to understand this verse by remembering the practical, congregational emphasis of the Sermon. This verse almost surely speaks to a particular dilemma in Matthew's church, and the fact that it follows immediately after the warning not to judge others but to reach out to them with empathy and compassion may indicate a connection to that saying.

What if a congregation is careful not to judge others harshly and self-righteously, careful to follow the process of compassion and moral care, but to no avail? What if all attempts to provide empathetic moral guidance are met with indifference, resentment, or anger? There are people who, for whatever reason, are hostile to the ministry of the church (and sometimes, we must admit, this is for good reason; see the previous commentary on judging others), and there are others who feign obedience to the kingdom while distorting its every claim. When the church has done all it knows how to do to claim and reclaim such people and failed, it needs to be prepared to admit that some things are beyond our power to help and heal.

"Do not throw your pearls before swine," states Jesus. His language is tough (as it often is in Matthew), and a similar tone can be heard later in the Gospel: "If the offender refuses to listen even to the church, let such a one be to you as a Gentile and a tax collector" (Matt. 18:17). It sometimes takes tough talk, though, to get good news across. The good news here is that the certainty of the kingdom does not depend upon the success of the church or the grateful response of every person we encounter. We are called to show compassion, but often our compassion is not enough. We are called to be the light, but there are places of gloom that our light cannot make cheerful. But because the world is in God's hands, and not the church's, the church can be free, when it has exhausted every ounce of mercy it can muster, to walk away from failure and leave it to the grace of God.

THE DISTRACTION OF TIMID PRAYER
Matthew 7:7–11

> 7:7 "Ask, and it will be given you; search, and you will find; knock, and the door will be opened for you. [8] For everyone who asks receives, and everyone who searches finds, and for everyone who knocks, the door will be opened. [9] Is there anyone among you who, if your child asks for bread, will give a stone? [10] Or if the child asks for a fish, will give a snake? [11] If you then, who are evil, know how to give good gifts to your children, how much more will your Father in heaven give good things to those who ask him!

In this passage Jesus seeks to replace hesitant and bashful prayer with bold, venturesome, even audacious communication with God. Jesus is concerned with those who pray timidly; not those who do so because they are afraid to pray, but rather those who do so because they are afraid of *God*. Those who think of God as punitive, who imagine that God is as ready to curse as to bless, who picture God as a divine lion ready to pounce, will tiptoe carefully around the lion's den. Their prayers, if they dare to pray at all, will sound like the fearful calculations of a clerk asking the boss for a day off. To the contrary, Jesus insists that God is not a ravenous lion, a prison guard, or a truant officer; God is a loving parent who promises to provide good gifts to those who ask in prayer.

The passage begins with a rhythmic invitation to prayer: ask . . . search . . . knock. These three verbs work to sound out the constancy of prayer like the beats of a drum. Prayer is built into the rhythms of the Christian life. Prayer is confident and regular communication with God, and it punctuates the passing of time like the regular and reassuring ticking of a clock: ask . . . search . . . knock.

Also, these three verbs represent distinct moods or attitudes of prayer. Sometimes we know what we need—or, at least, think we know—and we name our needs to God in prayer. That is, we ask. On other occasions, however, our praying is not nearly so focused or direct. We simply reach out to God, thoughts tumbling out randomly, our prayer words sighing and seeking a center. In this case, prayer is a movement toward discovery. Thus, we search, and only in the act of praying as seeking do we find God's will and blessing. On still other occasions, prayer assumes a desperate voice, a cry for help, a shout of rage and pain. We knock, beggars rapping urgently on the doorway of God's house of mercy.

Sometimes people wonder about what is appropriate to ask for in prayer. Is it fitting to pray for rain, for help on an exam, for strength to forgive, for healing? The line between what we genuinely need and what we merely want is often quite thin. Should we try to edit our prayers to remove all flecks of self-gratification? Jesus' word in this passage pushes us the other way, toward prayer that is daring, even brash. We can spill out our prayers to God, not attempting to sift the wheat from the chaff, because God hears beneath our words to our deepest needs and knows how to give good gifts.

Overly careful prayers betray an assumption that we, the ones who do the praying, are in control. We must then be cautious and meticulous about our prayers lest we pray for something we shouldn't. What are we thinking? That our prayers will somehow put God in a bind or that prayers are magic words that manipulate God's will? Jesus calls for an open, free, venturesome prayer, a communion with God that is like a child curling up in the lap of a parent, pouring out fears, dreams, desires, needs, and wishes. If earthly parents know how to give good gifts—bread and fish, not stones and snakes (Matt. 7:9–11)—how much more will God, who is wise and loving, hear the rushing torrents of our undisciplined prayers and respond by supplying us with all good things!

A SUMMARY WORD—
THE "GOLDEN RULE"
Matthew 7:12

7:12 **"In everything do to others as you would have them do to you; for this is the law and the prophets.**

With this verse, most often called "The Golden Rule," the Sermon on the Mount moves toward its conclusion. We recognize that this saying functions as a summary statement because it is introduced by the word "therefore" (present in the original Greek but omitted in the NRSV) and it is described as the epitome of "the law and the prophets" (compare Matt. 5:17).

But the Golden Rule forms something of a puzzle for interpretation. Even though this is among the most widely known and best-loved sayings in the New Testament, it is not easy to say why it stands in such an important culminating position in the Sermon. Taken in isolation, it was most often interpreted in a "you scratch my back and I'll scratch yours" fashion; if you want someone to do something for you, then the way to make that possible is to do the same for them. "You get what you give" hardly seems a fitting motto for the climax to the magnificence of the Sermon on the Mount.

The crucial point, though, is that, in the Sermon on the Mount, the Golden Rule does not stand in isolation. In the Sermon, the Golden Rule no longer functions as a piece of common workaday wisdom but as a saying of the kingdom of heaven. We have seen before how the arrival of the kingdom of heaven takes conventional morality and revolutionizes it ("you have heard it said . . . but I say to you"), takes customary religious practices and renews them ("whenever you pray, do not be like the hypocrites . . . "), and takes habitual ways of seeing the world and calls them into radical question ("therefore, do not worry . . . ").

Just so, when Jesus fishes the Golden Rule out of the stream of popular principle and sets it free in the heavenly sea, it flashes through the water with new and brighter colors. "In everything do to others as you would have them do to you"—what does this mean for citizens of the kingdom of heaven? What do the children of God want others to do to them? Of course, they want to be recognized as who they are, God's very own people, and they want to live in a world where mercy, meekness, and peace prevail. So, Jesus now calls them to treat the world in the same way, to treat the world as if it were already restored, as if it were already what it one day surely will be, a place where the merciful God is all in all and humanity is gathered at the great and joyous banquet.

THE THREE WARNINGS
Matthew 7:13–29

7:13 **"Enter through the narrow gate; for the gate is wide and the road is easy that leads to destruction, and there are many who take it.** [14] **For the** gate is narrow and the road is hard that leads to life, and there are few who find it.

[15] "Beware of false prophets, who come to you in sheep's clothing but inwardly are ravenous wolves. [16] You will know them by their fruits. Are grapes gathered from thorns, or figs from thistles? [17] In the same way, every good tree bears good fruit, but the bad tree bears bad fruit. [18] A good tree cannot bear bad fruit, nor can a bad tree bear good fruit. [19] Every tree that does not bear good fruit is cut down and thrown into the fire. [20] Thus you will know them by their fruits.

[21] "Not everyone who says to me, 'Lord, Lord,' will enter the kingdom of heaven, but only the one who does the will of my Father in heaven. [22] On that day many will say to me, 'Lord, Lord, did we not prophesy in your name, and cast out demons in your name, and do many deeds of power in your name?' [23] Then I will declare to them, 'I never knew you; go away from me, you evildoers.'

[24] "Everyone then who hears these words of mine and acts on them will be like a wise man who built his house on rock. [25] The rain fell, the floods came, and the winds blew and beat on that house, but it did not fall, because it had been founded on rock. [26] And everyone who hears these words of mine and does not act on them will be like a foolish man who built his house on sand. [27] The rain fell, and the floods came, and the winds blew and beat against that house, and it fell—and great was its fall!"

[28] Now when Jesus had finished saying these things, the crowds were astounded at his teaching, [29] for he taught them as one having authority, and not as their scribes.

The substance of the Sermon on the Mount is now finished. For nearly three chapters, Matthew has recorded Jesus' inaugural vision of the kingdom of heaven and of the life demanded of those who are citizens of that kingdom. Now, as the Sermon is brought to a close, Jesus candidly warns about the difficulties and risks involved in being a kingdom person.

The Two Gates
(Matthew 7:13–14)

Jesus first imagines two entrances into a city. One consists of a rough and difficult road leading to a narrow gate; the other is a smooth, easily traveled road rolling through a wide gate. Most people on a journey would, of course, select the broad highway passing through the spacious, accessible gate. Jesus, however, calls those who heed his words to "enter through the narrow gate" (Matt. 7:13). Only the rough road and the narrow gate lead to life; the other way leads to destruction.

But why is the way to life, the way of the kingdom of heaven, depicted as narrow and rough? There are two reasons. First, it often takes us to those places where we must make some painful and difficult choices. Imagine that a person in an office, in order to enhance his own position, is doing his best to undermine a co-worker. Rumors are being spread; vital information is hidden; needed support is withheld. What should the co-worker do about this treachery? There are a number of strategies that the co-worker could take, but "love your enemies and pray for those who persecute you" (Matt. 5:44) is surely the most difficult option one could imagine. Choosing to live the kind of life depicted in the Sermon on the Mount is difficult.

But suppose that this co-worker did decide to try to live out the ethic of the Sermon on the Mount. Making the choice to love this interoffice foe would surely be difficult, but that would only be the beginning of the hardship. Sticking with the decision to put this love into actual practice would be even more challenging. Christian love is not merely a matter of smiling and being nice. Sometimes Christian love calls for nonresistance and submission, but in other circumstances love invokes the voice of protest, calls for taking a firm stand. There are no clear compass readings to signal which way to turn; disciples have to make hard choices in the midst of ambiguous circumstances. The kingdom road has beautiful scenery—peace, joy, hope, forgiveness—but the road itself is long, hard, and rough.

Second, the gate to discipleship is described as narrow because in any given situation, full of many possibilities, disciples are beckoned to choose God's will and God's will alone. Belonging to God simply makes some choices not available to us. When, for example, a church finds itself in a community with heightened racial tension, it could ignore the situation, looking the other way, or it could make things worse, throwing gasoline on the fire of racial mistrust. But, because the kingdom of heaven is a society of peacemakers (Matt. 5:9), these are not real choices for a Christian congregation. Of all the approaches it could take, this church has but one, narrow option—to roll up its sleeves and to work in every way it can for reconciliation. The kingdom road is a narrow road, but it is the road that leads to life.

The Two Kinds of Leaders
(Matthew 7:15–23)

In this text, Jesus addresses the question of the integrity of leadership in the church. How can the church tell the difference between solid, responsible, faithful leadership and teachers and guides who are shallow and unwise? Jesus maintains that good leaders ("prophets") are known by "their fruits" (Matt. 7:16), that is, by what they produce in themselves and in those they lead. A true leader, an authentic leader of the faithful community, will work to ensure that the church looks and acts like the kingdom rather than just "sounding like" the kingdom. A true leader will show the mercy and forgiveness of the gospel and not just preach beautiful sermons about mercy and forgiveness. This does not mean that genuine leaders in the church are perfect; it does mean that they are always seeking to bring their lives and the lives of their congregations into accord with the message they teach.

Discerning whether or not a leader is authentic is not easy. It takes time, insight, and wisdom, for false leaders look genuine (they are in "sheep's clothing," Matt. 7:15), sound genuine (they cry, "Lord, Lord," Matt. 7:22), and act on the surface in genuine ways (they do "deeds of power," Matt. 7:22). What they lack, however, is a vital communion with Christ ("I will declare to them, 'I never knew you,'" Matt. 7:23), a relationship of faithful intimacy that creates inner transformation.

The Two Houses
(Matthew 7:24–29)

The last lines of the Sermon on the Mount warn those who have heard the Sermon—the disciples and the crowds, but also the readers of Matthew's Gospel—that they must not just listen to Jesus' words and then forget them, or even listen to Jesus' words and merely cherish them as lovely ideas, but they must put Jesus' words into action. A contrast is set up between the wise person who puts Jesus' teaching into practice and the foolish person who does not do so (see also Matt. 25:1–13). The wise person is like someone who builds a house on a rock foundation, but the foolish person is like someone who chooses a sandy lot for a building site. Things go well for both until the torrential downpours of the rainy season; then, as the deluge washes away all that is not solidly based, the difference in foundations becomes all too apparent.

Jesus calls those who hear his message to put his words into practice, because the Sermon on the Mount expresses God's will not just for the church but also for the world. The commands of the Sermon describe what it means to be fully *human*, not just what it means to be *religious*. Only a life based upon the vision embodied in the Sermon can stand firm and true when all the storms of life have done their worst. There are many houses in the human community. The house of greed washes away when the rains of economic crisis come. The house of power collapses when the political climate changes. The house of pragmatic living-for-the-moment slips off the foundation when life opens up with a mystery like birth, deep suffering, or death. Only those who "strive first for the kingdom of God and his righteousness" (Matt. 6:33) build a dwelling that tempests cannot shake and the gates of hell cannot destroy.

The Sermon formally closes with the somewhat solemn statement "when Jesus had finished saying these things." This formula is employed at the end of every one of the major teaching sections in Matthew (see also Matt. 11:1; 13:53; 19:1; 26:1), and it signals that what we have just heard is of great importance. Matthew also reports that "the crowds were astounded at his teaching." Their astonishment comes because Jesus teaches without footnotes; he teaches on the basis of his own authority. He does not justify what he teaches by appealing to a patchwork of previous statements by revered teachers. He even dares to go beneath the surface of scripture to the heart of God's will: "You have heard it said . . . but *I* say to you. . . ."

Now, the Sermon completed, the reader must follow Jesus and leave the mountain. We must go on to the rest of the story to see if the astonishment of the crowds—and our own amazement—at the words of Jesus is transformed into true discipleship.

5. Three Sets of Mighty Works
Matthew 8:1–9:34

Jesus has completed the Sermon on the Mount, and he is described by Matthew as coming down from the mountain trailed again by large crowds (Matt. 8:1). By depicting the crowds' response to Jesus, Matthew shows his readers that Jesus' words have received a positive reception among the people, and the "great crowds" that gathered around him at the beginning of his public ministry have not waned but have continued to be attracted to him and his message (see Matt. 4:25). Later, the crowds will be offended by Jesus and will turn against him (see Matt. 27:25), but for the moment they are receptive to his teaching.

Now, having spoken the words of the kingdom of heaven, Jesus puts those words into action—indeed, puts the kingdom itself into action—through a series of dramatic healings, miracles, and works of wonder. There are nine miracle stories in all (although one of the nine, Matthew 9:18–26, seems to be composed of two healing stories woven into one). Scholars generally agree that Matthew has grouped these nine stories into a deliberate pattern, although there has been a good bit of debate about just what that pattern is. The most plausible suggestion is that Matthew has arranged these miracles into three sets of mighty works: Matthew 8:1–17; 8:23–9:8; and 9:18–34—each group containing three stories and each group having its own emphasis. Not all of Matthew 8—9 is taken up with miracle stories, of course, but the other stories and sayings in these chapters are woven in to help the readers understand the significance of Jesus' miracles.

THE FIRST GROUP
OF MIGHTY WORKS
Matthew 8:1–17

8:1 **When Jesus had come down from the mountain, great crowds followed him; 2 and there was a leper who came to him and knelt before him, saying,**

"Lord, if you choose, you can make me clean." [3] He stretched out his hand and touched him, saying, "I do choose. Be made clean!" Immediately his leprosy was cleansed. [4] Then Jesus said to him, "See that you say nothing to anyone; but go, show yourself to the priest, and offer the gift that Moses commanded, as a testimony to them."

[5] When he entered Capernaum, a centurion came to him, appealing to him [6] and saying, "Lord, my servant is lying at home paralyzed, in terrible distress." [7] And he said to him, "I will come and cure him." [8] The centurion answered, "Lord, I am not worthy to have you come under my roof; but only speak the word, and my servant will be healed. [9] For I also am a man under authority, with soldiers under me; and I say to one, 'Go,' and he goes, and to another, 'Come,' and he comes, and to my slave, 'Do this,' and the slave does it." [10] When Jesus heard him, he was amazed and said to those who followed him, "Truly I tell you, in no one in Israel have I found such faith. [11] I tell you, many will come from east and west and will eat with Abraham and Isaac and Jacob in the kingdom of heaven, [12] while the heirs of the kingdom will be thrown into the outer darkness, where there will be weeping and gnashing of teeth." [13] And to the centurion Jesus said, "Go; let it be done for you according to your faith." And the servant was healed in that hour.

[14] When Jesus entered Peter's house, he saw his mother-in-law lying in bed with a fever; [15] he touched her hand, and the fever left her, and she got up and began to serve him. [16] That evening they brought to him many who were possessed with demons; and he cast out the spirits with a word, and cured all who were sick. [17] This was to fulfill what had been spoken through the prophet Isaiah, "He took our infirmities and bore our diseases."

In this first group of three mighty works, or miracles, Jesus heals a leper, the slave of a Roman military officer, and the mother-in-law of Peter. Each of these stories in its own way emphasizes not only the power of Jesus, who can heal instantly with a touch or even from a distance by uttering the word, but especially his authority (acknowledged in different ways by each of the persons healed). Moreover, we already see here how the kingdom of heaven reaches out beyond the margins of the established religious community. Each of the persons healed—a leper, a Gentile, and a woman—is on the edges of Israelite society.

The Healing of a Leper
(Matthew 8:2–4)

In the first story, a leper comes to Jesus and asks to be healed. In the ancient world, a leper was not only a person who was diseased but also a person who was socially and religiously outcast. There was a firm boundary of custom and religious taboo separating unclean lepers from the rest of society (see Leviticus 13, especially 13:45–46).

The way this leper makes his request to Jesus is quite significant. He begins by calling Jesus "Lord," which sounds to our ears like a good thing, but this is not necessarily so. Just one chapter before, in the Sermon on the Mount, Jesus has announced that not everyone who says "Lord, Lord" is on the side of the kingdom, only those who do God's will (Matt. 7:21–23). So, the fact that the leper calls Jesus "Lord" is ambiguous; we cannot tell at first hearing whether it is positive or negative until we know how it is connected to the issue of God's will. But the next words from the leper seem to tilt the equation in his favor: "If you choose," he states, "you can make me clean" (Matt. 8:2). This humble approach ("If you choose") is a sign, surely, of the leper's modesty, but it is even more a recognition that any healing would be utterly dependent upon Jesus' will. The leper is, in at least a tentative way, acknowledging Jesus' authority.

Indeed, it is this statement by the leper that seems to turn the key in the lock, since Jesus immediately and directly responds to it by touching the leper and saying, "I do choose. Be made clean!" (Matt. 8:3). It is no small matter that, when he touched the leper, Jesus transgressed the social and religious boundaries and broke the strict commandments of the Old Testament law. The Mosaic law declares that one who knowingly touches an unclean person becomes unclean, too, and guilty of sin (see Lev. 5:1–3). Matthew wants to highlight the fact that Jesus stepped over the line in this way, and Matthew shows the significance of this later when he affirms that Jesus joined himself with human sin and "bore our diseases" (Matt. 8:17). Jesus did not stand at a distance from the leper, but drew close and touched him, becoming not an "antiseptic healer" but one who joined himself to human brokenness.

Ironically, Jesus, who has violated the law, turns around and commands the leper to obey the law. Jesus technically violated the Mosaic law by touching the leper, but he firmly orders the leper, now healed, to obey the law of Moses, to follow the procedures set out in the Old Testament by taking an offering and showing himself to the priest (Matt. 8:4; see Leviticus 14).

This seeming contradiction begins to make sense, however, when we understand that, in this healing, Jesus is putting into action the words of the Sermon on the Mount, "You have heard that it was said . . . but I say to you . . . ," words that reveal Jesus' intent to move beyond the surface of the law (even to contradict the superficial legal requirements) in order to move to the center of the law's purpose (see comments on Matt. 5:21–47). In the touching and healing of the leper, Jesus has, once again, gone beneath the technical legal requirements to the heart of God's commandments. He has not come to abolish the law, but to fulfill its deepest intent (Matt. 5:17), and the true intent of the law in this case is the restoration of the leper both as a well human being and as a vital part of society.

So, Jesus steps over the taboo line and touches the leper—in violation of one aspect of the law—in order to fulfill the deeper intent of God to restore the leper as a human being; and Jesus sends him to the priest—in accordance with another aspect of the law—in order to fulfill God's intention to restore the leper to his community. Thus, both when he breaks the specifics of the law and when he follows them to the letter, Jesus is focused like a laser beam on the will of God.

The Healing of a Servant
(Matthew 8:5–13)

In the second story, Jesus heals the servant of a Roman centurion, a military officer in charge of one hundred men in a Roman legion. Three aspects of this healing miracle are especially significant:

First, the centurion, like the leper in the previous story, recognizes Jesus' authority, but even more directly and explicitly. The centurion's statement "Lord, I am not worthy" (Matt. 8:8–9) not only displays his humility but also reveals the source of this humility—his awareness that, in standing before Jesus, he is in the presence of a person of extraordinary authority.

The centurion makes an analogy between his own circumstances and those of Jesus. As a military officer, the centurion knows he has authority; he orders his soldiers to "go" and to "come," and they do. But the centurion not only has rank; he is also "a man under authority." Any authority he has is delegated and comes from higher up; thus he recognizes Jesus as a person of great authority, an authority that comes from "higher up," from God. The centurion also knows that Jesus can issue a command to a "subordinate" power, such as illness, and it will obey. So, he modestly refuses to let Jesus travel to his home to perform the healing and urges him instead to "only speak the word, and my servant will be healed" (Matt. 8:8). Jesus marvels at the centurion's discernment and calls it faith, "Truly I tell you, in no one in Israel have I found such faith" (Matt. 8:10).

Second, the centurion is a Gentile (Matthew doesn't need to spell this out for his readers, because the centurion's occupation in the Roman military gives him away); he is an outsider in Israel. Even so, he is a person of faith, prompting Jesus' amazement (Matt. 8:10).

Though we have essentially lost the capacity to be shocked by this story of a Gentile coming in faith to Jesus here at the beginning of his ministry, it was, in its original setting, a surprising and somewhat disturbing turn of events. Matthew presents Jesus as the Jewish messiah in every way. He is not an anonymous, traditionless, universal religious figure; he is "the son of David, the son of Abraham" (Matt. 1:1)—Jewish to the core.

In the finale of Matthew's Gospel, the risen Jesus, the vindicated Jewish messiah, will send his disciples out past the borders of Israel on a worldwide mission to make followers even of the Gentile nations (see Matt. 28:19). But here, twenty chapters too early, so to speak, this Gentile army officer, who makes an entrance into the drama of Jesus' ministry, possesses faith greater than Jesus has found in Israel. He is like a character in a play who, scheduled to appear in Act III, somehow wanders prematurely on stage in Act I, bewildering the audience. All will become clear, but only later.

The centurion's faith, then, anticipates the fruit of the later missionary work of the church, the coming into the kingdom of the Gentiles; people "will come from east and west and will eat with Abraham and Isaac and Jacob in the kingdom of heaven" (Matt. 8:11). On the other hand, the centurion's great faith, which contrasts with the lack of faith in Israel, anticipates the rejection of Jesus by the religious authorities of Israel and by others (Matt. 8:12), and perhaps serves to warn Matthew's readers that the church itself is always in danger of becoming faithless, too.

Third, when Jesus heals the centurion's servant from afar with a word (Matt. 8:13), he tells the centurion that he is doing so "according to your faith." The phrase does not mean that the centurion's faith somehow made it possible for Jesus to perform the healing, but that Jesus, who possesses all power and authority, nonetheless fits that power and authority to the shape of human expectation, to the situation addressed. A leper wants to be touched by Jesus, and he is touched. The centurion expects a person of authority to send a command from afar, and, in this case, that is what Jesus does. Later in Matthew, Jesus will go to his hometown, Nazareth; there the citizens believe nothing and expect nothing from him—which is precisely what they get (Matt. 13:58). Jesus is portrayed exercising the power of God in ways that are not coercive or overwhelming; Jesus responds gently to human initiative and invitation and draws back where he is unwelcome.

The Healing of a Woman
(Matthew 8:14–17)

In the last story of the first group of miracle stories, Jesus heals Peter's mother-in-law. In this story there is no prior interaction with Jesus, no request from the sick woman to be healed; Jesus simply sees the need and responds. In fact, the healing itself is described in very terse language, and the important aspects of this story seem to come *after* the healing.

When she was healed, Peter's mother-in-law "began to serve" Jesus (Matt. 8:15). It is easy for us to misunderstand this, even to be offended by it. Here is a woman, sick with fever and chills, who, as soon as she is healed, jumps up to serve. Are we to picture her rising from her sick bed to cook dinner, wash the dishes, and scrub the floors? No, Matthew means that she served Jesus in the sense of discipleship. In fact, Matthew, who borrowed this story from the Gospel of Mark, tries to make this clear by changing Mark's language. Mark says that Peter's mother-in-law served "them"; that is, all the disciples (see Mark 1:31). Matthew changes that to read that she served *him*, that is, Jesus.

In fact, in this account of Peter's mother-in-law serving Jesus, this section of healing stories moves to its climax. The leper acknowledged Jesus' authority, but only faintly. The centurion made an advance by defining Jesus' authority in terms of his own.

Also, the healing of Peter's mother-in-law forms a bridge to the healing of many people who were possessed by demons and who were sick (Matt. 8:16). Jesus, who has healed a leper, a centurion's servant, and a woman—symbols of those on the margins of society—now cures all who come to him. Jesus heals not just to make people well for the moment; his healings are signs of his deeper mission to save people from their sins (Matt. 1:21): "He took our infirmities and bore our diseases" (Matt. 8:17; Isa. 53:4).

Taken together, then, these first three mighty acts of Jesus—in which people who were considered not to be at the center of society, are, nonetheless, the focus of Jesus' healing work—remind us that God's will to save extends beyond all social and religious boundaries. We also discover in these stories the true meaning of faith in Jesus as the Christ. To be faithful is more than merely saying "I believe in Jesus Christ"; it is turning that conviction into practical obedience by doing God's will.

INTERLUDE:
THE COST OF FOLLOWING JESUS
Matthew 8:18–22

8:18 **Now when Jesus saw great crowds around him, he gave orders to go over to the other side.** [19] **A scribe then approached and said, "Teacher, I will follow you wherever you go."** [20] **And Jesus said to him, "Foxes have holes, and birds of the air have nests; but the Son of Man has nowhere to lay his**

head." ²¹ Another of his disciples said to him, "Lord, first let me go and bury my father." ²² But Jesus said to him, "Follow me, and let the dead bury their own dead."

In between the first and the second set of miracle stories comes this account of two would-be followers of Jesus who are taught about the great cost of discipleship. Matthew introduces the story with the curious fact that "when Jesus saw great crowds around him, he gave orders to go over to the other side" of the Sea of Galilee, that is, from the western shore to the eastern side (Matt. 8:18). Why does the sight of the crowds prompt Jesus to cross the sea? Is he trying to get away from them and their pressing needs? Is he trying to quell their enthusiastic, but perhaps misplaced, response to him?

This question can be answered only by putting together several pieces of the puzzle. First, it is clear that Jesus' departure is a deliberate and significant event, for he does not do it on a whim; he "gave orders" for it to happen. Second, this is not the first time that Jesus has responded with decisive action to the sight of the crowds. Earlier, when Jesus saw the crowds, he went up on the mountain and taught them in the Sermon on the Mount (Matt. 5:1–2). Third, we have already seen that, in this section of Matthew, Jesus is putting the teachings of the kingdom of heaven into action.

So, the pieces begin to fit. Jesus gives orders to cross the sea not to get away from the crowds but, rather, to teach them through action. The crowds have heard the Sermon on the Mount, but hearing alone is not sufficient. To hear Jesus' words and, then, not act on them would be "like a foolish man who built his house on sand" (Matt. 7:26). Jesus does not want mere hearers; he wants followers. The crowds around Jesus are large, and the only way to distinguish the true disciples from those who are only auditing the course is to leave them and see who follows—and that is precisely what Jesus does.

On cue, then, a man shows up volunteering for duty as one of Jesus' followers. He is a scribe, one of a group of religious leaders learned in the law of Moses, who approaches Jesus by saying, "Teacher, I will follow you wherever you go" (Matt. 8:19). The fact that he addresses Jesus by the title "teacher" is a dead giveaway; he is impressed by Jesus' teaching, and he wants to be a student in Jesus' class, to enroll in Jesus' academy. In his reply, Jesus makes it clear that being a true disciple is not like attending boarding school; indeed, "the Son of Man has nowhere to lay his head" (Matt. 8:20).

Next, another man engages Jesus on the issue of being a follower (Matt. 8:21–22). If the first would-be follower is overly eager to be a disciple (because he misunderstands), the second is already a disciple (Matt. 8:21), but he hesitates to make the full sacrifices of discipleship (maybe because he *does* understand).

What happens is that this disciple asks Jesus for permission to arrange for the burial of his father. The implication is that he will follow Jesus later, once the funeral and family obligations are finished. This incident calls to mind Elisha's request to Elijah, "Let me kiss my father and my mother, and then I will follow you" (1 Kings 19:20), a plea Elijah granted. Permission would surely have been even more readily forthcoming if Elisha had asked to take care of the burial of his parents. In today's society, attending to the burial of one's parents is a sacred obligation, and this was even more the case among first-century Jews. The holy law called for one to "honor thy mother and father," and the death of a parent was certainly a time when this commandment was to be solemnly observed. Not to give one's energy and care to the funeral of a parent would be scandalous, negligent, sacrilegious, unthinkable.

Jesus' reply, "Follow me, and let the dead bury their own dead" (Matt. 8:22), has always been troubling, even outrageous. It would be a mistake to attempt to soften Jesus' command; it is intended to shock. But it is also important to pay close attention to Jesus' choice of words. When Jesus says "let the dead bury their own dead," he implies that what is truly at stake for this would-be follower is more than a matter of a family obligation. What is at stake is no less than the challenge of the kingdom, and that is a matter of life and death.

In Jesus, the kingdom of heaven has drawn near, and everything is changed. The old world has passed away; it is dead and gone, and the new reign of God has begun. The only true response is to turn around, leave the old behind, and become a part of the new: "Repent, for the kingdom of heaven has come near" (Matt. 4:17). Thus, the critical question for everyone is: To which realm do you belong, to which epoch do you give your loyalties—the old age, which is dead, or the kingdom of heaven, embodied in Jesus? Many of us, like this disciple, want to keep a foot in both ages; we want to have a good life, but we also want *the* good life. We have one foot on the dock and one in the boat, and Jesus warns us: The boat of the kingdom is launching out to sea.

THE SECOND GROUP OF MIGHTY WORKS
Matthew 8:23–9:8

8:23 **And when he got into the boat, his disciples followed him. ²⁴ A windstorm arose on the sea, so great that the boat was being swamped by the** waves; but he was asleep. [25] And they went and woke him up, saying, "Lord, save us! We are perishing!" [26] And he said to them, "Why are you afraid, you of little faith?" Then he got up and rebuked the winds and the sea; and there was a dead calm. [27] They were amazed, saying, "What sort of man is this, that even the winds and the sea obey him?"

[28] When he came to the other side, to the country of the Gadarenes, two demoniacs coming out of the tombs met him. They were so fierce that no one could pass that way. [29] Suddenly they shouted, "What have you to do with us, Son of God? Have you come here to torment us before the time?" [30] Now a large herd of swine was feeding at some distance from them. [31] The demons begged him, "If you cast us out, send us into the herd of swine." [32] And he said to them, "Go!" So they came out and entered the swine; and suddenly, the whole herd rushed down the steep bank into the sea and perished in the water. [33] The swineherds ran off, and on going into the town, they told the whole story about what had happened to the demoniacs. [34] Then the whole town came out to meet Jesus; and when they saw him, they begged him to leave their neighborhood. [9:1] And after getting into a boat he crossed the sea and came to his own town.

[2] And just then some people were carrying a paralyzed man lying on a bed. When Jesus saw their faith, he said to the paralytic, "Take heart, son; your sins are forgiven." [3] Then some of the scribes said to themselves, "This man is blaspheming." [4] But Jesus, perceiving their thoughts, said, "Why do you think evil in your hearts? [5] For which is easier, to say, 'Your sins are forgiven,' or to say, 'Stand up and walk'? [6] But so that you may know that the Son of Man has authority on earth to forgive sins" —he then said to the paralytic—"Stand up, take your bed and go to your home." [7] And he stood up and went to his home. [8] When the crowds saw it, they were filled with awe, and they glorified God, who had given such authority to human beings.

In the first group of miracle stories, Jesus performed healings for three people on the edges of Israelite society—a leper, a Gentile, and a woman (Peter's mother-in-law). Now, in the second group of miracle stories, Jesus takes on the wild and chaotic powers of evil: a violent storm, raging demons, and the perversity of sin. By mastering these vicious forces, Jesus shows his authority over not just the more personal ills that plague human life but over all forms of destruction, every insidious power that tears at the heart of God's good creation.

The Calming of a Storm (Matthew 8:23–27)

The first of these mighty works involves a terrifying experience on the sea. Jesus gets into a boat to travel from Capernaum on the western shore over to the eastern side of the sea. Matthew tells us that "his disciples followed him" (Matt. 8:23), a phrase that is both literal and figurative. That is, the disciples actually followed him into the boat, but they are also to be seen representative of all true followers—authentic disciples—of Jesus, unlike the two would-be disciples described in the previous story (Matt. 8:18–22).

As they set out on the water, a sudden storm whips up. The NRSV says that "a windstorm arose on the sea, so great that the boat was being swamped by the waves" (Matt. 8:24), but the original Greek is even more frightening and evocative: The sea "shook" like an earthquake so that the boat was "hidden" by the waves. Jesus was asleep, so the disciples woke him up and cried out to him for help. Like the leper and the centurion before (Matt. 8:1–13), they appeal to him as "Lord" (Matt. 8:25).

After chastising them for their fear and the smallness of their faith, Jesus calms the raging storm with a word. The disciples are amazed and wonder, "What sort of man is this, that even the winds and the sea obey him?" (Matt. 8:27). The disciples do not answer their own rhetorical question (Peter will give a clear answer later; see Matt. 16:13–20), but Matthew hopes that his readers will supply their own response and that, by this point, they will be able to affirm, "He is Jesus, the Messiah, the Son of God, God-with-us."

Ancient people feared the wind and the sea as untamed, life-threatening, and chaotic forces—emblems of arbitrary, uncontrollable evil. This story, then, is an account of Jesus' divine power over these forces, but it is more than just a nature miracle. Matthew probably tells this stormy sea story in such a way that he wants it to be understood also as a parable of the life of the church. The picture of the disciples in a boat tossed about on the angry sea is a revealing symbol of the church, ever shaken by the battering wind and waves of the world. The disciples, like all followers of Jesus in stressful times, are terrified, and even though they know that Jesus is with them (see Matt. 28:20), he is asleep and silent, apparently distant, passive, and unconcerned.

The disciples' desperate cry to Jesus is the constant and urgent prayer of the church, "Lord, save us! We are perishing!" (Matt. 8:25). Jesus replies, "Why are you afraid, you of little faith?" a reminder to the church that the boiling sea and the howling winds of the world are to be expected and nothing to fear. When all is said and done, at the end of time, even the gales and the tempests, even the most malignant powers the world can conjure up against the community of faith, will themselves bow down and obediently serve the Lord of all creation (Matt. 8:27).

The Destruction of Demons
(Matthew 8:28–34)

In the previous mighty work, Jesus took on the random power of nature, which was loosing its devastation through a storm on the restless sea. Now, in a cemetery set in the farming country outside of a Gadarene town, Jesus confronts the screaming, hellish forces of the demonic. Two men, possessed by demons, encounter Jesus. The demons ravaging the men recognize, in the presence of Jesus, that they are threatened, and they suddenly shriek out in fear and defensiveness, begging to be cast into a herd of pigs. A single word from Jesus sends the demons flying into the swine, and that sends the pigs hurtling over an embankment into the sea. What is the meaning of this curious story?

We can spot one of Matthew's concerns when we compare his telling of this story with that of Mark (Mark 5:1–20). In Mark the emphasis falls upon the restoration of the demon-possessed man (there is only one demon-possessed man in Mark, compared with two in Matthew). Mark shows us the man "before"—in a chaotic frenzy, bruising himself with rocks and forcefully bursting loose from his restraining chains—and "after"—restored, "sitting there, clothed and in his right mind" (Mark 5:15). In other words, Mark wants us to see that the man is healed, calmed, made whole.

Matthew, however, does not focus nearly as much on the healing of the demon-possessed men, but on Jesus and on his strength to destroy demonic power. In fact, once the demons have been cast out of them, the possessed men are strangely never even mentioned again. Even though the demons at work in the men make them ferociously powerful, so much so that no one can safely travel the road by the cemetery where they lived (Matt. 8:28), Jesus is even more powerful. He is so potent that he can banish the demons with a single word (Matt. 8:32); he is so mighty that his strength frightens a whole town (Matt. 8:34).

This means that the community of faith does not ever need to be afraid. There is no power loose in the world that can finally overwhelm the power of Jesus Christ, no word forceful enough to outshout the gospel, no evil so insidious that it can vanquish the merciful will of God.

Matthew also tells this story so that it is full of irony and possesses perhaps even a measure of wit. Because of what has already happened in the Gospel, the readers of Matthew are aware, of course, of the theological truth that Jesus is the Son of God, the bearer of the kingdom of heaven, but the pig farmers and the townspeople in this story do not know this. Jesus is a stranger in this Gentile territory, and the residents have no idea of his messianic significance.

Amazingly, ironically, and somewhat humorously, it is the demons, and not the local folk, who discern the true identity of Jesus. They recognize him as "the Son of God" (Matt. 8:29); they are the ones who know whom they are up against. Amusingly, then, it is the demons who are the theologians in this story, members of the theological faculty of hell. They have their pet theology, but, as is fitting their demonic status, their theology is twisted and distorted—half right and all wrong.

On the correct side, they are realistic; they know that on the last day, at the end of time, God will ultimately triumph, that their freedom to roam around the earth working evil mischief is limited. But—on the wrong side— they mistakenly believe that, until that last day, they have an unfettered license to wreak destruction. They can torment as many souls as they can inhabit, wreck as many institutions as they can infiltrate, cause as much pain and sorrow as they can imagine. In short, the demons are well aware that the party will not last forever, but in the meantime they can hang around the tombs and dead places of the world and raise all the hell they want.

But, then, Jesus gets out of the boat, walks up the path right into their demonic lair and announces by his presence, "The party is over." Everybody in the area was terrified of these two demoniacs and gave them wide berth. They are wild-eyed, frenzied, and violent, and people took long detours around the tombs where they live. Jesus, however, strides right up to these ferocious demons who are bedeviling these men, rips off their flimsy Halloween masks and lets them know by his presence as God's own Son that their trick-or-treat privileges have been permanently revoked.

The demons squeal in hysterical protest that Jesus is not playing fair, that he has blown the whistle on them too soon, that, according to their theological calendar, they are supposed to have more time left to roam the earth performing foul deeds. "Have you come here to torment us before the time?" they screech (Matt. 8:29). But in Jesus the kingdom of heaven has invaded the present age of evil, and knowing they are no match for Jesus, the demons beg to be allowed to be cast into a herd of pigs. Since, to Jews, pigs were unclean and forbidden animals (see Lev. 11:7), the demons' request to be cast into Gentile-owned, unclean pigs would probably be amusing to Matthew's Jewish-oriented readers, something like asking to be cast into a cluster of skunks. There is a comic air of the expected about the next scene: The demons fly into the pigs, and the consequently panicked pigs, of course, rush headlong into the sea (over which Jesus has already demonstrated his power, Matt. 8:27). Stampeding over the cliff is exactly what one would expect from a bunch of "Gentile pigs." The demons look dumb here; they should have known better.

This story, then, is a supreme practical joke on the demonic powers, and the laughter it provokes is a holy laughter. Indeed, the mirth of Matthew's readers at the confused demons trapped in a pack of swine tumbling into the sea anticipates an even richer laugh at an even finer joke—the defeat of death and sin in the resurrection of Jesus Christ.

When the pig farmers run into town with the news of what has happened, the whole town responds by coming out to meet Jesus (Matt. 8:33–34). Matthew uses here the same verb in Greek that he used when he earlier described the demoniacs coming out to meet Jesus (Matt. 8:28), perhaps hinting that the resistance Jesus encountered in the demons he is about to face in the townspeople. Indeed, the local folk are afraid of Jesus. Perhaps Jesus was dangerous and defeated these demons because he was possessed by an even stronger demon. The demons "begged" Jesus to cast them out into the pigs; now the town, taking no chances, "begged" Jesus to cast himself out of their town. Like many communities before and since, this town prefers the demons they know to the power of God they do not know.

Healing and Forgiveness of Sins
(Matthew 9:1–8)

In the third, and last, mighty work in this group, Jesus heals a paralyzed man, but even more than this, he displays his command over the raging power of sin. In order to understand this story, we must recover the wider range of the theological concept of sin and, especially, the biblical linkage between sin and sickness.

REFLECTION
Sin and Sickness

We tend to have a view of sin that is too small; to many of us sin is a word that simply describes the naughty deeds people perform. Sin is more, much more. It is larger than bad actions, more than misdeeds, bigger than the things we do that we should not do. It is a power that captures us, that infects society, that pollutes nature, that enslaves the human heart, that destroys life. To say that someone has "sinned" means something larger than that he or she has stepped over a moral line and has done something he or she should not have done. To sin is to be captivated and captured by the larger forces that oppose God and to join them in doing their bidding.

Human beings cannot stop sinning merely by deciding to do so. Sin is a force that enslaves and destroys human life, and it employs many devices and servants: chaos, the demonic, illness, and death. Sin is the biggest word we have to describe all the powers loose in the world that oppose God's will. It is, for example, God's will that all nature exist in harmony, that the winds blow cool and gentle, that the fruits ripen in fatness on the vine, that the plants flower in ever-surprising beauty, that the lion and the lamb lie down together in peace. In the New Testament, then, a sudden and violent storm on the sea, a disruption of the peacefulness of the natural world, was more than just a low pressure system; it was an expression of sin, a loose and random power in rebellion against the will of God. So, Jesus exerts God's will and commands the winds and the waves to obey and to be calm (Matt. 8:27). This is more than just a "nature miracle"; it is a subduing of the chaotic powers derived from the forces of sin.

Likewise, the will of God is for people to live with purpose and dignity in joyful communion with others. So, the two homeless men who slept in the cemetery and whose bedeviled minds caused them to attack innocent people on the road (Matt. 8:28) were more than just psychiatric cases who were the victims of chemical imbalance; they were the casualties of forces at war with the will of God. Jesus acted in a way far greater than merely comforting or counseling these troubled men; he destroyed the evil and sinful powers that dominated them (Matt. 8:32).

In the story of the healing of the paralyzed man (Matt. 9:1–8), Jesus confronts sin in yet another guise—bodily illness. Sin is a force that opposes the will of God, and one of its weapons is illness. The will of God is for people to have life and to have it abundantly, but sin is the enemy of God's will, and its servants, disease and death, are sent forth as the enemies of life. They are more than viruses, bacteria, and cells gone awry. Disease and death are agents of rebellion against God, shock troops under the command of the power of sin.

So, before illness is something that happens to a person, it is something that happens to the whole creation. Sin is out to destroy God's good work, and illness is one of its devices of destruction. The whole creation is in "bondage to decay" (Rom. 8:21); in other words, the whole creation is ill. There is disease in the marrow of nature.

How, then, should we think of the connection between sin and sickness in human beings? The biblical witness has two claims. First, people who are sick, like all creatures in nature that experience disease, are suffering at the hands of a force larger than themselves, larger than any personal sense of blame or fault. When people get sick, we do not say, like Job's friends, that they must have done something evil to have somehow caused or merited this. People who are sick are the victims of an enemy, the enemy of God and the enemy of human life.

The second claim, however, is that human beings are a special case because, unlike flowers, trees, and animals, which do not commit sin, we can, and do, join forces with the foe. Like a prisoner of war who, through fear and weakness, collaborates with the enemy, we who are the victims of sin's power turn around and become the willful agents of sin's intent. We are not the authors of disease and death, but we sometimes do help them write their destructive scripts. To fill the atmosphere and our lungs with grime, to pour toxins into our seas and into our bodies, to drive ourselves mercilessly, to plague our minds with anxiety—these and other actions do not, in the deepest sense, *cause* illness, but they do cooperate with it.

The biblical witness, then, is a balance between the idea of people enslaved by sin and, nonetheless, freely deciding to collaborate with sin, choosing to become "sinners." It is easy for us, as contemporary people, to lose this sense of balance and to misunderstand this biblical view of the connection between sin and sickness. Sometimes we can miss the linkage altogether. In our technological world, we can think of illness only in the clinical sense, thereby missing the theological depths, viewing disease only as a physical process without moral or spiritual meaning.

Mostly, however, we are prone to think too narrowly, too mechanically, about the connection between sin and illness, trying to find the bond between a particular person's illness and some specific sin they must have committed. For example, a three-pack-a-day smoker develops lung cancer, and we wag the finger knowingly, as if to say, "Well, that's that. We have discovered the obvious tie between sin and disease in this case." But sin is not that obvious; it is larger than this apparent moral linkage. The savage effects of the illness, the insidious damage of malignancy, the pain and suffering of the one who is ill and of loved ones, the ever-present threat of death and loss of meaning—these are penalties too severe to be accounted for strictly in terms of personal morality. To smoke three packs of cigarettes a day is to become but a foot soldier in a vast and overwhelming army of destruction that seeks the death of all human life.

Moreover, it is often the sins of others that affects suffering in people. A coal miner contracts black lung disease or a child in a tenement develops brain damage through lead in the wall paint. In these cases, the sins of a whole society augment personal illness and suffering.

In the deepest sense, though, illness is a part of the human condition, a devastation that touches us all. The point is not to go from bed to bed in the hospital trying to discover what sin each patient has committed. That sort of one-to-one connection between sin and suffering is explicitly rejected in the New Testament (see John 9:1–3). To the contrary, the point is that we *all* ultimately end up in the sick bed; we *all* eventually are struck down by disease; we *all* finally die. No human being is free from the forces of illness and death. They have us cornered and trapped. Modern medicine can, at best, delay the inevitable, but no human power can deliver us from the grip of disease and death. They stalk human life until they conquer it; they oppose the will of God for the wholeness of humanity. They are, therefore, devious expressions of the overwhelming power of sin, and we need something more than an antibiotic; we need a deliverer. This is why biblical writers can move seamlessly between the language of illness and the language of sin. "Bless the LORD, O my soul," sings the psalmist, "and do not forget all his benefits—who forgives all your iniquity, who heals all your diseases" (Psalm 103:2–3). That is also why Jesus responds to the man's illness not only by healing his paralysis, but also by pronouncing that his sins are forgiven (Matt. 9:2). This man becomes a forerunner of all humanity. We need more than a temporary reprieve from our viruses, lifeless limbs, and cancers; we need for God to defeat the very power of sin that employs illness as its weapon.

In this story, a group of people bring a bedridden, paralyzed man to Jesus (Matt. 9:2). They obviously hope that Jesus will heal the man, but, surprisingly, Jesus goes far deeper than the man's physical need: "Take heart, son; your sins are forgiven" (Matt. 9:2). This remark about sins causes some of the religious authorities, the scribes, to think to themselves that Jesus had uttered blasphemy.

What is blasphemy? It is speaking in an intensely irreverent way, and it can assume several forms: It can be cursing God, or claiming for oneself the authority of God, or speaking about holy things lightly and frivolously. Matthew does not tell us what the scribes have in mind in Jesus' case, but it is probably one of the latter two cases. In their view, in pronouncing forgiveness of the man's sins, either Jesus had claimed for himself something that only God has the authority to do or Jesus' reply about forgiveness of sins was glib, a speaking of solemn, holy, godly matters in a flippant and irresponsible way.

Jesus reads the minds of the scribes, perceives that they thought "evil in their hearts" (Matt. 9:4), and challenges them with a curious question: "[W]hich is easier, to say, 'Your sins are forgiven,' or to say, 'Stand up and walk'?" Though today we may wonder about the correct response to Jesus' question, from a theological vantage point, what is genuinely difficult is the vanquishing of sin, more so than curing a bodily ill. Curing a paralyzed limb is holding back a wave; eradicating the power of sin is sweeping back the ocean. Jesus has already taken on physical illness and shown his powers as a healer; he has cured a leper, a centurion's paralyzed servant, a woman with a fever, and many other sick people (see Matt. 8:1–17). Now he takes on a greater foe—sin itself. He has moved from the symptom to the source. His question, then, phrased in other words is, "Which is the mightier foe, an illness that paralyzes a limb, or sin itself that consumes the very essence of life?"

So, the logic of the story is that Jesus says to a paralyzed man that his sins are forgiven. The scribes think of this as a cheap remark, a glib religious sentiment, an empty and blasphemous promise that Jesus has no authority to make. Jesus responds to them with a counterchallenge: It takes more authority to pronounce the forgiveness of sins than it does to heal sickness. Indeed, Jesus heals the man, but he prefaces the healing with the advance notice that it is to be seen as a manifestation of his greater authority, his wider power, to take on the ancient enemy of sin.

INTERLUDE:
THE SHOCKING NEWNESS OF JESUS' MINISTRY
Matthew 9:9–17

> 9:9 As Jesus was walking along, he saw a man called Matthew sitting at the tax booth; and he said to him, "Follow me." And he got up and followed him. [10] And as he sat at dinner in the house, many tax collectors and sinners came and were sitting with him and his disciples. [11] When the Pharisees saw this, they said to his disciples, "Why does your teacher eat with tax collectors and sinners?" [12] But when he heard this, he said, "Those who are well have no need of a physician, but those who are sick. [13] Go and learn what this means, 'I desire mercy, not sacrifice.' For I have come to call not the righteous but sinners."
>
> [14] Then the disciples of John came to him, saying, "Why do we and the Pharisees fast often, but your disciples do not fast?" [15] And Jesus said to them, "The wedding guests cannot mourn as long as the bridegroom is with them, can they? The days will come when the bridegroom is taken away from them, and then they will fast. [16] No one sews a piece of unshrunk cloth on an old cloak, for the patch pulls away from the cloak, and a worse tear is made. [17] Neither is new wine put into old wineskins; otherwise, the skins burst, and the wine is spilled, and the skins are destroyed; but new wine is put into fresh wineskins, and so both are preserved."

Here, between the second and third trio of miracle stories, Matthew inserts another interlude, arranged in three scenes. This one emphasizes the newness of Jesus' ministry, the fact that Jesus breaks the usual categories and defies accepted religious custom. As such, this interlude also forms a bridge. The newness in Jesus' ministry emerged at the end of the second group of miracle stories, where the crowds expressed astonishment because they witnessed in Jesus something they had not seen before, that "such authority [had been given] to human beings" (Matt. 9:8). This wonder over the unprecedented character of Jesus' ministry is a major theme of the third group of miracles, climaxing with the crowds exclaiming, "Never has anything like this been seen in Israel" (Matt. 9:33).

But what is this newness? Is it that Jesus is simply a religious maverick, an iconoclast who refuses to observe the expected standards? No, the task of this interlude section is to show that what strikes Jesus' critics as disturbingly novel is actually his fidelity to the will of God. What is unprecedented is that in this human being Jesus, God's will is embodied in its purity and fullness. In and through Jesus, God is engaging in a wide-ranging assault on the powers that infect human life, a mission of compassion that crosses old racial and religious boundaries, a display of holiness that shatters former taboos—something never before seen in Israel, or anywhere else either.

Scene One: The Call of a Tax Collector (Matthew 9:9)

The interlude section is set into motion by a terse account of Jesus' call of a tax collector named Matthew to be a follower, a disciple (Matt. 9:9). We are not given much detail here. Matthew the tax collector, sitting at the tax booth, is spotted by Jesus. Jesus says only the words "Follow me," and Matthew follows.

One of the details we are given has puzzled many readers—the name of the tax collector, Matthew. This story is taken from the Gospel of Mark (see Mark 2:14), but there the tax collector's name is Levi, not Matthew. Why the name change? The idea that the author of the Gospel of Matthew is here telling his own story is appealing, but not likely (see Introduction). Perhaps this tax collector had two names, Levi *and* Matthew, a rare but not unprecedented possibility. Maybe the name Matthew, which is derived from a Hebrew word meaning "gift of God," was a name given to Levi after he became a disciple, or perhaps the author of the Gospel preferred to connect this call story to one of the original twelve disciples rather than to the otherwise unknown "Levi." There are many speculations, but we simply do not have enough evidence to know for certain.

The more important details in the story, however, are that this tax collector named Matthew got up from his tax booth and followed Jesus. Because we live in a psychologically sophisticated age, we want to know why he responded this way, and we are tempted to try to read his mind and his motivations. We cannot imagine someone immediately getting up from his job and following Jesus without some significant subconscious reason, some prior inner need that was being met. In our world, people simply do not move instantly from busy bureaucrat to devoted disciple without psychological cause.

We should not, however, force our modern categories on the Gospel of Matthew. If Matthew the Gospel writer had wanted us to see inside the heart of Matthew the tax collector, he would have described the inner workings of Matthew's thoughts. The main point of this story is not to speculate about what is happening inside Matthew; it is to perceive what is happening outside through Jesus. His words "Follow me" are powerful and accomplish their mission simply by being spoken. Jesus, who healed a paralyzed servant with a word, calmed the raging winds with a word, sent howling demons hurtling into squealing swine with a word, and rolled back the tidal wave of human sin with a word, now begins to form a community, a church, with a word.

This is why services of Christian worship even today begin not with a psychological inventory ("How many of you out there feel like being here today?"), but with a call to worship ("Serve the Lord with gladness; come into God's presence with singing!"). Even now, the word from Christ, the word from beyond us, comes to us, powerfully beckoning us from our workplaces and our ordinary routines into a life of faithful following.

Another important aspect of this brief story of the call of Matthew is his occupation—tax collector. We have become so accustomed to the fact that Jesus associated with tax collectors that we have lost the shock value of that affiliation. In first-century, Roman-occupied Palestine one would probably not utter the words "tax collector" without spitting. Tax collectors, or publicans as they were sometimes called, were contract workers for the Roman government. They were personally responsible for paying the taxes due from their area, but they were permitted to gather those taxes by gouging as much extra from the citizenry as they could manage. Opportunities for graft, extortion, and theft were almost unlimited, and people simply assumed that every tax collector had his greasy hands deep into other people's pockets.

Tax collectors, then, were carp feeding off the river bottom of Roman rule. For Jesus to call a tax collector as a disciple would be as if he were today to call a political ward heeler in a bribery-saturated precinct, a narcotics detective on the take, a mafia don on the CIA payroll. The very act of extending any sort of invitation to such a shady character makes decent people wonder about Jesus' own character, which is precisely what happens next.

Scene Two: A Question about Sinners (Matthew 9:10–13)

In the next scene, we see Jesus reclining at dinner in "the house" (whose house is not clear); the call of Matthew the tax collector was evidently just the beginning, because Jesus is now surrounded by many tax collectors and other sinners (Matt. 9:10). The Pharisees, no doubt offended by this sight of Jesus in the midst of social rabble, interrogate Jesus' disciples about it (Matt. 9:11). Why would their teacher allow his table to be sullied by such unrighteous people? Jesus overhears their question and responds in three ways: with a proverb, with a quotation from the prophets, and with a statement about the nature of his ministry (Matt. 9:12–13).

The proverb "those who are well have no need of a physician, but those who are sick" points to Jesus' healing and saving role. He is a physician of the kingdom of heaven, and, as a physician, his work is among the sick. His purpose is to touch the diseased—in body, mind, and soul—and to restore them to full health. The quotation from the prophets, "I desire steadfast love and not sacrifice" (Hosea 6:6), seems, at first, out of place, since sacrifice is not at issue in this story. On closer inspection, however, the quotation is apt, because it is drawn from a section in Hosea describing God as the healer of Israel (see especially Hos. 6:1). God is a loving and merciful healer, and God's true servants will be those who themselves are genuinely loving and merciful, not merely ceremonially religious.

The proverb about the sick and the quotation from Hosea set the stage for Jesus' third response to the Pharisees' question, the breathtaking and shocking declaration "For I have come to call not the righteous but sinners" (Matt. 9:13). We must not allow an easy familiarity with the Gospel to cause us to miss the startling, outrageous quality of this statement. Jesus has here turned the customary reading of the Old Testament on its head. Over against the repeated Old Testament message that "sinners [will not stand] in the congregation of the righteous" (Psalm 1:5) and that God loves "righteousness and hate[s] wickedness" (Psalm 45:7), Jesus announces to the Pharisees that his whole ministry is based on the reverse, that his physician's office is open to the wicked and not to the righteous.

Righteousness is a concept that operates at two levels: the surface level of practice and the deeper level of vision and motivation. At the surface, righteousness means living a particular way: doing certain things, such as worshiping and giving alms for the poor, and not doing certain other things, such as committing acts of violence or stealing other people's property. Beneath these superficial righteous deeds, however, lies a profound and more basic vision of God's will; namely, that to be righteous is to "love the LORD your God with all your heart, and with all your soul, and with all your might . . . [and to] love your neighbor as yourself" (Deut. 6:5 and Lev. 19:18; see Matt. 22:37–39).

Righteous practices, then, are the surface expressions of this deeper love of God and neighbor. The danger, however, is that the two levels can easily get separated in the religious life so that righteous practices become isolated from the vision of God and neighbor, and therefore become ends in themselves. Or perhaps worse, righteous practices can become expressions not of a love of God and neighbor, but of our love of ourselves and our own self-affirmed goodness; in short, self-righteousness.

The Pharisees' protest about Jesus' association with tax collectors and sinners discloses that they have allowed righteousness as a practice to be split from righteousness as a vision. They have defined righteousness in terms of retreat rather than action, as separation from sinners rather than as love of God and neighbor. The psalmist, however, describes a different picture: "Restore to me the joy of your salvation. . . . Then I will teach transgressors your ways, and sinners will return to you" (Psalm 51:12–13). What we see in the ministry of Jesus is a stunning portrayal of sinners being restored, of true righteousness in action, righteousness so astoundingly faithful to the heart of the Old Testament and to the will of God that it comes across to Jesus' contemporaries as dramatically innovative.

Scene Three: A Question about Fasting (Matthew 9:14–17)

Continuing the theme of the newness of Jesus' ministry, the next episode concerns an exchange with the disciples of John the Baptist (Matt. 9:14–17). Even though John himself called the Pharisees a "brood of vipers" (Matt. 3:7), his disciples link themselves with the Pharisees (a clue, perhaps, that their attitude is adversarial and not neutral) when they ask, "Why do we and the Pharisees fast often, but your disciples do not fast?" (Matt. 9:14).

Jesus' reply, "The wedding guests cannot mourn as long as the bridegroom is with them" (Matt. 9:15), makes sense when we recognize that fasting was most often done in connection with periods of mourning or acts of sorrowful penance. There is, in other words, an appropriate time for fasting, but not when the party is in full swing. In the ministry of Jesus, all the stops have been pulled out in the celebration of God's presence and the joyful activity of the kingdom of heaven. To fast when Jesus is around would be like weeping at a victory celebration.

There will come a time, of course, when fasting will be fitting, when Jesus is no longer present, "when the bridegroom is taken away from them" (Matt. 9:15). This surely refers to Jesus' coming violent death, when the disciples of Jesus will mourn, but it may also refer to the experience of the church, whose service in a broken world includes fasting, sharing in the sorrow and suffering of the world while anticipating in hope the approaching victory of God's kingdom (see Matt. 6:16–18).

Jesus ends his remarks to John's disciples with two images describing the incompatibility between new and old: sewing a patch on a garment and putting wine into wineskins (Matt. 9:16–17). These images actually apply to the whole of Jesus' ministry and not just to the exchange with John's disciples about fasting. In the first, Jesus observes that no reasonable person would sew an unshrunk patch onto an old piece of clothing. Obviously, the first time the garment was washed, the new patch would shrink and make a worse tear. Likewise, no sensible person would pour young, green wine into old, seasoned wineskins. The new and still-fermenting wine would expand and burst the old skins. New wineskins are required for new wine. These are pictures that describe the surprising freshness of Jesus' ministry and the futility of trying to make Jesus' way of living out the will of God fit into conventional, rigid religious expectations. The point is not that Jesus destroys what has gone before; indeed, Jesus has not "come to abolish the law or the prophets . . . but to fulfill" (Matt. 5:17). The point, rather, is that human understandings of God are too small, too confined to our own limited horizons, and that Jesus fulfills the ancient promises of God in ways that shatter those expectations. Thus, Jesus fulfills the old in surprising new ways. Therefore "both [the old and new] are preserved" (Matt. 9:17).

THE THIRD GROUP OF MIGHTY WORKS
Matthew 9:18–34

9:18 **While he was saying these things to them, suddenly a leader of the synagogue came in and knelt before him, saying, "My daughter has just died; but come and lay your hand on her, and she will live."** [19] **And Jesus got up and followed him, with his disciples.** [20] **Then suddenly a woman who had been suffering from hemorrhages for twelve years came up behind him and touched the fringe of his cloak,** [21] **for she said to herself, "If I only touch his cloak, I will be made well."** [22] **Jesus turned, and seeing her he said, "Take heart, daughter; your faith has made you well." And instantly the woman was made well.** [23] **When Jesus came to the leader's house and saw the flute players and the crowd making a commotion,** [24] **he said, "Go away; for the girl is not dead but sleeping." And they laughed at him.** [25] **But when the crowd had been put outside, he went in and took her by the hand, and the girl got up.** [26] **And the report of this spread throughout that district.**

[27] **As Jesus went on from there, two blind men followed him, crying loudly, "Have mercy on us, Son of David!"** [28] **When he entered the house, the blind men came to him; and Jesus said to them, "Do you believe that I am able to do this?" They said to him, "Yes, Lord."** [29] **Then he touched their eyes and said, "According to your faith let it be done to you."** [30] **And their eyes were opened. Then Jesus sternly ordered them, "See that no one knows of this."** [31] **But they went away and spread the news about him throughout that district.**

[32] **After they had gone away, a demoniac who was mute was brought to**

him. [33] And when the demon had been cast out, the one who had been mute spoke; and the crowds were amazed and said, "Never has anything like this been seen in Israel." [34] But the Pharisees said, "By the ruler of the demons he casts out the demons."

We have seen in the first group of miracle stories (Matt. 8:1–17) how Jesus healed people on the edges of Israelite society, and, in the second group of miracle stories (Matt. 8:23–9:8), how Jesus took on the chaotic powers of evil. Now, in the third and final trio of miracle stories, we see the ministry of Jesus pushing beyond the expected boundaries—beyond the local area, beyond the bounds of Israel's hopes, even beyond the limits of death. Here the "new patch" of Jesus' activity dramatically tears away from the old and shrunken fabric, and the "new wine" of the kingdom fermenting in Jesus' mighty deeds bursts through the frail old wineskins and pours out with life-giving force over the whole earth.

The Healing of Two "Daughters" (Matthew 9:18–26)

A man identified only as "a leader" rushes up to Jesus with an urgent request: His daughter is dead, and the saving power of Jesus is desperately needed. The NRSV indicates that he is "a leader of the synagogue," but the words "of the synagogue," which appear in Mark's version of the story (Mark 5:22), are not present in the original Greek of Matthew. The tensions between Matthew's church and the Jewish community (see Introduction) probably caused Matthew to eliminate any reference to the synagogue.

This man, however, is more than just "a man"; he is a "leader," in some way a representative of the people. Whether Matthew wants us to think of him as a synagogue leader or as a public political official does not matter. Either way, he represents the community; he symbolizes the way things are. He stands for the "old"; he is about to encounter the dramatically "new."

Like the wise men and the leper before him, the leader bows down worshipfully before Jesus (Matt. 9:18). When Mark tells this story, the man requests a healing, for his daughter is "at the point of death" (Mark 5:23), but here in Matthew the man asks for far more than a healing. The daughter is already dead, and her father boldly calls for a resurrection, "[C]ome and lay your hand on her, and she will live" (Matt. 8:18).

On the way to the leader's house, Jesus encounters another urgent need. A woman with a flow of blood for a dozen years modestly comes up behind Jesus and touches the fringe of his cloak. Because of her constant bleeding, this woman is ritually unclean (see Lev. 15:25–33) and not allowed human touch. She reasons to herself, however, that touching the outer portion of Jesus' clothing will be sufficient for her to be made well (Matt. 9:21). When she does so, Jesus turns, sees her, and says (in wording parallel to that spoken to the paralyzed man in Matthew 9:2), "Take heart, daughter; your faith has made you well" (Matt. 9:22). In other words, her healing was not the result of any magic conjured up by her touching his garment, but the result of her faith in Jesus' power to heal.

Returning to the story of the leader's daughter, Matthew records that Jesus, when he arrived at the leader's house, found a wake in full progress, the paid flute players and grief-stricken mourners in noisy sorrow (Matt. 9:23). But, as Jesus taught earlier, people "cannot mourn as long as the bridegroom is with them" (Matt. 9:15), and he waves away the mourners with the astonishing announcement that "the girl is not dead but sleeping" (Matt. 9:24).

This provokes merry laughter all right, but of the mocking sort rather than the joyful kind. The citizens of the land laugh scornfully at Jesus because they know how to face reality. In the framework of the old age, when people die, they stay dead, and, face it, this little girl, sad to say, is dead as a doornail. "No, no," says Jesus, "a new reality is happening before your eyes; she's only sleeping." This remark naturally causes them to snicker, to laugh themselves to death, so to speak. But the citizens of the kingdom of heaven have the last, the best, and the most healing laugh, however, when Jesus goes into the house, takes the girl by the hand, and raises her up full of new life. Not surprisingly, "the report of this spread throughout that district" (Matt. 9:26).

The Healing of Two Blind Men
(Matthew 9:27–31)

In this story, two blind men, who are described as "following" Jesus (Matt. 9:27), cry out, "Have mercy on us, Son of David!" The wording of their appeal shows that they have at least a partial understanding of who Jesus is, a worker of mercy and the true son of David (see Matt. 1:1; 9:13). Jesus asks them if they believe he is able to heal them, and their "Yes, Lord" shows an even deeper recognition about Jesus: He is Lord, and he has the power and authority to heal. Jesus responds, "According to your faith let it be done to you" (Matt. 9:29), and the men receive sight. Once again, as in the case of the centurion's servant (Matt. 8:10) and the hemorrhaging woman (Matt. 9:22), healing is explicitly connected to a person's faith.

After the healing, Jesus abruptly and sternly orders the men to keep quiet about what has happened. Scholars have wondered about this, since, in Matthew, Jesus is generally not so secretive about his acts of ministry. Telling people not to spread the news is more a feature of the Gospel of Mark than Matthew. Indeed, in Matthew, only on one other occasion has Jesus ordered silence. That was in the case of the leper, and there it seemed to be connected to a need for the leper to appear before the priest to be declared fully restored to his community (Matt. 8:4).

It is probable that the main point of Jesus' command to silence is not to display Jesus' humility but is found in the final verse of the story: "But they went away and spread the news about him throughout that district" (Matt. 9:31). This statement virtually repeats the content of the final verse of the previous story, "And the report of this spread throughout that district" (Matt. 9:26), and the key idea seems to be that word about Jesus was spreading like wildfire, with or without his permission. At this point, Jesus is aiming his ministry exclusively to "the lost sheep of the house of Israel" (Matt. 10:6), but, even when he says nothing or flatly forbids a public fuss, the news of his ministry is already a prairie fire spreading rapidly across the countryside. Even now, at least one Gentile has been healed, the whole district is buzzing about Jesus, and the "new wine" is beginning to strain against the old skins.

The Healing of One Who Was Mute (Matthew 9:32–34)

This, the final healing story in this section of Matthew, is so brief, it barely takes a sentence and a half to describe. The details are sparse. A man who is possessed by demons and, thus, ill (the Greek word for his illness can signify that he was deaf, mute, or both) is brought to Jesus. The demon is cast out, and the man shows that he is healed by speaking (Matt. 9:32–33).

Matthew's primary interest appears to be in portraying the two opposing reactions to this healing (and, by implication, to the whole string of Jesus' mighty works in chapters 8–9). The crowds, which have been following Jesus since the beginning of his ministry, exclaim in amazement, "Never has anything like this been seen in Israel" (Matt. 9:33). The Pharisees, however, accuse Jesus of being himself under the power of demons: "By the ruler of the demons he casts out the demons" (Matt. 9:34).

These diametrically opposed reactions to Jesus name the chief issue of the Gospel of Matthew to this point—the source of Jesus' authority and power. Everybody recognizes the amazing works that Jesus performs; the question is, Where does he get the strength to do them—from God or from the demons? From the Pharisees' point of view, the answer can only be that Jesus is in league with Satan, because he certainly doesn't act like their image of a godly person. In their minds, God wants a righteous and holy people, people who are careful to keep separate from Gentiles, and people who are scrupulous to avoid unholy agents, like lepers, swine, menstruating women, and the dead. Jesus, of course, has already reached out his hand to a leper, healed a Gentile, ministered in a pig- and demon-infested region, been touched by a bleeding woman, and taken a dead girl by the hand. Jesus has stepped over every boundary separating the holy from the unholy, the clean from the unclean, and, in the Pharisees' view, only a servant of the demons would so trample down the fences in the holy garden.

But in Jesus the framework of holiness has been changed; in him "the kingdom of heaven has come near" (Matt. 4:17). Jesus' ministry is one of mercy, not of judgment and ritual purity. He is the merciful will of God in action, reaching out to lepers and demoniacs, overturning the forces that devalue women, paying no attention to the barriers that segregate Gentiles, calling sinners to follow him and to join him at table. Indeed, nothing like this, no *one* like this, has ever been seen in Israel. The wineskins have now burst, and the new wine of the kingdom is flowing across the land, irrigating the parched fields and preparing the way for the great harvest of God. In fact, it is to that harvest that Matthew next turns.

6. Laborers for the Plentiful Harvest
Matthew 9:35–10:42

At this point in Matthew's Gospel, Jesus is about to begin a new phase of his ministry—sending out his disciples to share in his mission. Matthew marks this development by repeating, almost word for word, the same statement he used several chapters earlier, at the outset of Jesus' ministerial journey: "Then Jesus went about all the cities and villages, teaching in their synagogues, and proclaiming the good news of the kingdom, and curing every disease and sickness" (Matt. 9:35; compare to Matt. 4:23). This not only serves as a directional signal, alerting the reader to a turn in the narrative road, a new stage in the story of Jesus, but it also makes an early connection between the ministry of the disciples (and, subsequently, the church) and that of Jesus. Despite controversy and conflict, Jesus is steady on his path, still teaching, preaching, and healing, and that will be both the lot and the work of the disciples, too. They, too, will be embroiled in controversy, but they are not to be deterred from the service of the kingdom—preaching, teaching, and healing—as they work toward the harvest that Jesus has assured will be "plentiful" (see Matt. 10:37).

SHEPHERDS AND FARM WORKERS
Matthew 9:35–38

> 9:35 **Then Jesus went about all the cities and villages, teaching in their synagogues, and proclaiming the good news of the kingdom, and curing every disease and every sickness.** [36] **When he saw the crowds, he had compassion for them, because they were harassed and helpless, like sheep without a shepherd.** [37] **Then he said to his disciples, "The harvest is plentiful, but the laborers are few;** [38] **therefore ask the Lord of the harvest to send out laborers into his harvest."**

"When he saw the crowds," Matthew writes, "he had compassion for them" (Matt. 9:36). Taken literally, this is a curious statement, since surely this is not the first occasion for Jesus to see the crowds, which have been pressing around him from the beginning. Obviously, Jesus does not suddenly become aware that there are crowds of people around him; here, he sees and describes the ever-present crowds in a new way. They are no longer simply "crowds"; they are people who are "harassed and helpless, like sheep without a shepherd" (Matt. 9:36).

This image of Israel as a flock of sheep wandering helplessly without a shepherd is a well-known Old Testament image, one that appears several times (for example, Num. 27:16–17; 1 Kings 22:17; 2 Chron. 18:16; Zech. 10:2). Jesus is on a mission of mercy to Israel, and, indeed, his response to this sight of a leaderless Israel is "compassion" (Matt. 9:36).

Jesus not only describes the people as "sheep without a shepherd"; in a sudden shift of images, Jesus also sees them as a field nearing the harvest and needing farm laborers (Matt. 9:37). These two pictures of the people—sheep without a shepherd and crops ready for the harvest—though agriculturally quite diverse, actually work well together to describe the nature of Jesus' mission. The shepherding image lifts up the theme of God's compassion for Israel. God has never left Israel without a shepherd, and, in fact, God is identified as the good and merciful divine shepherd (see Psalm 23). So, Jesus, the embodiment of God's will, is the compassionate shepherd for leaderless Israel (see Matt. 2:6; 25:32; and 26:31), and his disciples (and, finally, the church) will also be given the mission of shepherding with mercy and compassion.

The image of the harvest adds to this theme of compassion by introducing the urgency of time into the picture. When a crop is ready for the harvest, there is no time to waste. Reapers are needed on the spot and without delay. As Jesus looks over the crowds, he sees them as a bumper crop ready for the harvesting. Laborers, and plenty of them, were needed immediately. So, Jesus tells his disciples, "[A]sk the Lord of the harvest to send out laborers into his harvest" (Matt. 9:37). This is addressed to the disciples, but the church in every age has always heard Jesus speaking these words. The people wander "harassed and helpless," needing the kingdom ministry of compassion. Moreover, it is a mission that cannot wait for a more opportune time—when the church is stronger, richer, or more confident. The harvest time has come, and laborers are needed in the fields today.

THE TWELVE DISCIPLES
Matthew 10:1–4

10:1 **Then Jesus summoned his twelve disciples and gave them authority over unclean spirits, to cast them out, and to cure every disease and every** sickness. [2] **These are the names of the twelve apostles: first, Simon, also known as Peter, and his brother Andrew; James son of Zebedee, and his brother John;** [3] **Philip and Bartholomew; Thomas and Matthew the tax collector; James son of Alphaeus, and Thaddaeus;** [4] **Simon the Cananaean, and Judas Iscariot, the one who betrayed him.**

In the previous passage, Jesus told his disciples to pray that God would send laborers into the harvest (Matt. 9:38). Now, in this passage, it becomes clear that the disciples are to be the answer to their own prayer. Jesus calls them forward and gives them authority to cast out demons and to cure sickness (Matt. 10:1)—in other words, to continue and to spread the ministry that Jesus has been doing in Matthew 8–9.

Then Matthew lists the names of the Twelve, copying with slight modifications the list of the disciples in Mark 3:13–19. There are several interesting features of this roster of the disciples:

1. If we had only the Gospel of Matthew, we would be surprised that there were twelve disciples. Up to this point, Matthew has not specified how many disciples Jesus had, and he has written about the calling of only five disciples (see Matt. 4:18–22 and 9:9). The fact that the writer of Matthew can so suddenly and casually refer to the number twelve is a clear signal that he assumes his readers already know that Jesus had twelve disciples—no doubt from sermons, oral tradition, and probably the Gospel of Mark.

2. Here the twelve disciples are called "the twelve *apostles*" (Matt. 10:2), the only time in Matthew the word "apostles" is used. The reason Matthew substitutes "apostles" for "disciples" here is probably that the disciples are about to be sent out to do ministry, and "apostle" literally means "the one who is sent." A disciple is not a passive student of kingdom principles, but an active doer of kingdom ministry, one who follows Jesus by engaging in the very actions of Jesus.

3. Matthew places the word "first" before the name of Simon Peter (10:2), both because Simon was the one of the first two disciples called by Jesus (Matt. 4:18–20) and because Peter will increasingly take on a leadership role among the Twelve (see especially Matt. 16:18).

4. The twelve disciples are listed in pairs, probably a faint echo of the tradition that they were sent out to do ministry two-by-two (see Mark 6:7).

5. Several of the disciples are identified in family terms, as "son" or "brother," but three of the disciples have labels identifying them in non-familial ways: Matthew, Simon (not Peter), and Judas. Judas, of course, is forever remembered—then and now—by the tragic role he played in the death of Jesus: "the one who betrayed him" (Matt. 10:4). (Scholars are not

sure what the other word used to describe Judas, "Iscariot," means. It may be a geographical term, that is, "a man from Kerioth," a village in southern Judea. Others, however, have translated the word to mean "ruddy," "deceiver," or "assassin.") Matthew is named as "the tax collector," connecting him to the previous account of his call by Jesus (see comment on Matt. 9:9), and Simon is specified as "the Cananaean," probably a title reflecting his participation in a zealous group of Jewish nationalists ready to throw off the shackles of Roman occupation with force if necessary. To find the former Roman hireling Matthew and the revolutionary Simon together among the disciples is quite striking. As John Meier states, "The startling juxtaposition of this former Rome-hater with Matthew, a former lackey of Rome, shows that the new community of Jesus has embraced and transcended the tensions in the old community of Israel" (Meier, *Matthew*, 105).

A MANUAL FOR MISSIONARIES
Matthew 10:5–15

10:5 **These twelve Jesus sent out with the following instructions: "Go nowhere among the Gentiles, and enter no town of the Samaritans, ⁶ but go rather to the lost sheep of the house of Israel. ⁷ As you go, proclaim the good news, 'The kingdom of heaven has come near.' ⁸ Cure the sick, raise the dead, cleanse the lepers, cast out demons. You received without payment; give without payment. ⁹ Take no gold, or silver, or copper in your belts, ¹⁰ no bag for your journey, or two tunics, or sandals, or a staff; for laborers deserve their food. ¹¹ Whatever town or village you enter, find out who in it is worthy, and stay there until you leave. ¹² As you enter the house, greet it. ¹³ If the house is worthy, let your peace come upon it; but if it is not worthy, let your peace return to you. ¹⁴ If anyone will not welcome you or listen to your words, shake off the dust from your feet as you leave that house or town. ¹⁵ Truly I tell you, it will be more tolerable for the land of Sodom and Gomorrah on the day of judgment than for that town.**

A distinctive characteristic of the Gospel of Matthew is that it includes longish sections of the teachings of Jesus (see Introduction). There are five of these discourses in all; the first of these is the Sermon on the Mount (Matt. 5:1–7:29), and the second is this section of instructions to the disciples as they are sent out as missionaries of the kingdom of heaven. Even though these teachings of Jesus are addressed to the twelve disciples, Matthew's church surely heard them as words intended to shape their own mission work.

This section serves, then, as a manual of instruction for missionaries, and it includes the following lessons.

1. The disciples are to go only to "the lost sheep of the house of Israel," and not to Gentiles or to Samaritans (Matt. 10:5–6). How are we to understand this, given Jesus' own openness to Gentiles (see Matt. 8:5–13) and his ultimate mandate to "make disciples of all nations" (Matt. 28:19)? Many in the early church, Matthew among them, believed that God's plan to save the world involved, first, an appeal for the repentance and renewal of Israel and, only then, the proclamation of the gospel to the Gentiles. According to Paul "the gospel . . . is the power of God for salvation to everyone who has faith, to the Jew first and also to the Greek" (Rom. 1:16). God had made promises to Israel, and God remains faithful to those promises. Thus, God refuses to abandon Israel, and the gospel is given first for the refreshment of Israel, then to the Gentiles.

So, following this conviction about the order of salvation, Matthew, who wrote his Gospel in part to encourage his church to engage in a vigorous mission to Gentiles, here preserves what could have been for him a somewhat embarrassing truth—the statement of Jesus that his mission and, subsequently, that of his disciples was directed exclusively to the Jews. Some commentators have suggested that conservative Jewish Christians in the earliest church may well have seized upon this saying of Jesus as a "proof text" against opening the doors of the church to Gentiles (see Meier, *Matthew*, 106). The main point, however, is not exclusivity, but timing. The gospel is not just for Israel; it is to be proclaimed *first* to Israel in order that it may then be proclaimed, through Israel, to the Gentiles.

2. Matthew has portrayed Jesus in action preaching the gospel of the kingdom (Matt. 4:17), healing the sick (Matt. 9:27–34), raising the dead (Matt. 9:18–26), cleansing lepers (Matt. 8:1–4), and casting out demons (Matt. 8:28–34). Now, Jesus calls upon the disciples to take on those very same tasks (Matt. 10:7–8).

This means, first, that the mission of the church is a continuation of the ministry of its Lord. This is, of course, a tall order. In order to understand this command, two points need to be made. The first, and the easier to make, is that the ministry of the church, like the ministry of Jesus, is a comprehensive ministry addressed to the whole range of human need. Any notion that the church ought to quit getting involved in nonspiritual matters and get back to its "real job" of preaching the gospel and saving souls misses the point. "Preaching the gospel and saving souls" means grappling with disease and the demonic, with social segregation and the powers of death. It means, therefore, wrestling with issues of public health care, with racial and social alienation, with the powers of domination and oppression that bleed the life out of a community.

But this still leaves unanswered the harder question. To be sure, Jesus healed people, cast out demons, raised the dead, and performed many other mighty deeds, but we are not Jesus. So how, in the name of heaven, is the church supposed to do what he did? The second point, then, to be made is that our perceptions of our own weakness are accurate. We do not, in fact, have the power to touch lepers or cancer patients and cause them to be healed in an instant; we cannot shout "Be gone!" at the raging forces afflicting a diseased mind and expect the illness to flee; we are not able to stride into a funeral home and, with a word, raise the dead from their caskets.

The point, then, is not that Jesus used to do these mighty deeds, and, now that he is gone, we are supposed to try to imitate him and do them, too. The point, rather, is that God, who was at work in the world in Jesus, is still at work in the world in Christ. Wherever there is disease, evil, hope, unbelief, and death, Christ the merciful savior is at work to proclaim the gospel of hope, to heal people from every disease, to cast out the demonic forces of evil, to defeat the ruthless grip of death. The risen Christ is "with [us] always, to the end of the age" (Matt. 28:20). The task of the church is not somehow to replace Jesus but to join Christ in the work that he is doing in the world.

3. The disciples are to provide their ministry without charge (Matt. 10:8). They are to "take [or, perhaps 'acquire'—the Greek word can mean either] no gold, or silver, or copper" for their money belts, and they are not to pack luggage, take an extra change of clothing, wear sandals, or carry a stick for protection (Matt. 10:9–10).

The language of these verses may well make its point through hyperbole. It would be hard, for example, to imagine going very far in rocky Palestine without sandals, and any missionary journey of more than a few miles would require the carrying of food and water. The main theme, however, of these instructions is that the missionaries of the kingdom of heaven are not to roll into town like a self-sufficient corporation seeking to expand its power base. Ministers of mercy are to carry themselves humbly; they are to be vulnerable, depending upon the providence of God. Evangelists who show up in a Ferrari with a suitcase full of designer clothes cannot expect to have their gospel call to repent taken seriously.

Money is not the only issue here, though. Jesus seems to be urging his disciples to depend not only upon God but also upon the people to whom they are ministering. If they go out without money, food, extra clothing, or a stick for protection, then they must rely upon others for food, lodging, and safety. The phrase "laborers deserve their food" (Matt. 10:10) is drawn, of course, from the world of work and wages. If laborers perform some work, then they are deserving of being fed (and paid) by their employer. Just so, if missionaries bring the gospel to people, then they are worthy of being cared for. This principle is more than "you scratch my back, and I'll scratch yours." If people feed and care for the missionaries of the gospel, then they are both acknowledging that they have received something of value and participating in the ministry that brought it to them. To care for one who preaches the kingdom of heaven is already to become an active participant in that kingdom.

4. As we saw in the section above, the disciples are to be dependent upon those to whom they minister for food, care, and safety. This called for some special rules regarding the rather delicate matter of hospitality and lodging. Disciples, when they enter a town or village, are to be sensitive to these signals of welcome or rejection—in this case, welcome or rejection of the gospel and its proclaimer. The process seems to begin with a greeting (Matt. 10:12), and then with a kingdom benediction ("Peace be unto you," Matt. 10:13). If the greeting and the benediction, the message and the messenger, are welcomed and received, then this is a "worthy house" (Matt. 10:11), and the disciple is to stay in that house until the time of departure (not seeking a better place to stay as the days go by).

What happens, however, if there is rejection? The disciple is to "shake off the dust from your feet as you leave that house or town" (Matt. 10:14). In the first century, when Jews returned from traveling in Gentile areas, they would sometime shake the dust off their feet as a symbol of their disgust and rejection. The disciples, venturing only into a Jewish area, are to do the same.

We see here an early recognition of the fragility and reciprocal nature of the evangelistic situation. The gospel does not coerce or bulldoze its way intrusively into people's lives. It always depends upon a responsiveness, a sense of being welcomed. The wise witness is not simply pasting gold stars on a chart of discipleship deeds well done but is listening to the world, attentive to the ones to whom ministry is offered, waiting for the opportune moment when those who are to hear and experience the gospel are ready to receive it.

Always to reject the gospel, however, is a tragic loss. In a fashion typical of the language of the Gospel of Matthew, Jesus warns that "it will be more tolerable for the land of Sodom and Gomorrah on the day of judgment" than for a town that rejects the missionaries of the kingdom (Matt. 10:15). The reference is to the destruction of two wicked cities in the Old Testament (see Genesis 19). Despite the way this passage is phrased, the point here is not damnation—that somehow every town, every village, every person gets one and only one chance at the gospel, and if the response is not positive the first time, then there is eternal condemnation. No human community and few human beings could finally pass that test. The point, rather, is encouragement for the disciples. They are about the urgent work of Jesus Christ, and what they do and how people respond to what they do really count. To accept the witness of the faithful church is, in effect, to receive Jesus Christ; to reject that faithful witness, on the other hand, is a dire loss, a lamentable missing of the treasure of the kingdom of heaven.

DISCIPLES CAN EXPECT PERSECUTION
Matthew 10:16–39

10:16 "See, I am sending you out like sheep into the midst of wolves; so be wise as serpents and innocent as doves. [17] Beware of them, for they will hand you over to councils and flog you in their synagogues; [18] and you will be dragged before governors and kings because of me, as a testimony to them and the Gentiles. [19] When they hand you over, do not worry about how you are to speak or what you are to say; for what you are to say will be given to you at that time; [20] for it is not you who speak, but the Spirit of your Father speaking through you. [21] Brother will betray brother to death, and a father his child, and children will rise against parents and have them put to death; [22] and you will be hated by all because of my name. But the one who endures to the end will be saved. [23] When they persecute you in one town, flee to the next; for truly I tell you, you will not have gone through all the towns of Israel before the Son of Man comes.

[24] "A disciple is not above the teacher, nor a slave above the master; [25] it is enough for the disciple to be like the teacher, and the slave like the master. If they have called the master of the house Beelzebul, how much more will they malign those of his household!

[26] "So have no fear of them; for nothing is covered up that will not be uncovered, and nothing secret that will not become known. [27] What I say to you in the dark, tell in the light; and what you hear whispered, proclaim from the housetops. [28] Do not fear those who kill the body but cannot kill the soul; rather fear him who can destroy both soul and body in hell. [29] Are not two sparrows sold for a penny? Yet not one of them will fall to the ground apart from your Father. [30] And even the hairs of your head are all counted. [31] So do not be afraid; you are of more value than many sparrows.

[32] "Everyone therefore who acknowledges me before others, I also will acknowledge before my Father in heaven; [33] but whoever denies me before others, I also will deny before my Father in heaven.

[34] "Do not think that I have come to bring peace to the earth; I have not come to bring peace, but a sword.
[35] For I have come to set a man against his father,
    and a daughter against her mother,
    and a daughter-in-law against her mother-in-law;
[36] and one's foes will be members of one's own household.
[37] Whoever loves father or mother more than me is not worthy of me; and whoever loves son or daughter more than me is not worthy of me; [38] and whoever does not take up the cross and follow me is not worthy of me. [39] Those who find their life will lose it, and those who lose their life for my sake will find it.

Jesus has been instructing his disciples as they are sent out to do the work of the kingdom. Now, in a compelling mixture of images, Jesus warns them that he is sending them out "like sheep into the midst of wolves," so they are to be "wise as serpents and innocent as doves" (Matt. 10:16). In pulling these three animals into the same picture—vulnerable sheep, crafty serpents, and gentle doves—Jesus is being both candid about the dangers of discipleship and wise about the approach disciples should take in the face of that danger. Christians have learned through the generations that there is no guarantee of safety, that the world has made them pay for their witness by being the victims of social ostracizing, malicious rumors, the teeth of police dogs, the assassin's bullet, and gas chambers. They are sent like vulnerable "sheep into the midst of wolves." They are not to be surprised or naive about opposition—they are to be "wise as serpents"—but they are not to resort to violence or the destructive strategies of their opponents. They are to be "innocent as doves." One thinks of the nonviolent approach of the civil rights movement in the American South. Drawing upon the resources of the gospel, the movement, in terms of submitting to the violent actions of the hostile culture, was "innocent as doves," but, in terms of being effective against the evil of segregation, the movement was "wise as serpents."

The reason, of course, that the disciples can expect conflict and even persecution is that they are representatives of Jesus. Sharing in his ministry, they also share in his suffering. A "disciple [is] like the teacher, and the slave like the master" (Matt. 10:25). If they have slandered Jesus, the "master of the house," with charges of demon possession, then they will say even worse things about "those of his household" (Matt. 10:25).

Jesus names some of the painful experiences that the disciples can anticipate, and surely the first readers of Matthew's Gospel recognized them. In the volatile religious and cultural situation of the first century, missionaries from Matthew's church had undoubtedly been disciplined by religious councils, called on the carpet before public officials, rejected by members of their own families, and hated by many for their mission labors (Matt. 10:17–22).

Many readers have been troubled by the enigmatic word "When they persecute you in one town, flee to the next; for truly I tell you, you will not have gone through all the towns of Israel before the Son of Man comes" (Matt. 10:23). This verse is puzzling because it seems to advocate a fast-moving mission effort, since the time will be exceedingly short until the coming of the kingdom. Matthew, writing some half a century after the death of Jesus, knows, of course, that the kingdom has not yet come even in his day, so the verse must have some other significance for him. The most likely explanation is that Matthew interprets the saying to refer to Jesus' postresurrection appearance to the disciples (Matt. 28:16–20). Here the earthly Jesus now comes as the risen Son of Man to call his disciples to a wider mission, beyond the borders of Israel, to "all nations."

In the face of the conflict that disciples and other Christian missionaries can expect, Jesus provides four themes of encouragement.

1. The Holy Spirit will be always present with them and will never abandon them. Therefore, they do not need to worry about what to say before hostile officials; the Spirit will provide the words (Matt. 10:19). Not only that, as the faithful bear witness on behalf of the kingdom, Jesus himself will bear witness on their behalf to God (Matt. 10:32).

2. Their suffering is not wasted but, rather, is itself a testimony both to Jews and Gentiles (Matt. 10:18). Even though at this point the disciples are being sent only "to the lost sheep of the house of Israel" (Matt. 10:6), already the announcement of the gospel to "all nations" (see Matt. 28:19) is anticipated. Moreover, the disciples' experience of persecution will replicate that of Jesus; they first will be handed over to religious councils and then to secular political officials, as a light both to Israel and to the Gentiles (see Matt. 20:17–19).

3. There is nothing that the world can do that is able to eradicate the gospel or destroy God's loving and watchful care over the faithful. The world can forbid missionary activity and enforce it by throwing those who bear witness to the kingdom in jail, but "nothing is covered up that will not be uncovered, and nothing secret that will not become known" (Matt. 10:26). The world can even kill those who serve the gospel, but the murderers are not to be ultimately feared. They may have momentary power over bodily life, but they have no power over the soul. Only God has that. Only God is to be feared, and God, who counts the hairs on our heads and who does not fail to note even the falling of a single common sparrow, can be trusted to treasure those who serve the kingdom (Matt. 10:28–31).

So, proclaim the gospel without dread. What has been learned in times of private instruction ("in the dark," "whispered") must be announced fearlessly and openly to the world ("in the light," "from the housetops"). "The body they may kill," wrote Luther in his famous hymn, but "God's truth abideth still, His kingdom is forever."

4. Jesus assures his disciples that even disruptions in families are to be expected as a result of the crisis of the kingdom. The prophet Micah bemoaned the family strife of his day as a sign of slackening faith: "[F]or the son treats the father with contempt, the daughter rises up against her mother, the daughter-in-law against her mother-in-law; your enemies are members of your own household" (Micah 7:6). Jesus puts a surprising twist on this familiar text when he tells his disciples that the sort of family division Micah lamented is, in fact, one of the reasons for his coming: "I have come to set a man against his father, and a daughter against her mother, and a daughter-in-law against her mother-in-law" (Matt. 10:35).

Does this mean that Jesus came to wreck homes? Yes and no. No, Jesus is not against the family in and of itself. Jesus will teach later in Matthew that it is God who joins husband and wife (Matt. 19:3–6), and he will cite with favor the commandment to "honor your father and mother" (Matt. 19:19). But, yes, Jesus does divide families in the sense that his coming causes a crisis of loyalty and forces a decision. Does one belong to the kingdom of heaven and share in its values, or not? One cannot decide for the kingdom in one compartment of life and leave everything else in a separate compartment unchanged. It is simply a fact that the gospel shakes up values, rearranges priorities, reorients goals. The gospel is not a salve; it is a sword that pares away all that is not aligned to the kingdom (Matt. 10:34), and this often causes strain and strife in family relationships.

The reference to "the cross" (Matt. 10:38) is the first use of this term in Matthew, and it is the most dramatic and drastic symbol of the disciples' call to be like their master. They are to be ready to place their lives on the line, just as Jesus will do himself. To live with all one's energies focused in upon oneself is to lose the life one seeks; to give one's life away in the name of Christ is to be given all that makes life free, holy, and good.

THE REWARDS
Matthew 10:40–42

> 10:40 **"Whoever welcomes you welcomes me, and whoever welcomes me welcomes the one who sent me. ⁴¹ Whoever welcomes a prophet in the name of a prophet will receive a prophet's reward; and whoever welcomes**

a righteous person in the name of a righteous person will receive the reward of the righteous; ⁴² and whoever gives even a cup of cold water to one of these little ones in the name of a disciple—truly I tell you, none of these will lose their reward."

Jesus closes this teaching session with his disciples by announcing what is in store for those who receive their ministry. The whole passage can be summed up by the opening words: "Whoever welcomes you welcomes me, and whoever welcomes me welcomes the one who sent me" (Matt. 10:40). In other words, to show hospitality and receptivity to a disciple of Jesus is the same thing as showing hospitality to Jesus himself and, therefore, hospitality to God.

Some scholars have suggested that the mention of "prophet" and "righteous person" as well as "disciple" (Matt. 10:41–42) signals different kinds of missionaries in the early church, but probably these words of Jesus simply employ poetic repetition to emphasize that whoever welcomes any follower of Jesus in effect welcomes Jesus. The phrase "these little ones in the name of a disciple" (Matt. 10:42) actually means "these little ones who are disciples." In Matthew, the learners, beginners, and ordinary followers of Jesus are called "these little ones" (see Matt. 18:6, 10, and 14). Later the disciples will be placed in the position that Jesus now occupies, as a teacher of "the little ones," but now the disciples themselves are just beginning. They are "these little ones," and even a small gesture of hospitality to them, like giving "a cup of cold water," will be rewarded (Matt. 10:42). Later, this idea becomes the central motif of the parable of the sheep and the goats (Matt. 25:31–46).

7. The Road Becomes Hard
Matthew 11:1–12:50

Having completed his instructions to the disciples about their missionary labors, Jesus resumes his own ministry, teaching and preaching in the towns of the area (Matt. 11:1). Jesus has warned his disciples that their work on behalf of the kingdom of heaven will be greeted with resistance, outright conflict, false charges, and painful divisions even in their own families (Matt. 10:16–39). Now Jesus faces these forces of dissension himself. There have been flare-ups of doubt and antagonism earlier (see Matt. 8:34; 9:3, 11, 14, 24, and 34), but now the conflict will be intensified, and the looming shadow of the cross will fall more heavily over Jesus. Jesus' journey now takes him over a perilous and rocky stretch of highway.

THE DOUBTS OF JOHN THE BAPTIST
Matthew 11:1–6

> 11:1 **Now when Jesus had finished instructing his twelve disciples, he went on from there to teach and proclaim his message in their cities.**
> [2] **When John heard in prison what the Messiah was doing, he sent word by his disciples** [3] **and said to him, "Are you the one who is to come, or are we to wait for another?"** [4] **Jesus answered them, "Go and tell John what you hear and see:** [5] **the blind receive their sight, the lame walk, the lepers are cleansed, the deaf hear, the dead are raised, and the poor have good news brought to them.** [6] **And blessed is anyone who takes no offense at me."**

The first one in this section of Matthew's Gospel to voice doubts about Jesus is a friend, John the Baptist. The last we heard of John, he had been arrested and was, presumably, in Herod's prison (Matt. 4:12). Now he reappears in Matthew, staring over the prison walls and pondering the question that Matthew wants all who read his Gospel to consider, Is Jesus truly the one?

Earlier, of course, John had baptized Jesus and had identified Jesus as the "one who . . . is coming," the "more powerful" one, the one who "will baptize . . . with the Holy Spirit and fire," the one who carries a "winnowing fork . . . in his hand" to separate the wheat from the chaff (Matt. 3:11–12). But now, he is not so sure, and he sends his disciples to Jesus with his agonizing query, "Are you the one who is to come, or are we to wait for another?" (Matt. 11:3).

What has provoked this doubt in John? Every indication is that his wariness grows out of the fact that Jesus has not lived up to John's expectations.

John has read his Bible, and he knows what to look for in a messiah. He knows the prophetic promises, that "a fire will come out against all the house of Israel" (Ezek. 5:4) and "if any nation will not listen, then I will completely uproot it and destroy it, says the LORD" (Jer. 12:17). He looks and he listens, but he sees no fire and he hears no uprooting.

Jesus' reply to John's disciples—"Go and tell John what you hear and see: the blind receive their sight, the lame walk, the lepers are cleansed, the deaf hear, the dead are raised, and the poor have good news brought to them" (Matt. 11:4–5)—is not only a description of Jesus' ministry; it is also a word of guidance about how to read scripture. Anyone who reads the Old Testament and finds it to be a book solely about God's wrath and vengeance has seen a few trees, but missed the forest. To expect God to come only as a destroyer and not as a savior is to distort the essential message of the Old Testament and to miss the character of God.

Surely, some portions of scripture could lead one to think that the authentic mark of the messianic age is unbridled wrath and sweeping judgment, but the true scriptural vision of the messiah is one who will bring a time of healing and deeds of mercy. In Jesus' reply to John, one can hear the echo of these prophetic promises of restoration, especially as given in the prophet Isaiah: the blind will see, the lame will walk, and the deaf will hear (Isa. 29:18; 35:5–6), the dead will be raised (Isa. 26:19), and the poor will receive good news (Isa. 61:1). Jesus is saying that, despite John's misgivings and selective reading of scripture, what God is doing in and through Jesus is a fulfillment of the deepest promises of the prophets.

The closing saying, or proverb—"Blessed is anyone who takes no offense at me" (Matt. 11:6)—is both a warning and a promise. It warns that the presence and activity of Christ is always surprising, precedent setting, agenda shattering, and, thus, potentially offensive. Anyone who expects the work of God or the work of Christ's church to be safe and free of controversy simply misunderstands the nature of Christ's mission in the world. It will never be neat, tidy, and pretty, and there will always be controversy swirling around it. However, "Blessed is anyone who takes no offense at me" is also an encouraging promise to those who remain faithful to the gospel; that even when the world is scandalized or offended by acts of mercy and peace, those who swim past the waves of shock slapping them in the face will find themselves in a deep sea of blessing.

John represents, of course, all who are disappointed in Jesus because he fails to meet their expectations. Most of us are, on occasion, impatient with the ways of God in the world; we wish that God were more vigorous in punishing evil, swifter in response to prayer, clearer in renewing creation.

THE ROLE OF JOHN THE BAPTIST
Matthew 11:7–19

> 11:7 As they went away, Jesus began to speak to the crowds about John: "What did you go out into the wilderness to look at? A reed shaken by the wind? 8 What then did you go out to see? Someone dressed in soft robes? Look, those who wear soft robes are in royal palaces. 9 What then did you go out to see? A prophet? Yes, I tell you, and more than a prophet. 10 This is the one about whom it is written,
>
> > 'See, I am sending my messenger ahead of you,
> >   who will prepare your way before you.'
>
> 11 Truly I tell you, among those born of women no one has arisen greater than John the Baptist; yet the least in the kingdom of heaven is greater than he. 12 From the days of John the Baptist until now the kingdom of heaven has suffered violence, and the violent take it by force. 13 For all the prophets and the law prophesied until John came; 14 and if you are willing to accept it, he is Elijah who is to come. 15 Let anyone with ears listen!
> 16 "But to what will I compare this generation? It is like children sitting in the marketplaces and calling to one another,
>
> > 17 'We played the flute for you, and you did not dance;
> >   we wailed, and you did not mourn.'
>
> 18 For John came neither eating nor drinking, and they say, 'He has a demon'; 19 the Son of Man came eating and drinking, and they say, 'Look, a glutton and a drunkard, a friend of tax collectors and sinners!' Yet wisdom is vindicated by her deeds."

John the Baptist has raised the question, Who is Jesus? Now Jesus raises the question, Who is John? Jesus addresses this question to the crowds, and he begins by appealing to their own intuitive understanding of John's identity. When they went out into the wilderness to hear John preach (Matt. 3:1), Jesus asks, Whom did they think they were going to hear? A couple of tongue-in-cheek, satirical answers are suggested. Did they go out to see "a reed shaken by the wind" (Matt. 11:7); that is, to see a wishy-washy spokesman of the status quo, afraid of his own shadow, always putting his finger in the breeze to catch the prevailing popular opinion? Hardly. Or did they go out to see some dandy prancing around the desert in velvet robes (Matt. 11:8)? Definitely not. The place to see that, Jesus quips, is in a palace, not a wilderness or a prison. What they went to see, of course, was a *prophet*, and that is the first claim to make about John; he is a prophet in the great tradition of Isaiah and Jeremiah (Matt. 11:9).

Yes, John is a prophet, but he is more than a prophet. He is the last in the line of the great prophets, but he is also the first to point to the shifting of the ages, to the arrival of the Messiah. Jesus quotes the prophet Malachi to describe John's role: "See, I am sending my messenger ahead of you, who will prepare your way before you" (Matt. 11:10, citing Mal. 3:1). With the coming of Jesus, the world has shifted on its axis. Everything before Jesus is the old era; now, in him, all things have become new. The dawn has begun to break; the light of the kingdom of heaven, which will in time bathe the whole creation in its glow, has begun to shine.

So John is a prophet, the last of the great prophets, Elijah returned, indeed, the greatest person born of woman in the former age (Matt. 11:11). But, even though no one in the old order can claim more stature than John, in the new order, in the kingdom of heaven, even the least significant follower of Jesus is greater than John (Matt. 11:11). This is a staggering claim. This is not simply a statement about John the Baptist's place in history; it is a statement about what truly counts in human life. What this means is that the measuring standard for human greatness has been transformed by the kingdom of heaven. It is not fame, power, wealth, or any of the other scales of value that operate in the old order; it is fidelity to the kingdom of heaven, being a follower of Jesus. This means that what is going on in a primary Sunday school classroom is ultimately of more worth than a corporate merger or a political power play.

This section on the place of John the Baptist contains two passages that are ambiguous and, thus, difficult to interpret. The first is Matthew 11:12: "From the days of John the Baptist until now the kingdom of heaven has suffered violence, and the violent take it by force." An alternative translation of this verse is that "the kingdom has been coming violently." The first translation implies that violence has been done to the kingdom, but the second translation maintains that it is the kingdom that causes the violence, by exploding onto the landscape of history as a crisis. The most plausible interpretation of this saying, however, is based upon the first translation: Opponents of Jesus (some of whom we have already met in

Matthew) are attempting to thwart Jesus' ministry and message. Their forceful antagonism, now verbal, will eventually become violent in the physical sense, leading finally to Jesus' crucifixion.

The other ambiguous passage involves the brief parable of the children playing in the marketplace. Jesus compares "this generation" to a children's game, which involves a taunting song: "We played the flute for you, and you did not dance; we wailed, and you did not mourn" (Matt. 11:16–17). In other words, some performers—flute players and melancholy singers—played and wailed, but people did not respond to them. Now, the question for interpretation here is whether "this generation" is being compared to the performers—that is, to those who played and wailed—or whether "this generation" corresponds to the people who wouldn't respond, that is, to those who would not dance or mourn.

The latter is correct. "This generation" did not respond either to John or to Jesus, even though these two proclaimed the kingdom in contrasting ways. John was a wailer; he had an ascetic, even mournful, style. He came "neither eating nor drinking" (Matt. 11:18), but this generation would not repent and mourn. "He has a demon," they sneered (Matt. 11:18). Jesus, on the other hand, was a flute player. He came with merriment, kingdom joy, and compassion. His ministry was one of "eating and drinking" with all sorts of people (Matt. 9:10–11), but this generation stayed glued to their chairs, wallflowers at the kingdom dance. "Look," they said, "a glutton and a drunkard, a friend of tax collectors and sinners!" (Matt. 11:19).

It is not, of course, that "this generation" does not want to respond, does not want to be redeemed. Every generation wants something good for itself. The problem is packaging; John and Jesus do not look like saviors. They have, people say, the wrong diet, the wrong music, the wrong companions, the wrong words. "This generation," like all generations, is scanning the screen of history, looking for hope, searching for salvation. But they cannot commit to either John or Jesus on stylistic grounds alone, not to mention philosophical and theological differences. It would not be wise, they think. Jesus, knowing this is the core issue, hurls a proverb in their direction: "[W]isdom is vindicated by her deeds" (Matt. 11:19). In other words, just as he told John in prison, the proof of the kingdom is in the action, in what is happening in the world through Jesus. So, sit out the dance in your pseudo-wisdom if you want to, but the blind are seeing, the deaf are hearing, the lepers are made new, the dead are raised, and the poor have finally heard some music they can kick up their heels to—and *that* is the essence of wisdom.

JESUS REBUKES THE CITIES
Matthew 11:20–24

11:20 **Then he began to reproach the cities in which most of his deeds of power had been done, because they did not repent.** [21] **"Woe to you, Chorazin! Woe to you, Bethsaida! For if the deeds of power done in you had been done in Tyre and Sidon, they would have repented long ago in sackcloth and ashes.** [22] **But I tell you, on the day of judgment it will be more tolerable for Tyre and Sidon than for you.**
[23] **And you, Capernaum,**
> **will you be exalted to heaven?**
> **No, you will be brought down to Hades.**
For if the deeds of power done in you had been done in Sodom, it would have remained until this day. [24] **But I tell you that on the day of judgment it will be more tolerable for the land of Sodom than for you."**

The theme of the negative response to Jesus' ministry continues here. John the Baptist has doubts about him (Matt. 11:1–6), the present generation is indifferent (Matt. 11:16–19), and, now, the Galilean towns of Chorazin, Bethsaida, and Capernaum are singled out for reprimands because of their lack of repentance.

Jesus compares these three towns to a trio of notorious Old Testament cities: Tyre, Sidon, and Sodom. Tyre and Sidon, prosperous seacoast towns located about twenty miles apart on the Mediterranean, were favorite targets of the prophets for their pride and affluent arrogance (see Isa. 23:1–12; Jer. 25:22; Ezek. 29:11–23; Joel 4:4–8; Zech. 9:1–4). Sodom, whose sad story is told in Genesis 19, is, of course, the most famous symbol of urban iniquity in scripture (see Isa. 1:9–10; Amos 4:11). Jesus announces to Chorazin and Bethsaida that if the mighty deeds performed in them had been done in Tyre and Sidon, those cities would have rushed down the aisle of repentance. Likewise, Jesus informs his hometown, Capernaum, that if Sodom had been given the opportunity to see the works of power they have seen, Sodom, instead of being a rubbish heap, would still be standing (the saying addressed to Capernaum about being "brought down to Hades" in Matthew 11:23 is a paraphrase of a jab at Babylon found in Isaiah 14:13–15). The message here is that Tyre, Sidon, and Sodom were tough towns, all right, but, after all, they never had the benefit of the gospel of the kingdom and the mighty works of Jesus. All in all, judgment day will be more tolerable for them than for the cities of Galilee, which have turned a cold shoulder to the good news.

These harsh words toward Chorazin, Bethsaida, and Capernaum come as something of a surprise, since Matthew has not recorded any activity of

Jesus in Chorazin or Bethsaida, and his reception in Capernaum was more positive than negative (see, for example, Matt. 9:8). Perhaps Matthew assumes that his readers will know other stories of Jesus' activity in these towns. In any case, the three cities are treated as representative of places that were at the center of Jesus' ministry, that have been favored with displays of kingdom works, that have seen the gospel in action but have not repented. As such, these cities are used to teach a larger lesson: To experience the gospel firsthand and, then, to turn away unrepentant is a fearful tragedy. To be blind to the truth is surely a sad thing, but to have one's eyes opened and then to choose to shut them tight again is to be liable to the judgment of God.

The main point appears to be that the public ministry of Jesus is not going well. There is growing resistance on every front, and events are hurtling toward an inevitable showdown. The full extent of the crisis is not yet seen, but, like a movie soundtrack that plays ominous music foreboding terrors to come, these early warning signs of the rejection of Jesus alert us to the forces building even now that will eventually coalesce with a vengeance to murder Jesus. The viper is beginning to coil before the strike.

JESUS' PRAYER OF THANKSGIVING
Matthew 11:25–27

> 11:25 At that time Jesus said, "I thank you, Father, Lord of heaven and earth, because you have hidden these things from the wise and the intelligent and have revealed them to infants; [26] yes, Father, for such was your gracious will. [27] All things have been handed over to me by my Father; and no one knows the Son except the Father, and no one knows the Father except the Son and anyone to whom the Son chooses to reveal him.

It is clear that these are gloomy days in the ministry of Jesus. At this low point in his ministry, however, Jesus amazingly gives thanks in prayer that God is gathering around him a community of the lowly, the poor, and the weak, even if this inevitably means rejection by the mighty, the rich, and the self-sufficient. God has chosen to reveal the saving knowledge of the gospel to the most unlikely of candidates, to infants (that is, to spiritual babies), and to hide it from the very people who would consider themselves learned in the ways of God (the scribes, Pharisees, the noble cities of Israel). Jesus is nearing a turning point in his ministry. Instead of appealing to the whole of Israel, Jesus increasingly will focus upon his disciples, carrying out his mission by building upon this smaller community of "little ones."

The theology of this passage is somewhat complex. It is centered on the deep, mutual, and intimate sharing of knowledge between Jesus the Son and God the Father. No human being really knows who Jesus is, not in the full sense—not John, not the scribes and Pharisees, not the unrepentant towns, not the wavering crowds, not even the disciples. God is the only one who knows truly who Jesus is; "no one knows the Son except the Father" (Matt. 11:27). Likewise, no human being, save Jesus, fully knows God; "no one knows the Father except the Son" (Matt. 11:27).

God, who is known truly only by the Son, wants, however, to be known by others. Indeed, the mission of Jesus is to impart the deep and saving knowledge of God to all the world. According to Jesus' prayer language, the knowledge of God is communicated through Jesus the Son to "anyone to whom the Son chooses to reveal him." These words sound, at first, as if Jesus has the secret knowledge of God and then makes independent decisions about passing this knowledge to others of his own choosing. But this does not reflect the sense of the whole passage; the Son and the Father are so joined in relationship that a decision of the Son is an expression of the will of the Father, and, conversely, the will of the Father is embodied in the life of the Son.

What does the notion of God "hiding" the gospel from the wise and the intelligent say about the character of God and about the nature of human freedom? If God wants to be known by humanity, then why does God conceal that very knowledge from people just because they happen to be smart or powerful? And if the knowledge of God is a well-guarded divine secret, how can the scribes and the Pharisees and others be blamed for being bullheaded and resistant to the ministry of Jesus? Deprived of the essential revelation, were they really free to do anything other than reject Jesus?

This theological dilemma is created by a clash between ancient and contemporary thought patterns. Ancient theological writers, like Matthew, were not constrained by our need for tidy and systematic logic. Matthew believed both that people were free and responsible, on the one hand, and that God was in complete control of human history, on the other. We tend to pit human freedom and God's omnipotence as logically incompatible opposites. Matthew, however, could hold these truths together.

First, Jesus is giving thanks that the gospel generates a positive response among the lowly and those in need—the "infants." There is something about being aware of need, something about knowing that one cannot depend upon one's own strength alone, that opens people to the good news of God's gift of mercy. Second, Jesus' prayer honestly acknowledges that, even though the gospel is proclaimed freely and openly to all, the fact is that many of the people who consider themselves wise and self-sufficient turn it aside. There is something about the kingdom that is hard to receive from a position of power (see Matt. 19:23); it can be seen only by those who are infants, those who are willing to "change and become like children" (Matt. 18:3). Third, Jesus' prayer confesses that this aspect of the gospel that gathers the weak and the helpless and is scorned by the rich and the mighty is not an accident; it is essential to the nature of the good news and to the nature of God. Moreover, human rejection of the gospel, even by the powerful in the world, cannot overturn God's merciful will. God remains Lord over human history, and no amount of scorn can thwart God's intention to save. Therefore, without damaging the idea of human freedom to respond to the kingdom or to reject it, Jesus can speak of response and rejection as still within the will of God, as God's "hiding" these things from some and revealing them to others.

JESUS' APPEAL TO THE WEARY
Matthew 11:28–30

> 11:28 **"Come to me, all you that are weary and are carrying heavy burdens, and I will give you rest. ²⁹ Take my yoke upon you, and learn from me; for I am gentle and humble in heart, and you will find rest for your souls. ³⁰ For my yoke is easy, and my burden is light."**

Since God has chosen to reveal the secrets of the kingdom to the weak, to the poor, and to spiritual babes (Matt. 11:25), Jesus invites those who "are weary and are carrying heavy burdens" to come and find rest (Matt. 11:28).

What Jesus offers, however, is not a hammock, but a yoke. In Judaism, the yoke was a symbol of obedience to the law and wisdom of God. Likewise, Jesus' yoke is obedience to the commandments of the kingdom of heaven, a willingness to serve others with humility and mercy. Jesus' yoke is "easy," and his burden is "light" (Matt. 11:30) not because there is little to do or the way is safely paved. To the contrary, there is a cross to be carried (Matt. 16:24), and the world is full of wolves (Matt. 10:16). The yoke of Jesus is easy and his burden is light because it is the way of God, and it is profoundly satisfying to the human soul.

To come to Jesus is to be taught gentleness and humility (Matt. 12:29). It is to join with Jesus himself in serving the world in the name of God, and it is to hear, at the end of the day, the divine voice of blessing, "Well done, good and faithful servant."

JESUS AS LORD OF THE SABBATH
Matthew 12:1–14

12:1 **At that time Jesus went through the grainfields on the sabbath; his disciples were hungry, and they began to pluck heads of grain and to eat.** [2] **When the Pharisees saw it, they said to him, "Look, your disciples are doing what is not lawful to do on the sabbath."** [3] **He said to them, "Have you not read what David did when he and his companions were hungry?** [4] **He entered the house of God and ate the bread of the Presence, which it was not lawful for him or his companions to eat, but only for the priests.** [5] **Or have you not read in the law that on the sabbath the priests in the temple break the sabbath and yet are guiltless?** [6] **I tell you, something greater than the temple is here.** [7] **But if you had known what this means, 'I desire mercy and not sacrifice,' you would not have condemned the guiltless.** [8] **For the Son of Man is lord of the sabbath."**

[9] **He left that place and entered their synagogue;** [10] **a man was there with a withered hand, and they asked him, "Is it lawful to cure on the sabbath?" so that they might accuse him.** [11] **He said to them, "Suppose one of you has only one sheep and it falls into a pit on the sabbath; will you not lay hold of it and lift it out?** [12] **How much more valuable is a human being than a sheep! So it is lawful to do good on the sabbath."** [13] **Then he said to the man, "Stretch out your hand." He stretched it out, and it was restored, as sound as the other.** [14] **But the Pharisees went out and conspired against him, how to destroy him.**

After prayer, Jesus joins the fray once more as the winds of controversy pick up again. In two separate incidents, he wrangles with the Pharisees about right behavior on the sabbath day.

The first incident is provoked when Jesus' disciples, because they were hungry, ate grain they had picked from a grainfield as they traveled. There was nothing wrong with this, except for the fact that they did it on the sabbath. The Fourth Commandment forbade work on the sabbath day (Exod. 20:8–11; Deut. 5:12–15), and the teachers of the law had explicitly decided that plucking grain constituted work. So, what the disciples had done was an open and shut case, and the religious leaders came to Jesus and laid out the charges, "Look, your disciples are doing what is not lawful to do on the sabbath" (Matt. 12:2).

The Pharisees had a point, a good point as a matter of fact. Today, we probably find it difficult to take the Pharisees' concern seriously. In our culture, with Sunday schedules packed—soccer practice on Sunday morning, the mall open late, and the video store handily around the corner—any notion of a sabbath, a national day set aside exclusively for praise, feasting, and holy rest is a faint memory at best. The Pharisees who are offended by this tiny violation of the sabbath laws look to our eyes like fusty prudes who want to throw cold water on an innocent sabbath picnic.

Nothing could be further from the truth. Taken at its best, the sabbath was a significant and joyous festival. The sabbath was a gift of rest, spiritual refreshment, and freedom that God had given to Israel; it was a treasure not to be taken lightly, a well-guarded symbol of what it meant to be God's chosen people. The Pharisees had every reason to put Jesus under the lamp of interrogation: "What's going on with your disciples and the sabbath?" Jesus answers them in three ways:

The Example of David
(Matthew 12:3–4)

Jesus reminds the Pharisees about the time that David and the men accompanying him were given holy bread from the tabernacle because they were hungry and no other bread was available (1 Sam. 21:1–6). When they ate the holy bread, argues Jesus, they actually were in violation of the ceremonial religious law. But what is Jesus' point here? How does this Old Testament story about what David did long ago apply to Jesus and his disciples? There are two main ways to see the connection. The first possible link is that the story shows that human need is more important than the ritual law. When David and his men showed up at the tabernacle, they were evidently famished, and their hunger took precedence over the fact that the bread in the tabernacle was for religious use.

But, in Matthew, Jesus does not say "the sabbath was made for humankind." Matthew also wants to make another point. Of course, Matthew would agree with Mark's theme of the importance of human need (indeed, that will be the accent in the next story, Matthew 12:9–14), but here Matthew wants to highlight another truth—the authority of David and the parallel authority of Jesus, the son of David. When David's men were allowed to eat the holy bread, it was not just because they were hungry; it was also because they were with *David*. So, in Matthew, Jesus is, in effect, saying to the Pharisees, "You say my disciples are breaking the holy law? Well, David's companions did, too. So, like David's men, my disciples can break the ceremonial sabbath law because they are with me."

Of course, such an argument virtually begs for the retort, "Sure, David broke the holy law. But, after all, David was David. Who are you?"

This question silently hangs in the air. The reader already knows the answer, of course—has known it from the very first verse of Matthew's Gospel. This is Jesus, the Messiah, royal David's even greater son (see Matt. 1:1).

Something Greater Is Here
(Matthew 12:5–6)

Next, Jesus argues that the law itself allows for a violation of the sabbath. The law makes exceptions for the temple priests who must go about their religious chores on the sabbath. Nobody raises an eyebrow about this because it is understood that the requirements of temple worship outrank the legal stipulations of the sabbath.

"I tell you," argues Jesus, "something greater than the temple is here" (Matt. 12:6). The "something greater" is, of course, Jesus himself, and the logic is, if the temple is greater than the sabbath and Jesus is greater than the temple, then Jesus is "lord of the sabbath" (Matt. 12:8). Those who know Jesus' true identity as the Messiah recognize that he "*is* the law in these parts." If the law is an expression of the will of God, Jesus is God's will in flesh and blood.

This brings us close to the heart of this controversy. What most divides Jesus and his opponents is their understanding of what it means to be "godly." Jesus' opponents are not trying to be wicked; they are trying their best to be God's people in the world. Ironically, they have tried so hard to be godly on their own terms that they have missed what God was actually doing in the world on God's terms—acting in and through Jesus. This leads to Jesus' third response.

Mercy, Not Sacrifice
(Matthew 12:7–8)

Jesus and his disciples are on a mission of mercy, and the religious authorities are attempting to rein them in with rules and regulations. Jesus and the disciples are in an ambulance rushing to rescue a stricken world, and the religious leaders want to ticket them for speeding. They have missed the point and have declared "guilty" the very ones who are at work doing God's will. Indeed, Jesus' ministry of mercy is the essence of what the sabbath is all about. Therefore, it can be said that "the Son of Man is lord of the sabbath."

This whole episode demonstrates that it is sometimes God's greatest admirers who become God's bitterest foes. Loving God can easily become loving our own understanding of God, and eagerness to serve God can slide into an overconfidence about what does and does not count as authentic service.

After having tangled on the sabbath with the religious leaders in a grainfield, Jesus marches that same day right into the enemy camp—"their synagogue" (Matt. 12:9). In the congregation on that sabbath is a man who has a shriveled hand, a man who will serve as a test case for the issue named in the previous passage—mercy versus sacrifice (see Matt. 12:7).

Undoubtedly making sure that they can be heard by everybody in the synagogue, the opponents of Jesus pose the critical question, "Is it lawful to cure on the sabbath?" (Matt. 12:10). This was a trick question, since everybody already knew the answer—or thought they did. At that time, the generally accepted answer to this question was that it was lawful to attend to an illness on the sabbath only if it were life threatening. Since a shriveled hand is a long-term condition and not immediately life threatening, any medical attention would definitely have to wait until after the sabbath. The religious leaders have already seen Jesus in action in the grainfield; thus, they have reason to suspect that he will be equally permissive here in the more public arena of the synagogue. This provides, then, a wonderful opportunity to snare Jesus with his own words.

Once again, however, the authorities have underestimated Jesus. Jesus responds to their question with a question of his own, "Suppose one of you has only one sheep and it falls into a pit on the sabbath; will you not lay hold of it and lift it out?" (Matt. 12:11). Here Jesus has pitted common-sense religion against the technical rules. Although some of the rabbis interpreted the Old Testament law to forbid even the rescue of an imperiled animal, many interpreters of the law allowed an exception in this case. Jesus' question seems to assume that his hearers would agree that in this case the sheep should be rescued, even on the sabbath. After all, a person who owns only one sheep is poor, and if his one and only sheep falls into a cistern on the sabbath, his livelihood is at peril.

Then comes the clincher. "How much more valuable is a human being than a sheep!" proclaims Jesus. "So it is lawful to do good on the sabbath" (Matt. 12:12). The point was made that mercy and urgency supersede the sabbath law in the case of a poor person's sheep; who could challenge it, then, in the case of a human being? To attest this, Jesus says to the afflicted man, "Stretch out your hand." When he did, the withered hand was restored to soundness (Matt. 12:13).

Jesus clearly won the verbal duel, but the Pharisees have seen and heard enough. They slink away from the synagogue and begin to plot the murder of Jesus (Matt. 12:14). Note the strong irony. The religious leaders have accused Jesus of being a sabbath breaker, but how have the two parties spent this sabbath? Jesus has spent this sabbath day doing good—healing and giving life. The authorities, on the other hand, have used their sabbath doing evil, hatching plots, scheming to take a human life.

THE SERVANT OF GOD
Matthew 12:15–21

12:15 **When Jesus became aware of this, he departed. Many crowds followed him, and he cured all of them,** [16] **and he ordered them not to make him known.** [17] **This was to fulfill what had been spoken through the prophet Isaiah:**

> [18] **"Here is my servant, whom I have chosen,**
> **my beloved, with whom my soul is well pleased.**
> **I will put my Spirit upon him,**
> **and he will proclaim justice to the Gentiles.**
> [19] **He will not wrangle or cry aloud,**
> **nor will anyone hear his voice in the streets.**
> [20] **He will not break a bruised reed**
> **or quench a smoldering wick**
> **until he brings justice to victory.**
> [21] **And in his name the Gentiles will hope."**

We have just seen, in the previous passage, an example of Jesus' ability to outmaneuver his opponents verbally. In a joust of words, the religious authorities are no match for Jesus, so why doesn't he press his advantage? His ability to make sense to the common people combined with his ministry of healing would surely create a popular following that would outflank any attempt to do him harm. Why, then, doesn't he pursue his opponents, now that he has them on the run?

The answer Matthew gives to this question is that Jesus is obedient to God's will, not to any personal urge for combat or public approval. That point is made in this passage, which indicates that Jesus' response to the deadly intrigue of the Pharisees was withdrawal from the confrontation while continuing the kingdom work of healing. Moreover, this withdrawal, this refusal to engage in pitched battle, is taken by Matthew to be a fulfillment of Old Testament prophecy. Matthew paraphrases Isaiah 42:1–4 to assert that Jesus is God's servant who lives in the power of the Holy Spirit (Matt. 12:18). He does not seek an opportunity to "wrangle or cry aloud" (Matt. 12:19), to engage in a public skirmish with the religious leaders (although he will not cower either; see Matthew 23), because his approach is compassion. "He will not break a bruised reed or quench a smoldering wick" (Matt. 12:20). Jesus' intent—in sum, God's will—is not to defeat Israel's religious leadership. It is, rather, to proclaim justice and to give hope to all nations, including the Gentiles (Matt. 12:18, 21).

This paraphrase from Isaiah is the longest of Matthew's Old Testament references, and it contains a summary portrait of Matthew's depiction of

Jesus. It describes who Jesus is—God's chosen and Spirit-anointed servant with whom God is well pleased (language reminiscent of Jesus' baptism—Matthew 3:17). It presents Jesus' mission—to proclaim justice and to give hope to all the nations. And it portrays the style of Jesus' ministry: merciful, meek, and determined.

DOES JESUS' POWER COME FROM GOD OR SATAN?
Matthew 12:22–37

12:22 **Then they brought to him a demoniac who was blind and mute; and he cured him, so that the one who had been mute could speak and see.** 23 **All the crowds were amazed and said, "Can this be the Son of David?"** 24 **But when the Pharisees heard it, they said, "It is only by Beelzebul, the ruler of the demons, that this fellow casts out the demons."** 25 **He knew what they were thinking and said to them, "Every kingdom divided against itself is laid waste, and no city or house divided against itself will stand.** 26 **If Satan casts out Satan, he is divided against himself; how then will his kingdom stand?** 27 **If I cast out demons by Beelzebul, by whom do your own exorcists cast them out? Therefore they will be your judges.** 28 **But if it is by the Spirit of God that I cast out demons, then the kingdom of God has come to you.** 29 **Or how can one enter a strong man's house and plunder his property, without first tying up the strong man? Then indeed the house can be plundered.** 30 **Whoever is not with me is against me, and whoever does not gather with me scatters.** 31 **Therefore I tell you, people will be forgiven for every sin and blasphemy, but blasphemy against the Spirit will not be forgiven.** 32 **Whoever speaks a word against the Son of Man will be forgiven, but whoever speaks against the Holy Spirit will not be forgiven, either in this age or in the age to come.**
33 **"Either make the tree good, and its fruit good; or make the tree bad, and its fruit bad; for the tree is known by its fruit.** 34 **You brood of vipers! How can you speak good things, when you are evil? For out of the abundance of the heart the mouth speaks.** 35 **The good person brings good things out of a good treasure, and the evil person brings evil things out of an evil treasure.** 36 **I tell you, on the day of judgment you will have to give an account for every careless word you utter;** 37 **for by your words you will be justified, and by your words you will be condemned."**

One almost feels sorry for the religious authorities in this narrative. They are persuaded that Jesus is a deep threat to the peace and stability of Israel, and they want to do all they can to keep his popularity from spreading. But, here Jesus puts their public relations skills to a severe test; Jesus heals a man who, possessed by a demon, is blind, mute, and probably deaf as well. The crowds who witness this astounding healing and exorcism are "amazed" (literally "beside themselves") and come close to proclaiming that Jesus is the Messiah: "Can this be the Son of David?" (Matt. 12:23).

This is, to say the least, a setback for Jesus' opponents, but what rejoinder can they come up with to such an obviously wonderful event? It is difficult to criticize the physician when the patient has just leapt from the deathbed full of new vigor. So, they pull out their old trump card, the one they used the last time Jesus healed a mute demoniac (see Matt. 9:34): They accuse him of fighting fire with fire, of using demonic power to cast out demons.

Before, when the religious leaders accused him of demon possession, Jesus did not attempt to vindicate himself. This time, though, he responds with a fivefold defense:

1. Jesus' first reply has a note of humor in it. What the Pharisees are suggesting is that, in Jesus' ministry, Satan is casting out Satan, that the power of the demonic is working to destroy the demonic. Surely, Jesus counters, the Pharisees do not think that Satan is that stupid. "If Satan casts out Satan, he is divided against himself; how then will his kingdom stand?" (Matt. 12:26).

2. Jesus' second reply turns the tables on the Pharisees by noting that some of the Pharisees themselves are exorcists and have cast out demons (Matt. 12:27). Evidently there were Jewish exorcists about (see Acts 19:13–16), and some of them were Pharisees. If the Pharisees claim that Jesus' exorcism is performed with demonic power, what would they say about similar acts by their own people?

The Jewish exorcists would obviously vigorously affirm that exorcisms are performed by the power of God's Spirit. Just so, if Jesus casts out demons by that same Spirit, then no one can deny that the "kingdom of God has come to you" in Jesus' ministry as well (Matt. 12:28).

3. In his third reply to the Pharisees (Matt. 12:29), Jesus spins an image to interpret his work of casting out demons. Satan, he suggests, is like a "strong man" who holds humanity captive as "his property." Jesus is like a thief who breaks into the strong man's house, ties him up, and makes off with the property. In other words, the ministry of Jesus is an act of strength, breaking and entering, plundering the household of Satan and liberating captive humanity.

4. The fourth reply of Jesus contains one of the most troubling words in the Bible: "blasphemy against the Spirit will not be forgiven" (Matt. 12:31). What sin could possibly be so evil that not even God would forgive it? What is "blasphemy against the Spirit"?

This strong statement is based upon a distinction between knowing and not knowing the truth about Jesus' identity. The ministry of Jesus—healing, teaching, preaching, casting out demons—is the promised kingdom of heaven in action, but in the present, Jesus' work is surrounded by ambiguity. It is not difficult to miss the significance of Jesus, for he does not look like who he is—God come in power. He is meek and merciful, and even John the Baptist was uncertain if Jesus was the promised strong one of God, the Messiah (see Matt. 11:2–6). So, there are those who see Jesus and reject him because they misunderstand him. If anyone observes the teaching and healing of Jesus and still says "no" to him, that is a sin to be sure, but one that will be forgiven: "Whoever speaks a word against the Son of Man will be forgiven" (Matt. 12:32).

But, there is coming a day when the curtain will be pulled back and all will be revealed. There is coming a day in the future when God will shine the light of heaven upon the work of Jesus, and the Holy Spirit will disclose the truth to everyone that the ministry of Jesus was an embodiment of the kingdom of heaven. To say "no" to Jesus in ignorance is a forgivable sin. To say "no" to Jesus in honest doubt is forgivable. But to know the full truth, to know that Jesus is the expression of God's will, to be fully aware that the Spirit of God breathed in every word he spoke and energized his every deed, to know that Jesus is the very Son of God with whom God is well pleased—to know all this and, then, to say "no" is the one sin that will not be forgiven.

By this word, then, Jesus warns the Pharisees that they are perilously close to committing this unpardonable sin against the Holy Spirit. Jesus is implying that their accusations are not a case of mistaken identity. They know who he is, and they know in their secret hearts that his casting out of demons is by the Spirit of God. In short, they see Jesus rightly but still hurl curses at him. To see the light and yet call down the darkness runs the risk of being unforgiven.

5. The fifth, and final, response of Jesus to the Pharisees is equally harsh. Jesus makes an analogy to trees; trees are either good or bad. There aren't any such things as "in between" trees. Good trees produce good fruit, and bad trees produce bad fruit; it is as simple as that. The Pharisees, claims Jesus, are definitely bad trees (Matt. 12:34), and, even when they try to make their language sound pious and holy, the fruit of their words is rotten. To switch the image, the Pharisees have only an "evil treasure," and when they open their mouths to speak gems, only tawdry costume jewelry pours out (Matt. 12:35).

Jesus' warning to the Pharisees about the impact of their words (Matt. 12:36–37) is also a warning to the church. The old children's song "sticks and stones may break my bones, but words will never hurt me" is not true. Words do hurt; words do count. A word of rejection, a cruel word spoken in anger, a word that spreads hopelessness among people who desperately need a word of promise to cling to—such words matter greatly. Kingdom people need to speak the language of the kingdom—words of mercy, forgiveness, peace, and hope.

THIS "EVIL GENERATION" DEMANDS A SIGN
Matthew 12:38–45

12:38 **Then some of the scribes and Pharisees said to him, "Teacher, we wish to see a sign from you."** 39 **But he answered them, "An evil and adulterous generation asks for a sign, but no sign will be given to it except the sign of the prophet Jonah.** 40 **For just as Jonah was three days and three nights in the belly of the sea monster, so for three days and three nights the Son of Man will be in the heart of the earth.** 41 **The people of Nineveh will rise up at the judgment with this generation and condemn it, because they repented at the proclamation of Jonah, and see, something greater than Jonah is here!** 42 **The queen of the South will rise up at the judgment with this generation and condemn it, because she came from the ends of the earth to listen to the wisdom of Solomon, and see, something greater than Solomon is here!**

43 **"When the unclean spirit has gone out of a person, it wanders through waterless regions looking for a resting place, but it finds none.** 44 **Then it says, 'I will return to my house from which I came.' When it comes, it finds it empty, swept, and put in order.** 45 **Then it goes and brings along seven other spirits more evil than itself, and they enter and live there; and the last state of that person is worse than the first. So will it be also with this evil generation."**

Matthew has reported a series of confrontations between Jesus and the religious leaders. Having tangled with Jesus, the leaders now demand to see some credentials. Jesus has argued with them, and the Pharisees, along with their cohorts the scribes, have now pulled him over and want to see his license. "Teacher," they say, "we wish to see a sign from you" (Matt. 12:38).

What do they have in mind? What else in the way of a sign could they conceivably expect? They have already seen miracles of every imaginable type: The blind see, the deaf hear, lepers are cleansed, the mute speak, the paralyzed walk, the demon-possessed are made whole. They obviously want something more, something even more dramatic that will assure them that Jesus is from God. Maybe a light shining from heaven would do the trick, or perhaps a voice from the skies.

But there will be no sign—at least not of the sort they want. If they expected Jesus to comply with their request, they were sadly mistaken. "An evil and adulterous generation asks for a sign," Jesus replies, "but no sign will be given to it except the sign of the prophet Jonah" (Matt. 12:39). This statement of Jesus raises two questions. First, why would Jesus not give the religious leaders what they asked for? Why would he not give them a sign? And, second, what is "the sign of the prophet Jonah"?

In regard to the first question, Jesus refuses to give a sign because no quantity of signs would remove the scales from their eyes. Jesus has made the action of God visible in every deed he has performed, and they refused to see it.

There is, however, one sign that Jesus is willing to promise—the sign of the prophet Jonah (Matt. 12:39). The sign of the prophet Jonah is the ultimate sign, the most decisive disclosure of God's action in Jesus—Jesus' death and resurrection. "For just as Jonah was three days and three nights in the belly of the sea monster, so for three days and three nights the Son of Man will be in the heart of the earth" (Matt. 12:40).

The phrase "three days and three nights" comes from Jonah 1:17, and commentators through the centuries have observed that, in the case of Jesus, the math does not quite work. Jesus was buried on Friday and rose on Sunday, so he was "in the heart of the earth" for portions of three days, but only for two nights. Matthew knows this, of course, and he probably considers "three days and three nights" to be a poetic way of saying "three days."

When Jesus told the scribes and Pharisees, in response to their request for a sign, that they could expect to see "the sign of the prophet Jonah," it is important to understand that he was *not* saying, "You may not have been convinced by the little signs—the healings and the exorcisms—but just wait until you see the big sign—the resurrection. That will knock you off your feet!" As a matter of fact, the resurrection was no more convincing to the authorities than were any of the other miracles (see Matt. 28:11–15). The resurrection is not a "super miracle" designed to persuade people who are skeptical of Jesus and his deeds, to win over cynics who are unmoved by the "lesser miracles." To the contrary, the resurrection will serve to confirm Jesus' ministry, to place the stamp of validation upon all his acts of mercy. The resurrection will announce to the whole world what should already be plain to the eye: Jesus' teaching, preaching, and healing are expressions of the kingdom of heaven drawn near.

This whole dispute with the religious officials was touched off by the fact that Jesus cast out a demon. Now, Jesus turns this event into a warning to "this generation" (Matt. 12:43–45). When a demon has been cast out of a person, Jesus says, it wanders around looking for a new home. If it comes back to its former residence and finds a "vacancy" sign still hanging in the window, it gathers seven even nastier spirits and moves back in with a vengeance. Jesus' point is that, even though there is one fewer demon in Israel than there was the day before, unless the people fill that vacated space with a positive seeking of the kingdom of heaven, this generation will end up in even worse shape than before.

What Jesus said to his own generation is true for every generation. The Christian life is not merely the absence of bad things; it is the presence of good things. The life of faith is not a vacant lot where sin used to be; it is an active neighborhood where justice, mercy, and peace live together.

WHO IS ON THE LORD'S SIDE?
Matthew 12:46–50

12:46 **While he was still speaking to the crowds, his mother and his brothers were standing outside, wanting to speak to him.** [47] **Someone told him, "Look, your mother and your brothers are standing outside, wanting to speak to you."** [48] **But to the one who had told him this, Jesus replied, "Who is my mother, and who are my brothers?"** [49] **And pointing to his disciples, he said, "Here are my mother and my brothers!** [50] **For whoever does the will of my Father in heaven is my brother and sister and mother."**

In Matthew 11–12, we have seen the opposition to Jesus expand and intensify. John the Baptist has doubts; the general populace is intrigued, but unrepentant; and now, the authorities have accused Jesus of being a tool of Satan and are actively planning his death. Is there anyone left in Jesus' camp?

Perhaps Jesus can count on his family; after all, blood is thicker than water. Almost as if on cue, as the hostility toward Jesus surges, his mother and brothers suddenly appear on the edge of the crowd asking to speak to him. Matthew does not tell us what is on their minds; that is not what interests him. What interests him is Jesus' startling response. "Who is my mother, and who are my brothers?" Jesus asks. Then, pointing toward his disciples, he announces, "Here are my mother and my brothers!" (Matt. 12:48–49).

With these words, Jesus makes a cut with the sword he described earlier, the one that divides children of the kingdom from their own households (Matt.10:34–39). Even in the face of murderous opposition, Jesus will not retreat to the familiar comforts and protections of his biological family. He moves ahead, even to the cross, gathering around him a new family, one forged out of faith and obedience. Yes, Jesus is the son of Mary, but what is more definitive for him is that word spoken at his baptism, "This is my Son, the Beloved, with whom I am well pleased" (Matt. 3:17). He is God's Son, and his family is not bound to bloodlines but is open to all. He is brother to countless people who, through baptism, are joined to God through him: "For whoever does the will of my Father in heaven is my brother and sister and mother" (Matt. 12:50).

8. Jesus Teaches in Parables
Matthew 13:1–53

It is a distinct feature of the Gospel of Matthew to alternate between sections of action stories and sections of teaching and instruction (see Introduction). Now, in Matthew 13, school is once again in session, and Jesus has resumed his role as teacher.

Matthew 13 forms the third great teaching discourse in the Gospel of Matthew (there will be five in all). Jesus is back in his familiar role as instructor, but there is an unfamiliar sound in his voice. Jesus' style of teaching has changed. He speaks with a new cadence; his instructional methods have shifted. Now, for the first time in Matthew, Jesus begins to teach in *parables.* The direct approach of the Sermon on the Mount—for example, "Do not judge, so that you may not be judged"—is replaced by the indirect, by tales about farmers, seeds, and soils, by images of women at work baking bread and fishermen casting their nets. A cast of imaginative characters arrives on the scene—masters and merchants, reapers and plowmen. Somewhat abruptly at this juncture in his ministry, Jesus has become a spinner of parables.

Why here, in the middle of his ministry, is there a shift in Jesus' style of discourse? The disciples pose the question for us: "Why," they ask, "do you speak to them in parables?" (Matt. 13:10). Jesus probably had as many reasons for speaking in parables as preachers today have for using sermon illustrations: to be more graphic, to make points clearer, to stimulate the imagination, to make contact with the realities of everyday life, and more. Matthew, however, is not writing a historical analysis of Jesus' teaching methods; he is writing a Gospel. Jesus, as a historical figure, may well have used parables for many reasons, but Matthew is making a theological point, and he underscores one and only one reason for Jesus' teaching in parables—the fact that many of the people around Jesus have closed their ears and stopped listening.

Jesus has been rejected by many of the people and their leaders; the resistance to Jesus has been growing, and some among the people would rather be "blind" and "deaf" than see and hear that the kingdom has drawn near in Jesus. So, Jesus begins now to focus upon those who *will* hear and who *do* see, namely, his own disciples. Jesus does not withdraw or become reclusive; he continues to speak to the crowds and maintains his wide-ranging ministry of healing. Jesus persists in his public ministry, but, in terms of kingdom instruction, the inner circle of disciples increasingly move to the head of the class.

Parables are particularly apt for advanced learners. They are simply profound; that is, they are simple, but, for those with eyes to see and ears to hear, they are also profound, opening up deep insights about the ways of God. For those who are ready learners of the gospel, parables unlock the secrets of the kingdom; for those whose minds are closed, parables remain bolted shut. Jesus begins to speak in parables at this critical juncture in his ministry because he is turning his energies toward the disciples, those who are prepared to move to a higher level of wisdom, Jesus' truest followers.

From Matthew's point of view, then, it is no accident that Jesus changes his teaching style and becomes a teller of parables right at the moment that his ministry is experiencing its strongest repudiation. The reason Jesus speaks in parables, he tells his disciples, is precisely because the people have become hard of heart: "seeing they do not perceive, and hearing they do not listen, nor do they understand" (Matt. 13:13).

THE PARABLE OF THE SOWER
Matthew 13:1–9

> 13:1 **That same day Jesus went out of the house and sat beside the sea.**
> 2 **Such great crowds gathered around him that he got into a boat and sat there, while the whole crowd stood on the beach.** 3 **And he told them many things in parables, saying: "Listen! A sower went out to sow.** 4 **And as he sowed, some seeds fell on the path, and the birds came and ate them up.** 5 **Other seeds fell on rocky ground, where they did not have much soil, and they sprang up quickly, since they had no depth of soil.** 6 **But when the sun rose, they were scorched; and since they had no root, they withered away.** 7 **Other seeds fell among thorns, and the thorns grew up and choked them.** 8 **Other seeds fell on good soil and brought forth grain, some a hundredfold, some sixty, some thirty.** 9 **Let anyone with ears listen!"**

In the previous passage (Matt. 12:46–50), Jesus has been inside a house speaking to the crowds, but, now, Jesus "went out of the house" in order to teach an even larger multitude (Matt. 13:1). The crowd was so large that Jesus got into a boat and sat down (the posture of authority; see Matt. 5:1), addressing the crowd of people as they stood on the shoreline.

Jesus began at this point to teach in parables, and his first parable concerned a certain farmer who "went out to sow" (Matt. 13:3). The Greek term translated "went out" is the same one used about Jesus, that he "went out" to teach (Matt. 13:1). Matthew pictures Jesus as a "farmer" for the kingdom, going out, like the farmer in the parable, to sow the seed.

But notice how the farmer in the parable sows the seed! This is no careful, prudent planter. Far from cautious, this farmer throws seed around with abandon. It flies in all directions and lands everywhere—on the hard path, all over a rock-littered patch, into the thorn bushes, as well as onto the good, rich topsoil. In other words, the farmer in this parable is not a normal planter; he is a farmer whose methods reflect the kingdom of heaven. He sows the seed extravagantly, as widely as he can, oblivious to the risks, much as God lavishes mercy upon humanity. To be sure, the farmer takes some losses—birds snatch the seed off the sun-baked pathway, the sun scorches the young plants springing up in the shallows of the rocky soil, and tender sprouts are no match for the choking thorns—but never mind. Despite the wasted efforts and the squandered seed, the farmer nonetheless achieves a bumper crop—a hundredfold, sixtyfold, thirtyfold.

Later, this parable will receive a detailed interpretation (see Matt. 13:18–23), but, even before the specifics fall into place, it is clear that this is a joyful, encouraging, while at the same time realistic, parable. The work of the kingdom, like the work of the farmer, will take its share of blows, will have a series of seemingly overwhelming setbacks, but the abundant harvest is sure.

The church knows the truth of this parable. It takes the gospel into the world, hardly knowing where to cast the seed. A new idea for youth ministry falls flat on its face. A proposal for a needed neighborhood day-care center is choked out by bureaucratic regulations. A door-to-door evangelism program encounters locked doors and generates no new church members. Hard soil. Scorching sun. Sharp thorns. The church knows the truth of this parable.

But the church can also hear the promise of this parable. Keep on spreading the seed; keep on preaching the gospel and showing the compassion of the kingdom. In ways that we do not always know and in places we cannot always see, the gospel is falling on good soil, and even now the great harvest of God is growing rich and full in the fields.

WHY DO YOU SPEAK IN PARABLES?
Matthew 13:10–17

13:10 **Then the disciples came and asked him, "Why do you speak to them in parables?"** [11] **He answered, "To you it has been given to know the secrets of the kingdom of heaven, but to them it has not been given.** [12] **For to those who have, more will be given, and they will have an abundance; but from those who have nothing, even what they have will be taken away.** [13] **The reason I speak to them in parables is that 'seeing they do not perceive, and hearing they do not listen, nor do they understand.'** [14] **With them indeed is fulfilled the prophecy of Isaiah that says:**

'You will indeed listen, but never understand,
      and you will indeed look, but never perceive.
[15] **For this people's heart has grown dull,**
      and their ears are hard of hearing,
         and they have shut their eyes;
      so that they might not look with their eyes,
      and listen with their ears,
      and understand with their heart and turn—
      and I would heal them.'
[16] **But blessed are your eyes, for they see, and your ears, for they hear.** [17] **Truly I tell you, many prophets and righteous people longed to see what you see, but did not see it, and to hear what you hear, but did not hear it.**

The parable of the sower is the first parable Jesus has employed in Matthew, and this strange, new kind of speech from the lips of Jesus naturally provokes curiosity among the disciples. As we have already noted, the disciples come to Jesus with the obvious question, "Why do you speak to them in parables?" (Matt. 13:10).

Matthew is following the Gospel of Mark here, and, in Mark, Jesus gives a shocking response to the question about parables. He tells the disciples that he employs parables *so that* people will not understand; the disciples will get the message, but outsiders will miss the point (Mark 4:10–12). In other words, in Mark, Jesus speaks in parables deliberately to muddy the water.

This idea of purposeful secrecy and calculated obfuscation fits in with one of Mark's larger theological ideas, namely, that the full revelation about Jesus was withheld until the resurrection. But Mark's theological design is not Matthew's, and Matthew cannot conceive that Jesus would tell parables intentionally to cloud people's understanding. So, he makes a crucial change in Mark's language. In Matthew, Jesus states that he speaks in parables not "in order that" people will not perceive the truth of the kingdom, but *because* they do not perceive (Matt. 13:13).

The parables, then, are language specially fitted for the occasion—a time of dullness and lack of response to Jesus on the part of Israel. There are two reasons for this. First, rejected by the people, Jesus turns his attention to the disciples.

The second reason for Jesus' parables also concerns the fact that the ministry of Jesus has encountered opposition. Many of the parables are about trouble—seed falling onto poor soil, weeds growing up in a field of wheat, a net pulling up bad fish among the good—and the message of these parables enables the disciples to understand why Jesus has encountered trouble, why the good news of the kingdom has not been received with joy by everyone. Indeed, Matthew quotes Isaiah 6:9–10 to show that the people's hard-hearted response to Jesus, like all else in his ministry, is a fulfillment of Old Testament prophecy.

INTERPRETATION OF THE PARABLE OF THE SOWER
Matthew 13:18–23

13:18 **"Hear then the parable of the sower. [19] When anyone hears the word of the kingdom and does not understand it, the evil one comes and snatches away what is sown in the heart; this is what was sown on the path. [20] As for what was sown on rocky ground, this is the one who hears the word and immediately receives it with joy; [21] yet such a person has no root, but endures only for a while, and when trouble or persecution arises on account of the word, that person immediately falls away. [22] As for what was sown among thorns, this is the one who hears the word, but the cares of the world and the lure of wealth choke the word, and it yields nothing. [23] But as for what was sown on good soil, this is the one who hears the word and understands it, who indeed bears fruit and yields, in one case a hundredfold, in another sixty, and in another thirty."**

Although he is still speaking privately to his disciples, Jesus provides an interpretation of his first parable, the parable of the sower (see Matt. 13:1–9). He has just told the disciples that "many prophets and righteous people longed to see what you see . . . and to hear what you hear" (Matt. 13:17), and, now, as a realization of this saying, he lets them in on the secrets of the parable of the sower.

Two features of this interpretation are important to observe. First, although there are several ways to interpret a parable, the interpretation given here is an allegory, that is, almost each and every detail of the parable is given a meaning—the seed means this, the rocky soil signifies that, the thorns symbolize something else, and so on.

Second, this allegorical interpretation is not very smooth. We can note the roughness when we see how the symbol of the "seed" changes identity in the interpretation. First it is compared to the "word of the kingdom" (Matt. 13:19), but then the seed becomes, not the word, but certain types of people to whom the word is preached: the one who "receives [the word] with joy; yet . . . has no root" (Matt. 13:20–21), the one "who hears the word, but the cares of the world and the lure of wealth choke the word" (Matt. 13:22); and "the one who hears the word and understands it" (Matt. 13:23).

Most scholars agree that this abrupt shift is a sign that this allegorical interpretation, at least in its present form, did not originate with Jesus but comes from the early church. The interpretation is a kind of "sermon," applying Jesus' parable to the concrete circumstances faced by the early church. What had they experienced? They experienced what Jesus' own ministry experienced—some positive response amid much rejection. People were responding to the gospel and becoming a part of the Christian community, but the growth curve was not always up. Sometimes new converts to the Christian faith would suddenly, seemingly without cause, grow cold and fall away. Others would be ardent Christians until it began to cost them something, or persecution arose, or the anxious cares of life weighed them down; then they would leave their once enthusiastic faith behind.

All of these discouragements are reflected in the experience of the sower. Most of the seed he sowed fell onto unproductive soil. The parable contains a surprise, though. Just at the point when the pattern of defeat seems confirmed, when one disaster after another would lead most sowers to give up farming altogether—and most evangelists to despair of kingdom work—a few seeds take root in good soil and burst forth with an unexpectedly abundant harvest. So it is with the kingdom. The work is hard, often disheartening, but the great harvest is sure.

It is important to remember that this is a parable of the *kingdom* and not a story about conventional wisdom. The message of the parable to the church is not "Be diligent and play the percentages. Spread the word widely enough and a certain portion will surely yield results." No, in this parable the great harvest comes unexpectedly and is much more extravagant than could ever have been anticipated. The farmer in this parable would not congratulate himself that his hard work had finally paid off; he would be astonished at the gift he had received, a harvest more lavish than he could ever have dreamed.

The message to the church is that the gift of a great harvest awaits them, that when the kingdom of heaven comes in power, the witness and discipleship of the people of God, always fragile and at peril in the world, will be magnified by the generosity of God into a fruitful, extravagant, and altogether gracious yield. Therefore, the church is called to "waste itself," to throw grace around like there is no tomorrow, precisely because there is a tomorrow, and it belongs to God.

THE PARABLE OF THE WEEDS AND THE WHEAT
Matthew 13:24–30

13:24 **He put before them another parable: "The kingdom of heaven may be compared to someone who sowed good seed in his field;** 25 **but while everybody was asleep, an enemy came and sowed weeds among the wheat, and then went away.** 26 **So when the plants came up and bore grain, then the weeds appeared as well.** 27 **And the slaves of the householder came and said to him, 'Master, did you not sow good seed in your field? Where, then, did these weeds come from?'** 28 **He answered, 'An enemy has done this.' The slaves said to him, 'Then do you want us to go and gather them?'** 29 **But he replied, 'No; for in gathering the weeds you would uproot the wheat along with them.** 30 **Let both of them grow together until the harvest; and at harvest time I will tell the reapers, Collect the weeds first and bind them in bundles to be burned, but gather the wheat into my barn.'"**

Jesus' next parable is also an agricultural tale, and there are three places where this parable applies: to the ministry of Jesus himself, to the life of the church, and to the future judgment at the end of the world. In terms of Jesus' ministry, the parable assures the disciples that the rejection he is receiving (the weeds threatening to overwhelm the just sprouting wheat) is the result of enemy action and not a defect in the message and work of Jesus.

In terms of the life of the church, the parable presents the realities of the church; there are weeds as well as wheat "in the pews." The church is like the field in the parable. Weeds are entangled in the wheat; good and evil are mixed together. What does the parable say to such a situation? It assures us that this is not the way God wants it to be, nor will it always be this way. Selfishness, abuse, greed, and hatred are the enemies of God, and the fact that they are an inevitable part of God's people does not mean that they are a part of God's will. The simple fact that the church always has its share of hypocrites does not make the gospel hypocritical, nor does it destroy the integrity of God. When all is said and done, this evil will not endure; the goodness of God will prevail; the tender wheat will be protected and saved.

Moreover, the parable frees us from the burden of having to "play God" and set things right all by ourselves. The slaves in the parable wonder what they should do and are assured that it will be all right to leave the weeds growing in the field. The weeds will not choke out the wheat; the farmer is confidently in control of the situation and knows what to do; the weeds will be destroyed in due time at the harvest, and the success of the harvest is still sure.

This does not mean that the church sits complacently and does nothing in the face of corruption in its own ranks (indeed, later in Matthew Jesus spells out a process for dealing with internal problems in the church's life; see Matthew 18:15–20). It does mean that the ultimate victory of the kingdom of heaven does not depend upon stainless purity in the church. This allows the church to be patient and confident and not to launch any fearful and destructive inquisitions, ripping itself apart out of a puritanical zeal to punish wrongdoers.

The third application of this parable, to the future judgment of the world, is explored when Jesus explains this parable to the disciples later in Matthew 13 (see comments on Matt. 13:36–43).

THE PARABLES OF THE MUSTARD SEED AND THE YEAST
Matthew 13:31–33

> 13:31 **He put before them another parable: "The kingdom of heaven is like a mustard seed that someone took and sowed in his field; ³² it is the smallest of all the seeds, but when it has grown it is the greatest of shrubs and becomes a tree, so that the birds of the air come and make nests in its branches."**
>
> ³³ **He told them another parable: "The kingdom of heaven is like yeast that a woman took and mixed in with three measures of flour until all of it was leavened."**

In the first two of his parables, Jesus has spoken of the certain victory of the kingdom of heaven despite its many hardships and obstacles.

In these next two parables, the theme shifts to the amazing growth of the kingdom despite its humble beginnings. In the first, the kingdom is compared to a mustard seed (Matt. 13:31–32). In the second, the kingdom is like a handful of yeast that a woman uses to leaven three measures of flour.

At first glance, then, the message of these two parables is quite simple. The kingdom of heaven starts very small (one man, Jesus, preaching in an out-of-the-way corner of the world); but, like a tiny seed developing into a mighty tree or a little leaven permeating the whole ball of dough, the kingdom will expand to magnificent size.

This plain message becomes a bit more convoluted, however, when one looks more closely at these parables. To begin with, the parable of the mustard seed is saturated with hyperbole. A mustard seed is small, to be sure, but it is not the smallest of all seeds. Moreover, it is a gross exaggeration to say that a mustard seed grows into the "greatest of shrubs," and it certainly does not become a tree vast enough for flocks of nesting birds. Jesus probably has a twinkle in his eye as he plays on the popular image, drawn from the Old Testament, that a mighty political kingdom is like a great and strong tree. In fact, Jesus may be alluding to the depiction in Daniel of Babylon as a tree standing majestically at the center of the earth, with a top that reached to heaven, a tree that was visible to the ends of the earth, abundant enough that "the birds of the air nested in its branches, and from it all living beings were fed" (Dan. 4:10–12).

So, great kingdoms are supposed to look like the massive cedars of Lebanon or towering sequoias; instead, Jesus offers the humble image of a mustard bush. The kingdom of heaven is like . . . a mustard bush? The main point remains intact—the kingdom grows to great size from very small beginnings—but another point gets made as well: This greatness does not come in the form we expect. As David Garland has remarked, "Jesus' parable hints that the kingdom is breaking into the world in a disarming and, for many, disenchanting form. We do not sing, 'A mighty mustard bush is our God.' The parable implies that the kingdom . . . will not come 'as a mighty cedar astride the lofty mountain height' reaching to the topmost part of the sky but as a lowly mustard bush" (Garland, *Reading Matthew*, 149–50).

As it turns out, the parable of the yeast contains the same sort of unexpected twist. To our ears, it sounds like a gentle cooking illustration, but this is not so. In Jesus' day, yeast was a popular symbol for corruption (Matthew himself uses "yeast" this way; see Matt. 16:6). To observe that "a little yeast leavens the loaf" was equivalent to saying "one bad apple spoils the barrel" (see, for example, Paul's negative use of "yeast" in 1 Corinthians 5:6). So, as Garland observes, saying that the kingdom of heaven is like "yeast" is akin to saying that it is like "rust" or "a virus" (Garland, *Reading Matthew*, 150).

Not only that, but what the woman does with this yeast implies a bit of stealth. Despite the translation given in the NRSV, the woman doesn't innocently mix or blend the yeast into the flour; according to the original Greek, she *hides* it. And she is evidently baking for an army, because she hides the yeast in "three measures of flour"—that's about fifty pounds of flour, enough to make bread for a hundred people!

Putting all of this together, the parable of the yeast pictures the king-dom as a hidden force, working silently to "corrupt" the world—that is, to corrupt the corruption or, as the whimsical lyrics of a country song once put it, "You're gonna ruin my bad reputation." One cannot see the king-dom pervading the world, but when its covert fermentation is accom-plished, the bland flour of the world will have been transformed into the joyous bread of life.

JESUS AND THE PARABLES
Matthew 13:34–35

13:34 Jesus told the crowds all these things in parables; without a parable he told them nothing. [35] This was to fulfill what had been spoken through the prophet:
  "I will open my mouth to speak in parables;
    I will proclaim what has been hidden from the foundation of the
    world."

At this point in his ministry, Jesus teaches the crowds exclusively with parables. Matthew, as he has done several times before, describes Jesus' ministry as a fulfillment of Old Testament prophecy. The purpose of Jesus' parables is to "proclaim what has been hidden from the foundation of the world" (Matt. 13:35, paraphrasing Psalm 78:2). In the parable of the yeast (Matt. 13:33), Jesus likened the kingdom of heaven to yeast that a woman hid in flour. Now Matthew, through this Old Testament refer-ence, informs his readers that the purpose of Jesus' parables was to make this hidden kingdom visible.

INTERPRETATION
OF THE PARABLE OF THE WEEDS
Matthew 13:36–43

13:36 Then he left the crowds and went into the house. And his disciples ap-proached him, saying, "Explain to us the parable of the weeds of the field." [37] He answered, "The one who sows the good seed is the Son of Man; [38] the field is the world, and the good seed are the children of the kingdom; the weeds are the children of the evil one, [39] and the enemy who sowed them is the devil; the harvest is the end of the age, and the reapers are angels. [40] Just as the weeds are collected and burned up with fire, so will it be at the end of the age. [41] The Son of Man will send his angels, and they will collect

out of his kingdom all causes of sin and all evildoers, [42] and they will throw them into the furnace of fire, where there will be weeping and gnashing of teeth. [43] Then the righteous will shine like the sun in the kingdom of their Father. Let anyone with ears listen!"

Having finished his public sermon-in-parables, Jesus now withdraws to the privacy of a house and the company of his own disciples. The teaching continues, however, as Jesus instructs his disciples about the meaning of one of the parables he told earlier, the parable of the weeds (Matt. 13:24–30), and, then, adds three more parables intended especially for the disciples.

We saw earlier how the parable of the weeds could be taken in three ways: as applying to the ministry of Jesus, to the life of the church, and to the future of the whole world (see comments on Matt. 13:24–30). It is on this third, and largest, canvas that this parable is now interpreted to the disciples. Again, as was the case with the explanation of the parable of the sower (Matt. 13:18–23), the parable of the weeds is treated allegorically—that is, every feature of the parable is given a symbolic interpretation.

Jesus himself is the farmer who sows good seed, the children of the kingdom, in the field, which is the world. The enemy, who is the devil, sows wicked children in the same field. The good and the bad grow side-by-side until the harvest, the end of the age, at which time the reapers, the angels, are sent to divide the wheat from the chaff. They throw the evildoers and their works into the fiery furnace of judgment, but the children of the kingdom will be preserved and "will shine like the sun in the kingdom of their Father" (Matt. 13:43).

This is, of course, dramatic stuff—the children of Satan being jerked up at the end of time and tossed unceremoniously into a furnace of flaming misery. The expressions are typical of Matthew—stark, uncompromising, unequivocal pictures of good and bad spiced up with plenty of weeping and gnashing of teeth.

Reading this strange language today is like walking along the peak of a sharply sloped roof; we can easily slip off one side or the other. On the one hand, many have been afraid of this language, misunderstanding it as a terrifying vision of a fiery judgment and a God who dangles sinners over blazing pits. We must remember that Jesus is giving this interpretation of the parable to the disciples, to the faithful ones, to his closest followers. The language is graphic, to be sure, but its intent is to encourage the disciples by reassuring them that all that opposes the gospel is impermanent and destined for oblivion.

That leads to the second misunderstanding. It is easy for Christians to look through the church windows at the world and to think of ourselves as God's special insiders, the ones who will "shine like the sun" in the end. We can relish with smug self-satisfaction the thought of worldly types being rounded up at the great finale, collected like weeds and burned up in the everlasting fire.

However, we are, ourselves, a mixture of good and evil. Sometimes we are faithful, and sometimes we are not; one moment we can be God's loyal disciples, and the next we can be champions of all that opposes the kingdom. Even Peter was capable of moving from being a solid "rock" to a treacherous "Satan" within a few breaths (Matt. 16:18–23).

Even with all of its sensational images, this interpretation of the parable of the weeds is good news for frail human beings struggling to be faithful amid the ambiguities of life. It discloses a God who is a careful, wise, and loving farmer cultivating and nurturing the world and caring for us as well. "The glory of God," said the ancient Christian theologian Irenaeus, "is humanity fully alive," and the promise of this parable is that God will finally not tolerate anything that deadens humanity or corrupts God's world. Whatever is in the world, or in us, that poisons our humanity and breaks our relationship with God will, thank the Lord, be burned up in the fires of God's everlasting love.

THE PARABLES OF THE TREASURE AND THE PEARL
Matthew 13:44–46

13:44 "The kingdom of heaven is like treasure hidden in a field, which someone found and hid; then in his joy he goes and sells all that he has and buys that field.

45 "Again, the kingdom of heaven is like a merchant in search of fine pearls; 46 on finding one pearl of great value, he went and sold all that he had and bought it.

Jesus now whispers to his disciples privately two brief parables: the parable of the treasure and the parable of the pearl. The parables are similar in the sense that, in each of them, someone discovers something of precious and compelling value—in one case a hidden treasure and in the other case a magnificent pearl—and sells everything that he has in order to possess it.

The point, of course, for both parables is that the kingdom is like this. When people truly encounter it and realize what it is, it enters their hearts, seizes their imaginations, and overwhelms them with its precious value. No price is too great; nothing that they own can rival its value. Everything they possess goes on the auction block for the sake of possessing the kingdom.

But there the similarities between the two parables end. In the first parable, someone—probably a poor man, given the fact that he had to sell everything he owned to purchase one field—simply stumbles across a treasure. He wasn't looking for a treasure; he was probably plowing, and the blade of the plow struck a jar containing buried valuables. The treasure is a surprise, a dazzling and unexpected event.

In the second parable, however, the pearl merchant is a seeker, a wealthy merchant in search of one of the ancient world's most valued objects—fine pearls. Unlike the man who finds the treasure by surprise, the merchant finds exactly what he is looking for, and he knows precisely what he has found.

So it is with the kingdom of heaven. Some people are on a quest. They are hungry for meaning, and, when the kingdom is found, they recognize its priceless pearly gleam immediately. They have been reading widely or studying hard or asking countless questions, and, then, they discover the depths of the gospel. Perhaps they were raised in the church but never found it satisfying; so, they went in pursuit of something more profound, only to discover that the priceless pearl was at home all along.

But others are not on a quest at all. They have enough to handle simply to cope with life. They are plowing or filing or cooking or tightening bolts or raising children or going to meetings. They expect nothing but the routine, anticipate no more today than a variation on yesterday. But, then, something wonderful and surprising happens. Maybe a baby is born, and the preciousness of human life as a gift from God breaks into the routine. Or maybe a line from a book or a stray remark by somebody at work breaks through the gloom and shines an unexpectedly gracious light on everything. Or maybe a phrase from an old hymn drifts across the memory like the scent of costly perfume. All at once life becomes holy, God seems near, and everything pales before this new and breathtakingly priceless truth.

Taken together, these two parables bear witness to the many ways the Spirit brings God close, to the diversity of God's advent in our lives. However it happens, whenever it occurs, it is the event of a lifetime. Whatever we have considered valuable before is transformed from a legacy to a means to obtain the one, unparalleled treasure of the kingdom of heaven.

THE PARABLE OF THE NET
Matthew 13:47–50

13:47 **"Again, the kingdom of heaven is like a net that was thrown into the sea and caught fish of every kind;** [48] **when it was full, they drew it ashore,**

sat down, and put the good into baskets but threw out the bad. ⁴⁹ So it will be at the end of the age. The angels will come out and separate the evil from the righteous ⁵⁰ and throw them into the furnace of fire, where there will be weeping and gnashing of teeth.

This parable is another word encouraging the church to adopt an open and freewheeling approach to evangelism. The kingdom of heaven, Jesus says, is like a fisherman's net. When the fisherman casts it into the sea, he doesn't have any idea what kind of fish will be caught. Game fish, meat fish, tropical fish, trash fish—they all are gathered up in the net. The fisherman doesn't hesitate to cast the net for fear that the wrong kind of fish will be caught. He casts his net wide and deep. The sorting out of the good fish from the bad takes place later.

So it is with the kingdom; so it is with the church. The doors are thrown open; the programs are open to all; the net is cast wide and deep. Into the church come people who are deeply serious about the things of God and people who are looking for a pretty sanctuary in which to get married. People show up who are hungry to do righteousness, and people come because their spouse sings in the choir and they can't figure out what to do with themselves. The life of God's people is wonderfully nondiscriminatory. Everybody is welcome to come along for the ride; the job of sifting the serious from the frivolous, the authentic from the fraudulent, is left to the angels. In the meantime, the grace of God flows freely and hopefully. Who knows whether the fish that would, at first glance, have hastily been thrown back will, in time, turn out to be the best catch of the day?

SCRIBES FOR THE KINGDOM
Matthew 13:51–53

> 13:51 **"Have you understood all this?" They answered, "Yes." ⁵² And he said to them, "Therefore every scribe who has been trained for the kingdom of heaven is like the master of a household who brings out of his treasure what is new and what is old." ⁵³ When Jesus had finished these parables, he left that place.**

Jesus has been teaching in parables all day. First he taught the crowds; then he spoke privately to the disciples. Now, he has come to the end of the day, and he asks the disciples, those closest to him, if they have "understood all this" (Matt. 13:51). This is an astounding question, because "all this" means, of course, the most profound truths of God. Jesus is asking if the disciples—fishermen and common folk—understand the deepest mystery of life—the secrets of the kingdom of heaven.

Have the disciples understood "all this"? If we were reading the Gospel of Mark, the answer would definitely be "no." In Mark, the disciples never get it. In fact, they do not even understand Jesus' very first parable (see Mark 4:13), much less the rest of them. In Matthew, however, the situation is different. The disciples in Matthew have the capacity to understand, to respond, to be trustworthy in the life of faith. They have heard seven difficult parables and now Jesus wants to know if they have grasped the full range of kingdom truths these parables contain. Knowing Matthew's emphasis on discipleship, we are somehow not surprised by their answer: "Yes," they say. "We understand."

At this moment, the disciples show themselves to be examples of the kind of people Matthew hopes that all of his readers will be. They are scribes "who [have] been trained for the kingdom of heaven" (Matt. 13:52). What this means is that they take out of their treasure "what is new and what is old" (Matt. 13:52). Notice the word order. The usual way to speak of this pair is of the "old and the new," but here Jesus reverses the order—the "new and the old." In the kingdom of heaven, the new sets the bearings, while the old is fitted into this fresh orientation.

So, the disciples are those who have set the compass of their lives by the new—the inbreaking of the kingdom in Jesus—but who have not abandoned the old—the Law and the Prophets. They are like Joseph, whose story was told at the beginning of the Gospel of Matthew (see Matt. 1:18–25). He was open to the new thing that God was doing in Jesus, but he remained faithful in the deepest sense to the righteousness of God as revealed in the law. The disciples form the core of God's new community, and around these "scribes trained for the kingdom of heaven" Jesus will build the church.

9. Forming the New Community
Matthew 13:54–16:20

As the gloom of rejection gathers around Jesus, the first rays of dawn are already beginning to break through. Jesus will form a new community of God. It will not be a rejection of Israel. To the contrary, it will be the fulfillment of Israel, a community that trusts God's faithfulness in the past and is open to the new thing God is doing in the present. The "scribes" of this new community will be the disciples, who know how to reach into the treasure chest of God's wisdom and bring out "what is new and what is old" (Matt. 13:52).

Here the energies of Matthew's Gospel shift toward this new community. As a sign of this, Matthew now reports that Jesus returns to his hometown Nazareth (we last saw Nazareth at the beginning of Jesus' ministry, in Matthew 4:12–13; the Jesus story is, in a sense, starting over, this time with the focus on the new community). In rapid fashion, Matthew tells us that Jesus is rejected by his own home synagogue and, in a flashback, narrates the story of the death of John the Baptist, the last of the "old" prophets. In other words, the old has passed away—John is dead, and even Nazareth refuses to receive Jesus—and the new is about to come.

REJECTED AT HOME
Matthew 13:54–58

> 13:54 **He came to his hometown and began to teach the people in their synagogue, so that they were astounded and said, "Where did this man get this wisdom and these deeds of power?** [55] **Is not this the carpenter's son? Is not his mother called Mary? And are not his brothers James and Joseph and Simon and Judas?** [56] **And are not all his sisters with us? Where then did this man get all this?"** [57] **And they took offense at him. But Jesus said to them, "Prophets are not without honor except in their own country and in their**

own house." [58] **And he did not do many deeds of power there, because of their unbelief.**

After instructing the crowds and the disciples with parables, Jesus moves his teaching ministry to the synagogue in his hometown of Nazareth. The classes, however, do not go well. Unlike the disciples, who were good students (Matt. 13:51), the locals of Nazareth are offended (the Greek means "scandalized") by Jesus (Matt. 13:57) and end up as kingdom school dropouts.

What scandalized the local folk about Jesus? What was it about him that they found so offensive? It was not what he said or what he did. Like the crowds who heard the Sermon on the Mount, the citizens of Nazareth were "astounded" by Jesus' teaching, and they clearly recognized that he spoke words of "wisdom" and performed "deeds of power" (Matt. 13:54; compare Matt. 7:28).

No, the folk were not provoked because Jesus was unimpressive. To the contrary, what offended them was precisely that this fellow they had known for years *was* impressive, that such powerful and spiritual words and deeds were coming from a local carpenter's son. They knew Jesus, knew his family, knew his origins (Matt. 13:55–56). If God were actually working and speaking through this hometown boy, then they would have to change their understanding of God's ways in the world; that is, alter their theology. In their view, God could speak forcefully through the smoke and the cloud at Sinai but not on an ordinary sabbath at the synagogue. God could make a path in the waters of the Red Sea but surely not in the streets of Nazareth. And most of all, God's prophets were legendary figures from other places, people like Elijah and Jeremiah, certainly not like Jesus, Joseph's boy, who grew up just around the corner and who used to play with his brothers and sisters in that pasture right over there.

But now, in Jesus, Sinai has happened at the door of the synagogue, the path through the Red Sea has become Main Street in Nazareth, and the people were thrown into theological crisis. As long as God works deeds of power somewhere else and through strangers, one can keep a safe distance. But now, God has acted dramatically right in the local synagogue and through a neighbor's son.

So, as a way of keeping their distance from the God who insists on becoming perilously local, the hometown citizens scoff, "Where then did this man get all this?" (Matt. 13:56). Jesus cites the old saying about prophets having honor everywhere except at home (Matt. 13:57), and then he gives the people of Nazareth exactly what they want and expect from God—very little (Matt. 13:58).

THE DEATH OF JOHN THE BAPTIST
Matthew 14:1–12

14:1 At that time Herod the ruler heard reports about Jesus; [2] and he said to his servants, "This is John the Baptist; he has been raised from the dead, and for this reason these powers are at work in him." [3] For Herod had arrested John, bound him, and put him in prison on account of Herodias, his brother Philip's wife, [4] because John had been telling him, "It is not lawful for you to have her." [5] Though Herod wanted to put him to death, he feared the crowd, because they regarded him as a prophet. [6] But when Herod's birthday came, the daughter of Herodias danced before the company, and she pleased Herod [7] so much that he promised on oath to grant her whatever she might ask. [8] Prompted by her mother, she said, "Give me the head of John the Baptist here on a platter." [9] The king was grieved, yet out of regard for his oaths and for the guests, he commanded it to be given; [10] he sent and had John beheaded in the prison. [11] The head was brought on a platter and given to the girl, who brought it to her mother. [12] His disciples came and took the body and buried it; then they went and told Jesus.

When Herod Antipas, the Galilean ruler during Jesus' ministry (see comment on Matt. 2:1), heard rumors about the activity of Jesus, he assumed that one of his old enemies had come back to haunt him. "This is John the Baptist," he muttered; "he has been raised from the dead" (Matt. 14:2).

It was an understandable mistake. Ambitious politicians rarely have the time to make fine theological distinctions. Both John and Jesus were powerful preachers of the kingdom of heaven; both gave stirring calls to repent, and their dramatic ministries roused the same sort of passions among the Jews. From the faraway vantage of the palace porch, both must have looked the same to Herod, and he jumped to the conclusion that a problem, long buried, had been raised again.

But it was not a case of governmental mistaken identity that caused the early church to remember and to retell this story of the fate of John the Baptist. The first Christians recounted this story because of the ways in which it spoke of death and resurrection.

Death, of course, is what happened to John, and the flashback of his beheading is artfully, if gruesomely, recounted. By telling this story, the early church remembered the death of John the Baptist, but, perhaps more important, they saw how John's death at the hand of Herod anticipated Jesus' own death and also served to warn the church of the dangers that befall all who dare to represent the kingdom. John was the last and greatest of the old prophets (Matt. 11:11–16), but, in the world's economy, that counted less than the swirl of a dancer's skirt and a reckless oath uttered in the heat of desire at a politician's birthday party. Jesus was God's own Son, but he, too, became "inconvenient" to the rulers of this age.

"Blessed are those who are persecuted for righteousness' sake," Jesus taught in the Sermon on the Mount (Matt. 5:10). John was so persecuted; so was Jesus; and the new kingdom community, the church, should be ready for persecution as well. "Blessed are you when people revile you and persecute you . . . for in the same way they persecuted the prophets who were before you" (Matt. 5:11–12).

But persecution and death are not the only themes of this passage. When Herod, hearing of Jesus, mutters that "John the Baptist . . . has been raised from the dead" (Matt. 14:2), he is closer to the truth than he knows. God was at work in the world through John the Baptist, but, though they had "killed off" John, they had not killed God. God was active in an even more powerful way in Jesus. Moreover, by his remark Herod ironically foreshadows Jesus' actual resurrection, and he reveals the deepest fear of the rulers of the present age—that there is a power loose in the world that cannot be controlled by tyranny and cannot be stilled by the sword. Herod's father had already learned that truth at Bethlehem (Matt. 2:1–21), and all of the worldly powers will learn it most dramatically on Easter.

FEEDING THE CROWDS
Matthew 14:13–21

14:13 **Now when Jesus heard this, he withdrew from there in a boat to a deserted place by himself. But when the crowds heard it, they followed him on foot from the towns.** [14] **When he went ashore, he saw a great crowd; and he had compassion for them and cured their sick.** [15] **When it was evening, the disciples came to him and said, "This is a deserted place, and the hour is now late; send the crowds away so that they may go into the villages and buy food for themselves."** [16] **Jesus said to them, "They need not go away; you give them something to eat."** [17] **They replied, "We have nothing here but five loaves and two fish."** [18] **And he said, "Bring them here to me."** [19] **Then he ordered the crowds to sit down on the grass. Taking the five loaves and the two fish, he looked up to heaven, and blessed and broke the loaves, and gave them to the disciples, and the disciples gave them to the crowds.** [20] **And all ate and were filled; and they took up what was left over of the broken pieces, twelve baskets full.** [21] **And those who ate were about five thousand men, besides women and children.**

This story of the desert feeding of the multitude is the only story of a miracle of Jesus that is included in all four Gospels, a clue that it was a very important memory for the early church. The story is sometimes called "The Feeding of the Five Thousand," but Matthew makes it clear that there were more people fed than that. Matthew employs the Gospel of Mark, which says only that there were "five thousand men" (Mark 6:44), because the ancient custom was to count only the men in a large group. Matthew, however, takes a welcome editorial step by modifying Mark's language to read "about five thousand men, besides women and children" (Matt. 14:21). Even here, though, the women and children were still not counted, and, as Dale Bruner observed, "Today we know that this 'not counting' is patriarchal. Next time the women and children must be counted!" (Bruner, *Matthew*, vol. 2: *The Churchbook*, 531).

This feeding story is rich in symbolism, and, as Matthew tells it, the narrative stands as a fine expression of the "new and old" in the kingdom of heaven. In terms of the "old," the account of the desert feeding reminds the reader of several Old Testament feeding stories, especially two. First, there is the story of the children of Israel, their narrow escape from the Egyptian army fresh on their minds, heading out into the wilderness and experiencing their first deep pangs of hunger. With the empty wasteland ahead of them, what lay behind them looked suddenly appealing. Egypt may have been the land of oppression and slavery, but it was also the land of the full stew pot and plentiful bread. "You have brought us out into this wilderness," they whined to Moses and Aaron, "to kill this whole assembly with hunger." In order that the people may know "that I am the LORD your God," God feeds the people with bread in the desert, with "manna" (Exodus 16). Just so, God's Son feeds the multitude in the desert.

The second "old" memory recalled by this passage is the story about the day a man brought an offering of a few loaves and some ears of grain to the prophet Elisha. There was a famine at that time, so Elisha ordered the man to give the food offering to the people. The man is astounded. He has one grocery sack, and there are a hundred hungry people pressing around him. "How can I set this before a hundred people?" he stammers. Speaking for God, Elisha replies, "They shall eat and have some left," which, when the man spread out the food, is exactly what happened (2 Kings 4:42–44).

It is easy to see the parallels between this story and the one in Matthew. The disciples, like the man in the Elisha story, are skeptical about their small supply of food satisfying a large crowd (Matt. 14:17), but, just as in the earlier story, Jesus' meal includes leftovers (Matt. 14:20).

In terms of the "new," this story clearly connects to the church's experience of being fed by the risen Christ at the Eucharist, the Lord's Supper. Students of worship have noted that four verbs, four liturgical actions, have been a part of the holy meal ever since the beginning of Christian worship: *taking* bread, *blessing* bread, *breaking* bread, and *giving* bread to the worshipers. They appear in the New Testament accounts of the Last Supper (see Matt. 26:26) and in virtually all subsequent Christian eucharistic liturgies.

Indeed, the church is always in the desert, the place where it cannot rely upon its own resources, which are few. The church is hungry itself and is surrounded by a world of deep cravings, people who are lonely, disoriented, and poor in many different ways. Against the savage realities of human need, the church sees only small numbers on the membership roles and even smaller ones in the mission budget. It is no wonder, then, that the church joins the disciples in crying, "This is a desert. Send the crowds away to fend for themselves" (see Matt. 14:15).

Jesus is still the teacher, though, and there is a lesson for the disciples—and the church—to learn: God is compassionate and abundantly able to provide. With desperate and hungry people camped all over the church lawn, Jesus turns, then and now, to his followers and speaks what is either a cruel joke or lavish divine humor: "They need not go away; you give them something to eat" (Matt. 14:16). The disciples, fully aware that their own resources are not up to the magnitude of the need (Matt. 14:17), nonetheless trust that the jest is a divine one and obey Jesus. Indeed, the picture of the disciples moving among the now-nourished multitude, tugging twelve hefty baskets of leftovers back to their compassionate Lord, is surely enough to provoke peals of joyous laughter in the reader, perhaps even in heaven.

JESUS WALKS ON THE WATER
Matthew 14:22–33

14:22 **Immediately he made the disciples get into the boat and go on ahead to the other side, while he dismissed the crowds.** 23 **And after he had dismissed the crowds, he went up the mountain by himself to pray. When evening came, he was there alone,** 24 **but by this time the boat, battered by the waves, was far from the land, for the wind was against them.** 25 **And early in the morning he came walking toward them on the sea.** 26 **But when the disciples saw him walking on the sea, they were terrified, saying, "It is a ghost!" And they cried out in fear.** 27 **But immediately Jesus spoke to them and said, "Take heart, it is I; do not be afraid."**

28 **Peter answered him, "Lord, if it is you, command me to come to you on the water."** 29 **He said, "Come." So Peter got out of the boat, started walking on the water, and came toward Jesus.** 30 **But when he noticed the strong wind, he became frightened, and beginning to sink, he cried out, "Lord, save**

me!" [31] **Jesus immediately reached out his hand and caught him, saying to him, "You of little faith, why did you doubt?"** [32] **When they got into the boat, the wind ceased.** [33] **And those in the boat worshiped him, saying, "Truly you are the Son of God."**

On the surface, this is a story about the disciples' traveling across the Sea of Galilee in rough water and Jesus' ability to walk on the sea. In a deeper sense, however, Matthew (like Mark before him) has shaped this story into a parable about the church and a disclosure about the nature of Jesus.

First we get a symbolic picture of the church—the disciples in a boat on the unpredictable sea. Jesus, we are told, "made the disciples get into the boat and go on ahead to the other side" (Matt. 14:22). The point here is not that Jesus coerced the disciples into the boat (that is, the church) but, rather, that their being in the boat at all was because of a command of Jesus. Unlike a bowling league or the Coalition to Save Historic Buildings, the church is not a group of like-minded people who, on their own initiative, rally around a common desire or a worthy cause. The church, rather, is a peculiar people, called by God and sent onto a dangerous sea. Were it not for the authoritative command of Christ, no one would volunteer to climb into the boat.

Indeed, the journey to the other side is no lazy summer sail. The boat is "battered by the waves" and fights the wind as it struggles toward a difficult landfall (Matt. 14:24). Such is the recurrent experience of the church, straining to be faithful in perilous times. But we get more than a snapshot of the church; we also are given in this passage a picture of Jesus as Lord. As the stormy night wears on toward dawn, Jesus goes out to the disciples, walking on the sea. The emphasis here is not on Jesus' ability to perform an amazing deed, his capacity to do a dazzling circus stunt that shows off his supernatural powers, but rather on who Jesus is theologically. Like the demons, disease, and death, the raging sea is one of the unruly powers, but Jesus is Lord even over the sea; he is Lord over all the powers of chaos and destruction that threaten the life of the church, the mission of God's people, and the victory of the kingdom of heaven (see comment on Matt. 8:23–27).

As Jesus strides over the waves, he speaks in a voice like that of God in the Old Testament. His words "It is I" (literally, "I am") echo the words spoken to Moses by God out of the burning bush (see Exod. 3:14). The disciples, at first fearfully mistaking Jesus for a ghost, soon discover that they are not at the mercy of the angry sea; they are in the mercy of their compassionate Savior. "Take heart," he tells them, "it is I; do not be afraid" (Matt. 14:27).

Peter responds to this by asking permission to come to Jesus on the sea (Matt. 14:28). Peter does not vault impetuously over the gunwale; he waits for the command from Jesus: "Come" (Matt. 14:28–29). And when he does step out of the boat, Peter is enabled, for a moment at least, to walk, like his Lord, on the boisterous waters (Matt. 14:29). In this instant, then, we catch a brief glimpse of what Matthew believes discipleship is all about—obeying Jesus, sharing the fullness of his life and ministry, moving toward him confidently even in the teeth of the storm.

But Peter cannot maintain this posture. He catches sight of the wind, and now there are two rival powers symbolically in view: Jesus and chaos. Peter's faith is now mixed with fear; he has, as Daniel Patte has phrased it, "a faith with a divided mind" (Patte, *The Gospel According to Matthew*, 212), and, wondering whether Jesus or the raging wind will finally prevail, he begins to sink beneath the waters. Even when disciples falter, however, Jesus continues to save. He rescues Peter from the waves. Jesus and Peter join the others in the boat, and the final scene on the now becalmed sea is one of worship and confession: "Truly you are the Son of God" (Matt. 14:33).

In every case, the picture of the church we see in this passage is derived from the character of Jesus. The church is what it is because Jesus is who he is. Jesus is portrayed as: *Lord*, walking magisterially over the sea, authoritatively ruling over the wild, fearsome, humanly untamed powers loose in the world; *Savior*, reaching out to deliver a frightened, failing disciple; and *Son of God*, as Emmanuel ("God with us"), one who is worthy of worship and faithful confession. Indeed, the image of the disciples in the boat with Jesus on a tranquil sea, worshiping and confessing their faith, may well reflect the church on the Lord's Day, at sabbath rest. But Sunday is not the only day of the week, and the church does not exist to float around in a sabbath sea all by itself praising Jesus. The boat comes eventually to land, and the healing work of Jesus (and the church) continues (Matt. 14:34–35).

JESUS' HEALING MINISTRY
IN GENNESARET
Matthew 14:34–36

14:34 **When they had crossed over, they came to land at Gennesaret.** [35] **After the people of that place recognized him, they sent word throughout the region and brought all who were sick to him,** [36] **and begged him that they might touch even the fringe of his cloak; and all who touched it were healed.**

As Jesus arrives with the disciples in Gennesaret (a region or a town on the northwest shore of the Sea of Galilee), we see yet another picture of "ideal faith." We see a whole section of the countryside bringing sick people to Jesus, confident that merely a touch of Jesus' garment will be enough to heal (Matt. 14:35–36).

Dale Bruner (*Matthew*, vol. 2, 537) has pointed out that this brief passage contains "five excited absolutes": (1) word about Jesus goes out through the *entire* region; (2) *all* the sick people were brought to Jesus; (3) they begged Jesus to touch *only* the fringe of his cloak; (4) *all* were healed; (5) all were healed *completely* (the Greek word translated "healed" in the NRSV is an unusual one, probably conveying the sense of a total restoration of health). In other words, through this description of the model response of Gennesaret, we are given a peek into the future. One day, "all nations" will claim Jesus as the Son of God and become disciples (see Matt. 28:19); "every knee should bend . . . and every tongue should confess that Jesus Christ is Lord" (Phil. 2:10–11).

GOD'S COMMANDMENTS
VERSUS TRADITION
Matthew 15:1–20

15:1 **Then Pharisees and scribes came to Jesus from Jerusalem and said,** [2] **"Why do your disciples break the tradition of the elders? For they do not wash their hands before they eat."** [3] **He answered them, "And why do you break the commandment of God for the sake of your tradition?** [4] **For God said, 'Honor your father and your mother,' and, 'Whoever speaks evil of father or mother must surely die.'** [5] **But you say that whoever tells father or mother, 'Whatever support you might have had from me is given to God,' then that person need not honor the father.** [6] **So, for the sake of your tradition, you make void the word of God.** [7] **You hypocrites! Isaiah prophesied rightly about you when he said:**
   [8] **'This people honors me with their lips,**
        but their hearts are far from me;
   [9] **in vain do they worship me,**
        teaching human precepts as doctrines.'"
   [10] **Then he called the crowd to him and said to them, "Listen and understand:** [11] **it is not what goes into the mouth that defiles a person, but it is what comes out of the mouth that defiles."** [12] **Then the disciples approached and said to him, "Do you know that the Pharisees took offense when they heard what you said?"** [13] **He answered, "Every plant that my heavenly Father has not planted will be uprooted.** [14] **Let them alone; they are blind**

guides of the blind. And if one blind person guides another, both will fall into a pit." [15] But Peter said to him, "Explain this parable to us." [16] Then he said, "Are you also still without understanding? [17] Do you not see that whatever goes into the mouth enters the stomach, and goes out into the sewer? [18] But what comes out of the mouth proceeds from the heart, and this is what defiles. [19] For out of the heart come evil intentions, murder, adultery, fornication, theft, false witness, slander. [20] These are what defile a person, but to eat with unwashed hands does not defile."

This relatively lengthy passage involves a rather complicated dispute between Jesus and some of the Jewish leaders. The point of the debate is over the clash between ceremonial religious ritual and the deeper will of God. As noted in the Introduction, a good portion of the first readers of Matthew's Gospel ("Matthew's church") were almost surely Jewish in background, and many of the practices and thought forms from Jewish tradition were quite naturally carried over into their Christian life.

One can imagine, then, that on countless occasions Matthew's church faced the problem of determining how much of what they formerly believed and practiced was to be continued in their new life of faith. They had no "New Testament" as we know it; what we call the Old Testament was, to a great extent, their scripture. But how much of the Old Testament law applied to them in their situation now? As we observed before, the way Matthew's church framed this question gradually changed. In their early days as Christians, they wondered how to weave their new trust in Jesus as messiah into the well-worn cloth of their Judaism. Now, with time and distance growing between them and the synagogue, the question was reversed: How do we weave the strands of our Jewish heritage into the new fabric of the Christian faith?

Matthew addresses this question several times and in a variety of ways in his Gospel, and his overall answer never varies: Christians do not throw out the Old Testament law; to the contrary, through faith in Christ they are able to discern the intention of God that lies at the heart of the law. God's will is a straight and steady line from Moses to Jesus. "Do not think that I have come to abolish the law or the prophets," Jesus declares in the Sermon on the Mount. "I have come not to abolish but to fulfill" (Matt. 5:17).

But even though Jesus did not come to abolish the Law and the Prophets, this did not mean that each and every aspect of the Mosaic law and Jewish tradition was to be continued and honored. Things were more complex than that. Sometimes, in order to give expression to what was at the center of the law—God's will—Jesus challenged and transgressed what was on the surface of the law.

But what about the hundreds of everyday practices and customs that were the warp and woof of Judaism as Matthew's readers knew it? Was a Christian to continue the observances about food, offerings, holy days, and the like? How many of these carried over, and to what extent? In this passage, the dispute is over only one such practice—the ritual washing of hands before eating. But the first readers of Matthew probably understood this dispute as a "test case" the results of which could be applied broadly whenever similar questions were raised.

The passage begins with the arrival of "Pharisees and scribes" from Jerusalem (Matt. 15:1). Even though Matthew lumps them together, scribes and Pharisees were not the same. Scribes were trained scholars in the fine points of the Mosaic law. Pharisees were a religious party within Judaism committed to pure and total obedience to God's will as expressed in the law. By blending Jesus' opponents and calling them "Pharisees and scribes . . . from Jerusalem," Matthew presents them as a broad and united front of the official religious establishment and wants his readers to recognize that Jesus was about to be confronted by the "brass from headquarters."

The confrontation involves what Jesus' disciples were *not* doing. It was a "tradition of the elders" (Matt. 15:2) to wash one's hands before eating, and the disciples of Jesus were not observing this ceremonial custom. Hand-washing, in this context, had nothing to do with hygiene or cleanliness in today's sense; it was a practice designed to provide ritual purification in case a person had touched anything that the Old Testament law declares "unclean" (for example, unclean animals, a corpse, certain forbidden foods, or diseased persons).

Even though the Old Testament law does speak of ritual washing, even hand-washing, it makes no mention of the specific custom that has these officials from Jerusalem in a swivet. There is no Old Testament law that requires ordinary folk to wash their hands before daily meals. If the Old Testament doesn't require it, how, then, did hand-washing before meals become a "tradition of the elders"?

Probably the custom developed in stages. The first stage involved the ongoing process of applying the Mosaic law to everyday life. Many faithful Jews, particularly the Pharisees, thought of the law as a living tradition that needed to be related and applied to the changing issues of the day. Much as Christians today would want to know how an ancient biblical text—for example, Paul's admonitions about eating meat offered to idols (1 Cor. 8:1–11:1)—applies to their lives even though the specific issue addressed in the text is no longer current, just so, these devout Jews wanted to know how every law in the scriptures, no matter how remote it seemed, spoke to them. They wanted to be obedient to every aspect of God's will at every moment of the day.

So, their leaders would study the ancient law and, then, update it by saying what they thought this or that provision of the law required now, even in situations not mentioned in the scriptures. This process created an oral tradition of legal cases and teachings, called the "traditions of the elders," that grew up alongside the Mosaic law itself.

The matter of concern in our text—the ritual of hand-washing before meals—is a typical example of this process. The Mosaic law requires that priests, and only priests, wash to avoid uncleanness, but when the legal experts applied this principle to everyday life, it led logically to the idea that all faithful Jews should wash when they have come into contact with something or someone unclean.

Then, in a second stage, zealous persons would take these teachings even further and more stringently. Not wanting to break God's law even by accident, they would develop practices to ensure no violations of the commandments whatsoever, even unintentional ones. So, instead of washing their hands only when they knew for sure they had touched something unclean, they began to wash their hands before every meal, just in case.

In the final stage, these extraordinary measures of the super-righteous would gradually become the accepted practice for everyone. Thus, in some quarters, the ritual custom of hand-washing before each meal gradually became the community norm for pious folk, the established "tradition of the elders," the standard by which truly faithful behavior was judged.

The officials who come to Jesus from Jerusalem have caught Jesus' disciples in the act of eating without washing their hands. By raising this as a challenge, they imply that the disciples (and, by association, Jesus) have no regard for the law of God. In other words, if they don't wash their hands, they must not love God; if they don't carry their Bibles on the top of the stack, they surely don't love God's Word.

Jesus' response is two-pronged. First, he turns the tables on the Pharisees and scribes by attacking their motives. These religious leaders have suggested that Jesus' disciples do not love the will of God because they do not honor the tradition. Jesus reverses this and accuses the leaders of loving the tradition *instead* of the will of God, indeed, of being willing to break the true commandments of God for the sake of their tradition (Matt. 15:3).

As a case in point, Jesus cites two commandments about children's responsibility to honor their parents (Exod. 20:12 and 21:17). These commandments express God's will that children should respect, care for, support, and speak well of their parents. In the ancient world, the well-being of the aged depended upon financial and social support from the younger generation.

But what if a child, in a moment of spiteful rage or misplaced religious zeal, should say to a parent, "I have decided to give to God all of the money and property that I would normally use to support you. I declare that I am going to donate it all to the temple"? According to the tradition, this statement, because it involved a vow to God, would take precedence over the commandments to honor one's parents. The temple would get a hefty donation, and the parents would be left out in the cold. Here, in other words, the "tradition of the elders" ended up actually sanctioning what the law of God strictly forbade—neglect and abuse of one's parents. Not only was this tradition not a true expression of the law of God; it also worked to vandalize the commandments of God.

So, these religious officials had a shell game going. They would deftly whisk around their knowledge of the words of scripture, but when they actually lifted up a commandment, the true will of God often would have vanished, leaving only the husk of tradition. Jesus did not mince words about them. "For the sake of your tradition," he charged, "you make void the word of God" (Matt. 15:6). The religious authorities came from Jerusalem with their pious questions, pretending to be God's advocates, but Jesus exposes their true identity. They are not district attorneys for the law of God; they are saboteurs of the Word. "Hypocrites," Jesus calls them, using one of his favorite words (we have heard it before in Matt. 6:2, 5, 10; 7:5; see comments on Matt. 6:2), and he lets them know that, centuries ago, the great prophet Isaiah was on to their type and well acquainted with their game of empty lip service (Matt. 15:8–9, quoting Isa. 29:13).

So much for the character of Jesus' opponents, but what about the substance of their question? Even if the religious leaders were hypocrites, it is possible that they have a good point. How could the disciples be "clean" before God if they did not observe the custom of hand-washing? Thus, in the second prong of Jesus' response, he addresses the central issue in this hand-washing question—the theological matter of clean and unclean; that is, what makes a person fit or unfit to be in the presence of God.

Turning away from his opponents to address the crowd, Jesus announces that the Pharisees and the scribes have it backwards; people are not made unclean from the outside in but from the inside out. "It is not what goes into the mouth that defiles a person," he says, "but it is what comes out of the mouth that defiles" (Matt. 15:11).

This statement of Jesus is so contrary to the usual ways of thinking about purity that it enrages the Pharisees and puzzles the disciples. The Pharisees' anger provides Jesus the opportunity to jab at them once again. These pompous leaders, he claims, are actually weeds in God's garden and "blind guides of the blind," Jesus quips. When God finds a weed, what happens? God uproots it, naturally. When a blind tourist is led around by a blind tour guide, what happens? Both of them end up in a pit (see Matt. 15:13–14).

The disciples, however, are Jesus' students, and they want to understand the meaning of his strange statement. "Explain this parable to us," begs Peter, acting as spokesman for the group (Matt. 15:15). Here the word "parable" means something like "riddle," a mysterious, hard-to-understand saying. Jesus responds by revealing the logic of his words: Something that enters a person's mouth from the outside simply passes through the digestive tract and is eliminated from the body. The moral core of the person remains untouched. But what comes *out* of a person's mouth comes from the heart, and when a person's heart is evil, the whole person is defiled (Matt. 15:17–18). An evil heart, says Jesus, leads to evil deeds—"murder, adultery, fornication, theft, false witness, slander" (Matt. 15:19), a list of vices that seems to approximate the order of the second half of the Ten Commandments. (Earlier in Matthew, Jesus has made a similar moral argument, namely, that what is inside a person determines external morality; see comments on Matthew 6:22–23 and 7:15–20.)

At the primary level, then, this text, in which Jesus declares that "to eat with unwashed hands does not defile" (Matt. 15:20) provided practical guidance to Matthew's church about the extent to which the old religious customs were to be followed in the new Christian context. It loosened the bonds of ritual and ceremony while, at the same time, strengthening the deeper moral ties to God and neighbor. In Matthew's Gospel, however, this word about hand-washing operates at a second, even deeper level, giving the freedom to Matthew's church to move without dread into the larger Gentile world. The passage reassures them that they cannot become tainted by anything—or by anybody—out there, because it is what comes out of a person, not what goes in from the outside, that defiles. The passage is, then, one more anticipation of the mission to the Gentiles, and, right on cue, a Gentile woman arrives on the scene in the very next passage.

THE GREAT FAITH
OF A CANAANITE WOMAN
Matthew 15:21–28

15:21 Jesus left that place and went away to the district of Tyre and Sidon. ²² Just then a Canaanite woman from that region came out and started shouting, "Have mercy on me, Lord, Son of David; my daughter is tormented by a demon." [23] But he did not answer her at all. And his disciples came and urged him, saying, "Send her away, for she keeps shouting after us." [24] He answered, "I was sent only to the lost sheep of the house of Israel." [25] But she came and knelt before him, saying, "Lord, help me." [26] He answered, "It is not fair to take the children's food and throw it to the dogs." [27] She said, "Yes, Lord, yet even the dogs eat the crumbs that fall from their masters' table." [28] Then Jesus answered her, "Woman, great is your faith! Let it be done for you as you wish." And her daughter was healed instantly.

Few New Testament stories have proved as troublesome to contemporary readers as this description of Jesus' encounter with a Gentile woman. What is bothersome is that, by today's standards, Jesus at first appears to be narrow-minded, brusque, and unconcerned about the woman's urgent need. But we must remember that the story does not occur in our day; it takes place instead in the first-century context of the strained, often painful relations between Jews and Gentiles. When we explore this story in its own context, we find a surprising account carefully crafted to highlight the profound messianic identity of Jesus as well as the strength, tenacity, and great faith of a Gentile woman who finds hope and mercy in the Jewish Messiah.

What happens is this: Fresh from his confrontation with the Pharisees and scribes (Matt. 15:1–20), Jesus heads out for the far borders of Israel, northwest toward Gentile territory, in the direction of the Phoenician cities of Tyre and Sidon. Out there in the borderlands, he is suddenly approached by a local woman noisily appealing on behalf of her daughter, a victim of demon possession. In Mark's Gospel, this woman is described simply as "a Gentile, of Syrophoenician origin" (Mark 7:26), but Matthew ups the stakes by calling her "a Canaanite"—thereby identifying her with the Old Testament enemies of Israel (see, for example, Judg. 1:1).

It is difficult to overstate the drama here. Jesus has withdrawn from an angry confrontation with official Israel over the "tradition of the elders" (Matt. 15:1–20) only to run into a woman who wears the label of Israel's notorious ancient foe—Canaan. This encounter between Jesus and the Canaanite woman is situated in every way "on the border"—on the boundary between the old and the new, between male and female, between Jew and Gentile, between friend and enemy, between the holy and the demonic. The story develops swiftly through a series of four linked verbal exchanges:

First, the woman begs Jesus for mercy, her voice raised to an urgent shout (the word translated "shouting" in Matthew 15:22 can also mean "scream" or "shriek" and is employed in Revelation 12:2 to describe the cries of a woman in labor pains). Just as she groaned in pain when her daughter was born, she now cries out again for her daughter, lifting her voice in desperate hope to Jesus, whom she calls both "Lord" and "Son of David" (Matt. 15:22). Thus, one of the main themes of the story can already be seen—the woman's amazing faith. In contrast to the Pharisees and scribes who find fault with Jesus and keep their distance, this foreign "enemy" woman recognizes, in the depths of her need, that Jesus is the royal and messianic Son of David, the Lord, the Savior.

Astonishingly, Jesus speaks not a word to her in return. His silence is stunning, deafening. At the surface level, the fact that Jesus does not respond to her initial appeal simply serves to underscore the woman's persistence when she cries out again. At the deeper level, though, this is the mysterious and fearsome silence of God spoken of by the psalmist: "O my God, I cry by day, but you do not answer" (Psalm 22:2). "Great faith" endures not only when God's presence and help are readily available but also in the wintry season of God's silence—a silence that Jesus himself will experience on the cross.

In the second exchange, the disciples urge Jesus to get rid of this bothersome, clamorous woman. It is not clear whether they want him simply to dismiss her outright or whether they are asking Jesus to shut her up by giving her the healing she wants. They probably prefer the latter, for this makes better sense of Jesus' refusal: "I was sent only to the lost sheep of the house of Israel" (Matt. 15:24).

In either case, it is apparent that the woman is now facing at least three obstacles: the silence of Jesus, the annoyance of Jesus' followers, and a definition of the mission of the Messiah that apparently includes "the lost sheep of the house of Israel" but not her and her daughter. Under similar circumstances, most people would have retreated in dismay or disgust. However, this is a woman of "great faith," and she is not dissuaded. She ignores the disciples' irritation; she dares to break the silence with her renewed cry; and, what is most amazing, this Gentile responds to Jesus' Jewish messianic identity with reverence and worship. Matthew reports that the woman "knelt before" Jesus (Matt. 15:25), employing the same Greek word used to describe others in the Gospel who have rightly bowed down before Jesus, including the Magi (Matt. 2:11), a leper (Matt. 8:2), a synagogue leader (Matt. 9:18), and the disciples themselves (Matt. 14:33).

The woman's worship of Jesus further develops the motif of her great faith and sets up the third exchange, in which she repeats her plea for help (Matt. 15:25). Jesus finally breaks his silence toward her, but his word comes across as a harsh rebuff: "It is not fair to take the children's food and throw it to the dogs." The meaning is clear: The people of Israel are the "children," Gentiles are "dogs," and what Jesus has to give is intended for the "children." Some have tried to soften the blow by pointing out that the Greek word for "dogs" actually means "little dogs" or "house dogs," but the sting remains. To call Gentiles "dogs" was a common and well-known term of scorn.

What, then, are we to make of Jesus' retort? Is even he sometimes blinded by nationalism and racism? Is Jesus being callously dismissive of this Gentile woman in her time of need? No, we must be careful not to apply modern standards of delicacy and politeness to the language of this passage. Despite their blunt tone, Jesus' words are, in sharp and stark terms, an expression of his true identity. By the use of the metaphor of the children and the dogs, Jesus is graphically reaffirming what he said to the disciples. He *is* Israel's messiah, and he *has* been sent to the lost sheep of the house of Israel. Before anything else may be said of him, this must be acknowledged.

Jesus is not a generic savior, an anonymous Superman from a distant planet somewhere in space. Jesus is a Jew; indeed, he is *the* Jew who stands as the culmination of all of Israel's history. Thus, another main theme of this passage is beginning to emerge: Jesus can be the savior of all people only by remaining faithful to God's chosen people Israel, even in the face of their rejection of him.

Imagine a woman who founded and continues to manage a shelter for battered women. She has carefully defined the mission of the shelter and energetically cultivated contributions and sources of financial support for that mission. There are other agencies that serve children, the homeless, and the hungry, but this shelter is dedicated to the needs of abused women. One day, however, the woman answers a knock at the door of the shelter only to find a desperately needy man asking for food and money. No matter how much her heart goes out to this man, surely she would wonder about the propriety of taking money donated for the care of abused women and giving it to him, however worthy he may be.

Just so, the messiah of God, sent to the lost sheep of the house of Israel, is confronted by a Canaanite woman in need. Her need is worthy, but what she wants belongs properly to the children of Israel. This woman's repeated request has brought us, then, to the turning point of the story, indeed to the turning point of the history of God's people. What happens when the Gentiles knock on the door of the God of Israel? What happens when the old enemies of God's chosen people kneel before Israel's messiah and beg for mercy?

Everything hinges on what this woman's plea means. On the one hand, Jesus is out near the border, in every sense. This Canaanite's appeal for healing can be taken as an invitation to blur the boundaries and, thus, as a threat to his clear Jewish messianic identity. In Old Testament terms, she is from the "enemy" camp, and her request for help could imply that Jesus should face the fact that Israel has rejected him, that he should turn his back on Israel and forget the promises of God to his people, that he should leave behind his role as Jewish messiah and instead become a general wonder-worker for all peoples. If this is what her appeal means, this is a new temptation (see Matt. 4:1–11), but Jesus' reply makes it clear that he will not fall, that he will not deny his baptismal vocation. However, this is not what the woman's petition means. Everything about her request demonstrates that she grasps the essential theological point: Jesus is Lord of all because he is the promised Son of David. It is Jesus' obedience to his role as the messiah of Israel that renders him the savior of all nations.

In the fourth exchange, the story moves to this resolution. The woman does not challenge Jesus' definition of himself or his mission. Indeed, her reply indicates that she is willing to stand on his ground, willing to accept his identity as Israel's messiah, as the one sent to the lost sheep of Israel, but that she understands, in all humility, this to include her, too: "Yes, Lord, yet even the dogs eat the crumbs that fall from their masters' table" (Matt. 15:27). Her response captures the essence of Matthew's theology: Because Jesus is the obedient Son of God, the messiah of Israel, he is the savior of the whole world. "Yes, Lord," the woman said, "but even the dogs—even the Gentiles—are fed from Israel's table." With that remark, the key turns in the lock. "Woman," Jesus exclaims, "great is your faith! Let it be done for you as you wish" (Matt. 15:28). Her daughter was healed immediately.

This, then, is a story about Jesus, who is savior of all through being faithful to his calling as messiah of Israel. It is also a story about a Canaanite woman whose great faith gave her perseverance and allowed her to discern that Israel's messiah was her messiah, too. But there is more. This story mirrors the development that Matthew's church itself was perhaps experiencing—from a silent separation from Gentiles, to an annoyed awareness of their presence, and ultimately to an active Gentile mission. Finally, though, this is a story for all Gentiles who read Matthew's Gospel—a reminder that God has not forsaken and abandoned Israel. Those of us who are Gentile Christians should remember that we are, as New Testament scholar Krister Stendahl has termed it, "honorary Jews" (quoted in Hare, *Matthew*, 179).

JESUS HEALS AND
FEEDS ON THE MOUNTAIN
Matthew 15:29–39

15:29 After Jesus had left that place, he passed along the Sea of Galilee, and he went up the mountain, where he sat down. [30] Great crowds came to him, bringing with them the lame, the maimed, the blind, the mute, and many others. They put them at his feet, and he cured them, [31] so that the crowd was amazed when they saw the mute speaking, the maimed whole, the lame walking, and the blind seeing. And they praised the God of Israel.

[32] Then Jesus called his disciples to him and said, "I have compassion for the crowd, because they have been with me now for three days and have nothing to eat; and I do not want to send them away hungry, for they might faint on the way." [33] The disciples said to him, "Where are we to get enough bread in the desert to feed so great a crowd?" [34] Jesus asked them, "How many loaves have you?" They said, "Seven, and a few small fish." [35] Then ordering the crowd to sit down on the ground, [36] he took the seven loaves and the fish; and after giving thanks he broke them and gave them to the disciples, and the disciples gave them to the crowds. [37] And all of them ate and were filled; and they took up the broken pieces left over, seven baskets full. [38] Those who had eaten were four thousand men, besides women and children. [39] After sending away the crowds, he got into the boat and went to the region of Magadan.

Once again a multitude gathers around Jesus, and Jesus performs two kinds of ministry among them: healing the sick and feeding the great crowd with bread and fish. Matthew models the description of the healings on key passages in Isaiah. Compare, for example, the list of infirmities in Matthew 15:30–31 with those found in Isaiah 35:5–6. Also, note that the response of the crowd, "they praised the God of Israel" (Matt. 15:31), is an echo of Isaiah 29:23b: "they . . . will stand in awe of the God of Israel." An important theme in Matthew is, thus, continued: The ministry of Jesus fulfills what was promised in the prophets.

A careful reader of Matthew will experience a sense of déjà vu when encountering the story of feeding the multitude, since just one chapter earlier Matthew also wrote of Jesus' curing the ill among a great crowd and then feeding them bread and fish (Matt. 14:13–21). The two feeding accounts probably derive from a single original story; they are certainly very similar in structure and content.

So why does Matthew tell essentially the same story twice? Partly, Matthew is using the Gospel of Mark as a pattern. Mark includes two feeding stories (Mark 6:30–44 and 8:1–10), and Matthew simply follows suit. In Mark, however, the doubling of stories seems to have a clear purpose:

The second feeding story accentuates its setting in Gentile territory, as if to say that Jesus had an all-encompassing mission, first feeding Jews and then Gentiles. Matthew, though, edits out the references to Gentile territory, so the Jewish-Gentile contrast is not a part of Matthew's aim.

For Mark, the contrast between the two feedings appears to be a change of *latitude* (from Jewish territory to a Gentile region), but Matthew seems to provide instead a contrast of *altitude* (from beside the sea to the top of the mountain). At the beginning of this passage, Matthew says that Jesus "went up the mountain, where he sat down" (Matt. 15:29), which is, of course, exactly what Jesus did at the opening of the Sermon on the Mount (Matt. 5:1). This change in elevation symbolizes a shift in importance, for mountaintop events in Matthew are times of significant revelation.

In the Sermon on the Mount, Jesus revealed God's ways through his words, his teachings. Here, Jesus reveals God's ways through his gracious deeds, through compassionate healing and feeding (Hare, *Matthew*, 180). Just like the first feeding, this one also connects both backward to feedings in the Old Testament and forward to the Lord's Supper and to the church's ministry (see comments on Matt. 14:13–21).

The accent in both feeding passages falls on the power of God, but the role played by the disciples in these events is also significant. To be sure, in the first feeding story the disciples want to send the crowds away unfed (Matt. 14:15), and they are still dubious the second time around about feeding such a multitude in a remote place (Matt. 15:33). But in both cases, it is the disciples who produce the loaves and fish and who actually take the food to the people.

We see, then, an anticipation of both the harsh limitations and the extravagant promises the work and mission of the church of Jesus Christ. Gather all the tithes and offerings of a congregation of Christian people, pool all of their energies and commitments, combine all the resources of any community of faith and stack them up against the pressing needs of the crowd restlessly gathered around the church's doorstep, and what is achieved amounts to a hill of beans—or, to put it biblically, a few loaves and some fish. No wonder the disciples sounded apologetic when they gave their statistical reports to Jesus. "We have nothing here but five loaves and two fish," they said on the first occasion, and, "We have seven loaves and a few small fish," they confessed on the second. Note the language of diminished resources: "nothing here but," "a few," "small."

"Nothing here but . . . " is precisely what the church always has, but, in the magnifying grace of God, it is enough—and more. So, the church, like the disciples in the feeding stories, distributes to the crowds what it has been given, confident that it will lavishly feed the hungry crowd.

SINISTER TESTS AND BAD YEAST
Matthew 16:1–12

16:1 **The Pharisees and Sadducees came, and to test Jesus they asked him to show them a sign from heaven. ² He answered them, "When it is evening, you say, 'It will be fair weather, for the sky is red.' ³ And in the morning, 'It will be stormy today, for the sky is red and threatening.' You know how to interpret the appearance of the sky, but you cannot interpret the signs of the times. ⁴ An evil and adulterous generation asks for a sign, but no sign will be given to it except the sign of Jonah." Then he left them and went away.**
⁵ **When the disciples reached the other side, they had forgotten to bring any bread. ⁶ Jesus said to them, "Watch out, and beware of the yeast of the Pharisees and Sadducees." ⁷ They said to one another, "It is because we have brought no bread." ⁸ And becoming aware of it, Jesus said, "You of little faith, why are you talking about having no bread? ⁹ Do you still not perceive? Do you not remember the five loaves for the five thousand, and how many baskets you gathered? ¹⁰ Or the seven loaves for the four thousand, and how many baskets you gathered? ¹¹ How could you fail to perceive that I was not speaking about bread? Beware of the yeast of the Pharisees and Sadducees!" ¹² Then they understood that he had not told them to beware of the yeast of bread, but of the teaching of the Pharisees and Sadducees.**

Here the Pharisees and the Sadducees make their second joint appearance in Matthew. The last time we saw this unlikely combination was on the banks of the Jordan River, as they angled toward John the Baptist (see the comments on Matthew 3:1–12, especially the section on the incompatibility of Pharisees and Sadducees). John took one look at them and suggested that they perhaps had slithered out of a pit. "You brood of vipers!" he shouted in their direction (Matt. 3:7).

Now they are back, this time to hiss at Jesus. Actually they want to "test" Jesus (Matt. 16:1), which may seem fair until we realize that the word translated "test" is a version of the one Matthew used earlier to describe the devil, the "tempter" (Matt. 4:3). The Pharisees and Sadducees test Jesus by asking for "a sign from heaven" (Matt. 16:1). This is not the first time the Pharisees have asked Jesus for a sign, for earlier they teamed up with the scribes on just such a request (Matt. 12:38). Jesus' response then was the same as here: "An evil and adulterous generation asks for a sign, but no sign will be given to it except the sign of Jonah" (Matt. 16:4; see comments on Matt. 12:38–45). The additional remarks about the weather (Matt. 16:2–3) may well be a later addition to the text of Matthew (see the footnote in the NRSV), but, as they stand, they serve to reinforce the idea of the blindness of Jesus' opponents. Jesus is, himself, God's "sign from heaven," but the Pharisees and Sadducees, though good at meteorology, are poor at theology and cannot perceive it.

Basically, then, this passage is a repeat of the earlier account of Jesus' refusal to provide a sign. Here again, just as with the feeding story in the previous passage, we are left to wonder, Why has Matthew essentially duplicated a previous story?

One reason, of course, is to demonstrate the widening range of Jesus' enemies. The Pharisees have been on the attack before, but now the Sadducees have been added to the list of foes. In the main, however, this repetition serves as a dark reminder that the narrative of Jesus is moving inexorably toward his death. The first time Jesus' opponents asked for a sign (Matt. 12:38), the hostility toward Jesus was deepening, and there were even death plots (Matt. 12:14). Now, the tempter has reentered the stage, and the testing of the Son of God has begun again. A grim bell tolls in our memory. Jesus gives the same reply to his interrogators: The only sign the world will get is the sign of Jonah (Matt. 12:39; 16:4). The reader remembers Jesus' own interpretation of this sign, that this sign entails the burial of the Son (compare Matt. 12:40). The readers of Matthew, then, are warned and forewarned. They are warned that the Pharisees and Sadducees are not on an innocent theological fishing expedition, and they are forewarned about the murderous undertones present in the Jesus story. The forces opposed to Jesus are beginning to gather, and Jesus is going to die.

The disciples, however, have been absent, traveling separately in a boat across the sea. They, too, must be warned, but Jesus' attempt to do so creates a labyrinth of communicational confusion (Matt. 16:5–12). When the disciples arrive, Jesus immediately attempts to alert them to the danger, only to be misunderstood. "Watch out," he cautions, "and beware of the yeast of the Pharisees and Sadducees" (Matt. 16:6). Jesus is, of course, using "yeast" figuratively—as a symbol for the penetrating power of false teaching—but the disciples take it literally and, therefore, mistakenly think that Jesus is scolding them for having forgotten to bring a supply of bread on the journey (Matt. 16:7).

Their literalism does prompt a rebuke from Jesus—"you of little faith"—a reprimand the disciples have heard before (see Matt. 6:30; 8:26; and 14:31). In Matthew, "little faith" is not agnosticism or unbelief. It is *distracted* faith, faith that is shaken because it has drifted away from its anchorage in the kingdom of God. Followers of Jesus have "little faith" when they are distracted by everyday worries about food and clothing (Matt. 6:25–33), lose their confidence in God's care when storms trouble life's sea (Matt. 8:23–27; 14:28–33), or, as in this passage, are preoccupied with concerns about daily bread.

If the disciples had greater faith, they would be perceptive, and they would know that Jesus was issuing an urgent warning about false teaching and not literally talking about bread. If they had "great faith," like the Canaanite woman encountered shortly before (Matt. 15:21–28), they would know that anxiety about bread is a spiritual distraction, since God can and will provide bread (even if, like that woman said, it is crumbs that fall from the master's table; see Matthew 15:27).

So, there are actually two warnings in this passage, two ways that discipleship can be distracted. First, discipleship can be seduced by false teaching. Disciples are to focus upon the teaching of Jesus and not that of the Pharisees and Sadducees (Matt. 16:12). This warning about false teaching should not be taken to mean that a congregation or a church school class must study only Bible and doctrine and never examine any other "teaching"—world religions, current social concerns, family issues, philosophy, or the like. It does mean that the gospel received from Jesus stands at the center of our lives, and all else is interpreted through it. The church is always tempted to lose confidence in the gospel and to search around for a replacement. In Matthew's world, this was the problem with the teaching of the Pharisees and Sadducees; it was a formidable rival to the teaching of Jesus. It was like "yeast"; a little bit could pervade and taint the whole.

If the first danger comes from without, the second comes from within. Faith can be distracted not only by false teachers but also by trivialization. Jesus spoke solemnly and urgently to his disciples about the kingdom of heaven, but they thought he was talking about lunch. Jesus' message is always urgent and life-giving, always beckoning his followers to step out of the safety of conventional compromise and into the wind-blown adventure of faith, to the thrill of self-denial, to the possibility of bearing a cross and of saving one's life by losing it for Christ's sake; but his passionate call is often trivialized into an invitation to join a religious club that meets for tea and conversation on Sundays.

PETER'S CONFESSION
Matthew 16:13–20

16:13 Now when Jesus came into the district of Caesarea Philippi, he asked his disciples, "Who do people say that the Son of Man is?" 14 And they said, "Some say John the Baptist, but others Elijah, and still others Jeremiah or one of the prophets." 15 He said to them, "But who do you say that I am?" 16 Simon Peter answered, "You are the Messiah, the Son of the living God." 17 And Jesus answered him, "Blessed are you, Simon son of Jonah! For flesh

and blood has not revealed this to you, but my Father in heaven. [18] **And I tell you, you are Peter, and on this rock I will build my church, and the gates of Hades will not prevail against it.** [19] **I will give you the keys of the kingdom of heaven, and whatever you bind on earth will be bound in heaven, and whatever you loose on earth will be loosed in heaven."** [20] **Then he sternly ordered the disciples not to tell anyone that he was the Messiah.**

This is one of the most dramatic scenes in the Gospel of Matthew. In a stirring exchange of speeches, Peter names the mystery and declares that Jesus is "the Messiah, the Son of the living God," and Jesus responds by blessing Peter and announcing that he is the "rock" upon which Jesus will establish his church. Occurring near the midpoint in the Gospel, this encounter has the feel of a turning point, a telling event of recognition upon which the story of Jesus pivots.

Even so, it is important to observe that this passage brings to clear expression only what has already been disclosed. Even though no disciple has yet called Jesus "the Messiah," we are not surprised to learn this about Jesus. We have known it since the first sentence of the Gospel (see Matt. 1:1). Peter also names Jesus the "Son of the living God" (Matt. 16:16), but this is not new either; the disciples made a similar confession previously (Matt. 14:33). Also, many chapters earlier the reader was told about Simon's nickname, "Peter" (see Matt. 4:18), and we are already aware that Jesus' disciples share the authority of his ministry (see Matt. 10:1). This passage, then, is a culmination of prior elements in the Gospel. Streams that have sprung forth earlier in Matthew now flow together into a deep and refreshing pool, from which the rest of the Gospel will draw.

The scene occurs at Caesarea Philippi, a Roman city in the far northern reaches of Israel. Jesus begins the dialogue by inquiring of all the disciples how the populace understands him: "Who do people say that the Son of Man is?" (Matt. 16:13). Jesus is not taking a poll, feeling for the pulse of popular opinion. Instead, the point of his question is to provide a contrast between the way the world views Jesus and the way Jesus appears to the eyes of faith.

Who *do* people say Jesus is? The disciples give four answers: Some think of Jesus as John the Baptist, others as Elijah, still others as Jeremiah, and some as one of the prophets (Matt. 16:14). Each identification makes sense in its own way. John the Baptist, like Jesus, was a startling and controversial preacher of the kingdom, and even Herod thought of Jesus as a resurrected John the Baptist (Matt. 14:2); Old Testament prophecy indicated that the old prophet Elijah would reappear at the end of the age, as a signal of the arrival of the "great and terrible day of the LORD" (Mal. 4:5);

the suffering prophet Jeremiah, like Jesus, tangled with the authorities and experienced painful rejection; and the classical prophets, like Jesus, spoke with power as they announced the new action of God in the world.

In other words, Jesus has a point of contact with all of these popular understandings of him; each of these public angles on Jesus shows an awareness of some aspect of Jesus' ministry and character. Nevertheless, they all operate at the surface and represent a failure to discern the depth and fullness of Jesus' identity. To the popular mind, Jesus is déjà vu: John, Jeremiah, Elijah, or whoever. We've seen all this before. Nothing about Jesus is new, unique, or challenging; he is merely one of the old prophets recycled. The people have turned Jesus, who is a window to the kingdom of heaven, into a mirror. They look at Jesus but see only the reflection of religious ideas from their past.

Every age is tempted to transform Jesus into its own image. Jesus has been described as a great teacher of wisdom, a social reformer, a champion of individual freedom and worth, a gentle nature lover, a mystic, or a streetwise revolutionary. There are grains of truth in all of these depictions, but, in each case, people have pounded a peg labeled "Jesus" into a hole drilled to fit their own religious preconceptions.

The partial, one-sided, and finally mistaken understandings of Jesus held by the populace of Jesus' day simply serve as a backdrop for the true and full confession of Peter. "Who do *you* say that I am?" Jesus asks the disciples, and Peter steps forward as spokesman. The entire Gospel of Matthew has been building up to his response: "You are the Messiah, the Son of the living God" (Matt. 16:16).

To call Jesus "Messiah" (in Greek, "Christ") is to know that Jesus is the savior, the one who rescues a world in peril. It is the claim that Jesus is the fulfillment of the deep hope that God would produce an *ideal* king for Israel, a king who would fulfill every hunger of the nation for well-being, one who would bring peace, wisdom, righteousness, and prosperity (see comment on Matt. 1:1). To call Jesus the "Son of the living God" has two primary meanings. First, Jesus is the "*Son*," the human being whose union with God is so intimate that he participates in the very nature of God. Second, Jesus is the Son of the "*living God*" of Israel (see Hos. 1:10), the God who is the source of all life, the God who confers the gift of life upon all creatures, the creator God who summons the winds and scatters light across the sky, the God who sustains and nourishes the world, the God who knows the falling of a sparrow and who counts the hairs of human heads, the God whose own image has been imparted to human beings— not the lifeless, inanimate, spiritless, and defunct gods of other peoples.

How did Peter know that Jesus is "the Messiah, the Son of the living

God"? Was he a theological genius, the smartest pupil in Jesus' master disciples class? No, Peter was not a high achiever; he was, in the truest sense, a "*gifted* student." Peter's discernment of Jesus' identity was, in every way, a gift from God and not a human accomplishment. "Blessed are you," Jesus says to Peter. "You did not obtain this insight from human beings, but as a revelation from my Father in heaven" (see Matt. 16:17).

The fact that Peter's confession was, at one and the same time, both *his* confession of faith and a gift from God, yields at least two important insights. First, to come to faith in Jesus as the Christ, the Son of the living God, is finally to relinquish any sense of merit in having done so. Faith is not a gold medal in the spiritual high jump. It is not a sign of our ability to leap to new sacred heights; it is a sign of God's willingness to bend down to us, to be "Emmanuel" in our world. Peter is able to say what he does only because God came near to Peter through Jesus, the Son. Peter is not merely informed about Jesus; Peter *knows* Jesus, an intimacy possible, of course, only because Jesus has entered into communion with Peter. Jesus has given himself, given the very self of God, to Peter, and Peter's confession, then, is not an answer to a theological riddle; it is the expression of a profound relationship.

In the second place, however, this does not mean that faith comes only through mystical experience, irrational illumination, or some kind of channeling of the divine Spirit. The Gospel of Matthew makes it absolutely clear that Jesus was a teacher and the disciples were diligent students under his instruction. Peter was in class every day, listening to Jesus' words, watching Jesus perform kingdom deeds. Peter's faith was a disciplined, "schooled," informed faith.

After blessing Peter, Jesus made a promise to him that has sparked controversy throughout the history of the Christian church: "And I tell you, you are Peter (in Greek, *Petros*), and on this rock (in Greek, *petra*) I will build my church" (Matt. 16:18). Since, in the original Greek, *Petros* and *petra* both mean "rock," it is easy to spot this statement as a pun, a play on words: "Your name is 'Rock,' and on this 'rock' I will build my church." Jesus' meaning is plain: Peter is the rock, the foundation, upon which he is going to erect his church.

However, many interpreters, particularly Protestants, have resisted this interpretation, mainly because it gives special importance to Peter and seems to reinforce later Roman Catholic claims about Peter as the first in a long line of popes. These interpreters have pointed, among other things, to the fact that *Petros* is masculine and *petra* feminine. This grammatical difference, they have argued, indicates that Jesus is referring not to Peter, but to some other "rock" on which he will build his church—maybe on

Peter's faith, or on the revelation given to him, or, perhaps, on Jesus Christ himself.

Jesus spoke Aramaic, however, not Greek. In Aramaic, the words for "Peter" and "rock" are the same (*Kepha*). Moreover, Reformation-era disputes should not be read back into this text. This is not a passage about the papacy; it is a story about Peter and Jesus, and the most plausible interpretation of the passage is that Jesus is, indeed, pointing to Peter as the foundation stone, the principal leader, of this new people of God. Peter continued, of course, to be the flawed, fearful, sink-in-the-sea human being that he had always been (in fact, this "rock" will, within minutes, become a "stumbling block"; see Matthew 16:23), but there is much evidence that he also played a primary leadership role in the early Christian church. He was the first disciple Jesus called (Matt. 4:18–20); he is named first in all lists of the disciples (see, for example, Matt. 10:1–4); on Pentecost, he serves as the preacher and interpreter of the Christian movement (see Acts 2:14); throughout the book of Acts, he can be seen exercising leadership in church deliberations (see, for example, Acts 15:6–7); and even Paul recognizes Peter's special place in the new community of faith (see Gal. 1:18; 1 Cor. 15:5). For the church, the new people of God, Peter was, indeed, the "rock," corresponding to Abraham of old, who was "the rock from which you were hewn" (Isa. 51:1).

To his promise to build the church on the foundation of Peter, the "rock," Jesus added two words. First, Jesus assured Peter that "the gates of Hades [hell] will not prevail against" the church (Matt. 16:18). The "gates of hell" is a symbol for everything that opposes God's will—the powers of death and destruction that ravage human life. Jesus' promise does not mean that the church will be free of trouble. Indeed, through the ages the church has experienced every kind of distress imaginable. The promise is not that the Christians will not go through hell; the promise is that hell does not hold the winning hand and that the powers of death will not have the last word. When all is said and done, hell's devastation will be exposed as an empty threat because Jesus, who calmed the savage winds, shouted out the chaotic demons, subdued the devastation of disease, and conquered death, will save and protect his own.

Second, Jesus gave to Peter (and, beyond, to the whole church; see Matthew 18:18) the "keys of the kingdom of heaven" (Matt. 16:19). The picture of Saint Peter, keys in hand, standing guard at the gates of heaven, the staple of a thousand jokes, is a misunderstanding of this passage. The "keys" are a symbol of the church's authority on earth, and the point here is that what the church does—the decisions it makes, the grace it expresses, the stands it takes, the truths it teaches—matters to God. When the church wrestles with a controversial issue, tries to speak the gospel to one who is alienated from God, provides hospitality to a stranger, teaches the faith to a child, or cares for those in need, it is not just "playing church"; it is acting out God's future—the kingdom of heaven—in the present and, thereby, participating in the very life of God, sharing in the power of God. When the church faithfully calls itself and the world to ethical responsibility ("whatever you bind on earth") and when the church truly proclaims God's free forgiveness to one who has failed to live up to that responsibility ("whatever you loose on earth"), it is not just the church that acts; God acts in and through the church.

To possess "the keys of the kingdom of heaven" does not mean, of course, that the church is never wrong, that the church somehow has God on a string, or that God promises to uphold everything the church does no matter what. What it does mean is that God will not abandon the church, indeed, that God works in the church to keep it faithful and through the church to give faith to the world.

This passage concludes with a mysterious message: Jesus sternly orders the disciples not to let the secret out that he is the Messiah (Matt. 16:20). Why? Why would Jesus not want his disciples to spread the good news? The reason is that there are two ways to distort and misunderstand Jesus: One is to get the word about him all wrong; the other is to get it half right. At this point, the disciples have it right, but only half right. They know that Jesus is truly the Messiah, but they do not yet understand the companion truth: Jesus, the Messiah, must suffer and die. If they were to become evangelists at this moment, they would proclaim a half truth—a cost-free gospel, Jesus without the cross. The disciples, as we will soon see, do not yet understand this. Until the story is complete, then, they are to remain silent; later they will be commanded to tell the whole truth to the whole world (see Matt. 28:19–20), but on this side of the cross, they have only half a truth.

10. The Cross Looms Ahead
Matthew 16:21–17:27

Matthew's story of Jesus now moves toward its conclusion as Jesus turns his face toward Jerusalem and toward his inevitable death. Death is no stranger to the Gospel of Matthew. Herod greeted the birth of Jesus with a bloodbath of children in Bethlehem (Matt. 2:16); Jesus has ominously predicted that his disciples will fast when the "bridegroom is taken away from them" (Matt. 9:15) and warned about those who would "kill the body"; Matthew has told of the Pharisees meeting to plot Jesus' doom (Matt. 12:14); Jesus himself has spoken of his Jonah-like burial (Matt. 12:40); and John the Baptist, who blazed the trail for Jesus with his preaching, also prepared the way for him in his death (Matt. 14:3–12; see Garland, *Reading Matthew*, 177). These foreshadowings of death now increase in volume as Jesus heads into Jerusalem, the city that kills prophets (Matt. 23:37).

JESUS ANNOUNCES
HIS IMPENDING DEATH
Matthew 16:21–23

16:21 **From that time on, Jesus began to show his disciples that he must go to Jerusalem and undergo great suffering at the hands of the elders and chief priests and scribes, and be killed, and on the third day be raised.** 22 **And Peter took him aside and began to rebuke him, saying, "God forbid it, Lord! This must never happen to you."** 23 **But he turned and said to Peter, "Get behind me, Satan! You are a stumbling block to me; for you are setting your mind not on divine things but on human things."**

Peter has just announced that Jesus is the "Messiah, the Son of the living God" (Matt. 16:16). Now Peter and the other disciples are told the other half of the gospel truth: The messianic road leads to the cross. The phrasing here—"Jesus began to show"—is significant, because this hard lesson about suffering and death will take more than one session to sink in. Indeed, on four separate occasions in Matthew, Jesus announces his impending death to his disciples (see also Matt. 17:22–23; 20:17–19; and 26:2).

Hearing this startling news for the first time, Peter, who only moments before was the solid rock upon which the church would be built (Matt. 16:18), suddenly crumbles into a lesser kind of stone—a stumbling block (Matt. 16:23). Unable to stand the thought that Jesus would suffer and be murdered, he scolds Jesus for having such ideas: "God forbid it, Lord! This must never happen to you" (Matt. 16:22). Peter said this to Jesus privately, taking him aside to talk some sense into his head. Jesus, however, saw it not as an attempt to "take him aside," but as an effort to "pull him off course" with human folly, or worse, as yet another Satanic temptation. Indeed, Peter's attempt to persuade Jesus that he could be the glorified Messiah without having to go through the messiness of suffering and death is a strong reminder of Satan's third temptation of Jesus, the seductive possibility that Jesus could instantly have "all the kingdoms of the world and their splendor" (Matt. 4:8) at low cost and with no pain (see comments on Matt. 4:1–11). Recognizing Peter's devilish suggestion for what it was, Jesus resisted him with verbal force, "Get behind me, Satan! . . . for you are setting your mind not on divine things but on human things" (Matt. 16:23).

This, then, is a contest of minds and wills—Peter's mind versus Jesus' mind; human will against the will of God. Thinking in human terms, Peter is shocked and offended by the announcement that Jesus will suffer and die. Peter is like a man who has just been named campaign manager of a promising presidential candidate who astonishingly hears the candidate proclaim that he can accomplish his goals only by being assassinated. Humanly speaking, the concept of a suffering, dying Messiah is absurd, a contradiction in terms. The Messiah is God's strong agent; suffering is weakness. The Messiah is supposed to save and liberate God's people, not be killed by the oppressors. The idea of a crucified Messiah violates religious expectation and defies reason. Jesus is to be God's strong Messiah through the weakness of suffering, and Jesus will liberate and save God's people through losing his own life. This is God's way, and Jesus, obedient to God's way, will not be swayed by human thoughts. If Peter cannot accept in trust the "stumbling block" of the cross, then he will himself become a "stumbling block" strewn in the pathway of God's Son.

THE CROSS AND GLORY
Matthew 16:24–28

16:24 **Then Jesus told his disciples, "If any want to become my followers, let them deny themselves and take up their cross and follow me.** 25 **For those who want to save their life will lose it, and those who lose their life for my sake will find it.** 26 **For what will it profit them if they gain the whole world but forfeit their life? Or what will they give in return for their life?**

27 **"For the Son of Man is to come with his angels in the glory of his Father, and then he will repay everyone for what has been done.** 28 **Truly I tell you, there are some standing here who will not taste death before they see the Son of Man coming in his kingdom."**

Peter was shocked and offended by the thought that the cross was God's will for Jesus (Matt. 16:21–23), and now Jesus deepens the offense by reminding the disciples that the cross is God's will for them, too (Matt. 16:24–26). This is the second time in Matthew that Jesus has called his followers to imitate him by taking up their own crosses (see comments on Matt. 10:38–39), but this time the cross, the symbol of suffering, is paired with a picture of triumph, the "Son of Man . . . [coming] with his angels in the glory of his Father" (Matt. 16:27). The effect of contrasting the humility of carrying a cross with the glory of God's victory is to highlight the difference for people of faith between appearance and reality, the distinction that Peter blurred between "divine things" and "human things" (Matt. 16:23).

This division between what the cross means in the eyes of the world and what it means in kingdom terms runs like a cord through the heart of this passage. On the one side, the command to bear a cross is a crisis for Jesus' followers because it appears to be the way of losers and the path to defeat. Bearing a cross means more than just reaching down to help struggling people; it means following in the way of Jesus, and that involves standing with those who are weak, opening the doors to those who are unacceptable, loving those who are unlovely. Cross bearers forfeit the game of power before the first inning; they are never selected as "Most Likely to Succeed." Cross bearers are dropouts in the school of self-promotion. They do not pick up their crosses as a means for personal fulfillment, career advancement, or self-expression; rather, they "deny themselves" (Matt. 16:24) and pick up their crosses, like their Lord, because of the needs of other people.

Most cross bearers do not literally pay the price with their own blood. Unlike Jesus, most of his followers are not actually killed for their faithful obedience to God, but it should not be forgotten that some are. Most Christians carry crosses of quiet self-sacrifice and compassionate service to the needs of others, but in every period of history there have always been Christians for whom the cross has been more than just a symbol, for whom "losing their life for Christ's sake" is more than a figure of speech.

So, from the vantage point of the world, nothing could be more self-defeating, foolish, and wasteful than laying down one's personal agenda and picking up a cross—the crude, cruel instrument of suffering and loss. When the curtain of the kingdom is drawn back, however, another picture is revealed. Bearing a cross may look to the world like a tragedy, but in God's eyes it is a triumph. Suffering on behalf of others may appear to be pouring one's life down the bottomless drain of human need, but in the kingdom it is what it means to save one's life (Matt. 16:25). It is the mystery of the gospel that what appears to crush everything one hopes to be as a human being—bearing the cross of service and suffering—is in fact the only way for a human being to be fully alive (Matt. 16:25–26).

Despite its ominous sound, Jesus' word that, when the Son of Man comes in glory, "he will repay everyone for what has been done" (Matt. 16:27) is a promise, not a threat. It is a word of assurance to Jesus' followers that, although the cross may look insignificant and foolish to the world, bearing a cross counts in the kingdom of heaven, counts to God. A life that is spent soothing the pain of the sick, caring for children in need, hammering nails in houses for those without shelter, sharing bread with the hungry, visiting those in prison, and denying oneself may seem like a squandered life in the economy of a self-centered age, but in the storehouse of heaven, it is a lavish treasure.

Many have been perplexed by the apparent contradiction of Jesus' closing statement that "there are some standing here who will not taste death before they see the Son of Man coming in his kingdom" (Matt. 16:28). Everyone who heard this statement is, of course, long since dead, and the kingdom has not yet come. Some scholars surmise that this statement is left over from the earliest days of the Christian movement, a time when Christians believed themselves to be living in the final days, when they expected the return of Jesus at any moment and the world to be brought to an end in their lifetimes. The problem with this view is that Matthew, who wrote several decades after the time of Jesus, would surely know better.

Matthew, then, probably understood this saying of Jesus to pertain not to the final victory of God at the end of time but to an event in which the disciples glimpsed this victory in advance, when they saw a foretaste of what the whole creation will eventually see. There are two likely possibilities: Jesus' appearance to the disciples after the resurrection and the transfiguration. Of these two, the latter is the more likely reference, for it follows immediately in Matthew.

THE TRANSFIGURATION OF JESUS
Matthew 17:1–13

17:1 Six days later, Jesus took with him Peter and James and his brother John and led them up a high mountain, by themselves. ² And he was transfigured before them, and his face shone like the sun, and his clothes became dazzling white. ³ Suddenly there appeared to them Moses and Elijah, talking with him. ⁴ Then Peter said to Jesus, "Lord, it is good for us to be here; if you wish, I will make three dwellings here, one for you, one for Moses, and one for Elijah." ⁵ While he was still speaking, suddenly a bright cloud overshadowed them, and from the cloud a voice said, "This is my Son, the Beloved; with him I am well pleased; listen to him!" ⁶ When the disciples heard this, they fell to the ground and were overcome by fear. ⁷ But Jesus came and touched them, saying, "Get up and do not be afraid." ⁸ And when they looked up, they saw no one except Jesus himself alone.

⁹ As they were coming down the mountain, Jesus ordered them, "Tell no one about the vision until after the Son of Man has been raised from the dead." ¹⁰ And the disciples asked him, "Why, then, do the scribes say that Elijah must come first?" ¹¹ He replied, "Elijah is indeed coming and will restore all things; ¹² but I tell you that Elijah has already come, and they did not recognize him, but they did to him whatever they pleased. So also the Son of Man is about to suffer at their hands." ¹³ Then the disciples understood that he was speaking to them about John the Baptist.

Many of the details of this story are strongly reminiscent of Moses' encounter with God on Mount Sinai (Exod. 24:12–34:35). Both were "mountaintop" events (Exod. 24:12; Matt. 17:1); both stories involve a divine manifestation "after six days" (Exod. 24:16; Matt. 17:1); both include God speaking out of a cloud (Exod. 24:16; Matt. 17:5); and the faces of both Moses and Jesus become luminous (Exod. 34:29; Matt. 17:2).

Even by New Testament standards, this is an unusual story. In some ways, it moves along like a regular narrative, but there are misty, dreamlike qualities in it as well. It seems both real and surreal. Later, Jesus himself will call it a "vision" (Matt. 17:9). In order to understand the full range of meaning in this curious passage, we must be alert to the kind of "vision" it is. We must pay attention not only to *what* this story says but also to *how* it says it, because this text uses the language and tactics of a very stylized form of visionary literature known as "apocalyptic."

One major purpose of apocalyptic literature is to pull back the curtain, to lift the veil, so that what is normally hidden—the action of God, the hidden ways of heaven—can be seen (in fact, the word *apocalypse* means "revelation"). Thus, apocalyptic texts often involve revelatory dreams and visions (see Dan. 7:1) in which the activity of God is disclosed. Because apocalyptic passages are about revelations and prophetic dreams of the heavenly world beyond the pale of human vision, they often employ strange language and fantastic symbols. Since God's activity is hidden from normal human sight, apocalyptic texts seek to provide extraordinary vision by pulling back the heavenly shroud to reveal, if only for an instant, the incognito activity of God, woven undetected into the fabric of human history and disguised in the ordinariness of life.

When Jesus' face begins to shine and his clothes become luminous, it is not because of some mutation in him; it is a disclosure of what is already true about him—a sign of his glory, an apocalyptic way of saying, "Look! This Jesus of splendor is who he really is." When Jesus is accompanied by Moses and Elijah, it is a pulling back of the curtains of time to show that Jesus is continuous with all that God has promised and given in the Law and the Prophets; when Jesus stands alone at the end of the story, it is a revelation of the truth that the Law and the Prophets have been fulfilled and magnified in him.

If someone stands on the bank of a lake and gazes into the water, often the glare of sunlight on the water allows only the surface to be seen. If a cloud passes overhead, however, suddenly the surface is made transparent and the depths of the lake revealed. Just so, the passing overhead of the divine cloud in this passage enables the disciples—and the readers—to see past the surface identity into the depths of the full nature of Jesus.

The difference between the surface and the depths, between the glare from Jesus that history can see and the profound Jesus revealed in this apocalyptic vision of faith, is striking. Historically speaking, Jesus is on a death march, entering the gloomiest season of his life. In the heavenly light, however, his face and clothes gleam with the favor of God. The earthly Jesus is headed toward his doom on the cross, but suddenly we see not a victim, but a victor; not the one despised and rejected by the world, but the one beloved and well pleasing to God.

The story of the transfiguration is positioned, theologically, between Jesus' baptism and his resurrection. Imagine that the life of Jesus is a highway and that, as we travel along, we come across three road signs with messages from God about Jesus. We see the first road sign at the very beginning of the journey, at Jesus' baptism, and it announces the heavenly identity of Jesus: "This is my Son, the Beloved, with whom I am well pleased" (Matt. 3:17). At the dawn of Jesus' ministry, before he has performed a single deed, healed a single person, or taught a single truth, he is already who he will show himself to be—the divine Son.

The second road sign occurs in the middle of the journey, here at the transfiguration, and it has a twofold message. Initially, this second sign simply repeats the message of the first: "This is my Son, the Beloved; with him I am well pleased" (Matt. 17:5). This repetition causes us, of course, to remember Jesus' baptism and to recognize that God is validating Jesus' ministry. God's word says, in effect, "This Jesus is *still* my Beloved Son, and with all that he has done—his teaching and his healing, his compassion and his conflict—I am indeed well pleased."

This second road sign does more, however, than merely repeat the message of the first; it adds a new word, a command to obey Jesus: "Listen to him!" (Matt. 17:5). This word is a preview of things to come, an anticipation of the victorious completion of Jesus' ministry and the authority that will be given to the risen Christ (Matt. 28:18).

Several students of the Gospel of Matthew have pointed to the contrasting parallels between Matthew's description of the transfiguration and the account of the crucifixion. In the transfiguration, Jesus' clothes shine with the glory of God; at the crucifixion, the soldiers gamble over his garments. In the transfiguration, Jesus is surrounded by Moses and Elijah, at the cross by two criminals. In the transfiguration, Jesus is declared to be "God's Son" by the voice of God from the cloud; at the crucifixion, the words "he said, 'I am God's Son'" become a taunt of mockery on the lips of the religious authorities. At the end of the transfiguration, Moses and Elijah have departed, leaving Jesus to stand in singular glory; at the end of the crucifixion, Jesus dies in humiliation while the crowd stands around waiting to see "whether Elijah will come to save him." In both events, three of Jesus' followers are specified as witnesses—the transfiguration by Peter, James, and John, and the crucifixion by Mary Magdalene, the other Mary, and Salome, the mother of Zebedee's sons. The parallels suggest that we are to read one story in the light of the other, anticipating in the shining splendor of the transfiguration the suffering by which this glory will be won and discerning in the shame of the cross the very glory of God (Garland, *Reading Matthew*, 183–84).

The three disciples—Peter, James, and John—play a significant and representative role in this story. They become gradually transfigured, too, shifting and changing through the story, modeling the stages of faith's development. In the first stage, they are dazzled, astounded before the gathering of the great three: Jesus, Moses, and Elijah. They were, in this moment, like all new converts, like all in the first blush of religious experience—intensely joyful and possessed of a feeling of fullness and completion. The presence of Jesus together with these two heroes of the faith was a sign that the messianic age had arrived; what the ages had expected and yearned for had, at last, arrived. No wonder Peter is glad to be pres ent and wants to halt the story here, to call for an orchestral swell and the rolling of the closing credits: Jesus . . . Moses . . . Elijah. His statement is a sign of contented obedience: "if you wish"; and satisfied devotion: "I will make three dwellings here" (Matt. 17:4).

But the story does not end here; there is more in store for the disciples. The vision of Jesus, Moses, and Elijah is but a call to worship, and the preaching is to follow: "This Jesus alone," the voice of God says sermonically, "is my Son, my Beloved, the One upon whom my blessing lies. Obey his teaching. Follow his commandments. Be his disciples. Listen to him!" At this the disciples fall down in fear (Matt. 17:6). Fear is a common reaction to apocalyptic visions (see, for example, Dan. 8:17; 10:7–9), but what was it, exactly, that frightened them? The presence of God, the voice of God? Yes, surely. But perhaps also they were frightened and overwhelmed by the command to listen to Jesus, by the thought that every word of Jesus—even the one, perhaps especially the one, about taking up a cross and following (Matthew 16:24; significantly, the next time that Peter, James, and John will be mentioned together is at Gethsemane, Matthew 26:37)—was more than a religious idea to be thoughtfully considered and debated. Rather, his words were ethical mandates to be obeyed. Stop the story; stop the kingdom; they wanted to get off.

But the story kept unfolding. Jesus, who touched the leper (Matt. 8:3), who touched the hand of the fevered woman (Matt. 8:15), who touched the eyes of the blind men (Matt. 9:29), now healingly touches Peter, James, and John. "Get up" (literally, "be raised"), Jesus says to them, "and do not be afraid" (Matt. 17:7). Daniel of old heard these same words after his vision (see Dan. 10:2–14), but the hopeful command not to fear would be most powerfully heard after the resurrection (see Matt. 28:5, 10).

Coming down the mountain, Jesus orders Peter, James, and John not to tell anyone about the vision they have seen until after the resurrection (Matt. 17:9; for an understanding of this command to secrecy, see comments on Matthew 16:20). These disciples then ask Jesus a question about biblical interpretation that must surely have mirrored a similar concern in Matthew's church. A well-known Old Testament text, Malachi 4:5–6, implied that Elijah would return before the messiah came. Probably, the early Christians in Matthew's church were embarrassed by the challenge from the synagogue that Jesus could not possibly be the messiah they claimed him to be since Elijah had not yet arrived.

Jesus' answer to this challenge is similar to his "you have heard that it was said . . . , but I say to you" formula in the Sermon on the Mount. He affirms the prophecy—"Elijah is indeed coming and will restore all things" (Matt. 17:11)—but then he reinterprets it in new, kingdom terms.

Elijah, in fact, has already come symbolically in the form of John the Baptist (Matt. 17:12; see Matt. 11:14). Because the literal-minded religious authorities lacked the vision of the kingdom, they could not see God fulfilling this old prophetic promise in a new way. When the kingdom encounters closed minds and eyes, violence often results, and, indeed, "they did to [John] whatever they pleased." Jesus, himself, will share his fate (Matt. 17:12).

THE EPILEPTIC BOY
AND THE DISCIPLES' "LITTLE FAITH"
Matthew 17:14–20

> 17:14 **When they came to the crowd, a man came to him, knelt before him,** [15] **and said, "Lord, have mercy on my son, for he is an epileptic and he suffers terribly; he often falls into the fire and often into the water.** [16] **And I brought him to your disciples, but they could not cure him."** [17] **Jesus answered, "You faithless and perverse generation, how much longer must I be with you? How much longer must I put up with you? Bring him here to me."** [18] **And Jesus rebuked the demon, and it came out of him, and the boy was cured instantly.** [19] **Then the disciples came to Jesus privately and said, "Why could we not cast it out?"** [20] **He said to them, "Because of your little faith. For truly I tell you, if you have faith the size of a mustard seed, you will say to this mountain, 'Move from here to there,' and it will move; and nothing will be impossible for you."**

Jesus and the disciples rejoin the crowd, and immediately a desperate father approaches Jesus on behalf of his diseased son. His appeal is more than an urgent request; it has the posture and the tone of worshipful prayer. The father kneels down before Jesus and addresses him as "Lord." In his petition he does not merely name his son's need; like one in heartfelt prayer, he honestly and movingly pours out a narrative of the boy's suffering.

The news of the disciples' failure evokes from Jesus an Old Testament-style lament in which Jesus echoes the bemoaning over rebellious Israel done by Moses ("You faithless and perverse generation"; see Deut. 32:5) but also by God ("how much longer must I put up with you?"; see Num. 14:27). In short, the disciples have become like a previous "generation" of God's people, Israel in the wilderness—contentious and disobedient. Even though Jesus has already given his disciples authority over demons (see Matt. 10:1), Jesus knows the disciples have faltered, and he must respond himself to the father's needs. Just as he rebuked the unruly powers in the winds and the waves (Matt. 8:26), Jesus rebukes the evil spirit in the boy, and he is, like others, instantly cured (see Matt. 8:13; 15:28).

The real point of interest in the story comes with the surely sad and abashed inquiry of the disciples, "Why could we not cast it out?" (Matt. 17:19). Previously Jesus told his disciples to "cast out demons" (Matt. 10:8), but now they have tried it, and something has gone awry. The problem, Jesus tells them, is a familiar one; their "little faith" has again deterred them (see Matt. 6:30; 8:26; 14:31; and 16:8). In Matthew, the phrase "little faith," we have already learned, is not disbelief, but distracted and divided faith (see comment on Matt. 16:1–12). The twelve have tried their hand at being disciples, at being ministers of Jesus, but they have become distracted by the difficulties; their trust in God has wavered, and they have become fearful.

Jesus says that the disciples' problem is "little faith." As a matter of logic, then, it would seem that what they need is "big faith." Seemingly, the cure for "little faith" is faith with some size, faith as massive as Mount Nebo, faith as large as a great cedar of Lebanon. But there is a surprise waiting in this story. Astonishingly, Jesus tells them that what they need is to have "faith the size of a mustard seed" (Matt. 17:20). But the mustard seed has already been described as "the smallest of all the seeds" (Matt. 13:32), so how is it that mustard–seed-sized faith can serve as a remedy for "little faith"?

The answer lies in the difference between "little faith" and "faith the size of a mustard seed." Both are small, but in different ways. "Little faith" is small in that it has lost confidence in God's promise and power. "Little faith" sees the demons very clearly, but it loses sight of God's saving purpose. "Little faith" is strong in the morning, setting out to show compassion to the poor, exercise mercy to the sick, stand for justice for the oppressed, and bring peace to places of strife. By the end of the day, though, spirits have sagged and knees have buckled. The poor are too many, disease seems always to have the last word, trips to the cemetery are too frequent, the unjust are too strong, and the roots of evil too deeply entrenched. The gospel appears too little to go on, disciples are too few to make a difference, and trying to follow Jesus in this kind of world begins to seem like bailing out the ocean with a leaky bucket. "Little faith" moves from distraction, to despair, and finally to defeat. The world is the way it is, and that's that.

Mustard-seed faith is small, too, but in a different way. Like "little faith," it knows that it is always surrounded by troubles of great size, but it rests its hope in the ultimate victory of God. Like a mustard seed, this kind of faith looks puny when planted in the soil of a troubled earth, but the gardener knows that the tiny mustard seed, by God's providence, will eventually grow into a great shrub. Mustard-seed faith is the faith that, even though compassion and mercy seem overwhelmed by the immense cruelty in the world, what is done in Christ's name really counts and that God's saving purpose will ultimately prevail over all that opposes it.

Jesus promises the disciples that, if they have faith the size of a mustard seed, they can command mountains to move—indeed, that "nothing will be impossible." Jesus is not telling his followers that they will become magicians, waving a wand and making the Rocky Mountains jump to the east coast. He is promising that the kingdom of heaven is sure, that one day all of the mountains that separate human life from God—evil, poverty, suffering, and death—will be shoved aside by the mercy of God, and the whole creation will become a plain of righteousness and peace. Therefore, what disciples of Jesus Christ do today genuinely matters to God; though they are few in number and frail, they can boldly walk up to the mountain range of sorrow and put their shoulders against the seemingly unyielding mass, confident that one day the boulders will shift and the mountain will yield to the glory of God.

THE SECOND ANNOUNCEMENT OF JESUS' DEATH
Matthew 17:22–23

17:22 **As they were gathering in Galilee, Jesus said to them, "The Son of Man is going to be betrayed into human hands,** [23] **and they will kill him, and on the third day he will be raised." And they were greatly distressed.**

For the second of four times, Jesus announces that he will die and be raised from the dead (see comment on Matt. 16:21–23). The NRSV translation reads the "Son of Man is going to be betrayed into human hands," and the verb "betrayed" serves apparently as a reference to Judas' act of treachery. An alternative, and perhaps more accurate, translation of the Greek verb is "the Son of Man is going to be *given up into* human hands," a probable reference not to Judas but to God's offering of Jesus on behalf of humanity. Paul employs the same verb in Romans 8:32 when he says that God did not withhold his own Son, "but gave him up for all of us."

The first time they heard this word, the disciples fastened only on the part about Jesus' suffering and death, and they resisted it (Matt. 16:22). This time, they still can hear only the bad news of Jesus' death and not the good news of his resurrection, but at least they have moved from stubborn resistance to heartfelt sorrow (Matt. 17:23). In short, they have grown, but they still have more to learn. In time, they will know and embrace the full and joyous truth—that this Jesus, murdered by human hands, has been raised by God, and all authority in heaven and on earth has been given to him (see Matt. 28:18).

JESUS AND THE TEMPLE TAX
Matthew 17:24–27

> 17:24 When they reached Capernaum, the collectors of the temple tax came to Peter and said, "Does your teacher not pay the temple tax?" 25 He said, "Yes, he does." And when he came home, Jesus spoke of it first, asking, "What do you think, Simon? From whom do kings of the earth take toll or tribute? From their children or from others?" 26 When Peter said, "From others," Jesus said to him, "Then the children are free. 27 However, so that we do not give offense to them, go to the sea and cast a hook; take the first fish that comes up; and when you open its mouth, you will find a coin; take that and give it to them for you and me."

The question about tax was a political hot potato. In Jesus' day, Jewish males nineteen and older were expected to pay an annual tax of two drachmas (equal to a half shekel) for the upkeep of the temple. This tax was rooted in the Old Testament law that required each male in Israel to give a half shekel of "atonement money" to be used for the support of the tent of meeting (Exod. 30:11–16). Like most taxes, however, this one was popular with few and actively resisted by some. Groups like the Pharisees supported the tax, but many other Jews found some way to claim an exemption, simply neglected to pay, or vigorously refused to pay as a matter of principle and an act of protest against the temple establishment.

So the tax collectors' question is not innocent. They want to know if Jesus is loyal to the temple or not. The tax collectors are not asking if Jesus' current tax bill is paid up; rather, they are asking whether he is an establishment man or a tax rebel, a part of the mainstream in Judaism or on the fringe.

Peter immediately answers that, yes, Jesus does pay the tax, but there is at least a hint that he is not really sure about this. Perhaps Peter is guessing that Jesus would surely obey the commandments, or maybe he was just dodging a confrontation with the revenuers. In any case, back at the house, Jesus initiates an exchange with Peter about the tax matter, beginning with the question, "What do you think, Simon?" This open-ended way of introducing the topic has a parablelike sound, and it is a clue that what is to follow is a parabolic lesson about the kingdom (see the similar "What do you think?" construction prefacing the parable of the lost sheep, Matthew 18:12).

What Jesus wants Peter to think about is not the mundane question of whether they ought to pay the temple tax, but the larger relationship between those who have the authority to levy taxes and those who have to pay them. Think about those who have the authority to tax, Jesus says. Do they squeeze taxes from their own children or from others? Peter gives the obvious answer, "From others." That is right, Jesus responds. No king would tax his own children; "the children are free" (Matt. 17:26).

Notice how Jesus has shifted this matter to a higher plain. Presumably the temple tax collectors would describe this tax not merely as maintenance money for the institution but, ultimately, as a tax paid to *God*. Ah, that is the real question Jesus wants Peter to ponder: Do we owe tax to God? The answer to that question, Jesus suggests, depends upon whether we think of ourselves as God's children or as God's vassals. Vassals pay tax; children do not. Jesus the Son has come to make people daughters and sons of God, and "the children are free."

So, the children of God are not taxed by God, and, if that were all there were to say, then Jesus and the disciples would pay no tax. But Jesus does not leave the matter there. Having staked out the freedom not to pay, Jesus turns around and commands Peter to pay the tax for both of them "so that we do not give offense to them" (Matt. 17:27). In other words, they are not obligated to pay the tax, but they are free to choose to pay. However, Peter is to get the money in a strange way. He is to go fishing and find the money to pay the tax in the mouth of the first fish he catches (Matt. 17:27).

What does this all mean? This story should probably be read on at least three levels. At the most practical level, this story no doubt reflects the struggle of Matthew's church to live in reasonable peace as a minority party within Judaism. The relationship between Matthew's group of Jewish Christians and other Jews in the area was undoubtedly strained (see Introduction), and the question must have arisen on a number of occasions and in a variety of ways, Are Christians still obliged to support the old religious structures they left behind? The message of this story is that, even though Christians are children of the heavenly king and free from such obligations, they are also free out of love for the neighbor (and in reverence for their Jewish roots) to give as a gift the support they are not legally bound to provide.

At a second, and deeper, level, however, this story is a metaphor of the freedom of the Christian life. This story contrasts what may be called "the world of taxation" with "the world of God's children." The world of taxation is a burden; we earn so much, we own so much, we control so much, but we are obliged to pay so much. This part is mine; that part, the tax, is theirs; it belongs to the government. Now if God is like a giant tax collector, then the main religious question is, "OK, God, how much do I owe?"

But what if we saw that we live in another world? What if we are not debtors to a potentate, but children at home in a household of love? If so, the question of life changes from "How much do we owe?" to "How can we, as God's cherished children of freedom, shower upon others the gifts we have freely received?"

Where will we get these gifts—the money, the mercy, the patience, the food, the time, and the whatever else needed? We will get them, Jesus promises, as unmerited gifts from God, something like finding an unexpected coin resting in the mouth of a fish that happens to swim by. Jesus is not talking about a magic trick or even a miracle in the typical sense; the coin in the fish's mouth is a parable of the whole Christian life. When we put aside any thoughts that we have earned this and deserved that, when we think about our lives as children of the heavenly king, then we see that pulling wonderful unmerited gifts from the endless bounty of God's merciful sea is the way everything comes to us—everything, every day.

There is a third, even more profound, level at which this story may be read. In its origins, the temple tax was "atonement money," or as Exodus puts it, "a reminder to the Israelites of the ransom given for your lives" (Exod. 30:16). It is, of course, Jesus, the true Son of God, the child of heaven who is genuinely free, who will himself be the ransom given for our lives. Now he instructs Peter to take the offering for the temple. Very soon, Jesus himself will go down from the Mount of Olives, enter the temple, and become himself the freely given offering of the atonement.

11. Living Together as the Church
Matthew 18:1–35

At the end of Matthew 17, Jesus was at home in Capernaum in Galilee. At the beginning of chapter 19, he will leave Galilee and begin his march toward Jerusalem, toward the cross, toward his death. Thus, Matthew 18—the fourth of five major sections of Jesus' teaching in the Gospel (see Introduction)—is poised at a critical juncture in the Gospel narrative. The Galilean ministry is finished; the story of the crucifixion is about to begin. As such, this chapter in Matthew describes an uncommon teaching moment as Jesus turns to instruct his disciples at the outset of his decisive journey to the cross.

And what does Jesus select as his topic at this dramatic turn? Jesus chooses this occasion to give his disciples lessons on church polity. He instructs them on such seemingly routine matters as the nature of leadership in the Christian community, the role of nurture and pastoral care, what to do when conflict breaks out in the congregation, and the importance of forgiveness among church members—the sorts of everyday practical and ethical concerns that all Christians trying to live together have. In fact, some interpreters have seen this section of the Gospel as something like "the book of church order" for Matthew's church.

Upon reflection, though, it is not really a surprise that Jesus teaches about church leadership and order at this climactic moment. Jesus' life is entering its last and fatal phase, but his ministry will not end with his death. Jesus' mission will continue—in and through the church. The church will extend Jesus' message and ministry beyond Israel to the ends of the earth (see Matt. 28:16–20). The church is not merely a religious institution or a society for the preservation of good ideas about God. Rather, the church is a colony of the kingdom of heaven, Christ's own saving presence in human society. In the terms of Matthew's Gospel, the church is the salt of the earth, the light of the world, the leaven of mercy in the loaf of the world's misery.

Therefore, how the church lives together is of crucial importance.

When the world looks at the church, it should see not simply another social organization trying to raise money and keep its membership up; it should see a living embodiment of the kingdom of heaven, a community of faith where leaders serve instead of swagger, where the weak are nourished instead of cast aside, where people who lose their way are not forgotten but sought and restored, where people cultivate mercy and forgiveness as if they were the rare flowers of heaven.

GREATNESS AND LEADERSHIP
Matthew 18:1–5

18:1 **At that time the disciples came to Jesus and asked, "Who is the greatest in the kingdom of heaven?"** [2] **He called a child, whom he put among them,** [3] **and said, "Truly I tell you, unless you change and become like children, you will never enter the kingdom of heaven.** [4] **Whoever becomes humble like this child is the greatest in the kingdom of heaven.** [5] **Whoever welcomes one such child in my name welcomes me.**

Matthew, Mark, and Luke all report that the disciples asked the question, Who is the greatest? That sounds to us, quite naturally, like a vain question, and, indeed, in the context of both Mark and Luke, it is. Matthew, however, is different. The disciples' question about who is the greatest is a *good* question. They are not caught like schoolboys whispering about a forbidden topic, and they are not embroiled in a jealous debate. They approach Jesus openly and forthrightly with their query about greatness. Moreover, the wording of their question is different in Matthew. The disciples don't ask about ordinary, worldly greatness, but "Who is the greatest *in the kingdom of heaven*?" (Matt. 18:1). Striving to be great in the kingdom of heaven is not a vain ambition but a worthy goal, one that Jesus himself set forth in the Sermon on the Mount (see Matt. 5:19).

So, here in Matthew, the disciples are asking a good question, not a selfish one. Jesus is about to teach them how to care for the "little ones" in the community (Matt. 18:6, 10, 14), and his teaching implies that there are "greater ones" who have the responsibility to do this caring. Thus, the disciples are right to want to know who these "greater ones" are and how they come to be "great" in the kingdom sense. In other words, they want to know how to be great *leaders* in the church.

So, the problem is not with their question, as such; it is with their assumed definition of greatness. The disciples think of greatness in terms of strength and superiority, and, in order to reshape their assumptions, Jesus answers them with a living illustration. He places a child in their midst and tells them that they will never enter the kingdom of heaven unless they, too, become like children.

What does it mean to "become like children"? We must be careful not to read into this command our own notions about children. In our culture, children are of central importance to many families. Parents sacrifice to see that their children receive the best life has to offer, and grandparents proudly display "brag photos" of grandchildren. Children are precious to us, and when the unimaginable happens—when a child dies—it is an almost unbearably sorrowful event.

It is difficult, then, for us to conceive how weak, vulnerable, and lowly children were in Jesus' day. Children were always at risk. According to some estimates, 30 percent of infants died at birth, another 30 percent perished by age 6, and 60 percent were gone by age 16. First-century parents cared for and loved their children, of course, but, when the odds were overwhelming that a child would not live to adulthood, society was reluctant to place much value on childhood. Indeed, a child was a "nobody," the social equal of a slave, and had to achieve adulthood before being considered a free person eligible to inherit the family estate (Malina and Rohrbaugh, *Social Science Commentary on the Synoptic Gospels*, 117).

In Jesus' day, any notion of a child-centered family or society would have been unthinkable. But, of course, by placing a child in the center, Jesus asks his disciples to think the unthinkable: A low, humble, and insignificant child is the model for greatness in the kingdom. Jesus is teaching his disciples that leaders in the community of faith must be humble and unassuming. Faithful leadership is not a matter of winning at church politics or acquiring the trappings of prestige. It is being childlike and humble. The "great ones" in the community of faith are not to be found tipping the maître d' at a power lunch but serving the Lord's Supper in a cancer ward. They are not seen stepping on the backs of others as they scramble to the top of the hill, but are seen in the valley binding up the wounds of the injured. The "great ones" in the community of faith know that what goes on in a church school class in the basement of the church is at least as important as what transpires in the boardroom of a Fortune 500 company.

When we pay attention to the visual aspects of this passage, an even more remarkable truth emerges. Imagine a circle drawn in the sand called "the kingdom of heaven." When the disciples ask, "Who is the greatest in the kingdom of heaven?" they assume, of course, that they are standing *inside* this circle. They want to know who, among the insiders, is the greatest. Startlingly, Jesus reaches *outside* the circle for his example. "Truly I tell you," Jesus states, calling a child and placing the child inside the circle, "unless you change and become like children, you will never enter the kingdom of heaven" (Matt. 18:3). Now, ironically, it is the disciples who are *outside* the circle, and the only way back in is for them to stoop low and become humble like children. "Whoever becomes humble like this child is the greatest in the kingdom of heaven" (Matt. 18:4).

But Jesus is not finished with the moves on this circle in the sand. If the disciples indeed become humble leaders, then they will demonstrate that by showing hospitality to those who are like children, the weak and lowly. Why? Because whoever shows hospitality to the powerless, "whoever welcomes one such child in my name" actually welcomes Jesus (Matt. 18:5). Astonishingly, Jesus is now *outside* the circle, hidden in the faces of the children, the "nobodies," the weak, the small, and the helpless. On the cross, Jesus became weak and vulnerable; Jesus became a "nobody" so that all who are broken and frail, all who are at risk and lost, may be saved. Whenever leaders in the church open the doors of hospitality to receive such "little ones," they are welcoming Jesus himself into their midst.

Putting all of this together, what do we see? No one stands in the middle of the circle, no one has the status of "great" in the kingdom of heaven who has not felt the sting of being on the outside, who does not realize that being inside the circle is a matter of mercy and not merit. When it comes to the kingdom of heaven, we are all outsiders. We have all stood like orphans in the dark and cold, pressing our noses against the window, only to have the door of the kingdom open and the master's gentle hand beckon us forward into the warmth of the hearth and the bounty of the table.

TAKING CARE
OF THE "LITTLE ONES"
Matthew 18:6–14

18:6 "If any of you put a stumbling block before one of these little ones who believe in me, it would be better for you if a great millstone were fastened around your neck and you were drowned in the depth of the sea. [7] Woe to the world because of stumbling blocks! Occasions for stumbling are bound to come, but woe to the one by whom the stumbling block comes!

[8] "If your hand or your foot causes you to stumble, cut it off and throw it away; it is better for you to enter life maimed or lame than to have two hands or two feet and to be thrown into the eternal fire. [9] And if your eye causes you to stumble, tear it out and throw it away; it is better for you to enter life with one eye than to have two eyes and to be thrown into the hell of fire.

[10] "Take care that you do not despise one of these little ones; for, I tell you, in heaven their angels continually see the face of my Father in heaven. [12] What do you think? If a shepherd has a hundred sheep, and one of them has gone astray, does he not leave the ninety-nine on the mountains and go in search of the one that went astray? [13] And if he finds it, truly I tell you, he rejoices over it more than over the ninety-nine that never went astray. [14] So it is not the will of your Father in heaven that one of these little ones should be lost.

Just as little children in Jesus' day were vulnerable and always in danger, so new converts to the Christian faith were also always at risk. They were like new seedlings, growing green and lovely, but shallow of root and imperiled by weeds, drought, and the scorching heat of the sun (see Matt. 13:18–22). A discouragement that someone seasoned in the faith could take in stride may well cause a new convert to lose hope, wither, and blow away.

In this passage, Jesus instructs his disciples about how to care for these "little ones"; that is, how to care for new converts and for others whose faith is not yet strong enough to withstand trial and temptation. When a physician is deciding how to treat a patient, the first rule of medical practice is to "do no harm"; don't make the patient any worse. Just so, Jesus' first word to the disciples was don't do any harm to vulnerable followers; don't cause the trouble. The world will cause enough distress for people whose faith is weak without church leaders adding to it.

Jesus is realistic here. The path of faith is a rocky path. Inevitably many instances will occur when "little ones" in the faith trip over "stumbling blocks" (the Greek is actually "scandals"), but God forbid that church leaders would be the ones who put the stumbling blocks in their paths (or, closer to the Greek, "causes them to be scandalized"; Matt. 18:7). To emphasize this, Jesus employs a dramatic image. If any leaders cause weak members of the community of faith to stumble, it would be better for such leaders to have heavy millstones tied around their necks and be dropped into the deep blue sea. This is hyperbole, of course, a sensational way of saying that, because the basic vocation of a church leader is to welcome and nurture faith in people, if a leader were to do the opposite and discourage faith, then it would be better for that person to drop out of sight altogether.

When church leaders wander off the path and stumble, others following behind them stumble, too. So, whatever causes a church leader to stumble must be cast aside. Jesus puts it very forcefully: "If your hand or your foot causes you to stumble, cut it off. . . . And if your eye causes you to stumble, tear it out" (Matt. 18:8–9). These are fearsome words, especially since we know that all Christians, no matter how earnest and committed, stumble somewhere along the way. No one walks a perfectly straight line into the kingdom of heaven. Cut off your foot? Tear out your eye? To take these words literally would result in a mutilated congregation—beginning with the church officers!

We get a better sense of Jesus' warnings when we recognize that they are phrased in a pattern of exaggerated contrast characteristic of Jewish teaching of his day. When Jesus says that it would be better for some terrible thing to happen—a hand cut off, an eye poked out—than to miss the life of the kingdom of heaven, the emphasis is supposed to fall on the glory of the life of the kingdom, not on the terrible thing. The point, in other words, is how wonderful the kingdom is, so wonderful that a person would be willing to sacrifice greatly to participate in it.

Thus, Jesus' first word to the disciples about caring for the "little ones," the weaker brothers and sisters in the church, is to do everything possible to avoid causing them to stumble. But, truth be told, they will still stumble. No matter how careful church leaders are to do no harm, there are simply too many temptations, distractions, and problems for some of them not to trip up somewhere. So the second word to church leaders is, when the "little ones" do stumble, don't sit passively by; go into action to seek and to restore them.

These newborn and tender followers are worthy of special attention, Jesus says, because "in heaven their angels continually see the face of my Father in heaven" (Matt. 18:10). The idea here is that the "little ones," those struggling in the faith, have guardian angels who watch over them and who are granted constant access to the very presence of God in heaven to plead and intercede on their behalf. The popular notion was that even angels only rarely glimpsed God's face, but here Jesus says that the angels who protect the "little ones" in the faith are exceptions and are given immediate access to God's throne.

It would be a mistake to make this language too literal, to imagine white-robed, winged creatures hovering over church members and hurtling back and forth between earth and heaven. In essence, "angel" is a powerful and graphic way of speaking about the presence and activity of God, and what Jesus is saying to his disciples is basically that God cares deeply about fragile children in the faith and watches over them constantly. Since God, like a vigilant mother, keeps a heedful eye on the "little ones," church leaders should care deeply and watch over them, too.

In order to make this point, Jesus tells the well-known parable of the shepherd with a hundred sheep. We are probably more familiar with this parable the way it is told in the Gospel of Luke (Luke 15:3–7) than with Matthew's version. In Luke, Jesus tells this parable to his opponents—to the Pharisees and the scribes, who are grumbling that Jesus "welcomes sinners and eats with them" (Luke 15:2). But in Matthew, Jesus tells the parable to his disciples, not to defend himself but to instruct them regarding their pastoral care responsibilities. In Matthew, the sheep stands for one of the "little ones," a weaker brother or sister in the church who has become fearful, confused, or full of doubt, and, therefore, is first described as "astray" (Matt. 18:12), a more fitting portrayal of the way that weaker church members can meander aimlessly off the desired path. In Luke, the shepherd symbolizes Jesus himself, and there is no doubt that he will find the lost sheep: "*When* he has found it . . . " (Luke 15:5). In Matthew, the shepherd represents the leadership of the Christian church, and there is the candid recognition that attempts to restore wandering Christians are not always successful: "*If* he finds it . . . " (Matt. 18:13).

In Matthew, then, the parable is a symbolic lesson to "shepherds" in the church: When a vulnerable member of the community goes astray, drop everything and do whatever you can to seek and to restore this wanderer. If such a command seems to have a dash of foolishness in it, given the exhausting variety of ways that members of the flock can go astray, the parable itself contains that same rashness. No reasonable shepherd would actually leave ninety-nine of his sheep unprotected in dangerous mountain country while he pursued a single wandering stray. Only a shepherd with an out-of-bounds passion for the lonely, the weak, and the lost would do such a thing—and that, of course, is the point. God is such a shepherd, and church leaders should model their leadership styles not after the latest corporate models, but after God. The goal of the church, after all, is not to be a well-oiled institution, a member of the ecclesiastical Fortune 500, but to do "the will of your Father in heaven that not one of these little ones should be lost" (Matt. 18:14).

TROUBLE IN THE CHURCH
Matthew 18:15–35

18:15 **"If another member of the church sins against you, go and point out the fault when the two of you are alone. If the member listens to you, you have regained that one. 16 But if you are not listened to, take one or two others along with you, so that every word may be confirmed by the evidence of two or three witnesses. 17 If the member refuses to listen to them, tell it to the church; and if the offender refuses to listen even to the church, let such a one be to you as a Gentile and a tax collector. 18 Truly I tell you, whatever you bind on earth will be bound in heaven, and whatever you loose on** earth will be loosed in heaven. ¹⁹ Again, truly I tell you, if two of you agree on earth about anything you ask, it will be done for you by my Father in heaven. ²⁰ For where two or three are gathered in my name, I am there among them."

²¹ Then Peter came and said to him, "Lord, if another member of the church sins against me, how often should I forgive? As many as seven times?" ²² Jesus said to him, "Not seven times, but, I tell you, seventy-seven times.

²³ "For this reason the kingdom of heaven may be compared to a king who wished to settle accounts with his slaves. ²⁴ When he began the reckoning, one who owed him ten thousand talents was brought to him; ²⁵ and, as he could not pay, his lord ordered him to be sold, together with his wife and children and all his possessions, and payment to be made. ²⁶ So the slave fell on his knees before him, saying, 'Have patience with me, and I will pay you everything.' ²⁷ And out of pity for him, the lord of that slave released him and forgave him the debt. ²⁸ But that same slave, as he went out, came upon one of his fellow slaves who owed him a hundred denarii; and seizing him by the throat, he said, 'Pay what you owe.' ²⁹ Then his fellow slave fell down and pleaded with him, 'Have patience with me, and I will pay you.' ³⁰ But he refused; then he went and threw him into prison until he would pay the debt. ³¹ When his fellow slaves saw what had happened, they were greatly distressed, and they went and reported to their lord all that had taken place. ³² Then his lord summoned him and said to him, 'You wicked slave! I forgave you all that debt because you pleaded with me. ³³ Should you not have had mercy on your fellow slave, as I had mercy on you?' ³⁴ And in anger his lord handed him over to be tortured until he would pay his entire debt. ³⁵ So my heavenly Father will also do to every one of you, if you do not forgive your brother or sister from your heart."

Matthew has no romantic illusions about the church. He knows that the church is not all sweet thoughts, endlessly patient saints, and cloudless skies. In Matthew's church, people—no matter how committed—are still people, and stormy weather is always a possible forecast. "Blest be the tie that binds our hearts in Christian love"; even so, painful breaks can occur in once tender and loving relationships. "We are one in the Spirit, we are one in the Lord"; nevertheless, sharp and cruel words can split a congregation into angry factions. "The church's one foundation is Jesus Christ her Lord"; but greed, lust, and envy can threaten to shake even a strong church off its footing. What happens when the menu at the church potluck includes such unwelcome entries as rage, hatred, and betrayal?

"If another member of the church sins against you," Jesus begins, and what follows is a detailed process for dealing with those bitter conflicts that realistically will arise in every Christian congregation. Many Christian groups and denominations have used this procedure as a model for church discipline and for handling conflict, and its most impressive feature is how persistent and time consuming it is. In this process, nobody is written off in haste, no one is fired on the spot, no one slams the door in another's face in rage; to the contrary, a sea of energy is expended trying, time and again, to make peace. In contrast to the attitudes of the prevailing culture ("If somebody hassles you, forget them. It's their problem, not yours"), relationships are of precious and enduring value in the church. When a relationship is broken, it is worth going back over and over to work toward reconciliation.

Also, the whole process is focused on the restoration of the offender, not revenge for the offended. Jesus has just provided the beautiful picture of a shepherd searching for a sheep who has gone astray, but this is not merely a sentimental idea to be preserved in stained glass. This painstaking, step-by-step process of trying to regain harmony between brothers and sisters in the church is one of the ways that this shepherd image comes alive in the rough and tumble of real congregational life. The point is to regain the brother or sister, to make the flock whole again, to bring the wandering sheep back into the protection and care of the fold.

But what happens if all efforts at reconciliation fail? What about sinners who, weary of the church's incessant knocking with offers of covered dishes of repentance and platters of restoration, shut the door and lock it, insisting upon the quarantine of sin rather than the healing power of forgiveness? Then, a genuinely fearful thing happens; they get what they want. "Let such a one," said Jesus, "be to you as a Gentile and a tax collector" (Matt. 18:17); in other words, the church takes the dire step of excommunication. A church member who does not wish to be in fellowship with the rest of the church is granted that wish and is, to employ theological irony, "left the hell alone."

Even here, though, the ultimate goal is restoration. Indeed, Matthew's readers may do a double take on the words "let such a one be to you as a Gentile and a tax collector," for Jesus himself ate with tax collectors (Matt. 9:10–11) and showed mercy to Gentiles (Matt. 8:5–13; 15:21–28). When all efforts to restore falter, the church solemnly recognizes that fellowship with the offending party is broken, and it does so by heavenly authority: "Whatever you bind on earth will be bound in heaven" (Matt. 18:18). Thus, it is not acting in its own name, not acting as a religious club petulantly expelling a quarrelsome troublemaker; to the contrary, it is acting in the name of God, the God who, in Jesus Christ, eternally seeks to restore sinners. As such, it acts humbly, prayerfully, courageously, and in response to the presence of the risen Christ: "For where two or three are gathered in my name, I am there among them" (Matt. 18:20).

As if to emphasize the point that forgiveness is the real issue here, a discussion about forgiveness follows immediately. No sooner has Jesus outlined the process for repairing broken relationships in the church than Peter, as the spokesman for the disciples, steps forward to ask for clarification. "I hear what you say about seeking restoration, but, supposing that I am the victim of someone else's sin," Peter wonders, "how often should I extend forgiveness?" Peter wants to know about the statute of limitations on sin. Given human nature, this sin-forgiveness dynamic could loop out endlessly. So, how many times does a follower of Jesus have to get on the forgiveness treadmill? "As many as seven times?" Peter asks, no doubt considering this to be a generous number (Matt. 18:21).

Jesus' answer is astonishing: "Not seven times, but, I tell you, seventy-seven times" (Matt. 18:22). The Greek is difficult here and, as the footnote in the NRSV indicates, the phrase can also be translated "seventy times seven," but the exact number is not the issue. In fact, whether Jesus says "seventy-seven" or "seventy times seven," either way, the number is enormous, and the point is that calculating limits on forgiveness is out of bounds.

To underscore this point, Jesus tells a rip-roaring tale about forgiveness, a parable involving circumstances so exaggerated that surely his listeners found it tremendously amusing (Matt. 18:23–34). The fun begins in the opening scene, when a king, settling accounts with his slaves, discovers one vassal who is on the books with a debt of ten thousand talents. Since a slave, even one belonging to the king, was hardly a high-powered wage earner and a single talent was worth more than fifteen years' worth of typical daily wages, we have here an outlandish debt, in fact, one unimaginably large. An Egyptian pharaoh couldn't come up with ten thousand talents, much less a slave. The situation is something like our saying that a lowly mail-room clerk owed the CEO of IBM a "bazillion dollars." It was hard to know who was more foolish—the slave, for getting into that size debt, or the king, for extending that sort of credit line to a slave. In any case, the king, realizing that repayment was out of the question, attempts at least to cut his losses by ordering the slave to be sold, along with the slave's family and all his worldly goods.

The second laugh comes when the slave, realizing his desperate predicament, falls to his knees and begs for an extension on his loan, "Have patience with me, and I will pay you everything" (Matt. 18:26). Right. The king must have been amused as well, because he responded to this ridiculous request with an even more preposterous response: He forgave the debt—every last penny of it—and set the slave free. No threats, no recriminations, nothing—just extravagant forgiveness, pure and free.

Now the story turns dark. This same slave, on his way out the door, the words of the king's forgiveness still ringing in the chamber, runs across a second slave who, as chance would have it, owes a debt to the first slave. This debt happens to be a hundred denarii, or, to make the math plain, over half a million times less than the first debt. But the first slave is ruthless. "Pay what you owe," he snarls. The second slave pleads for patience, using virtually the same desperate speech employed by the first slave, "Have patience with me, and I will pay you" (Matt. 18:28–29). But in this scene there is no mercy. The first slave throws the second into debtors' prison.

You can imagine the reaction Jesus' parable provoked at this point. Anyone who heard this story was surely enraged at the massive ingratitude of the first slave. How could that miserable creep come rolling out of the king's palace on a highway of mercy, fresh from being forgiven the equivalent of the national debt, only to shut off the water to his own debtor? There is, then, some deep satisfaction about the final scene of the parable. Other slaves, realizing what had happened, told the king about the slave's selfish reaction, and the king, mightily angered by this display of greed, cast the wicked and thankless slave into a torture chamber.

Good! Or is it? Suddenly Jesus turns the parable on his disciples—and on us. "So my heavenly Father will also do to every one of you, if you do not forgive your brother or sister from your heart" (Matt. 18:35). When we hold other people to a strict accounting, treating them only on the basis of what we think they "owe" or "merit," while forgetting that we ourselves have received unmerited grace and have had all our debts erased by the mercy of God, we are just as thankless as that ungrateful slave. Indeed, even good disciples who ask reasonable questions like "How often should I forgive?" are simply counting small change and tallying tiny debts, forgetting in a massive act of thoughtlessness that their own national debt load of sin has been graciously, astonishingly forgiven by a merciful God.

We have come, then, full circle in Matthew 18. The chapter began by letting us know that we will never enter the kingdom of heaven until we have stood in the shoes of a child, until we have felt what it means to be an outsider, a "nobody" suddenly made, by the grace of God, into a "somebody." Now, at the end of the chapter, this same humility and dependence take the shape of a slave whose debt is so enormous that only an act of majestic pardon could wipe it out. When one gets a sense of proportion, then, a sense of the size of our sinful debt and the immensity of God's mercy, no one would dare attempt to ration forgiveness. We know too well that the little boat in which we are sailing is floating on a deep sea of grace and that forgiveness is not to be dispensed with an eyedropper, but a fire hose.

12. Who Is Able?
The Narrow Gate to the Kingdom
Matthew 19:1–20:34

In the book of Revelation, the seer John is witness to a dramatic scene in which the whole of creation is being searched for one who is worthy to break the seals on the sacred, heavenly scroll. The angels explore high and low, but, alas, no one is qualified, no one is worthy, "no one in heaven or on earth or under the earth was able to open the scroll" (Rev. 5:3). John begins to weep because the great scroll must, it seems, remain unopened, its holy truths forever hidden. But suddenly, a joyful announcement is made. One who is worthy has at last been found to open the scroll—Jesus Christ, the Son of David. Quickly the word spreads throughout heaven, and soon the angelic chorus raises an ecstatic hymn of praise:

> "Worthy is the Lamb that was [slain]
> to receive power and wealth and wisdom and might
> and honor and glory and blessing!"
>
> (Rev. 5:12)

Worthy is the Lamb, and no one in heaven or on earth but the Lamb is worthy. Although the language of his Gospel is quite different from that of Revelation, Matthew shares this conviction that Jesus Christ alone is worthy, and, indeed, it is the theme of this section of the Gospel. As Jesus journeys toward the cross, Matthew makes it clear that this is a costly journey, and only Jesus is worthy and able to pay the price.

Jesus is leaving Galilee and heading toward a showdown with sin and death in Jerusalem. This is no dress rehearsal; this is the main event. The road to glory will be a rough road, a bloody road. The hard road to the kingdom of heaven passes through the constricted pass at Golgotha, and, in a series of exchanges in this section of Matthew, one question stands in the background: Who is worthy and able to make this sacrificial journey? The gate to the kingdom of heaven is narrow indeed (see Matt. 7:14), and one by one the fainthearted, the ambitious, and the half-hearted fall by the wayside. At the end, only Jesus is able to pass through the gate; only Jesus is left to carry the cross for all humanity, to walk the sacrificial path to victory. "Worthy is the Lamb that was slain. . . ."

MARRIAGE AND CELIBACY
Matthew 19:1–12

19:1 **When Jesus had finished saying these things, he left Galilee and went to the region of Judea beyond the Jordan.** [2] **Large crowds followed him, and he cured them there.**

[3] **Some Pharisees came to him, and to test him they asked, "Is it lawful for a man to divorce his wife for any cause?"** [4] **He answered, "Have you not read that the one who made them at the beginning 'made them male and female,'** [5] **and said, 'For this reason a man shall leave his father and mother and be joined to his wife, and the two shall become one flesh'?** [6] **So they are no longer two, but one flesh. Therefore what God has joined together, let no one separate."** [7] **They said to him, "Why then did Moses command us to give a certificate of dismissal and to divorce her?"** [8] **He said to them, "It was because you were so hard-hearted that Moses allowed you to divorce your wives, but from the beginning it was not so.** [9] **And I say to you, whoever divorces his wife, except for unchastity, and marries another commits adultery."**

[10] **His disciples said to him, "If such is the case of a man with his wife, it is better not to marry."** [11] **But he said to them, "Not everyone can accept this teaching, but only those to whom it is given.** [12] **For there are eunuchs who have been so from birth, and there are eunuchs who have been made eunuchs by others, and there are eunuchs who have made themselves eunuchs for the sake of the kingdom of heaven. Let anyone accept this who can."**

Jesus has just completed the fourth of five major teaching sessions (Matthew 18; see Introduction), and Matthew concludes this portion with the usual formula that appears at the end of a block of teaching material: "When Jesus had finished saying these things . . ." (see also Matt. 7:28; 11:1; 13:53; 26:1).

Now the story of Jesus arrives at a break point. The Galilean ministry is finished, and the death march to Jerusalem begins. Jesus leaves Galilee, Matthew tells us, and moves to Judea (Matt. 19:1). In other words, Jesus is beginning to close in on Jerusalem, where the forces of death will, in turn, close in on him. The crowds, who will all too soon shout for his death, are, for the moment, still following; and the work of the kingdom continues, as signified by Jesus' healing ministry (Matt. 19:2).

Quickly, the Pharisees reappear on the scene to put Jesus to the test, just as they did the last time we saw them (Matt. 16:1–4). This time they ask Jesus about the legality of divorce. Jesus answers them with essentially the same word about divorce he gave in the Sermon on the Mount (for a discussion of Jesus' view on divorce and possible meaning for today, see the comments on Matthew 5:31–32).

An important question here is, Why does Matthew include Jesus' word on divorce twice? Since we have already heard what Jesus has to say on the subject and there is basically nothing new here, why, then, the déjà vu? Perhaps this second word is for the Pharisees' benefit, since the first teaching about divorce, in the Sermon on the Mount, was addressed to the disciples and the crowd. Or maybe, as some have suggested, the matter of divorce was so urgent in Matthew's church it deserved repeated emphasis. A more telling clue, though, is found in the phrasing of the Pharisees' question: "Can a man divorce his wife for *any cause?*" In other words, the reader remembers that Jesus said in the Sermon on the Mount that divorce is against the will of God. Now, with that earlier teaching firmly in the background, the Pharisees want to know if there are *any* exceptions, can *any* compromises be struck, can we work *any* sort of deal on this matter?

In other words, the real issue in this exchange is not divorce per se— that has been addressed—but whether there is any negotiating room in the will of God. The Pharisees are probing to see if they can find cracks in Jesus' resolve. They could have picked any one of the key kingdom themes—anger, adultery, peacemaking, loving one's enemy; they chose divorce, which is, we are told, a *test* case (Matt. 19:3). The main issue at stake is whether Jesus' view of God's will includes the possibility of compromise, of cutting corners with heaven.

Can we make deals with God? This is a crucial issue at this juncture of the story of Jesus. Right at the moment when Jesus makes the critical turn in the road that will take him to the cross, right at the point that Jesus' own faith will allow no turning back, the Pharisees want to know if God strikes bargains, perhaps on a matter like divorce. Later at Gethsemane, Jesus will pray, "My Father, if it is possible, let this cup pass from me; yet not what I want but what you want" (Matt. 26:39). Here, the Pharisees want to know if we can mix a little of what "we want" with what God wants, if God is willing to make a little room for human avarice and craving. Take divorce as an example, say the Pharisees; is there any room here for negotiation with human desire?

"No," replies Jesus. God makes no deals. Because of human hardheartedness, Moses may have cut a bargain, but God will not adjust the divine will. It is God's will that human relationships be holy and abiding, that marriage be steadfast, that a man leave his parents and be joined to his wife, the two becoming one until death do them part—no compromises.

At first glance this may seem overly stern. Moses was at least reasonable. Moses could account for the frailties of actual human existence, but Jesus, it seems, stubbornly will not budge. Upon reflection, however, what appears to be divine intransigence turns out to be gracious good news. Remember, in Jesus' day, divorce was essentially the equivalent of abandonment. No certificate could cover up the fact that divorce involved, at least to some degree, the social desertion and the devaluing of another human being. These religious leaders are really asking, then, if God would be willing to wink at a little abandonment. Moreover, the Pharisees' "test" question about divorce spills over into every aspect of God's will. Would God tolerate a small dose of poison in the harmony of human relationships? Would God be willing to turn a blind eye to any instance of human destruction—to a small percentage of spouses being abused, a few children being molested, so long as it wasn't a very large slice of the population? Would God be willing to shrug the shoulder when a tiny number of homeless people freeze to death every winter, so long as the United Way keeps increasing each year? We know that God's will is peace and righteousness, justice and mercy, but is there any cause—*any* way—that God could do a discount deal?

And the reply of Jesus, the strong and gracious reply, is "No, God will not compromise one inch on the promises of the kingdom. Not one inch." The church is called to live in that volatile tension between God's uncompromised will and the realities of human frailty. In regard to marriage and divorce, the church should strive to live now as people of the kingdom of heaven, gratefully holding marriages to be places of sacred, steadfast, and unbreakable trust. It must also live as people who are on the pilgrim way, as people who see the kingdom of heaven but who have not yet arrived, as people whose relationships will sometimes erupt in anger, whose bonds of trust will sometimes be broken, whose marriages will sometimes falter, as people who need forgiveness time and time again (see Matt. 18:21–22).

Who can possibly say in every circumstance of life, "Not my will, but yours, O Lord"? Finally, only one human being was capable of that—Jesus. "Worthy is the Lamb that was slain. . . ." The disciples realize that they are in a no-compromise zone, that they are following Jesus along a hard, demanding path. "If such is the case," they cry, "it is better not to marry" (Matt. 19:10). Jesus replies, "Not everyone can accept this teaching, but only those to whom it is given" (Matt. 19:11). It is not entirely clear what Jesus means here by "this teaching." Is he referring to what he has just taught about marriage—the difficult word that divorce is, in every circumstance, outside God's will? Or does "this teaching" refer to the disciples' statement that "it is better not to marry"? In this latter case, Jesus would, in effect, be agreeing with them, "Yes, it *is* better to remain unmarried, but that is a hard teaching to swallow. Only a few can accept it."

So, does "this teaching" refer to divorce or to celibacy? The fact that the disciples have just registered astonishment over Jesus' uncompromising statement about divorce adds weight to the former, but most commentators agree that the fact that Jesus goes on to discuss celibacy adds greater weight to the latter. In either case, though, the main theological point is the same: The kingdom of heaven constitutes an urgent, uncompromising call to a new way of living.

In Matthew 19:12–13, Jesus develops this theme of celibacy. Some people, he says, are born eunuchs (that is, incapable of sexual intercourse), and other people have been "made eunuchs by others" (that is, castrated), but there are still others who have "made themselves eunuchs" (that is, chosen to be celibate) "for the sake of the kingdom of heaven." In the history of the church, this notion of celibacy for the sake of the kingdom has been connected to the vows of religious orders, but in Matthew's context the idea probably refers to missionaries who, for the sake of their vocation, have chosen to abstain from the comforts of marriage.

CHILDREN IN THE KINGDOM
Matthew 19:13–15

13 **Then little children were being brought to him in order that he might lay his hands on them and pray. The disciples spoke sternly to those who brought them;** [14] **but Jesus said, "Let the little children come to me, and do not stop them; for it is to such as these that the kingdom of heaven belongs."** [15] **And he laid his hands on them and went on his way.**

In the previous passage, the disciples were surprised to learn that the kingdom of heaven was so demanding. Now they are to be surprised that the kingdom is so encompassing. People—probably parents—were thrusting children toward Jesus so that he could lay his hands on them and give them a blessing. To our contemporary eyes, this seems to be a touching picture, something like parents bringing their delighted children to a department store Santa Claus, but to Matthew's first readers the scene would not be nearly so charming. Children were of little social significance in the first century (see comments on Matt. 18:1–5), and their sudden intrusive appearance here on the way to Jerusalem would be construed as a distraction.

So, the disciples try to act as bodyguards, shooing the parents away, shielding Jesus from being deterred by the inconsequential. But it is the disciples Jesus stops, not the children: "Let the little children come to me . . . for it is to such as these that the kingdom of heaven belongs" (Matt. 19:14).

Just as was the case in regard to the divorce saying (Matt. 19:3–9), the statement that the kingdom of heaven belongs to children is essentially a repetition of the earlier teaching in Matthew 18:1–5. Indeed, in that previous exchange, the disciples were clearly told, "Whoever welcomes one such child in my name welcomes me" (Matt. 18:5). Now, only a brief time later, the disciples are caught putting up a barbed-wire fence to keep children away from Jesus. The point here is not that the disciples lack short-term memory; the point, rather, is the very one that serves as the main theme of this section of Matthew: The demands of the kingdom are difficult. The disciples surely remember (as does the reader) the command to open the doors to children; it is just tough to do. It is yet another hard word, a narrow gate through which it is difficult to pass.

The reason for this, of course, is that the command to "let the little children come to me, and do not stop them" is, in effect, a command to knock down the barriers between the church and all the "little ones," all who lack worth and status in the eyes of the world. Decent people are willing to be charitable, willing to reach out and make a contribution to the downtrodden. Jesus' word, however, is much more radical. The little children, the migrant worker, the forgotten woman in the back ward of a nursing home, the teenager abandoned on the mean urban streets—these are the ones to whom the kingdom of heaven belongs. They have nothing, nothing except the care of a merciful God. Having nothing but God, then, they have everything. The mission of the church is not to pass a plate of food out the back door but to set a place for these little ones at the family feast. But who among us can do this, who can sustain the ministry of making one's life perfectly open and available to the abused, the broken, the neglected, and the forgotten of the earth? Finally, only one human being was capable of that—Jesus. "Worthy is the Lamb that was slain. . . . "

THE RICH YOUNG MAN
AND THE POOR DISCIPLES
Matthew 19:16–30

19:16 Then someone came to him and said, "Teacher, what good deed must I do to have eternal life?" 17 And he said to him, "Why do you ask me about what is good? There is only one who is good. If you wish to enter into life, keep the commandments." 18 He said to him, "Which ones?" And Jesus said,

"You shall not murder; You shall not commit adultery; You shall not steal; You shall not bear false witness; [19] Honor your father and mother; also, You shall love your neighbor as yourself." [20] The young man said to him, "I have kept all these; what do I still lack?" [21] Jesus said to him, "If you wish to be perfect, go, sell your possessions, and give the money to the poor, and you will have treasure in heaven; then come, follow me." [22] When the young man heard this word, he went away grieving, for he had many possessions.

[23] Then Jesus said to his disciples, "Truly I tell you, it will be hard for a rich person to enter the kingdom of heaven. [24] Again I tell you, it is easier for a camel to go through the eye of a needle than for someone who is rich to enter the kingdom of God." [25] When the disciples heard this, they were greatly astounded and said, "Then who can be saved?" [26] But Jesus looked at them and said, "For mortals it is impossible, but for God all things are possible."

[27] Then Peter said in reply, "Look, we have left everything and followed you. What then will we have?" [28] Jesus said to them, "Truly I tell you, at the renewal of all things, when the Son of Man is seated on the throne of his glory, you who have followed me will also sit on twelve thrones, judging the twelve tribes of Israel. [29] And everyone who has left houses or brothers or sisters or father or mother or children or fields, for my name's sake, will receive a hundredfold, and will inherit eternal life. [30] But many who are first will be last, and the last will be first.

The story of the man who approaches Jesus with a question about eternal life appears in Matthew, Mark, and Luke and is often called the tale of the rich, young ruler. But only in Luke is the man described as a ruler, and only in Matthew is he portrayed as young.

In order to follow the contours of the story, we must realize that, when the young man encounters Jesus, two very different worlds collide: this world, with all its prevailing customs and values, and the radical new way of life called for in the kingdom of heaven. The man has his feet firmly planted in the present age; for all of his religion, he is still a child of the dying order, of the world as it is. Jesus, on the other hand, is the agent of the new reality that God is bringing to bear, the Messiah through whom God's future kingdom breaks in.

When the man asks Jesus, "What good deed must I do to have eternal life?" (Matt. 19:16), the question is ambiguous. Does the man want to know how to cross over the bridge to the kingdom of heaven, or does he merely want to add one more possession to his already large collection? Does he want to move from one world to another, or is he simply standing in the same old world and checking out the price tag on eternal life? Jesus' curious response to the man—"Why do you ask me about what is good?" (Matt. 19:17)—is designed to expose this equivocation. Jesus wants the man to know that in the dictionary of the kingdom of heaven, "good" has a different meaning than in the vocabulary of the present age, that "good" changes definition when one crosses the border into the kingdom.

Jesus wants this young man to move to a new place, to see his life in the light of God's kingdom, not to ask about the "right thing" to do but to hunger and thirst for righteousness. Jesus knows that the man is talking about a "good deed" in the conventional sense, but Jesus wants him to be truly righteous, not merely respectable. "There is only one who is good" (Matt. 19:17), Jesus goes on to say, making it clear that, in the kingdom vocabulary, goodness is a radical virtue, defined by God alone.

"If you wish to enter into life," Jesus continues, "keep the commandments" (Matt. 19:17). These words must have been unsettling, because they imply that the young man has some traveling to do, that he needs to move from where he is to somewhere else, that he has not yet fully entered life. When the young man, no doubt puzzled, inquires which commandments Jesus means, Jesus cites the second table of the Ten Commandments, namely, those commandments that have to do with one's responsibilities toward other people, and then reinforces this ethical thrust by adding the command from Leviticus 19:18 to love one's neighbor. "I have kept all these," protests the young man; "what do I still lack?" (Matt. 19:20).

Jesus' response goes to the root of the issue: "If you wish to be perfect"—that is, if you who are young wish to be genuinely mature, if you who still lack something wish to be truly fulfilled, if you who stand in the world that is passing away wish to be a child of the kingdom of heaven— "sell your possessions, and give the money to the poor . . . ; then come; follow me" (Matt. 19:21). Jesus knows that the best way to reveal which world people are really invested in is to ask them to divest, to sell their portfolio. Alas, the young man is too heavily invested in the status quo, in the world as it is; he cannot bear to part with his land and goods, so he turns away, grieving. He is offered the adventure of being a disciple of Jesus, a child of God with great treasure in heaven; he decides instead to manage real estate in Palestine.

Jesus, then, turns to his disciples and observes, "It will be hard for a rich person to enter the kingdom of heaven" (Matt. 19:23). Jesus makes his point emphatic by using a piece of colorful hyperbole, indicating that a camel would have an easier time sliding through the eye of a needle than a rich man would have entering the kingdom (Matt. 19:24). This camel-through-a needle image is an example of Jesus' wit; Jesus is saying, in effect, "that for a rich man to get to heaven is about as easy as for a Cadillac to get through a revolving door" (Buechner, *Wishful Thinking: A Theological ABC*, 81).

Why is it hard for a rich person to enter the kingdom? If we take at face value the statements of the rich young man, it is not that he is an evil man, an oppressor, or an extortioner. He has kept the commandments—all of them—including the commandments not to steal, not to covet what belongs to somebody else, and to love his neighbor. The problem with this man is not that he is dishonorable; the problem is that he is rich. The problem is not with the evil he has done to others, but with the evil his wealth is doing to him. Because he is rich, it is hard for him to surrender to God. He finds it painfully difficult to become humble like a child. His wealth reinforces his commitment to the present age and to his own status in it; his wealth underscores his self-sufficiency. As one commentator has observed, "The young man asked, 'What good thing shall *I* do?' . . . and insisted, 'All these things *I* have observed, what do *I* still lack.' He assumes that entering into the kingdom of heaven is something that he can bid for and pull off on his own" (Garland, *Reading Matthew*, 203).

Being rich, therefore, simply intensifies the basic human desire for self-justification. The disciples, who are not rich, quickly realize that Jesus is speaking about more than the moneyed rich; Jesus' word embraces all those who, in any way, are rich unto themselves—in short, the whole of humanity. Astounded, the disciples cry, "Then who can be saved?" (Matt. 19:25). The kingdom calls for total surrender to the will of God, a demand forever defeated by human pride and self-sufficiency. If the kingdom really does demand that we divest ourselves of all our investments in the present age and throw ourselves in trust and hope upon God, then the disciples are right. Who can possibly do it? Finally, only one human being was capable of that—Jesus. "For you know," wrote the apostle Paul, "the generous act of our Lord Jesus Christ, that though he was rich, yet for your sakes he became poor, so that by his poverty you might become rich" (2 Cor. 8:9). "Worthy is the Lamb that was slain. . . . " Salvation is a divine gift, a work not of ordinary human beings, but of the faithful Son of God. "For mortals it is impossible, but for God all things are possible" (Matt. 19:26).

Even though it is Jesus alone who totally surrenders his wealth for the sake of poor humanity, there are those who follow him; there are those who do not, like the young man, turn away but who uproot themselves from the present age and seek to live as children of the kingdom. Jesus' disciples were the first among many to cut the bonds with the old order and to follow. "Look," said Peter to Jesus, "we have left everything and followed you" (Matt. 19:27). Some followers of Jesus leave their families and their homes to travel to distant fields of mission, and others leave their families and homes on Thursday evenings to tutor street kids. Some leave lucrative careers to become hospice workers and schoolteachers in troubled schools; others refuse to close on deals they know will hurt other people and decline to climb the corporate ladder by stepping on somebody's back.

"What then will we have?" Peter asks (Matt. 19:27). The question sounds self-serving on the surface, but it is Peter's way of asking if discipleship and sacrifice in Jesus' name really count. "We have left everything to travel the road of sacrifice with you," Peter says. "Now, where does the road lead?" Jesus responds by drawing a picture of the end of the road, the end of the world—the time of "the renewal of all things, when the Son of Man is seated on the throne of his glory" (Matt. 19:28). Then, the followers of Jesus who have chosen a life of humility will be in positions of power and authority (Jesus' image is that they will sit on thrones judging the ancient twelve tribes of Israel; see Matthew 19:28), and those who have sacrificed for the kingdom will become wealthy in kingdom treasure (Matt. 19:29).

Indeed, many of those who appear to be in the pole position in the race to heaven, like that earnest and successful young man who kept all the commandments, will turn out to be bringing up the rear, and those who seem to be dead last, like the poor, the disciples who have left everything to follow Jesus, children, and the little ones of the earth, will cross the finish line first. "But many who are first will be last, and the last will be first" (Matt. 19:30).

THE PARABLE OF THE
LABORERS IN THE VINEYARD
Matthew 20:1–16

20:1 **"For the kingdom of heaven is like a landowner who went out early in the morning to hire laborers for his vineyard. ² After agreeing with the laborers for the usual daily wage, he sent them into his vineyard. ³ When he went out about nine o'clock, he saw others standing idle in the marketplace; ⁴ and he said to them, 'You also go into the vineyard, and I will pay you whatever is right.' So they went. ⁵ When he went out again about noon and about three o'clock, he did the same. ⁶ And about five o'clock he went out and found others standing around; and he said to them, 'Why are you standing here idle all day?' ⁷ They said to him, 'Because no one has hired us.' He said to them, 'You also go into the vineyard.' ⁸ When evening came, the owner of the vineyard said to his manager, 'Call the laborers and give them their pay, beginning with the last and then going to the first.' ⁹ When those hired about five o'clock came, each of them received the usual daily wage. ¹⁰ Now** when the first came, they thought they would receive more; but each of them also received the usual daily wage. [11] And when they received it, they grumbled against the landowner, [12] saying, 'These last worked only one hour, and you have made them equal to us who have borne the burden of the day and the scorching heat.' [13] But he replied to one of them, 'Friend, I am doing you no wrong; did you not agree with me for the usual daily wage? [14] Take what belongs to you and go; I choose to give to this last the same as I give to you. [15] Am I not allowed to do what I choose with what belongs to me? Or are you envious because I am generous?' [16] So the last will be first, and the first will be last."

At the close of Matthew 19, Jesus reminded his disciples that the kingdom of heaven would be radically different from the way things are in this world. In the prevailing culture, "to the victor go the spoils" and "might makes right," but in the kingdom "many who are first will be last, and the last will be first" (Matt. 19:30).

To reinforce this claim that the kingdom turns the world's values topsy-turvy, Matthew adds Jesus' unsettling parable about laborers who were hired at various times in the day to work in a vineyard only to discover that they had hired on with a very unusual employer indeed.

Perhaps the first task in interpreting this parable is to say what it is *not* about. The parable is not a lesson in corporate economics or an example of how employers, even Christian ones, are to treat their employees. Any company that paid employees hired in December the same wage as those who worked a full twelve months would soon have trouble finding anybody in the office from January to November. Any teacher who gave an "A" to a student who registered for the course on the last day of class would face a justifiable revolt on the part of the students who showed up for class and handed in the required assignments.

No, the purpose of this parable is not to provide a practical guide for the management of a vineyard, a factory, or a classroom. Indeed, the aim of this parable is to be monumentally impractical, to fracture so thoroughly our expectations, our customary patterns of practicality, that we are forced to think new thoughts—new thoughts about ourselves, about other people, and about God.

Here are some of the ways the parable generates new insights:

1. The parable invites us to see the landowner as a symbol for God. This is not the same as saying that the landowner *is* God; the connection is more poetic than that, but the way the landowner operates in the parable is intended to evoke in our imaginations something of the character of God.

Notice, for instance, that the focus of the landowner's concern is always on the laborers, not on the crop or on his own profit. Ordinarily, one would expect the story to say that the landowner hired some harvesters early in the day, but, when he found out that there was more crop than these first workers could handle, he went out to secure extra help. But no, the story says that the owner hired more workers because he found them standing around, out of work (Matt. 20:3, 5, 6). In other words, the landowner is motivated by *their* need for work, not his need for workers.

Particularly touching is the exchange with the five o'clock crew. When the landowner found them still loitering in the market near the end of the day, he asked them, "Why are you standing here idle all day?" (Matt. 20:6). "Because no one needs us," they respond. A normal employer would say, "Well that's tough" or, perhaps more compassionately, "I wish I could use you, but we're full at the moment. The economy, you understand. Maybe it will pick up soon." But this is no normal employer. This divine landowner employs even those the world ignores and forgets. As he surveys these idle folk who stand there like the leftover kids on a ball field whom nobody wants on the team, he calls out graciously, "I can use you. You also go into the vineyard."

2. Because the landowner is a symbol for God, the parable also encourages us to place ourselves in the shoes of the laborers and to rethink how we relate to God. Notice how the various groups of workers operate out of quite different agreements with the landowner. The early morning group made a firm and clear contract for a regular day's wage. Before they would go into the vineyard, they wrangled a bargain for a denarius. The nine o'clock, noon, and three o'clock shifts, however, were less specific, perhaps a bit more trusting. They went into the vineyard only on the landowner's word that he would pay them "whatever is right" (Matt. 20:4). The five o'clock workers struck no deal whatsoever; all it took to get them into the vineyard was the simple invitation of the landowner, "You also go" (Matt. 20:7).

At the end of the day, the landowner gives all the workers what they need. Everybody gets a full day's wage; everybody gets a denarius; everybody gets enough to provide for life. When the all-day laborers grumble about the pay scale, carping that the one-hour crowd has been made their equals, the landowner merely reminds one of them that he got what he bargained for: "Friend, I am doing you no wrong; did you not agree with me for the usual daily wage?" (Matt. 20:13).

The parable dramatically contrasts these first-hour workers with those employed the last hour. The last-hour crew—those who have waited in vain throughout the day for a call, those who are desperate and needy and who know it, those who realize that they would stand idle and useless all day were it not for the benevolence of the landowner, those who in relief and joy and trust respond to the command of the landowner to go—are given sheer grace: a day's wage. The first-hour workers, even though they don't recognize it, are also given grace: a day's wage, the sustenance of life. But grace is not their framework. We have already seen that they are bargainers, contract workers. They think that life works according to deals and negotiations; they even strike bargains with the Almighty. They count up good deeds, check their time cards, and divvy out their devotion with measuring spoons. Their vocabulary is filled with cries of "I deserve" and "where's mine?" and "it is my God-given right." The contrast could not be greater. The bargainers are working for a denarius; the latecomers are working for the landowner, for God. Both get what they are working for.

3. In the ordinary sense, all the workers get a denarius, a typical daily wage for laborers. But this is a parable about the kingdom of heaven, and we are compelled to think beyond the ordinary sense. What is a "daily wage" in the kingdom of heaven? That question sends us back to the previous story, in which Peter asks Jesus about the "wages" of followers of Jesus, "What then will we have?" (Matt. 19:27). Jesus' answer? "A hundredfold, and . . . eternal life" (Matt. 19:29). In other words, at the end of the day all who have labored in God's vineyard, all who have served in the work of the kingdom, will be lavished with the "daily wage" of heaven: all the treasure of God.

Suddenly we see plainly the true poverty of the first-hour workers. Everybody in the parable is tendered with the wealth of the kingdom; the deep river of providence flows through everybody's life. God gives everyone a daily wage so extravagant that no one could ever spend it all. A deluge of grace descends on all; torrents of joy and blessing fall everywhere. And there these first-hour workers stand, drenched in God's mercy, an ocean of peace running down their faces, clutching their little contracts and whining that they deserve more rain.

4. The landowner's speech at the end of the parable could well serve as a summary of Matthew's theology. The landowner is free to do what he will with what he owns, and he uses this freedom to be generous (Matt. 20:15). The same is true of God. "The earth is the LORD's and all that is in it," and, despite our schemes of religious merit and competition, God chooses to be generous. To the leper, to the lame, to the Gentile, to the last and the least, God is merciful.

Now, the question is, What do we think of the way God uses the divine freedom? What do we think of this kind of gracious God? What do we really think about a God whose basic character is mercy and forgiveness? When it is shown toward us, of course, we like it fine, but the test comes when God shows mercy to people we do not think deserve it. When we look in our pay envelopes and find that we received the same measure of mercy as those who, in our opinion, have arrived too late with too little, then our response is a test of kingdom character.

The phrase "are you envious because I am generous?" (Matt. 20:15) can be more literally translated "is your eye evil because I am good?" This "evil eye" language takes us back to the Sermon on the Mount, where Jesus described the eye as a symbol for the spirit of the whole person (see comments on Matt. 6:23). In other words, when the landowner says to the first-hour workers, "Are you envious because I am generous?" he is really saying, "Does my generosity expose the poverty of your own spirit?" Indeed, this is a major theological theme in Matthew. In Jesus, the world sees the generosity of God, and everything depends upon how the human spirit responds to this divine display of good will.

Ever since Jesus left Galilee and began his long journey toward the cross (see Matt. 19:1), he has engaged in a series of exchanges that demonstrate the urgent nature of the kingdom and the insistent demands of the pilgrim way. At each juncture, some are offended by these exigencies and turn away.

Now, in this parable comes, ironically, the most challenging and offensive word of all: God is generous. God's generosity spills over the levees we have built to contain it and surges mercifully over the landscape of human life. The rush of God's generosity bears away in its flood every rickety shack built on human schemes of merit and this world's view of goodness. Whose spirit can match the mercy of God? Finally, only one human being was capable of that—Jesus. "Worthy is the Lamb that was slain. . . ."

THE CROSS AND THE CUP
Matthew 20:17–28

20:17 **While Jesus was going up to Jerusalem, he took the twelve disciples aside by themselves, and said to them on the way,** [18] **"See, we are going up to Jerusalem, and the Son of Man will be handed over to the chief priests and scribes, and they will condemn him to death;** [19] **then they will hand him over to the Gentiles to be mocked and flogged and crucified; and on the third day he will be raised."**

[20] **Then the mother of the sons of Zebedee came to him with her sons, and kneeling before him, she asked a favor of him.** [21] **And he said to her, "What do you want?" She said to him, "Declare that these two sons of mine will sit, one at your right hand and one at your left, in your kingdom."** [22] **But Jesus answered, "You do not know what you are asking. Are you able to**

drink the cup that I am about to drink?" They said to him, "We are able." [23] He said to them, "You will indeed drink my cup, but to sit at my right hand and at my left, this is not mine to grant, but it is for those for whom it has been prepared by my Father."

[24] When the ten heard it, they were angry with the two brothers. [25] But Jesus called them to him and said, "You know that the rulers of the Gentiles lord it over them, and their great ones are tyrants over them. [26] It will not be so among you; but whoever wishes to be great among you must be your servant, [27] and whoever wishes to be first among you must be your slave; [28] just as the Son of Man came not to be served but to serve, and to give his life a ransom for many."

Twice before, Jesus has warned his disciples that his life is moving inexorably toward suffering and death (see comments on Matt. 16:21 and Matt. 17:22–23). Now, as they walk along the road that leads up to Jerusalem, Jesus predicts his death for a third time. This prediction is somewhat more specific than the previous ones, for Jesus actually names the precise events that will occur: the mockery, the flogging, and crucifixion.

Once again, however, the point is not new information; the point is the cost of the kingdom. This whole section of Matthew, beginning with 19:1, is constructed like a series of increasingly narrow gates, each demanding a higher toll on the followers of Jesus. Now, the ultimate cost has been named: Following Jesus leads to the place of condemnation, mockery, torture, and death.

In a masterpiece of bad timing, the mother of James and John arrives on the scene to request that her sons be allowed to climb the kingdom ladder. With Jesus' speech about suffering, the cross, and the cost of discipleship still ringing in the air, she presses her request that Jesus give her sons the best seats at the kingdom feast table. At a formal banquet, the host was positioned in the middle, with the most honored guest on the right and the next most honored on the left. This mother wants to be sure that, when the place cards are set out in the kingdom, her two boys have the choice assignments.

When the Gospel of Mark tells this story, James and John themselves, in a dense moment of almost incredible misunderstanding, make the embarrassing request (see Mark 10:35–45). Matthew, however, generally creates a more positive impression of the disciples, and most scholars believe that Matthew has introduced the mother here as a buffer to preserve this view.

If so, it is a half-hearted device, because Jesus immediately addresses James and John directly, not their mother: "You do not know what you are asking. Are you able to drink the cup that I am about to drink?" (Matt. 20:22). In other words, if you want to sit next to Jesus at the kingdom banquet, you must drink from the same cup as he drinks, the cup of suffering. This image of a cup filled with the bitter wine of suffering is taken from the Old Testament (see especially Isa. 51:17, 22; Jer. 25:15; Lam. 4:21).

James and John respond to Jesus' question by vowing that they are, indeed, able to drink this cup, to share in Jesus' suffering. In a sense, they are correct. James and John, as leaders in the early Christian community, will endure its persecutions and suffer for their faith; James will die a martyr's death by Herod's sword (see Acts 12:2). As Jesus says, "You will indeed drink my cup . . ." (Matt. 20:23). In another sense, though, they are not able. After only a meager taste of the caustic wine, James and John, as well as all the others, threw down the cup and "deserted him and fled" (Matt. 26:56).

Who is able to drink the cup? Only one, and it was a deep crisis even for him. "My Father, if it is possible, let this cup pass from me," Jesus will later pray at Gethsemane (Matt. 26:39). But finally, and willingly, Jesus lifts the cup to his lips and freely drinks, "My Father, if this cannot pass unless I drink it, your will be done" (Matt. 26:42).

When the other disciples discovered the ambitious maneuver of James and John, they howled in protest, probably not because they were morally offended but because they feared the Zebedee brothers were jockeying ahead. Jesus used this occasion to teach once again the lesson of humble leadership (see Matt. 18:1–5). What is the model of leadership in the secular culture (that is, among "the rulers of the Gentiles")? The world is full of spiteful tyrants, power hungry CEOs, and top-down managers who "lord it over" people, but these are not the models to be emulated in the Christian community. The church should not have organizational charts with the influential at the top exerting their influence over the peons below. Indeed, in the Christian community, the great ones are the little ones, the servants (in Greek, "deacons," those who wait on tables) and slaves (Matt. 20:27).

It is, of course, very strenuous for the church to maintain the role of servant leadership. Instead of waiting on tables, the church often wants reserved parking places. Who among us is able perfectly to choose the role of humble service? Only Jesus, who "gave his life a ransom for many" (Matt. 20:28). Only the Son of Man, only Jesus lived totally the kind of life about which it could be said that he "came not to be served but to serve" (Matt. 20:28). Finally, only one human being was able. "Worthy is the Lamb that was slain. . . ."

THE HEALING SERVANT
Matthew 20:29–34

> 20:29 As they were leaving Jericho, a large crowd followed him. [30] There were two blind men sitting by the roadside. When they heard that Jesus was passing by, they shouted, "Lord, have mercy on us, Son of David!" [31] The crowd sternly ordered them to be quiet; but they shouted even more loudly, "Have mercy on us, Lord, Son of David!" [32] Jesus stood still and called them, saying, "What do you want me to do for you?" [33] They said to him, "Lord, let our eyes be opened." [34] Moved with compassion, Jesus touched their eyes. Immediately they regained their sight and followed him.

Jesus has just taught his disciples about servant leadership; now he practices what he preached. Leaving Jericho for Jerusalem, a large crowd following in their wake, Jesus and the disciples encounter two blind men by the road (Mark 10:46–52 presents only one blind man, but it is typical of Matthew to double up on the number of such folk; see the same thing in Matthew 8:28–34; 9:27–31).

The blind men cry out, "Lord, have mercy on us, Son of David!" (Matt. 20:30). In sum, they acknowledge Jesus' royal lineage and his lordly, messianic standing. By their cry, they defer to Jesus; they recognize that he is in the position of power. The rulers of this earth, Jesus told his disciples, use power to "lord it over" people (Matt. 20:25). Jesus, however, displays another kind of power. He "emptied himself, taking the form of a slave" (Phil. 2:7). Heading to the cross, he uses his power to serve, uses his status to "lord it under" these blind beggars. "What do you want me to do for you?" asks the servant king (Matt. 20:32). When they ask for their eyes to be opened, the Son of Man, who came not to be served but to serve, was moved with compassion, touched their eyes with healing, and gave them what they asked (Matt. 20:34).

By telling this story of the two blind men as he does, Matthew creates a vague sense of déjà vu. Somewhere in our memory, we faintly recall having met these blind men before, only to realize that, in a way, we have— not *these* blind men exactly, but two others quite like them, back in Matthew 9:27–31. In the earlier account, the two blind men cry out to Jesus in words very similar to the later story: "Have mercy on us, Son of David!" (Matt. 9:27). In the preceding story, though, the blind men began by following Jesus (Matt. 9:27) but ended up disobeying Jesus and heading off on their own (Matt. 9:31). In this subsequent story, they began as bystanders and ended up as followers. Symbolically, these two new followers of Jesus are a contrast to James and John. James and John have been told about the cross, but they still do not see. These two blind men have been given their sight, and now they follow Jesus with their eyes wide open. What they will see, of course, is the servant king, the Son of Man, heading down the road of suffering. The blind men have called him the majestic and the royal Lord and Son of David. Now they are following him on the road to his coronation, which will be a strange ceremony indeed: "the Son of Man will be handed over . . . condemned . . . mocked and flogged and crucified" (Matt. 20:18–19). "Worthy is the Lamb that was slain. . . ."

13. Something Greater than the Temple Is Here
Matthew 21:1–23:39

As Jesus begins the last week of his life, he enters Jerusalem, the city of his destiny, and moves swiftly to the temple, which is, ironically, both the house of God and the epicenter of the opposition to God's Son. Earlier, in a dispute with the Pharisees back in Galilee, Jesus referred to himself when he said, "I tell you, something greater than the temple is here" (Matt. 12:6). Now—in Jerusalem, in the temple itself—Jesus proceeds to demonstrate that one greater than the temple has, indeed, arrived.

At the beginning of Jesus' ministry, the devil had tempted Jesus to throw himself off of the temple confident that God would send angels to break his fall (Matt. 4:5–6). Instead, Jesus throws himself into the temple, into the teeth of those who would destroy him, and no angels are sent to rescue him.

THE HUMBLE KING
ENTERS JERUSALEM
Matthew 21:1–11

21:1 **When they had come near Jerusalem and had reached Bethphage, at the Mount of Olives, Jesus sent two disciples,** 2 **saying to them, "Go into the village ahead of you, and immediately you will find a donkey tied, and a colt with her; untie them and bring them to me.** 3 **If anyone says anything to you, just say this, 'The Lord needs them.' And he will send them immediately."** 4 **This took place to fulfill what had been spoken through the prophet, saying,**

> 5 **"Tell the daughter of Zion,**
> **Look, your king is coming to you,**
> **humble, and mounted on a donkey,**
> **and on a colt, the foal of a donkey."**

6 **The disciples went and did as Jesus had directed them;** 7 **they brought the donkey and the colt, and put their cloaks on them, and he sat on them.** 8 **A very large crowd spread their cloaks on the road, and others cut**

branches from the trees and spread them on the road. ⁹ The crowds that
went ahead of him and that followed were shouting,
    "Hosanna to the Son of David!
    Blessed is the one who comes in the name of the Lord!
    Hosanna in the highest heaven!"
¹⁰ When he entered Jerusalem, the whole city was in turmoil, asking, "Who
is this?" ¹¹ The crowds were saying, "This is the prophet Jesus from Nazareth
in Galilee."

Jesus at last enters Jerusalem, a city of profound contradictions. On the
one hand, Jerusalem is the Holy City, "the city of the great King" (Matt.
5:35). "Pray for the peace of Jerusalem," sings the psalmist: "'May they
prosper who love you'" (Psalm 122:6). But Jerusalem is also the center of
opposition to Jesus (Matt. 15:1) and "the city that kills the prophets and
stones those who are sent to it!" (Matt. 23:37). Although this is Jesus' first
appearance in Jerusalem, the city has been looming—both promisingly
and menacingly—on the horizon from the beginning. Twice Jesus has
told his disciples that Jerusalem will be the place where he will suffer and
die, and also the place where he will be raised from the dead (Matt. 16:21;
20:18). The whole city of Jerusalem shook with fear when Jesus was born
(Matt. 2:3); it will shake with apocalyptic dread and hope at his death
(Matt. 27:51–54).

    The story of Jesus' entry into Jerusalem begins with the curious account
of the securing of the two animals on which Jesus will ride. The story is
unusual in at least two respects. First, there is Jesus' strange instruction
that, if anyone should accuse the disciples of rustling these two beasts, they
are simply to say that "the Lord needs them" (Matt. 21:3) and all will be
fine. Does this mean that Jesus has previously made arrangements for the
animals, or does Jesus somehow (supernaturally?) know in advance what
will happen?

    Probably Matthew's theology is in high gear at this point, and the reader
is being invited to put on theological bifocals and to read these Jerusalem
events at two levels simultaneously. On one level we see the wild, even
chaotic, forces of the present age, forces that will spew out their bitter
venom at Jesus and in a terrifying frenzy crucify him. At this level everything is random, unpredictable. The disciples are sent out to gather up two
haphazardly placed animals wherever they can find them. The animals'
caretaker would have every reason to be alarmed to see the beasts being ab-
ducted. On the other level, however, is the steady, undeterred cadence of
the will of God. Everything that is occurring as Jesus enters Jerusalem is
according to divine plan, even as Jesus appears to be the victim of powers
beyond his control. At the first level, Herod is king, Caesar is lord, Pilate

is governor, the demons rule, and they all will team up to take Jesus' life. At the other level, Jesus is Lord and King and Messiah, the forces of heaven rule, and no one will take his life; he will give it freely. The first level is visible to all; the second is seen only through the eyes of faith.

As Jesus heads down the Mount of Olives, the city of Jerusalem lives at the first level. Jerusalem does not know who Jesus is (Matt. 21:10); the city does not recognize that its Lord and king is about to enter. Yet, even though this truth is hidden from the eyes of most, there is a growing community of those who discern at the second, deeper level. The disciples are the core of this new community; they confess that Jesus is Lord, and their eyes see what many prophets longed to see but did not see (Matt. 13:17). The two blind men just healed by Jesus (Matt. 20:29–34) also follow and know to call him "Lord." And now, still others will be added to the number of those who have eyes to see and ears to hear. Now another character is added to the cast of those who somehow recognize this deeper, truer level—the caretaker of the two animals. His willing response to the command "the Lord has need of them" is a tacit acknowledgment of the true currents of God running steady beneath the churning sea, an incipient response of faith and obedience. "The paschal glory is already shining through the narrative" (Meier, *Matthew*, 233).

The second curious thing about this story is the fact that Jesus sends his disciples after two animals instead of just one. We have the odd and potentially amusing picture of Jesus riding into Jerusalem astride both a donkey and a colt (in contrast to Mark 11:7; Luke 19:35; and John 12:14, where, more reasonably, Jesus rides only one animal). Almost all scholars agree that the reason Matthew depicts Jesus atop two animals is because he is at pains to show that Jesus' entry into Jerusalem was in every way a fulfillment of the scriptures (Matt. 21:5). Scholars do not agree, though, about whether or not Matthew got carried away here and made a mistake.

The scripture Matthew cites here is composed of phrases taken from two prophetic passages: Isaiah 62:11, "Say to daughter Zion . . . ," combined with a portion of Zechariah 9:9, "Lo, your king comes to you; . . . humble and riding on a donkey, on a colt, the foal of a donkey." Now, superficially it may appear that the Zechariah quotation describes *two* animals—a donkey and a colt. Actually, though, only one animal is meant. "On a donkey, on a colt" is a textbook example of parallelism, a common device in Hebrew poetry where something is said once and then repeated for emphasis in a slightly different fashion.

Some argue that Matthew simply misunderstands this parallelism and, thus, supplies two beasts instead of one. More likely, however, Matthew, in good rabbinical fashion, found hidden meaning in the two different words in the prophetic text, "donkey" and "colt." Garland has suggested that the donkey, a coronation animal, may have stood in Matthew's mind for Jesus' royal status as the Son of David, whereas the more humble colt may have represented Jesus' lowly servant role (Garland, *Reading Matthew*, 210). Whether or not this particular interpretation is correct, Matthew is conveying a theological truth here, and he risks the somewhat improbable picture of Jesus straddling two beasts in order to make his point: King Jesus' humble entrance into Jerusalem was, in the deepest sense, a fulfillment of God's intent to save humanity as declared in scripture.

As Jesus makes his way into the city, two discrete groups react: "the crowds" and "the whole city" (Matt. 21:9, 10). The crowds will eventually turn on Jesus, but, for the moment they are followers (Matt. 20:29), even if their understanding is flawed (Matt. 20:31). The crowds spread their cloaks and tree branches on the road as a royal and festive welcome (see 2 Kings 9:13) and greet Jesus with a joyful hosanna, the language of which is taken from Psalm 118:25–26. "The whole city," on the other hand," is "in turmoil"; the Greek actually reads "shaken," as in an earthquake (Matt. 21:10).

"The whole city," for their part, has no idea who Jesus is. When they ask about his identity, the crowds respond, "This is the prophet Jesus from Nazareth in Galilee" (Matt. 21:11). This exchange is reminiscent of the dialogue in Psalm 24:8: "Who is the King of glory? The LORD, strong and mighty." In this case, however, both the call and the response are incomplete. "The whole city" fails to recognize Jesus' kingship, and the "crowds" name him only as a prophet, a correct and important title, but one that goes only so far (see Matt. 16:14). Both "the whole city" and "the crowds" have much to learn.

THE LORD CHALLENGES
THE TEMPLE ESTABLISHMENT
Matthew 21:12–17

21:12 Then Jesus entered the temple and drove out all who were selling and buying in the temple, and he overturned the tables of the money changers and the seats of those who sold doves. [13] He said to them, "It is written,
'My house shall be called a house of prayer';
but you are making it a den of robbers."
[14] The blind and the lame came to him in the temple, and he cured them. [15] But when the chief priests and the scribes saw the amazing things that he did, and heard the children crying out in the temple, "Hosanna to the Son of David," they became angry [16] and said to him, "Do you hear what these are saying?" Jesus said to them, "Yes; have you never read,

'Out of the mouths of infants and nursing babies
you have prepared praise for yourself'?"
[17] He left them, went out of the city to Bethany, and spent the night there.

Jesus' first act upon entering the city is dramatic indeed. He creates a scene in the area of the temple, the sacred center of Jerusalem. The customary image in Sunday school art of Jesus striding dauntlessly into the very temple sanctuary itself to overturn tables is inaccurate. The word translated "temple" (Matt. 21:12) actually refers to the whole temple precinct, a crowded and bustling complex of courtyards and buildings. The temple proper, the "holy of holies," was the centerpiece of this cluster, but it was only one structure among many. Jesus' encounter took place not in the temple proper but in a large open arena called the "Court of the Gentiles," where the selling of animals and the exchange of foreign money—both necessary services for the temple sacrifices—took place.

Matthew clearly describes what Jesus did. He drove out all those involved in the sale of sacrificial animals, both the sellers and their customers, giving special attention to the sellers of doves (the offering of doves was permitted for women, lepers, and the poor). Furthermore, he overturned the tables of the money changers (Matt. 21:12). But why did Jesus do this? The answer is not so clear. The popular notion that the temple had become commercialized and Jesus was "cleansing" it, restoring it to its previous sacred purpose, is false. The sacred role of the temple *was* the offering of sacrifices and the making of offerings under the direction of the priests. If these functions were to be fulfilled, then someone had to provide the animals to be sacrificed, and someone had to change the Greek and Roman coins the pilgrims brought with them into Jewish coins suitable for offerings. The practice of selling animals and exchanging money in the temple area was no more impure than handing out pledge cards and offering envelopes in churches today. Jesus is not a reformer; he is a kingdom revolutionary. He is not improving the temple; he is attacking the temple, and it is doomed: "not one stone will be left here upon another; all will be thrown down" (Matt. 24:2).

In the Gospel of Matthew, Jesus demolishes the religious structures of his day, not in order to create havoc and to strew the landscape with wreckage, but in order to accomplish the deep sense of the will of God, to allow God's true intent for the world to emerge. We have already seen in his teaching and healing that Jesus fulfilled the law of God by tearing down the established view of the law and building up something new: "You have heard it said . . . but I say to you. . . ." Lest anyone misunderstand his goal, Jesus asserted, "Do not think that I have come to abolish the law or the prophets; I have come not to abolish but to fulfill" (Matt. 5:17). Now Jesus does the same with the whole temple system. In order to fulfill God's will, Jesus overturns the old edifice and erects something new. He is building a new temple out of his words and deeds. Jesus is vacating the old in order to clear out a space where the messiah reigns and the unprecedented reality of the kingdom of heaven holds sway. In Jesus, truly "something greater than the temple is here" (Matt. 12:6).

The key to understanding Jesus' actions is found in the two prophetic quotations he twines together to explain himself: "It is written, 'My house shall be called a house of prayer' [from Isa. 56:7]; but you are making it a den of robbers" (from Jer. 7:11). We see here the contrast between what the temple was supposed to represent and what the temple had become. For the Old Testament prophets, the temple was intended to be a means for people to draw near to God, not an end in itself. Indeed, the temple was the symbol of the deepest of all truths about Israel, that the distinctive character of Israel was its intimate and abiding relationship to God. In other words, Israel was defined by *prayer*, by its access and communion with God, and the temple was to be a "house of prayer," a place that symbolized and enacted this union between God and Israel.

But in actual operation, the temple was a "den of robbers." A robbers' den is not the place where thievery is committed; it is a hiding place where thieves go to be safe after committing their crimes. The prophet Jeremiah, who was the first to call the temple "a den of robbers," accused the people of Judah of the crime of breaking the Ten Commandments—stealing, murdering, bearing false witness, serving other gods—and then of sliding home to the temple, saying, "We are safe!" (Jer. 7:8–10).

What were the crimes in Jesus' day? Two chapters later (Matthew 23), Jesus will read out the charges in a bill of indictment, but we can already discern the broad contours. The people, led by the religious officials, had constructed not a "house of prayer" but a self-serving house of privilege. The prophet Isaiah had dreamed of a great highway providing access to God, the "Holy Way . . . for God's people" (Isa. 35:8), but the religious leaders had erected roadblocks and exit ramps.

The old temple was the place where "the blind and the lame shall not come into the house" (2 Sam. 5:8; see also Lev. 21:18). Now, however, the Messiah himself has pushed over the roadblocks and repaved the Holy Highway, and, astonishingly, "the blind and the lame came to him in the temple" (Matt. 21:14). The old temple was a place of privilege, where only those deemed righteous by the purity codes enforced by the priests could be considered worthy. Now the Son of David has cleared out the old temple and built the new, where even children, those counted of little value (see comments on Matt. 18:1–5), could sing "Hosanna to the Son of David," embodying the truth of Psalm 8:2: "Out of the mouths of infants . . . you have prepared praise" (Matt. 21:15–16). As Jesus said earlier in the Gospel, the so-called "wise and intelligent" have missed the meaning of his deeds, whereas God has "revealed them to infants" (Matt. 11:25). It is a sign of the sickness of the old regime that what angers the chief priests and the scribes about Jesus' temple assault is the sight of people being healed and the sound of children singing hosannas.

Jesus' attack on the temple establishment continues to serve as a warning to all religious institutions, especially to churches. The essential mission of the church is the increase of the love of God and neighbor, and when Christians live as people of mercy and peace, forgiveness and righteousness, prayer and justice, it allows the world to see the surprising ways of God and to draw near. The sign of a faithful church is that the hurting and bruised of the world—"the blind and the lame"—are healed and those whom the world counts of little value—"the children"—are gathered in to sing praises to the Son of David. However, when Christians simply mirror the grabbing and getting values of the world and then retreat to the safety of the sanctuary, then the living Christ enters this den of robbers and turns over the tables of religious respectability.

One puzzling aspect of this story is that, when Jesus quotes Isaiah, he abbreviates: "My house shall be called a house of prayer." Isaiah actually said, "My house shall be called a house of prayer *for all peoples*" (Isa. 56:7). According to Mark, Jesus in the temple uttered the full quotation from Isaiah (see Mark 11:17). Matthew, in other words, has intentionally edited out the words "for all peoples." Why? Some have suggested that Matthew eliminates the phrase as meaningless, because the temple had already been destroyed at the hand of the Romans by the time Matthew wrote his Gospel. It is more likely that Matthew has in mind a strict order of salvation history. At this point in his ministry, Jesus is Israel's messiah; he is fulfilling God's promises to Israel and renewing Israel's temple. After the resurrection, those promises will spill over to "all the peoples," that is, to the Gentiles (Matt. 28:19).

THE CONDEMNING
OF THE FIG TREE
Matthew 21:18–22

21:18 **In the morning, when he returned to the city, he was hungry.** [19] **And seeing a fig tree by the side of the road, he went to it and found nothing at** all on it but leaves. Then he said to it, "May no fruit ever come from you again!" And the fig tree withered at once. [20] When the disciples saw it, they were amazed, saying, "How did the fig tree wither at once?" [21] Jesus answered them, "Truly I tell you, if you have faith and do not doubt, not only will you do what has been done to the fig tree, but even if you say to this mountain, 'Be lifted up and thrown into the sea,' it will be done. [22] Whatever you ask for in prayer with faith, you will receive."

Admittedly this is a strange story, subject to confusion and misunderstanding. Viewed from the vantage point of contemporary psychology, Jesus potentially comes across as impetuous and destructive, not to mention ecologically insensitive. In Matthew's context, however, this is not the story of a rash Jesus dragged by his hunger into an impulsive tantrum; this is an enacted parable of God's judgment.

What Jesus does this day on the road into Jerusalem is, in a sense, a reprise of what he did in the temple the day before. When Jesus demonstrated the judgment of God by overturning the tables in the temple courtyard, he cited a prophetic cry of Jeremiah to the effect that the temple had become a "den of robbers" (Jer. 7:11). In the very next chapter of Jeremiah, the prophet continues the lament over the failings of God's own people: "When I wanted to gather them, says the LORD, there are no grapes on the vine, nor figs on the fig tree" (Jer. 8:13). Matthew's first readers would recognize that fig tree with no fruit not as an unlucky plant that happened to be in the wrong place at the wrong time but as a prophetic symbol of barren Jerusalem, of God's own people who resist what God is doing in the world.

The instant withering of the barren tree seems, of course, fearsome bad news, but, in the theological worldview of Matthew, it is actually quite good news. If we allow the symbolism to take hold and see the fig tree as a sign, first, of the holy but barren city of Jerusalem resisting the ministry of Jesus, but, beyond this, as representative of all that appears to offer nourishment, justice, and hope but finally gives only bitter disappointment, for all that seems to serve the saving and merciful purposes of God but is actually all show, then the act of withering becomes an announcement of God's promise for the redemption of all creation. Nothing that stands in the way of God's salvation will stand; only that which is good and fruitful, saving and merciful will endure.

The good news aspect of this story is underscored by Jesus' statement to the disciples about faith and prayer (Matt. 21:21–22). The theological point is that the church can trust the promises of God, can have confidence that God's saving purpose will prevail. Therefore, Jesus' followers can give evil and hatred a withering glare and can boldly head out to do the work of the kingdom even when seemingly insurmountable mountains stand in the way. They can take up causes every wise social critic says are hopeless. They can plant works of healing, peace, mercy, and justice even when every other tree on the lot is barren. They can go, as all must go, to the open grave and sneer in the barren face of death, saying to a mountain of grief, "Christ is the resurrection and the life! Despair be cast into the sea."

THE AUTHORITIES
CHALLENGE JESUS IN THE TEMPLE
Matthew 21:23–27

> 21:23 **When he entered the temple, the chief priests and the elders of the people came to him as he was teaching, and said, "By what authority are you doing these things, and who gave you this authority?"** [24] **Jesus said to them, "I will also ask you one question; if you tell me the answer, then I will also tell you by what authority I do these things.** [25] **Did the baptism of John come from heaven, or was it of human origin?" And they argued with one another, "If we say, 'From heaven,' he will say to us, 'Why then did you not believe him?'** [26] **But if we say, 'Of human origin,' we are afraid of the crowd; for all regard John as a prophet."** [27] **So they answered Jesus, "We do not know." And he said to them, "Neither will I tell you by what authority I am doing these things.**

Jesus has entered Jerusalem as messiah and king. He has been greeted by noisy hosannas from the crowd and has generated turmoil all over the city. He has cleared out the temple of business as usual and, in effect, put himself in its place. Now, as he enters the temple again—as teacher, king, messiah, and Lord—the religious officials, quite understandably, ask to see his credentials. "By what authority are you doing these things?" they challenge him (Matt. 21:23).

The reader of Matthew already knows the answer to their question. "All things," Jesus said before, "have been handed over to me by my Father" (Matt. 11:27), but this is not how he answers the religious officials. In traditional rabbinical fashion, he responds to their question with a question of his own: "Was John's ministry from God, or was he just a strong personality who held sway over the crowds?"

This was a tough question for the religious officials. If they answered that John was just a magnetic figure with merely human powers of persuasion and no more, then the people, who viewed John as one in the line of the great prophets, would be incensed. On the other hand, if they responded that John had a divine commission, then the people would rightly want to know why they, as keepers of the religious tradition, had not followed this God-ordained prophet, which, indeed, they had not (see Matt. 11:18). Damned if you do, and damned if you don't, so they decided to keep their mouths shut. "We do not know," they whimpered (Matt. 21:27).

Jesus' question was a sharp scalpel deftly dividing two different forms of authority. First, there is human authority. No matter how sophisticatedly it is packaged, human authority is a matter of raw power. If you have enough people behind you or guns with you, you have it, and what you say goes, period. Divine authority, on the other hand, has to do with truth, the truth of God, the truth about who God made us to be. In the short run, human authority can appear to overwhelm divine authority—even to crucify it—but, ultimately, God's truth prevails. When the Berlin Wall falls or when apartheid is toppled even when other people seem to have most of the guns and the might, then we see a foretaste of the triumph of divine authority. The powers-that-be are frightened, of course, by these early warning signs that earthly powers will not last forever. That is why one Herod tries to kill the child Jesus (Matt. 2:16) and the puppet of another Herod signs the death warrant of the man Jesus (Matt. 27:26). But God's truth is raised from the dead to announce that, when all is said and done, earthly authority has been gathered up into the divine: "All authority in heaven and on earth has been given to me" (Matt. 28:18).

When the religious leaders refuse to give Jesus an answer, he refuses to give them one. They have put their finger into the wind of popular opinion and played the human power game the best they can. Because they have thus disclosed that they define authority only on the human side of the equation, there is no way that they can comprehend Jesus' authority. "No one knows the Son except the Father, and no one knows the Father except the Son and anyone to whom the Son chooses to reveal him" (Matt. 11:27). "Neither will I tell you," said Jesus, "by what authority I am doing these things" (Matt. 21:27).

THREE PARABLES
ABOUT DISOBEDIENCE
Matthew 21:28–22:14

21:28 "What do you think? A man had two sons; he went to the first and said, 'Son, go and work in the vineyard today.' 29 He answered, 'I will not'; but later he changed his mind and went. 30 The father went to the second and said the same; and he answered, 'I go, sir'; but he did not go. [31] Which of the two did the will of his father?" They said, "The first." Jesus said to them, "Truly I tell you, the tax collectors and the prostitutes are going into the kingdom of God ahead of you. [32] For John came to you in the way of righteousness and you did not believe him, but the tax collectors and the prostitutes believed him; and even after you saw it, you did not change your minds and believe him.

[33] "Listen to another parable. There was a landowner who planted a vineyard, put a fence around it, dug a wine press in it, and built a watchtower. Then he leased it to tenants and went to another country. [34] When the harvest time had come, he sent his slaves to the tenants to collect his produce. [35] But the tenants seized his slaves and beat one, killed another, and stoned another. [36] Again he sent other slaves, more than the first; and they treated them in the same way. [37] Finally he sent his son to them, saying, 'They will respect my son.' [38] But when the tenants saw the son, they said to themselves, 'This is the heir; come, let us kill him and get his inheritance.' [39] So they seized him, threw him out of the vineyard, and killed him. [40] Now when the owner of the vineyard comes, what will he do to those tenants?" [41] They said to him, "He will put those wretches to a miserable death, and lease the vineyard to other tenants who will give him the produce at the harvest time."

[42] Jesus said to them, "Have you never read in the scriptures:
'The stone that the builders rejected
    has become the cornerstone;
this was the Lord's doing,
    and it is amazing in our eyes'?

[43] Therefore I tell you, the kingdom of God will be taken away from you and given to a people that produces the fruits of the kingdom. [44] The one who falls on this stone will be broken to pieces; and it will crush anyone on whom it falls."

[45] When the chief priests and the Pharisees heard his parables, they realized that he was speaking about them. [46] They wanted to arrest him, but they feared the crowds, because they regarded him as a prophet.

22:1 Once more Jesus spoke to them in parables, saying: [2] "The kingdom of heaven may be compared to a king who gave a wedding banquet for his son. [3] He sent his slaves to call those who had been invited to the wedding banquet, but they would not come. [4] Again he sent other slaves, saying, 'Tell those who have been invited: Look, I have prepared my dinner, my oxen and my fat calves have been slaughtered, and everything is ready; come to the wedding banquet.' [5] But they made light of it and went away, one to his farm, another to his business, [6] while the rest seized his slaves, mistreated them, and killed them. [7] The king was enraged. He sent his troops, destroyed those murderers, and burned their city. [8] Then he said to his slaves, 'The wedding is ready, but those invited were not worthy. [9] Go therefore into the main streets, and invite everyone you find to the wedding banquet.' [10] Those slaves went out into the streets and gathered all whom they found, both good and bad; so the wedding hall was filled with guests.

11 "But when the king came in to see the guests, he noticed a man there who was not wearing a wedding robe, 12 and he said to him, 'Friend, how did you get in here without a wedding robe?' And he was speechless. 13 Then the king said to the attendants, 'Bind him hand and foot, and throw him into the outer darkness, where there will be weeping and gnashing of teeth.' 14 For many are called, but few are chosen."

After having acted out a parable with the fig tree (Matt. 21:18–22), Jesus now adds three additional parables, these in more traditional narrated story form. The audience for these parables is the same group of religious leaders who have just challenged Jesus' authority in the temple (Matt. 21:23–27). While each of these parables has its own plot and set of characters, the basic theme of all three is the same as the moral of the fig tree incident—Israel's failure to respond to God's saving action in the messiah Jesus.

The Two Sons
(Matthew 21:28–32)

This brief parable is hardly a full story; it is more a vignette of agricultural family life. This parable is, in its own way, a narrative depiction of Jesus' earlier statement in the Sermon on the Mount: "Not everyone who says to me, 'Lord, Lord,' will enter the kingdom of heaven, but only the one who does the will of my Father in heaven" (Matt. 7:21). Matthew's earliest readers would undoubtedly have read this, at least the first time through, as a description of the church-synagogue tension in which they found themselves (see Introduction). Israel, in the form of the synagogue and its leaders, was like the second son in the parable, saying "yes, Lord," but rejecting Jesus as messiah. The church, especially with its new Gentile converts, was like the first son, those who once said "no" but changed their minds (converted) and joined the community gathered around Jesus Christ.

That was, at least, the simple interpretation of the parable. But parables are rarely as simple as they seem, and Jesus' opening question, "What do you think?" (Matt. 21:28), was addressed to the reader of Matthew as well as to the religious officials in the temple. Now it was the church that needed to think, that needed to be cautious. In the middle of patting themselves on the back for being those who, unlike the synagogue, responded positively to the kingdom, they would be caught up short by the realization that this self-congratulation potentially placed them in a new position in the parable. Now, the church possibly was in the role of the second son, saying, "Yes, Lord." But were they actually showing up for work in the vineyard? Were they doing the peacemaking, mercy-granting, justice-seeking work of the kingdom? It was food for thought.

Moreover, the self-serving notion that the "synagogue across the street" had said "no" to the kingdom, while they, the church, had said "yes" afforded yet another reversal in interpretation. Maybe the synagogue was now in the role of the first son, saying "no, I won't go," but poised to change its mind. As commentator John R. Donahue has noted, "The 'surprise' of this parable is that Matthew summons the Jewish leaders of his day to be like the first son and to join the heirs of tax collectors and harlots—the Christian community—while warning his own community not to say 'Lord' without doing the will of the Father" (Donahue, *The Gospel in Parable*, 88–89).

The Wicked Tenants
(Matthew 21:33–46)

This parable, as it stands in Matthew, is clearly an allegory; that is, it is a kind of code with each major element in the parable symbolizing something outside the story. We can recognize this right away because of the opening description of the landowner carefully preparing his vineyard. He "planted a vineyard, put a fence around it, dug a wine press in it, and built a watchtower" (Matt. 21:33). This almost exactly matches the description of the actions of a vineyard owner portrayed by the prophet Isaiah (Isa. 5:1–2), and Isaiah clearly announces that "the vineyard of the LORD of hosts is the house of Israel" (Isa. 5:7). The religious leaders who heard this parable from Jesus as well as the first readers of Matthew would know this familiar story from Isaiah and would readily make the allegorical connections: God is the vineyard owner and Israel is the vineyard.

What happens next is an astonishing cycle of violence and a thinly veiled allegory of the Christian story of God's relationship to Israel. The pieces fall neatly into place. The tenants of the vineyard, those responsible for the harvest, are clearly the authorities entrusted by God with leading Israel to fruitful obedience, but who do not. The slaves who are sent again and again, only to be rejected and abused, stand for the prophets calling the people to faithfulness. In the words of Jeremiah, "I [the Lord] have persistently sent all my servants the prophets to them, day after day; yet they did not listen to me, or pay attention, but they stiffened their necks" (Jer. 7:25–26). The owner's son is, of course, Jesus himself, who is thrown outside of the vineyard and killed (see Heb. 13:12).

Thus, when Jesus turns to his hearers and queries them about what the vineyard owner will do to these tenants who greet his servants with violence and murder even his own son, their verdict pronounced on these scoundrels is, in essence, their own judgment. Those wretched tenants, they say, will be put to a "miserable death" (would Matthew's readers connect this to the destruction of Jerusalem in A.D. 70?), and the vineyard will be leased to new occupants (the Jewish Christians in Matthew's church, a group that will eventually include Gentiles), tenants who will "give him the produce at the harvest time" (Matt. 21:40–41).

In case any of these allegorical links were missed, Jesus makes them clear in his postparable announcement to his hearers (Matt. 21:42–44). He cites Psalm 118:22–23 regarding the rejected building stone that has become the cornerstone, a passage that the early church frequently quoted to refer to Jesus (see Acts 4:11; 1 Peter 2:7). He also proclaims that the "kingdom (that is, the vineyard) of God will be taken away from you and given to a people that produces the fruits of the kingdom" (Matt. 21:43). Verse 44 is missing from some of the ancient manuscripts of Matthew, and seems a bit out of place in its present location. It would more logically follow verse 42 (as it does in Luke 20:17–18), since it describes the consequences of continuing to reject the cornerstone. Any who think they can thwart the redemptive will of God in and through Jesus are mistaken; the weight of the stone breaks anyone who opposes its momentum.

Now it dawns on the chief priests and the Pharisees that the parables of the two sons and the wicked tenants are really stories about them and their fruitless disobedience. This realization causes them to want to place Jesus under arrest, but, true to their political instincts, they fear to act because of the popular view that Jesus is a prophet (the same view they held of John the Baptist; see Matt. 21:26).

So, at the basic level, the parable of the wicked tenants is an allegory about the disobedience of the people of Israel, especially their leaders, and the consequent turn of God toward a new people, the followers of Jesus Christ. Once more, however, the parable allows no self-congratulation on the part of the church. The Christian church is now in the position of being the tenants, and the parable begins all over again. Now the church is responsible to God for the harvest of the vineyard; now the church is challenged truly to be "a people that produces the fruits of the kingdom" (Matt. 21:43).

Moreover, it would be a mistake to read this parable too quickly into contemporary Jewish-Christian relations. It is too easy to hear this parable as God's total dismissal of the Jews in favor of the Christian community. We should remember that for Matthew's readers the issue was not Jew versus Christian. Matthew's church was largely, perhaps entirely, Jewish in membership (see Introduction), and the division with Judaism was, for them, a difference of conviction among Jews. Also, note the character of the vineyard owner, who stands as a symbol for God. Again and again he sends agents to the vineyard. There is special pathos about the decision to send the son. This is a vineyard owner reluctant to give up on the tenants, even caring enough for them to be willing to risk his own son in a situation with a history of violence. To be sure, judgment falls upon all who finally oppose God's purposes, but judgment—even when it is expressed in harsh Matthean tones—is always aimed at restoration (see comments on Matt. 7:1–9). After all, Matthew is writing the story of Jesus, who is Israel's messiah first, and only then the messiah of all the nations. Matthew's story is the story of Jesus, whose essential mission is to "save his people from their sins" (Matt. 1:21).

The Wedding Banquet
(Matthew 22:1–14)

Jesus adds a third parable—actually a two-part parable—to the set. The first part concerns a king who gives a wedding banquet for his son, but the people invited make excuses and refuse to come. So the king scours the countryside for guests. Most scholars think that the original parable that Jesus told can be seen by deleting verses 6–7 and that Matthew, or his source, added these extra verses to turn the parable into yet another allegory of Christian history (see comments on Matt. 21:33–46).

The supplemental verses make the story highly improbable; people kill other people and a city is destroyed in a military action—all over some rejected party invitations. These implausibilities simply highlight the fact that Matthew intends this to be read as an allegory, and his first readers would know how to decode the details:

king = God

son = Jesus

marriage feast = the great marriage feast of the Lamb
of God at the end of time (see
Matt. 8:11 and Rev. 19:9)

slaves = prophets

those invited = Israel

violence = Israel's rejection of prophets

destroyed city = fall of Jerusalem in A.D. 70

gathering of good and bad = evangelistic mission of church

wedding hall = church

So, at the close of the first part of this parable, we have a symbolic picture of Matthew's church. Matthew's readers can recognize their own faces. There they are, gathered at the son's wedding banquet as last-minute replacements for the original guest list—the people of Israel. They are jammed into this churchly banquet hall, both good folk and bad.

At this point, however, a puzzling development takes place. The king himself arrives and surveys the hodgepodge collection of partygoers, only to spy a man not wearing a proper wedding suit. The king reacts harshly. "Friend," he says to the man (and, in Matthew, the word "friend" always has a negative connotation, something like "Buster"), "how did you get in here without a wedding robe?" The man is left speechless, so the king orders the man booted, not merely out the door but "into the outer darkness, where there will be weeping and gnashing of teeth" (Matt. 22:12–13).

The obvious objection to this strange twist in the story is to protest that the man could not be expected to have on a wedding garment, because he, like the other guests, was recruited off the streets. A man plowing a field or tending a shop cannot be expected to pack a wedding garment in his lunch box just in case a late-breaking invitation slides down the chute.

But this is no ordinary story; it is an allegorical parable, and things in this parable stand for other things. The "wedding garment" symbolizes the Christian life. Like other clothing metaphors in the New Testament, this garment represents putting on the baptismal garment of Christ (see Gal. 3:27), being attired in the new self created in God's own likeness (Eph. 4:24; Col. 3:10), clothing oneself with the compassion, kindness, humility, meekness, and patience of one who belongs to the kingdom (Col. 3:12). Thus, the scene in which the king catches the man without a wedding garment is actually a picture of the end of time, when God comes as judge. Those who cry, "Lord, Lord, look at me over here in your church" may do so to no avail. What is needed is not presence at the punch bowl but a "wedding garment"; what is required is doing God's will (see Matt. 7:21). The final line—"many are called, but few are chosen"—should not be read literally. It reflects a traditional Jewish saying that basically means "everybody gets called but not everybody ends up worthy of it," or, in the context of this parable, "God wants everybody at the party, but not everybody wants to come or knows how to behave when they get there."

This parable urgently reminds us that being a part of the Christian community should make a discernible difference in who we are and how we live. In other words, there should be a sense of awe and responsiveness about belonging to the church, belonging to the community of Christ, being a child of the kingdom of heaven. Sure, the spotlighted guest in the parable was pressed in off the street unexpectedly and was probably wearing cutoffs and clodhoppers, but, when he got inside, only a fool would fail to see the difference between what he wore and where he was. He was in the banquet hall of the king; he was at the wedding feast for the royal son. The table was set with the finest food; the best wine flowed from regal chalices. He is the recipient of massive grace. Where is his awe? Where is his wonder? Where is his regard for generosity? The other guests humbly, quietly trade in their street clothes for the festive wedding garments of worship and celebration, but there he is, bellying up to the punch bowl, stuffing his mouth with fig preserves, and wiping his hands on his T-shirt. When the host demands to know where his wedding garment is, he is speechless, and well he should be. In his self-absorption, he hadn't the foggiest idea until that very moment that he was at a wedding banquet at all. Just so, to come into the church in response to the gracious, altogether unmerited invitation of Christ and then not conform one's life to that mercy is to demonstrate spiritual narcissism so profound that one cannot tell the difference between the wedding feast of the Lamb of God and happy hour in a bus station bar.

JESUS' FINAL EXAM
Matthew 22:15–46

> 22:15 Then the Pharisees went and plotted to entrap him in what he said. [16] So they sent their disciples to him, along with the Herodians, saying, "Teacher, we know that you are sincere, and teach the way of God in accordance with truth, and show deference to no one; for you do not regard people with partiality. [17] Tell us, then, what you think. Is it lawful to pay taxes to the emperor, or not?" [18] But Jesus, aware of their malice, said, "Why are you putting me to the test, you hypocrites? [19] Show me the coin used for the tax." And they brought him a denarius. [20] Then he said to them, "Whose head is this, and whose title?" [21] They answered, "The emperor's." Then he said to them, "Give therefore to the emperor the things that are the emperor's, and to God the things that are God's." [22] When they heard this, they were amazed; and they left him and went away.
>
> [23] The same day some Sadducees came to him, saying there is no resurrection; and they asked him a question, saying, [24] "Teacher, Moses said, 'If a man dies childless, his brother shall marry the widow, and raise up children for his brother.' [25] Now there were seven brothers among us; the first married, and died childless, leaving the widow to his brother. [26] The second did the same, so also the third, down to the seventh. [27] Last of all, the woman herself died. [28] In the resurrection, then, whose wife of the seven will she be? For all of them had married her."

²⁹ Jesus answered them, "You are wrong, because you know neither the scriptures nor the power of God. ³⁰ For in the resurrection they neither marry nor are given in marriage, but are like angels in heaven. ³¹ And as for the resurrection of the dead, have you not read what was said to you by God, ³² 'I am the God of Abraham, the God of Isaac, and the God of Jacob'? He is God not of the dead, but of the living." ³³ And when the crowd heard it, they were astounded at his teaching.

³⁴ When the Pharisees heard that he had silenced the Sadducees, they gathered together, ³⁵ and one of them, a lawyer, asked him a question to test him. ³⁶ "Teacher, which commandment in the law is the greatest?" ³⁷ He said to him, "'You shall love the Lord your God with all your heart, and with all your soul, and with all your mind.' ³⁸ This is the greatest and first commandment. ³⁹ And a second is like it: 'You shall love your neighbor as yourself.' ⁴⁰ On these two commandments hang all the law and the prophets."

⁴¹ Now while the Pharisees were gathered together, Jesus asked them this question: ⁴² "What do you think of the Messiah? Whose son is he?" They said to him, "The son of David." ⁴³ He said to them, "How is it then that David by the Spirit calls him Lord, saying,

⁴⁴ 'The Lord said to my Lord,
    "Sit at my right hand,
        until I put your enemies under your feet"'?
⁴⁵ If David thus calls him Lord, how can he be his son?" ⁴⁶ No one was able to give him an answer, nor from that day did anyone dare to ask him any more questions.

The ancient rabbis and other Jewish teachers were constantly honing their religious knowledge by posing difficult questions and testing each other. Jewish teachers made a productive game of putting forth various "what ifs" and sharpening their wits by trying out possible answers from the Bible and tradition.

In this section of his Gospel, Matthew presents Jesus as the subject of a round of such testings. Representatives of the several strands of Judaism step forward in turn to pose a series of difficult theological problems, and Jesus responds with astonishing wisdom in each case. These exchanges are not, however, part of a benign academic exercise. The questioners have the not-so-hidden motive of discrediting Jesus, of putting him in an embarrassing position and thereby stripping him of his popular support. Indeed, the situations placed before Jesus are so challenging and tricky that this section could well be termed "Jesus' final exam," both in the sense of difficulty (these dialogues show Jesus to be wiser than the best and brightest among the religious leaders) and in the sense of finality (this astute outflanking of the authorities seals Jesus' doom).

There are four separate exchanges.

The Tax Question
(Matthew 22:15–22)

The first team of examiners is composed of Pharisees and Herodians, a strange and unlikely alliance indeed. Only a mutual distaste for Jesus could have pushed these two parties together. The Herodians were a priestly group whose power base in Israel was founded largely on a set of alliances forged with the occupying Roman government. The Pharisees, by contrast, were a lay group within Judaism with a fervor to obey the law of Moses and to keep alive the zeal of the prophets. For the Pharisees, compromises with the pagan Romans would have been theologically unthinkable. By Matthew's day, rabbis loyal to the Pharisaical view had become the dominant force in synagogue-based Judaism. Thus, Matthew, whose church was in tension with the synagogue (see Introduction), is at pains to show that this first dialogue with Jesus was actually a sinister trap masterminded by the Pharisees and their disciples (Matt. 22:15).

The exchange begins with a bit of flattery, which functions merely as a setup for the trick question that follows. The effect of their praise is to say, "OK mister truth-teller who never shies away from controversy, handle this hot potato." The hot potato in question has to do with the legality of paying taxes to the Roman emperor. For a quarter of a century, Jews had been forced to pay, in Roman currency, a head tax to the Roman government. Some Jews rested easy with Roman rule and supported the tax (probably including the Herodians), but most of the citizens of Judah reacted to the idea of paying money to the pagan emperor with distaste ranging from mild provocation to seething insurrection. Indeed, when the tax was established, in A.D. 6, there was a small-scale armed revolt. Adding insult to injury was the fact that the tax, which amounted to a denarius (about a day's wage for a laborer; see comments on Matt. 20:1–16), was most often paid with the common denarius coin. This coin was minted with the image of Caesar Tiberius and carried the odious (to a Jew) inscription "Tiberius Caesar, august son of the divine Augustus and high priest."

So, to raise the question of paying taxes to the emperor was to pull the scab off a political and theological wound, which is exactly what Jesus' questioners did. "Is it lawful to pay taxes to the emperor, or not?" they asked (Matt. 22:17), knowing full well that this question, posed in public, put Jesus in a precarious position. If Jesus were to say, "No, according to the law of God, it is not lawful to pay taxes to Caesar," then the Roman government would swiftly move in on him as a dangerous political agitator. On the other hand, if Jesus were to reply, "Yes, it is lawful to pay the

Roman tax," then he would lose credibility with many of the people, who paid the tax but who did so only begrudgingly, since they considered the tax an illegal act of an oppressor government and a moral affront to their religion.

Jesus, however, was aware of the treachery of his interrogators, and he cleverly sidestepped their snare. He asked them for one of the tax coins and, when they produced one, he asked them whose image it bore. When they answered "the emperor's," he stated, "Give therefore to the emperor the things that are the emperor's, and to God the things that are God's" (Matt. 22:21).

Basically, there are two ways to understand Jesus' statement: a mild way and a more radical version. The mild variation interprets Jesus' words to mean in essence, "Look, the tax is not the issue. You pay the tax with Roman coins, and they bear the emperor's image and belong to the emperor. So give the emperor his little coins back and get on about the weightier business of rendering your lives to God. The coin is created in the emperor's image, but you are created in God's image; so give your whole self to the God who owns you."

The more radical version, which is the likelier rendition, is that Jesus refuses to answer the question and actually turns the tables on his examiners, showing them up as two-faced hypocrites. The question they posed to Jesus was designed to allow Jesus two equally bad alternatives. In effect they ask, "Are you a foolish, uncompromising revolutionary whose allegiance to the kingdom of heaven is actually a political revolution in disguise, or are you a smooth-talking street preacher who stirs up people with glib talk of God's majesty but who underneath advocates a get-along-go-along policy with the Roman, Gentile pigs?"

Jesus responds to this trick with a gambit of his own. When he asks them for the tax coin, they unsuspectingly reach into their purses and withdraw the evidence that exposes them—not him—as deceptive and hypocritical compromisers. They are the ones carrying around Caesar's money, not Jesus; they are the ones who have the emperor's image in their pocketbooks; they are the ones who have already bought into the pagan system. In this more radical interpretation, Jesus' words mean, "Everybody has to decide between Caesar and God. No one can serve two masters (Matt. 6:24). You seem to have made your decision, forged your convenient compromise. But what about your obligation to God? Render to God what belongs to God. Choose this day whom you will serve."

What this more radical interpretation does is not to provide any formula for resolving the tension between God and secular pressures but, rather, to upset any neat schemes of division. Whether we call it taxation, tithing, or stewardship, there is the temptation to compartmentalize life ("I set aside this part for God, and the rest belongs to me and to Caesar"). What Jesus says is that, although we may have to live under this or that Caesar and we may have to plunk down this or that tax, we are never Caesar's. We belong, body and soul, to the living God, and we are to render to God what is God's.

The Resurrection Question
(Matthew 22:23–33)

The next round of questioning comes from a different party in first-century Judaism: the Sadducees. It is important in understanding this exchange with Jesus to remember that the Sadducees, as distinguished from the Pharisees, considered only the Pentateuch (the first five books of the Old Testament, sometimes called the books of Moses) to be authentic scripture and, consequently, rejected any idea they could not find supported in those writings—including the doctrine of the resurrection of the dead.

So it is not surprising that these interrogators frame their question in terms of Moses' teaching (Matt. 22:24). They set up the problem by citing the Mosaic marriage law that requires that if a man dies childless, his brother is to marry the widow and produce heirs (this is sometimes called "levirate" marriage, from *levir*, the Latin word for brother-in-law; see Genesis 38:8; Deuteronomy 25:5–10). Having set forth this statute, they then pose an extreme case for Jesus to ponder—a widowed woman who has married seven brothers and has had children by none of them. The question is, In the resurrection, whose wife is she?

This is a multiple choice question, and all of the options the Sadducees think Jesus has are poor. Choice "A" is to name one of the brothers. In the resurrection, she will be the first brother's wife, or the last brother's wife, or the fourth brother's wife; pick one. This is a bad choice because each brother was equally her husband. Why, in the resurrection, would one brother have more of a claim than any of the others?

Then there is choice "B." Choice "B"—namely, in the resurrection, she will be the wife of *all seven* brothers—is even worse, since it is too confusing, conflictual, and finally absurd to deserve serious consideration.

That leaves choice "C," the answer the Sadducees hope that Jesus will choose, indeed believe that he will be forced to choose, namely: "You got me there, fellows. Since I cannot reasonably figure out whose wife this woman would be if there were such a thing as a resurrection, I suppose the case renders preposterous the whole idea of resurrection. You Sadducees were right all along; the teaching of Moses pretty well closes the book on the concept of an afterlife, and the only perpetuation a person has is here on this earth through one's descendants."

But Jesus surprises the Sadducees. He will not be trapped by their limited choices; instead, he challenges their basic assumptions. The way the Sadducees set up their little puzzle implied two things: one, that they knew the scriptures (that is, the Pentateuch) backward and forward; and two, that the ways of God were predictable. In other words, their trap depended upon a closed theological system of which they were the masters. Once they set up the dominoes about this woman who married seven brothers, they were confident that they could predict how they would fall; thus, there was no way out for Jesus.

Jesus informs them, however, that they do not know as much about either the scriptures or the ways of God as they think (Matt. 22:29). In regard to the ways of God, their test case assumes that the afterlife, were there to be one, would be simply an extension of the present tense, that God's future would simply be an eternal version of the status quo. "Whose wife will she be?" they wonder, assuming that earthly institutions, such as marriage, would just keep on functioning in the age to come and that the woman would still be a first-century-style wife who would be the property of some man in the kingdom to come. But the resurrection power of God does more than preserve; it transforms. And the kingdom of heaven is not a mirror image of earthly conditions. There is no marriage in the resurrection, Jesus tells them (Matt. 22:30). He could well have added that there are no schools, or hospitals, not even any churches in the resurrection, for all the temporary earthly structures necessary to give hope and healing to people in pilgrimage will have been transcended by the saving victory of Christ who "is all and in all!" (Col. 3:11). Those who are gathered up in the resurrection power, Jesus says, are "like angels" (Matt. 22:30). This does not mean that people in the resurrection are disembodied spirits. The language of angels is a graphic way of saying that resurrection involves a radically new form of existence.

At least one commentator, Rachel Wahlberg, has pondered what this exchange between Jesus and the Sadducees over the unnamed woman with seven husbands sounds like to the ears of women. Women hear, she maintains, the trumpet sound of the radically new resurrection existence. They especially hear that the woman in the Sadducees' test case would, in the kingdom of heaven, no longer "be a man's appendage, a possession . . . that she is not someone's property, that she has equal status in the resurrection, that she has a position not relative to anyone else" (Wahlberg, *Jesus According to a Woman*, 64–65).

In regard to the Sadducees' knowledge of the scriptures, Jesus makes a case that the Pentateuch itself teaches the doctrine of the resurrection, and the Sadducees have been blind to it. To demonstrate his point, Jesus quotes God's own self-description from one of the books of Moses: "I am the God of Abraham, the God of Isaac, and the God of Jacob" (Exod. 3:6, 15–16), emphasizing the present tense of that identification. In other words, God does not say to Moses, "I used to be the God of Abraham when Abraham was alive," but "I *am* the God of Abraham . . . " now. This implies that, though Abraham, Isaac, and Jacob are already dead in an earthly sense, they are still alive in the presence of God, for God is "God not of the dead, but of the living" (Matt. 22:32). Thus, claims Jesus, the Sadducees' own scriptures, the books of Moses themselves, teach the resurrection.

When the crowds heard how Jesus outsmarted the Sadducees, they were left wagging their heads in astonishment (Matt. 22:33). As for the aristocratic Sadducees themselves, the irony, as Meier has noted, is that, having been bested on the issues of death and resurrection, they "will soon precipitate Jesus' own death and resurrection" (Meier, *Matthew*, 255).

The Greatest Commandment Question (Matthew 22:34–40)

The Pharisees send in a lawyer for this third round of examining. Actually the "lawyer" mentioned here (Matt. 22:35) is less like a modern attorney and more like a Bible professor, an expert in the law of Moses. The question this lawyer asks Jesus seems quite benign—"Teacher, which commandment in the law is the greatest?" (Matt. 22:36)—but it is not innocent at all. Matthew tells us that it was a "test," using a variant of the same Greek word translated "tempt" in the story of Jesus' temptations (Matt. 4:1–11). This time Jesus is not being tempted by the devil, but by a Pharisaical theology professor.

What is sinister about the lawyer's question? Jewish scholars who counted the laws of Moses came up with 613 separate commandments. The lawyer is asking Jesus to pick one out of this number as "the greatest," thereby exposing him to criticism over the 612 commandments he did not choose. The lawyer is licking his chops over the prospect of embarrassing Jesus with a follow-up question. But Jesus leaves no room for a follow-up. His answer shows that the lawyer, like the tempter in the wilderness, is no match for Jesus. The first part of Jesus' response quotes Deuteronomy 6:5: "'You shall love the Lord your God with all your heart, and with all your soul, and with all your mind.' This is the greatest and first commandment" (Matt. 22:37–38). This verse would have been well known to all his hearers, since it formed part of the Shema, a key element in Jewish worship. Devout Jews would have recited this verse several times a day and would have known it by heart. Then Jesus quotes Leviticus 19:18 as a second commandment, which is like the first, "'You shall love your neighbor as yourself.' On these two commandments hang all the law and the prophets" (Matt. 22:39–40).

Jesus accomplished two things by his answer. First, he showed himself to be completely orthodox by giving a response that was straight from the treasury of Jewish devotion and, in essence, beyond debate. Who could challenge the idea of loving God with heart, soul, and mind accompanied by the love of one's neighbor as the core of the law? One is reminded of the theologian Karl Barth's often-quoted response to the question, What is the most important truth you have learned in your theological study? The great theologian is reported to have answered, "Jesus loves me, this I know, for the Bible tells me so." Who can argue with that? Even the smallest child would recognize and praise the integrity of that answer.

But Jesus does more than establish his orthodox credentials. He also confounds the lawyer—and all like him. The lawyer's question implies a rule-based understanding of the law. "We have 613 rules here; now which is the most important?" the lawyer was asking. If the lawyer had been asking about baseball, and Jesus had replied that "three strikes and you're out" was the most important rule, the lawyer would have had reason to produce a counter argument. "How come the most important rule isn't 'four balls and you walk'?" he might have reasonably said. What Jesus' answer achieves, however, is to undermine the whole notion of the law as rules and regulations. What Jesus claims is that the whole law is about love, not rules, about really loving God and one's neighbor, not about figuring out how to avoid stepping on cracks in the legal sidewalk.

This understanding of the law is the reason Jesus can reach out in the name of God and with healing in his hands touch a neighbor who is a leper, even though some would have said that doing so broke one of the rules (see comments on Matt. 8:1–4). The whole law, said Jesus, every one of those 613 commandments, is really about love—loving God and loving neighbor. The scholars of the law had a picture in their minds of every law hanging by a strand to a peg, to some key passage of scripture. Jesus refreshes that image by portraying the whole law and the prophets, everything, as hanging by a cord to the twin pegs of love of God and love of neighbor (Matt. 22:40).

This part of Jesus' examination began with the statement that the Pharisees gathered together and thrust forward this sharp lawyer because they heard that Jesus "had silenced the Sadducees" (Matt. 22:34). It is interesting to note that the story ends in silence, without a retorting word from the lawyer. Jesus' response to his testy question has stilled his voice, and he has soundlessly slipped off the pages of Matthew never to be heard from again.

Whose Son Is the Messiah?
(Matthew 22:41–46)

Now that he has silenced and astonished his examiners, it is Jesus' turn to do the questioning, and he goes on the offensive. While the Pharisees are still gathered as a group (Matt. 22:41; see Matt. 22:34), he seizes the opportunity to put a question to them. "What do you think of the Messiah? Whose son is he?" (Matt. 22:42).

The Pharisees give the traditional answer: "The son of David" (Matt. 22:42; see 2 Chron. 17:10–14; Isa. 9:2–7; 11:1–9; Jer. 23:5–6). This is correct, as far as it goes, but it does not go far enough. In Matthew's theology, Jesus, as Messiah, is not only the son of David, he is also the Son of God (see Matt. 1:1; 16:16). Jesus is not only David's descendant; he is also David's ancestor, David's Lord and God.

In order to get at this issue, Jesus challenges the completeness of the Pharisees' answer. He quotes Psalm 110:1 (a favorite verse of early Christians and the most quoted Old Testament passage in the New Testament): "The Lord said to my Lord, 'Sit at my right hand, until I put your enemies under your feet.'" He then raises two additional questions: If the Messiah were only David's son, then how is it that David calls him "Lord," and if David calls him "Lord," how can he be his son?

Jews in that time believed that David, inspired by God, wrote all of the psalms (scholars today see multiple authors behind the composition of the psalter), and they probably considered Psalm 110 to be a psalm in praise of the Messiah. Therefore, the Pharisees would view "the Lord said to my Lord" as David's very own words and, as Jesus is suggesting here, this phrase could best be interpreted as meaning "When the Lord (that is, God) said to my Lord (that is, the Messiah)." In short, the argument, putting together the logical links, is that David refers to the Messiah as "my Lord"; so, if the Messiah is David's Lord, how can he be only David's son?

With this challenge, Jesus passes his "final exam" with flying colors. He is David's true son, but he is more. He is Messiah and Lord. The religious authorities cannot contain him, cannot hem him in with their traditional methods, and "no one was able to give him an answer, nor from that day did anyone dare to ask him any more questions" (Matt. 22:46). Jesus will not be tamed, will not be entrapped by their systems. Their snares foiled, their tricks upended, their test questions shredded, all that is left to them, all they can do now, is to kill him.

WOES UPON FALSE TEACHERS
Matthew 23:1–39

23:1 Then Jesus said to the crowds and to his disciples, [2] "The scribes and the Pharisees sit on Moses' seat; [3] therefore, do whatever they teach you and follow it; but do not do as they do, for they do not practice what they teach. [4] They tie up heavy burdens, hard to bear, and lay them on the shoulders of others; but they themselves are unwilling to lift a finger to move them. [5] They do all their deeds to be seen by others; for they make their phylacteries broad and their fringes long. [6] They love to have the place of honor at banquets and the best seats in the synagogues, [7] and to be greeted with respect in the marketplaces, and to have people call them rabbi. [8] But you are not to be called rabbi, for you have one teacher, and you are all students. [9] And call no one your father on earth, for you have one Father—the one in heaven. [10] Nor are you to be called instructors, for you have one instructor, the Messiah. [11] The greatest among you will be your servant. [12] All who exalt themselves will be humbled, and all who humble themselves will be exalted.

[13] "But woe to you, scribes and Pharisees, hypocrites! For you lock people out of the kingdom of heaven. For you do not go in yourselves, and when others are going in, you stop them. [15] Woe to you, scribes and Pharisees, hypocrites! For you cross sea and land to make a single convert, and you make the new convert twice as much a child of hell as yourselves.

[16] "Woe to you, blind guides, who say, 'Whoever swears by the sanctuary is bound by nothing, but whoever swears by the gold of the sanctuary is bound by the oath.' [17] You blind fools! For which is greater, the gold or the sanctuary that has made the gold sacred? [18] And you say, 'Whoever swears by the altar is bound by nothing, but whoever swears by the gift that is on the altar is bound by the oath.' [19] How blind you are! For which is greater, the gift or the altar that makes the gift sacred? [20] So whoever swears by the altar, swears by it and by everything on it; [21] and whoever swears by the sanctuary, swears by it and by the one who dwells in it; [22] and whoever swears by heaven, swears by the throne of God and by the one who is seated upon it.

[23] "Woe to you, scribes and Pharisees, hypocrites! For you tithe mint, dill, and cummin, and have neglected the weightier matters of the law: justice and mercy and faith. It is these you ought to have practiced without neglecting the others. [24] You blind guides! You strain out a gnat but swallow a camel!

[25] "Woe to you, scribes and Pharisees, hypocrites! For you clean the outside of the cup and of the plate, but inside they are full of greed and self-indulgence. [26] You blind Pharisee! First clean the inside of the cup, so that the outside also may become clean.

[27] "Woe to you, scribes and Pharisees, hypocrites! For you are like whitewashed tombs, which on the outside look beautiful, but inside they are full of the bones of the dead and of all kinds of filth. [28] So you also on

the outside look righteous to others, but inside you are full of hypocrisy and lawlessness.

[29] "Woe to you, scribes and Pharisees, hypocrites! For you build the tombs of the prophets and decorate the graves of the righteous, [30] and you say, 'If we had lived in the days of our ancestors, we would not have taken part with them in shedding the blood of the prophets.' [31] Thus you testify against yourselves that you are descendants of those who murdered the prophets. [32] Fill up, then, the measure of your ancestors. [33] You snakes, you brood of vipers! How can you escape being sentenced to hell? [34] Therefore I send you prophets, sages, and scribes, some of whom you will kill and crucify, and some you will flog in your synagogues and pursue from town to town, [35] so that upon you may come all the righteous blood shed on earth, from the blood of righteous Abel to the blood of Zechariah son of Barachiah, whom you murdered between the sanctuary and the altar. [36] Truly I tell you, all this will come upon this generation.

[37] "Jerusalem, Jerusalem, the city that kills the prophets and stones those who are sent to it! How often have I desired to gather your children together as a hen gathers her brood under her wings, and you were not willing! [38] See, your house is left to you, desolate. [39] For I tell you, you will not see me again until you say, 'Blessed is the one who comes in the name of the Lord.'"

In the last chapter, Jesus engaged in a series of adversarial encounters with the Herodians, the Pharisees, and the Sadducees, representatives of the major groups within Judaism at the time. These disputes served as Jesus' "final exam," and, in each case, he passed with honors and emerged as the uncontested victor. Now in this chapter of Matthew, Jesus turns toward these religious leaders with withering force, pronouncing judgment on them in unambiguous language. He saves special antipathy for the scribes and the Pharisees, but his words of reproach fall, finally, upon the whole city of Jerusalem. Again, the Christian interpreter must be cautious not to read these words in the light of today's Jewish-Christian relations. When Jesus excoriates the Jewish leaders, he does so as a Jew, as a prophet like Isaiah or Jeremiah, whose strong words denouncing Israel are spoken from within.

The first salvo, Matthew 23:1–12, is an attack on the Jewish religious leadership, but it is not addressed directly to them. Instead, Jesus speaks to "the crowds and to his disciples" (Matt. 23:1), and the main point of these verses seems to be to portray the religious authorities as bad examples and, thereby, to encourage Jesus' followers, and Matthew's church, not to imitate their remote and haughty leadership style.

The address begins with Jesus giving his foes their due. Jesus acknowledges that the scribes and Pharisees do, in fact, teach the Mosaic law; that is, they "sit on Moses' seat" (Matt. 23:2), and, therefore, they do impart some measure of the truth. Matthew, as we have seen, is no opponent of the Old Testament law. Indeed, he is convinced that Jesus, in the deepest sense possible, fulfills every letter and stroke of the law (Matt. 5:18).

According to Jesus, the basic problem with the scribes and the Pharisees is not with what they teach; it is with what they do or fail to do. "They do not practice what they teach," Jesus charges (Matt. 23:3), and he cites three specific examples of this. First, the scribes and Pharisees lay heavy burdens on the shoulders of others, but do not lift a finger to help (Matt. 23:4). This refers to the Pharisaic program for how people should live every day according to the law. It consisted of a myriad of rules, standards, and directives, and the whole process easily degenerated into moral bean counting. The procedures were so cumbersome that no human being could possibly accomplish them; no one could ever hope to keep the full weight of all these laws and carry the heavy freight of this ethical load, not even the scribes and the Pharisees themselves. Matthew's church, by contrast, took the law quite seriously but saw it in simpler, "love God and love your neighbor" terms. The small, nitpicking regulations were subsumed in favor of the larger moral vision of the law lived and taught by Jesus. The Pharisees turned the law into a burden too severe to be carried, but under the teaching of Jesus, the yoke was easy, the burden light, and the goal was rest for one's soul (Matt. 11:29–30).

Second, Jesus charges that the scribes and the Pharisees were more interested in appearance than in performance. "They do all their deeds to be seen by others; for they make their phylacteries broad and their fringes long" (Matt. 23:5). A number of passages in the Old Testament called for the keeping of the commandments of God "as a sign on your hand . . . an emblem on your forehead" (Deut. 6:8; see also Exod. 13:9 and Deut. 11:18), and in strict observance of this, many Jews wore small containers with verses of scripture ("phylacteries" in Matthew) on their arms or foreheads during prayer. Moreover, other passages in the Old Testament required the wearing of tassels (called "fringes" in Matthew) on one's cloak, also as a reminder of the commandments (Num. 15:38–41; Deut. 22:12). The true purpose of these phylacteries and fringes was to keep the faithful ever mindful of the laws of God, to assist the worshiper in prayer, but, according to Jesus, the scribes and Pharisees had turned them into fashion statements. Like a contemporary Christian wearing a two-pound cross or sporting a bumper sticker on the car reading "My God Is Alive, Sorry About Yours," the question can be raised: Is this faith or flash, praise or pomp?

The third indictment Jesus makes of the scribes and Pharisees is that they consider themselves to be superior to others, and they consistently pull rank. They insist on the best seats in the house at banquets and at worship, and they love to swagger through the marketplace, to be saluted and called by the title "rabbi" (which means "my lord").

In contrast, the followers of Jesus are not to be preoccupied with rank and prestige. Because Christ is their one true teacher and they are all equals in his classroom, they are not to elevate themselves with the teacher's titles "rabbi" and "instructor." Nor are they to speak of themselves as "father," a designation of reverence in Jesus' day, for God is their one true Father. Instead, they are to assume the role of servant, trusting that, in the coming kingdom, it will be humble service, not earthly prestige, that will be exalted (Matt. 23:8–12).

Jesus is addressing here the dynamics of power in the Christian community. The issue is not titles per se, but styles of leadership and interaction. Today, some of God's humblest servants bear the titles "rabbi," "father," and "reverend," and calling oneself "sister" or "brother" is certainly no guarantee of humility. However, whenever Christians, especially those in positions of leadership, begin to develop a hierarchical, "reserved parking space" mentality, lording their alleged rank over others in the church—in short, whenever "reverends" act like spiritual CEOs rather than servants or when "fathers" order others around like children—then they have, like the scribes and Pharisees of old, presumed for themselves the honor that belongs to God alone.

After the opening protest, Jesus next pronounces a set of seven "woes," specific complaints against the scribes and Pharisees. A "woe," Meier notes, "expresses both the seer's dismay and his threat of punishment" (Meier, *Matthew*, 267). In each of these "woes," Jesus addresses his opponents directly: "Woe to *you*. . . . " But did the scribes and Pharisees actually hear these? Were they even within earshot? Jesus was still in the temple area, to be sure, and the scribes and Pharisees may have been lurking in the shadows catching an earful of Jesus' words, but the primary audience has not changed. It is still the crowds and the disciples (Matt. 23:1), and what Jesus says is basically for their benefit. Jesus is like a piano teacher saying to a diligent student, "Woe to those who do not practice every day. They will soon lose the gift of music." The teacher's words are about people "out there" who don't practice every day, but the teacher's purpose is to encourage the student right there on the bench, the one who *is* disciplined and does the daily exercises. So, the scribes and Pharisees—who may or may not be present—form the target of Jesus' complaint, but the beneficiaries are the disciples and the crowd gathered immediately around him.

The first "woe" (Matt. 23:13–14) charges the leaders with blocking the door to the kingdom of heaven. The primary job of a religious teacher is to open doors to God, to set torches out along the path so that people can find their way to God. Not only do these religious leaders refuse to go into the kingdom themselves (as evidenced by their opposition to Jesus, the Messiah and Son of God), but, if others should begin to knock at heaven's door, these leaders try by their interference to lock them out.

The second "woe" (Matt. 23:15) concerns Jewish missionary activity. There is evidence that first-century Pharisaic Judaism engaged in efforts to convert Gentiles, calling upon them to be circumcised and to obey the laws of Moses. It is a well-known phenomenon that converts to a faith often turn out more zealous than the missionaries who proselytized them, and this is the charge that Jesus makes about the converts to Pharisaism. He has already asserted that the scribes and Pharisees have a heavy and burdensome religion (Matt. 23:4), and now he bemoans that they travel all over the place to make converts who are twice as hellish, twice as bound up in legalism, as they are. The fact that Matthew includes this "woe" may reflect the early church's problems caused by a collision between Christian missionaries and Gentile converts to Judaism. Some of the most intense resistance to Christian missionary activity among the Gentiles may well have come from Gentile converts to the law (see, for example, Galatians, especially Gal. 3:1–14).

In the third "woe" (Matt. 23:16–22), Jesus lampoons the Pharisees' system of oath taking. In contemporary society, if someone borrows money or agrees to do a task, there is usually a mortgage or a contract to back this up. In the ancient world, though, there were no contracts; there were oaths. People formed binding obligations by publicly swearing on their word to do thus and so. The most serious oaths were those taken in the name of God (such as when the President of the United States seals the oath of office by placing a hand on a Bible and saying the words "so help me God"), but devout Jews were opposed to this casual speaking of the name of God. Thus, a system developed by which sacred oaths could be spoken without actually saying God's name; the one taking the oath could swear not "by the name of God" but, rather, by some sacred object, something that was associated with God.

The Pharisees developed a whole scheme of such oaths, a list of sacred objects, so that, if they were named in an oath, the oath was considered binding. Jesus mocks this whole system as just another instance of the scribes and Pharisees missing the forest for the trees. For example, two items on the Pharisees' list of sacred oath objects were the gold in the temple sanctuary and gifts on the temple altar. However, the sanctuary itself and the altar were missing from the list. So, by the Pharisees' rules, if someone swore by the sanctuary gold, it would be binding, but if that same person swore by the sanctuary itself, the oath would be null and void (Matt. 23:16). This, said Jesus, is blind foolishness, "for which is greater, the gold or the sanctuary that has made the gold sacred?" (Matt. 23:17).

Jesus' point is not to create a better list of sacred objects, a more authentic system of oaths. Indeed, Jesus already condemned all oaths in the Sermon on the Mount (see comments on Matt. 5:33–37). The point is to demonstrate that the scribes and Pharisees cannot tell the difference between the weighty and the trivial, between the external procedures of religion and the deeper purposes of faith. There little rules and schemes operate on the periphery, blind to the majesty of God at the center of life (Matt. 23:22). An analogy to the Pharisees' system is the debate among some Christians about the correct formula for prayer. Some argue that, in order for a prayer to be heard by God, it must be spoken in Jesus' name; that is, it must include words like "in Jesus' name" or "in the name of Christ." Imagine saying to a mother whose sick child is hovering between life and death, who cries out in the middle of the night, "O God, save my child!" that this prayer was probably not heard because it lacked the proper formula. What is greater, "correct" prayer form or the God who hears people in distress and who makes all prayer holy?

In the fourth "woe" (Matt. 23:23–24), Jesus expands on the inability of the scribes and Pharisees to distinguish between the trivial and the consequential. In response to the law, the Pharisees tithed their possessions; indeed, they were so scrupulous that they even tithed their household spices—their "mint, dill, and cummin"—in observance of the law that required the setting apart of "a tithe of all the yield of your seed that is brought in yearly from the field" (Deut. 14:22; Matt. 23:23).

The problem, however, is that, while the scribes and the Pharisees were counting out seeds for the offering plate, they were neglecting the more important commandments—"justice and mercy and faith"—the very heart of God's law (Matt. 23:23). Jesus ridicules this failure to discriminate between what counts and what does not with a joke based on the commandments about unclean animals. Jews could not eat any animal that the law deemed unclean, and this included both the largest animal in Palestine, the camel (Lev. 11:4; Deut. 14:7), and one of the smallest, the gnat (Lev. 11:41–43). Jesus quips that the scribes and Pharisees are the kind of people who would painstakingly put a cloth over a jar of liquid to "strain out a gnat" while being willing to "swallow a camel" (Matt. 23:24).

The fifth "woe" (Matt. 23:25–26) is based on the Pharisees' practice of washing cups and plates used in ceremonial meals. In some ways, this custom was like polishing the Communion service on the altar or Communion table, because these vessels are set apart for sacred use. For the scribes and

Pharisees, however, this was an even more urgent matter, for a contaminant on the outside of a cup or dish could render it ritually unclean.

Jesus turns this into a metaphor about human life, indicating that the scribes and Pharisees do with themselves what they do with the cups and plates; that is, they meticulously polish the outside of their lives, putting on a clean, pious, and law-abiding face, while inside their hearts they are full of uncleanness—"greed and self-indulgence" (Matt. 23:25). Human lives, Jesus instructs, need to be cleaned from the inside out (Matt. 23:26).

The sixth "woe" (Matt. 23:27–28) extends the contrast, begun in the previous "woe," between inner and outer purity. In the law, a dead body was considered unclean (see Lev. 21:1, 11), and observant Jews were careful to avoid even unintentional contact with the deceased. In the well-known parable of the good Samaritan in Luke, it made a certain kind of sense for the priest and the Levite to have "passed by on the other side," because the wounded man appeared lifeless and they wanted to avoid contact with a dead body (see Luke 10:29–37).

Though the background of this sixth "woe" is somewhat uncertain, most scholars believe that on certain festival occasions, such as Passover, the tombs in Jerusalem were covered with whitewash in order to mark them clearly so that worshipers could steer clear of them and remain ritually pure. In any case, the image of a whitewashed tomb, lovely and pure on the outside and inside full of decay and dead bones, was a perfect one for Jesus to seize in his description of the scribes and Pharisees. On the outside, they wore a religious "smiley face," but on the inside they had spiritual dry rot.

In the seventh "woe" (Matt. 23:29–36) Jesus' denunciation of the scribes and Pharisees reaches a fever pitch as he essentially accuses them of being murderers. In Israel, the tombs of prophets and other fallen heroes were decorated as public monuments to commemorate their righteousness and faith. Like an American town renaming a street "Martin Luther King Jr. Boulevard," the Israel of Jesus' day wanted, by honoring the prophet martyrs, in part to atone for its past. To glorify the graves of the old prophets was, in essence, to say: "Our ancestors blindly murdered these prophets, but now we, their descendants, know better. We would never have taken part in the killing of the prophets."

Jesus will have none of this false penance; the scribes and Pharisees are, in his view, the descendants in every way of those who killed the prophets, and they have inherited every homicidal gene of their forebears (Matt. 23:30–31). Since that is who they are, Jesus thunders, they should just go ahead and fulfill their destructive destiny by filling up their cups with blood. If they are looking for fresh victims, they need look no further.

Jesus promises to send his own followers—"prophets, sages, and scribes"—and predicts that they will be persecuted, tortured, and even crucified (Matt. 23:32–34).

All this bloodshed, Jesus states, will be an extension of the line of murder drawn from "A to Z"—from Abel to Zechariah—in Israel's history. There is a slight problem with Matthew's text at this point. He has Jesus call Zechariah the "son of Barachiah"; in other words, the prophet Zechariah (see Zech. 1:1). But Jesus also describes this Zechariah as the one "whom you murdered between the sanctuary and the altar" (Matt. 23:35), an incident that almost surely refers to another Zechariah, the son of the priest Jehoiada, the last casualty of murder mentioned in the old Hebrew Bible (2 Chron. 24:20–22). Indeed, this Zechariah would make the most sense of Jesus' statement, for he would be tracing Israel's murderous past from the first innocent victim (Abel, Gen. 4:8–10) to the last.

Not very far beneath the surface of this seventh "woe" is the experience of Matthew's church. We do not know the full extent of this church's experience of persecution, but evidently missionaries and others from this congregation were in frequent conflict with the synagogue. Whatever else Christians take away from this text, we should be reminded of the tragic history of religious persecution. Sometimes Christians have been its victims, and Jesus' wrathful words should give us hope. On other occasions, however, Christians have been in positions of strength and tempted to use their power against others. In such cases Jesus' words serve as a warning.

The list of woes closes with a poignant lament over Jerusalem, "the city that kills the prophets and stones those who are sent to it!" (Matt. 23:37). Jesus speaks not only in his own voice but also in the very voice of God the Father: "How often have I desired to gather your children together as a hen gathers her brood under her wings, and you were not willing!" (Matt. 23:37). God is pictured as a mother hen, seeking over and over again to protect her brood, to gather her little ones under her protective wing, only to be rebuffed. Now, God has tried to care for Jerusalem again, this time through Jesus the Messiah. But again Jerusalem has rejected God's loving care, and Jerusalem's "house is . . . desolate" (Matt. 23:38).

"You will not see me again," Jesus says, "until you say, 'Blessed is the one who comes in the name of the Lord'" (Matt. 23:39). Then, when Jesus comes on the last day, he will not enter Jerusalem as a meek and humble servant on a donkey, but as the judge of all history. At that time, the Jerusalem, the city that cruelly and smugly rejected him when he came the first time, will be obliged by the force of God's victory to admit that Jesus is, indeed, Messiah, and to cry in astonished shame, "Blessed is the one who comes in the name of the Lord."

14. Jesus Teaches about the Future Judgment
Matthew 24:1–25:46

In Matthew 24–25 we find Jesus' fifth, and last, major section of teaching (see Introduction). In his previous sessions, he has delivered the Sermon on the Mount (Matthew 5–7), instructed missionaries (Matthew 10), taught in parables (Matthew 13), and schooled the disciples on church leadership (Matthew 18). This time his main theme is the final judgment and the ultimate victory of God at the end of time. With this material, we once again enter into the strange, symbolic world of apocalyptic literature. Jesus speaks in this chapter of the "second coming," of the consummation of human history, and of the time when all of the nations of the earth will be gathered before the triumphant Son of Man to be judged.

In order to teach people who were fully in the stream of history about a divine victory that is anchored out beyond history's edge, Jesus' language is stretched almost out of recognizable shape. He speaks here of the darkening of the sun and the shaking of the powers; of famines, earthquakes, lightning flashes, and rumors of wars. He warns of false prophets and counterfeit messiahs, and he promises that the Son of Man, who came the first time to a peasant girl and her dream-haunted, carpenter husband, would come again at the end of time riding the great clouds of power and glory. As with all apocalyptic literature, there is a fantastic, otherworldly quality about this section of Matthew. We are peering from the vantage point of our world through the looking glass to a time and place beyond our imagining—the world to come.

THE DESTRUCTION OF THE TEMPLE
Matthew 24:1–2

24:1 **As Jesus came out of the temple and was going away, his disciples came to point out to him the buildings of the temple.** [2] **Then he asked them, "You see all these, do you not? Truly I tell you, not one stone will be left here upon another; all will be thrown down."**

In the previous section of Matthew, Jesus has been embroiled in a series of controversial encounters in the temple. His parting words were a stern rebuke of the whole Jerusalem establishment, a "you will never see me again" speech (see Matt. 23:39), after which Jesus leaves the temple never to return. Jesus' exit was dramatic, but his disciples cannot resist lingering for one last look at the temple. The disciples—probably with a sweeping, panoramic gesture—point out the magnificent array of buildings on the temple grounds. The irony is unmistakable. Jesus has just denounced the temple; he has overturned the tables of the merchants and, on his way out, issued a string of withering curses on the whole temple enterprise, but his disciples pause for a final, longing glance back, as if to say, "You'll have to admit, Jesus, it is, after all, a pretty impressive place."

Captured symbolically in this gesture of the disciples is the ambivalence that consistently plagues God's people caught between God's formidable future and the seductions of the comfortable past. When God is doing something new in the world and God's people are beckoned to follow, there is the temptation, nonetheless, to gaze longingly back toward the seeming security of the way things used to be. Lot's wife, even as she fled toward deliverance, was unable to resist turning back toward doomed Sodom and Gomorrah (Gen. 19:24–26). The children of Israel in the wilderness, being led toward freedom in the promised land, still cast a wistful eye back toward the seeming stability of slavery in Egypt (Exod. 16:3).

Here, then, are the disciples in a familiar situation for God's people, between the seeming safety of the old and the frightening uncertainty of the new. The temple may have symbolized all that opposed Jesus as the Messiah, but it also represented all that was secure about the traditional patterns of worship and belief. So, the rock-solid temple with all its trusted and established structures was behind them; the cross with all its fearful uncertainties and demanding sacrifices was ahead of them. Given that location, no wonder the disciples turned back to admire the grandeur of the temple.

But Jesus would not allow them their nostalgic illusion. He no doubt astonished the disciples by announcing that the temple, which looked so appealing, so invulnerable, so secure, was destined for God's wrecking ball. The buildings of the temple, though appearing so magnificent and imposing, would soon be so much debris and rubble (Matt. 24:2).

Indeed, in A.D. 70, a decade or more before Matthew wrote his Gospel, Jesus' prophecy was literally fulfilled when the temple was burned by the Roman legions. But Jesus' doomsday saying over the temple was more far-reaching than merely a description of the military destruction of a few buildings. It was not just the temple that was doomed; the entire old world of which the temple was a part will ultimately pass away. Jesus condemned every institution that clings doggedly to the old patterns and resists the new thing that God is doing to bring mercy and redemption to human life. It will do no good to gaze longingly at the shimmering splendor of a dying world, even at its most cherished and sacred institutions. The only future is God's future; the only authentic choice is to follow.

THE COMING END OF THE AGE
Matthew 24:3–44

24:3 When he was sitting on the Mount of Olives, the disciples came to him privately, saying, "Tell us, when will this be, and what will be the sign of your coming and of the end of the age?" 4 Jesus answered them, "Beware that no one leads you astray. 5 For many will come in my name, saying, 'I am the Messiah!' and they will lead many astray. 6 And you will hear of wars and rumors of wars; see that you are not alarmed; for this must take place, but the end is not yet. 7 For nation will rise against nation, and kingdom against kingdom, and there will be famines and earthquakes in various places: 8 all this is but the beginning of the birthpangs.

9 "Then they will hand you over to be tortured and will put you to death, and you will be hated by all nations because of my name. 10 Then many will fall away, and they will betray one another and hate one another. 11 And many false prophets will arise and lead many astray. 12 And because of the increase of lawlessness, the love of many will grow cold. 13 But the one who endures to the end will be saved. 14 And this good news of the kingdom will be proclaimed throughout the world, as a testimony to all the nations; and then the end will come.

15 "So when you see the desolating sacrilege standing in the holy place, as was spoken of by the prophet Daniel (let the reader understand), 16 then those in Judea must flee to the mountains; 17 the one on the housetop must not go down to take what is in the house; 18 the one in the field must not turn back to get a coat. 19 Woe to those who are pregnant and to those who are nursing infants in those days! 20 Pray that your flight may not be in winter or on a sabbath. 21 For at that time there will be great suffering, such as has not been from the beginning of the world until now, no, and never will be. 22 And if those days had not been cut short, no one would be saved; but for the sake of the elect those days will be cut short. 23 Then if anyone says to you, 'Look! Here is the Messiah!' or 'There he is!' —do not believe it. 24 For false messiahs and false prophets will appear and produce great signs and omens, to lead astray, if possible, even the elect. 25 Take note, I have

told you beforehand. [26] So, if they say to you, 'Look! He is in the wilderness,' do not go out. If they say, 'Look! He is in the inner rooms,' do not believe it. [27] For as the lightning comes from the east and flashes as far as the west, so will be the coming of the Son of Man. [28] Wherever the corpse is, there the vultures will gather.

[29] "Immediately after the suffering of those days
> the sun will be darkened,
>> and the moon will not give its light;
> the stars will fall from heaven,
>> and the powers of heaven will be shaken.

[30] Then the sign of the Son of Man will appear in heaven, and then all the tribes of the earth will mourn, and they will see 'the Son of Man coming on the clouds of heaven' with power and great glory. [31] And he will send out his angels with a loud trumpet call, and they will gather his elect from the four winds, from one end of heaven to the other.

[32] "From the fig tree learn its lesson: as soon as its branch becomes tender and puts forth its leaves, you know that summer is near. [33] So also, when you see all these things, you know that he is near, at the very gates. [34] Truly I tell you, this generation will not pass away until all these things have taken place. [35] Heaven and earth will pass away, but my words will not pass away.

[36] "But about that day and hour no one knows, neither the angels of heaven, nor the Son, but only the Father. [37] For as the days of Noah were, so will be the coming of the Son of Man. [38] For as in those days before the flood they were eating and drinking, marrying and giving in marriage, until the day Noah entered the ark, [39] and they knew nothing until the flood came and swept them all away, so too will be the coming of the Son of Man. [40] Then two will be in the field; one will be taken and one will be left. [41] Two women will be grinding meal together; one will be taken and one will be left. [42] Keep awake therefore, for you do not know on what day your Lord is coming. [43] But understand this: if the owner of the house had known in what part of the night the thief was coming, he would have stayed awake and would not have let his house be broken into. [44] Therefore you also must be ready, for the Son of Man is coming at an unexpected hour.

The disciples recognize that Jesus' prediction of the destruction of the temple (Matt. 24:1–2) is really about more than just the temple; it is a prophecy about the end of the whole world as we know it, the time when the curtain will fall on the drama of human history and the messiah will return to inaugurate the kingdom of heaven. Thus, with some urgency they ask Jesus, "When will this be?" (Matt. 24:3).

Jesus responds with a long, apocalyptic statement about the end of the world. The statement can be divided into four sections.

What Will Happen before the End?
(Matthew 24:3–14)

Just as today's Christians read the newspaper with its daily accounts of war and violence, so Matthew's first readers looked out at a world of constant suffering and turmoil. Jesus' first word to the disciples about the end of the world is one of wary reassurance: Such events are to be expected, and they are not to be misled by the doomsayers who cry over every conflict and crisis, "The sky is falling! The sky is falling!"

When Matthew's church read these words, they surely thought of their own situation. Not many years before, in A.D. 70, the Jewish people had mounted an armed resistance against Rome ("nation will rise against nation," Matt. 24:7), and they had paid the price for it. The Roman army crushed the rebellion and poured vinegar in the wound by torching the beloved and sacred temple. In the volatile political environment of Palestine, several self-proclaimed "messiahs" appeared on the scene with this or that plan for the salvation of Israel. Also, Matthew's church itself had suffered, almost surely experiencing active resistance to its missionary activity ("you will be hated by all nations because of my name," Matt. 24:9) and painful internal dissension and conflict ("the love of many will grow cold," Matt. 24:12).

In other words, when Matthew's church saw Jesus' description of the bad news in the world and in the community of faith, they felt as though they were looking into a mirror. To this Jesus offers a word of deep comfort. He tells the disciples that the key to the future is not to be found in the bad news but in the good news, the gospel. Seasons of suffering—in the world and in the church—are not the culmination that God has in mind for the world; they are but the "birthpangs" (Matt. 24:8), the labor pains of the old creation groaning for the new, sighing for a mercy deeper than its own anguish, a redemption more hopeful than its sad despair. The God who knows the number of hairs we have on our heads and who sorrows over the fall of a single sparrow (Matt. 10:26–31) commands the sweep of time with providential care.

So, the church is not to be afraid, come what may (Matt. 24:6). The church is to follow its Lord with boldness, teaching and healing and preaching the kindness of God, steadfast to the end (Matt. 24:13). In fact, the truest sign of the end of the world is not an earthquake in Japan, a famine in the Sudan, a bombing in Oklahoma, or an outbreak of war in the Middle East, but the rising flood tide of the gospel across the landscape of history as the church preaches and teaches and serves with mercy: "And this good news of the kingdom will be proclaimed throughout the world, as a testimony to all the nations; and then the end will come" (Matt. 24:14).

The Great Suffering
(Matthew 24:15–28)

When the economy takes a sharp downturn and someone remarks, "It's hard times come around again," what they are saying is that some circumstances in life seem to have a way of recycling, of returning again and again in new form. Just so, when Jesus speaks of "the desolating sacrilege standing in the holy place" and Matthew signals "let the reader understand" (Matt. 24:15), what the reader is supposed to understand is that this is an event that happens time and again in history. Generation after generation, the powers that be in the world slip into the holiest of sanctuaries and make a sacrilegious display.

One of the most memorable of such events—and Matthew's first readers would remember it as Texans remember the Alamo—was the occasion, in 167 B.C., when Antiochus IV Epiphanes, the ruler of Syria, shocked and disgusted faithful Jews by erecting a shrine to the Greek god Zeus on the very altar of the Jerusalem temple. The book of Daniel was written during this period, and, even though it is ostensibly set as a story in Babylon in the sixth century B.C., it obviously alludes to the persecutions of Antiochus IV. Indeed, Daniel refers to this event in the temple as "an abomination that desolates" in the temple (see Dan. 9:27; 11:31; 12:11), and Jesus borrows Daniel's language when he speaks of the "desolating sacrilege in the holy place" (literally, "abomination of desolation").

But "hard times keep coming 'round," and Matthew's readers know that 167 B.C. was not the only time in history when such an outrage occurred. In 40 B.C., the Roman emperor Caligula had threatened to install a statue of himself in the Jerusalem temple and, in A.D. 70, the Roman general Titus had destroyed Jerusalem and burned the temple to the ground. Whether it is a statue of the emperor installed in the sanctuary, or the attempt by a totalitarian state to crush all religious fervor, or an effort by self-serving politicians to use Christianity to bolster their partisan political ambitions, in every generation the powers-that-be attempt to replace God with their own images in the holy place. "Let the reader understand," Matthew urges, and we do understand. We have seen the sacrilege in the holy place many times.

Just as Californians often think of each new earthquake that rumbles along the San Andreas fault as but a warning shot, a premonition of "the big one," just so, Jesus seems to indicate that the waves of sacrilege that surge through history are but warning signs of "the big one," the coming "great suffering, such as has not been from the beginning of the world until now" (Matt. 24:21). This is a common theme in apocalyptic literature—

that the evil forces are gathering themselves for a momentous struggle as God's triumph approaches. Like a doomed and surrounded battalion that fights all the more viciously the closer defeat comes, the powers of evil in the world cause more and more suffering the nearer God's ultimate victory draws.

So, all of the little "desolations" in history, all of the recurring seasons of strife and suffering, are signs pointing toward the "great suffering," the last dying but dangerous lashing out of this age as the kingdom of heaven finally dawns with mercy and peace. How is the church to respond to these "desolations," both small and large? First, the church should be aware that such times of suffering and conflict are indeed bad—indeed, they are, in their own ways, the end of the world—but they are not the end of God or of God's providence. The powers-that-be can do much damage and can cause great suffering, but they are not finally in control of human destiny. The world ends not in the destruction fomented by the forces of evil, but in the glory granted by a merciful God (see Matt. 24:30).

Second, the church should, at least figuratively, "flee to the mountains" (Matt. 24:16). But why? Why does Jesus say that the church should run in the face of trouble? In order to understand this, we must first realize that Matthew's church would remember that, when Jerusalem was destroyed in A.D. 70, the Roman legions smashed the walls, burned the city including the temple, and slaughtered innocent people in their homes. Many of the Christians who were in Jerusalem at the time were among the refugees who actually did flee for their lives from the fiery destruction. Their flight, in other words, was their means of salvation.

Thus, Jesus' command to "flee to the mountains" reflects a desire that the faithful community be protected and preserved through the danger. Moreover, their flight represents a freedom from the material world. What is being destroyed is the present age; it is the old world that is passing away, and those who belong to the kingdom of heaven are not to get caught up in trying to preserve structures that are doomed, not to cling to the possessions of the dying world. They are not to be like those foolish people who, when a devastating hurricane is blowing ashore, camp out in their beachfront condominiums, vainly trying to preserve their property. They are not to turn back with nostalgia, as Lot's wife did toward Sodom and Gomorrah or the disciples did toward the doomed temple (see comments on Matt. 24:1–2). They are to flee without returning "to take what is in the house" or "to get a coat" (Matt. 24:17–18). They are to give thanks that God does not allow the suffering to be prolonged (Matt. 24:22) and to pray that nothing will hinder their flight (in Matthew's day, pregnancy, the burden of nursing children, the bad weather of winter, and trying to escape on the Jewish sabbath, when Christians would be easily identifiable, were examples of such hindrances; see Matthew 24:19–20).

Third, they are not to be deceived by false messiahs. Every time of struggle and social upheaval produces a bevy of tinhorn saviors who, playing upon peoples' anxieties, announce that they can "save the imperiled country," "renew the faltering church," or "liberate the oppressed masses." So, if anyone tries to promise what only God can provide, the church is not to believe a word of it (Matt. 24:23). Moreover, if anyone tries to sell a "secret program of salvation," saying in effect, "Not everybody knows this, but the messiah is hidden out in the wilderness . . . or secreted away in an inner room . . . or to be found in a mystical growth group in the desert . . . or to be discovered through private communication with angels," the church is not to give such nonsense the time of day (Matt. 24:26). The return of the true messiah, the Son of Man, will be a clear, unambiguous, and public event. Like lightning flashing across the whole sky, it will be visible to everyone (Matt. 24:27). The curious saying, "wherever the corpse is, there the vultures will gather" (Matt. 24:28), is probably a proverbial saying meaning that a body cannot possibly be hidden because everybody for miles around can see the circling vultures. The point is the same: The coming of the messiah will not be a private event, but one for every eye to see.

The Appearance of the Son of Man (Matthew 24:29–31)

How will the world end? What will the "last day" of human history be like? Will the world go out with a "whimper or a bang"? Even to consider such an event strains ordinary language to the breaking point; words are the product of human history, and here they are pressed into the service of that which is beyond the edge of human history. Indeed, the fantastic word pictures in this section of Matthew are not to be read with strict literalism. A combination of images from such Old Testament books as Daniel, Isaiah, Ezekiel, Joel, and others is employed to describe what is finally ineffable—the final death throes of the old world and the fulfillment of all of the promises of God for the future.

In Matthew's day, people thought of the sun, moon, and stars as suspended above the earth and moved along their courses, day after day and night after night, by heavenly powers. At the end of time, suddenly, all of that seemingly timeless predictability and regularity will come crashing down. The "powers of heaven will be shaken," causing the moon to grow dark and the stars to fall from heaven (Matt. 24:29). Just as the birth of the child Jesus, his first advent, shook all of Jerusalem (Matt. 2:3), just so, the second advent of Jesus the Messiah will shake the very foundations of the present world. It will become clear that all those things that have seemed permanent and unwavering—the cycles of nature, the tides of history—are not eternal at all; all creation depends upon the free providence of God.

Then, what has been hidden except to the eyes of faith becomes visible to all; the triumphant Son of Man will appear on a cloud "with power and great glory" (Matt. 24:30). Because his coming marks the end of the worldly powers, all those who have invested themselves in the "things of this age" will lament and mourn the passing of the world (Matt. 24:30). But for those who have hoped in the promises of God—those who have hungered and thirsted for righteousness, prayed for peace, suffered for the sake of mercy, and hoped against hope for justice—the joyful trumpet blast will call them from all over creation into a great and joyful congregation (Matt. 24:31).

What are we to make of these pictures in our day? The ancient concept of stars and heavenly bodies suspended over the earth has given way to a vast and complex universe of galaxies, black holes, and quasars. Even so, we recognize in the first-century imagery—the notions of a heavenly canopy, the "four winds," and a trumpet blast loud enough to be heard over the earth—more than merely a quaint and obsolete worldview; in these images we hear a confidence in the power and providence of God, a hope that transcends historical vagaries and circumstances. The point is not to try to turn this passage into a timetable or into a description of what will happen when at the end of time. The point is to hear the basic theological affirmation that God's will, the will embodied in the ministry of Jesus, will not be overcome by the world but will prevail—that the goal of all human life and history is Jesus Christ. The gospel is essentially a matter of hope, hope that life is stronger than death, hope that justice will endure and not oppressive power, hope that the broken places in society and in the human heart will be knitted together with mercy. When all is said and done, when human history has said all that it can say, one more word will be spoken, and that word is Jesus Christ, validating the gospel promise of hope.

The description of the angels of God gathering "the elect" (Matt. 24:31) is best read not as some divine "choosing up sides"—the saved versus the damned, the elect versus the nonelect. Rather, it should be heard as the joyful validation of the ministry of God's people. Imagine a parole officer who tries to live the Sermon on the Mount in his work. He attempts not to get caught up in the paper shuffling and the bureaucracy, but instead to focus on the human side of the cases to which he is assigned. He cares for them; he works mercifully and tenderly with them; he mourns with them as they struggle and rejoices with them when they gain some foothold on life. Even so, the statistics are not good. He knows that most of them will eventually return to prison, and even the youngest of his clients are likely on their way to being career criminals. So, on many days he wonders, why care? Does it really matter? Why not just fill out the papers and put in my time until retirement? This word from Jesus about the angels gathering the elect is addressed precisely to such a struggle in the middle of human history. Jesus pulls back the curtain on the human drama to show the very angels of God scurrying around to honor and confirm all kingdom labor; the vision is to announce to faithful people working for mercy and peace in the middle of difficult circumstance, "It counts. It really counts."

The Timing of the End
(Matthew 24:32–44)

The whole of Matthew 24, a chapter in which Jesus teaches about the coming kingdom, was initiated by the disciples' question "When will this be?" (Matt. 24:3). Now Jesus returns specifically to their inquiry.

First, Jesus points to the fig tree as an illustration of when to expect the coming of the kingdom (Matt. 24:32–35). Unlike much of the other vegetation in Palestine, the fig tree sheds its leaves in the rainy winter season and grows new leaves just before summer. In other words, new growth on the fig tree signals a change in times and seasons. Just so, there will be signs in human events that will signal the coming of the messiah. "When you see all these things," Jesus teaches them, "you know that he is near, at the very gates" (Matt. 24:33).

But what exactly does Jesus mean by "all these things"? Perhaps he means each and every one of the events just mentioned in the previous verses—the appearance of false messiahs, the increase of crime, wars, and so on. However, Jesus has just made a point of stating that most of these events—"wars and rumors of wars . . . famines and earthquakes"—are red herrings; that is, they are *not* signs of the end (Matt. 24:6–8). If we comb through the whole of Matthew 24 looking for those events that are—like the new leaves on the fig tree—clearly set forth as signs of the changing of God's seasons, two emerge: the gospel proclaimed throughout the world to the nations (Matt. 24:14) and the profaning of the holy place (Matt. 24:15). In other words, the sign of the advent of the Son of Man is when the mission of the church to spread the good news is at flood tide and the powers of evil are at fever pitch.

Jesus' apparently inconvenient pledge that "this generation will not pass away until all these things have taken place" (Matt. 24:34) has created consternation through the ages. Many scholars think that Matthew (and perhaps Jesus) wrongly believed that the kingdom of heaven was coming very soon—in his own day, his own generation—and he was simply mistaken about the timing. The problem with this view is that the very next passage appears to disallow any speculation about the timing of the kingdom (Matt. 24:36–44), and there are other references that seem to indicate that Matthew was preparing his readers for a delayed arrival of the kingdom (Matt. 24:48; 25:5).

The verse is admittedly a hard one to interpret, but probably it is not the case that Matthew is misguided about the timing of the kingdom. Matthew almost surely was quite aware that the generation of people around Jesus would pass away well before the kingdom arrived. After all, Matthew wrote his Gospel about half a century after Jesus' death (see Introduction), and all but a very few of the people who were living in Jesus' day were already deceased. Also, the mission of preaching and teaching the good news "throughout the world, as a testimony to all the nations" (Matt. 24:14) was far from finished in Matthew's time; in some ways, it was just getting started. Matthew surely knew that many generations would pass before the gospel would spread to the whole inhabited world.

So what does it mean that "this generation will not pass away until all these things have taken place" (Matt. 24:34)? The best possibility is that Matthew believed that the kingdom of heaven would come in final and victorious form at the "last day," the ultimate end of the world, a day whose timing "no one knows." However, for the generation of people who were alive in Jesus' day, a window of vision would be opened for them, and they would be able to see an anticipatory glimpse of the forces of evil in full battle array and the Son of Man coming in great power and glory.

This window, of course, was the death of Jesus. Then, as at the end of time, a "desolating sacrilege" happened in the "holy place" of Jerusalem. Then, as at the end of time, a season of "great suffering" was followed by the darkening of the sun (Matt. 27:45), the shaking of the powers (Matt. 27:51), and the shining forth of the glory and power of the Son, so that even the Gentiles (the nations) confessed him to be God's own Son (Matt. 27:54). Matthew may even suggest that every generation of Christians is given this window of vision, at the Lord's Supper, where Jesus eats and drinks with his own children "in my Father's kingdom" (Matt. 26:29).

How is the church to wait for the coming kingdom? Jesus instructs his followers to be expectant but not to waste time trying to know what cannot be known—God's timetable (Matt. 24:36). Just as the flood surprised Noah's generation in the midst of their daily duties, so the arrival of the kingdom will also be a surprise, coming in the midst of such routine activities as working in the fields and grinding flour (Matt. 24:37–41). Since the church does not know when the kingdom will arrive any more than a householder knows when a burglar will slip through a window into the house, the task of the church is to be vigilant and ever ready.

What vigilance and readiness means is that the church must always be about the mission of Jesus in the world, preaching and teaching the gospel, showing mercy, working for justice, laboring for righteousness, never relaxing its intent to work toward God's coming victory. This is difficult to do under any circumstances, but it is especially hard when day after day passes and nothing happens. A bumper sticker reads, "Jesus is coming soon. Look busy!" It is one thing to be "busy" about God's work if Jesus is indeed coming soon, if tomorrow the Son of Man will arrive to say cheerfully, "Well done, good and faithful servant." But when tomorrow is just more of today and all labors of love seem poured into a bottomless pit of human suffering, indifference, and cynicism, then it is hard to march out the front door to be a disciple. In the face of the crushing needs of the world, the only way to preserve hope, the only way to maintain a willing sense of discipleship, is to trust that at any moment we may be surprised by the sudden presence of God. As we journey down the long and seemingly endless path of discipleship, we never know when we may encounter the living God waiting for us around the next bend. Indeed, each unexpected meeting, each moment of holy surprise, is but an anticipation of the great climax of all human history and longing, when the world, seemingly spinning along in ceaseless tedium, will find itself gathered into the extravagant mercy of God. "Therefore you also must be ready, for the Son of Man is coming at an unexpected hour" (Matt. 24:44).

FOUR ADVENT PARABLES
Matthew 24:45–25:46

24:45 "Who then is the faithful and wise slave, whom his master has put in charge of his household, to give the other slaves their allowance of food at the proper time? 46 Blessed is that slave whom his master will find at work when he arrives. 47 Truly I tell you, he will put that one in charge of all his possessions. 48 But if that wicked slave says to himself, 'My master is delayed,' 49 and he begins to beat his fellow slaves, and eats and drinks with drunkards, 50 the master of that slave will come on a day when he does not expect him and at an hour that he does not know. 51 He will cut him in pieces and put him with the hypocrites, where there will be weeping and gnashing of teeth.

25:1 "Then the kingdom of heaven will be like this. Ten bridesmaids took their lamps and went to meet the bridegroom. 2 Five of them were foolish, and five were wise. ³ When the foolish took their lamps, they took no oil with them; ⁴ but the wise took flasks of oil with their lamps. ⁵ As the bridegroom was delayed, all of them became drowsy and slept. ⁶ But at midnight there was a shout, 'Look! Here is the bridegroom! Come out to meet him.' ⁷ Then all those bridesmaids got up and trimmed their lamps. ⁸ The foolish said to the wise, 'Give us some of your oil, for our lamps are going out.' ⁹ But the wise replied, 'No! there will not be enough for you and for us; you had better go to the dealers and buy some for yourselves.' ¹⁰ And while they went to buy it, the bridegroom came, and those who were ready went with him into the wedding banquet; and the door was shut. ¹¹ Later the other bridesmaids came also, saying, 'Lord, lord, open to us.' ¹² But he replied, 'Truly I tell you, I do not know you.' ¹³ Keep awake therefore, for you know neither the day nor the hour.

¹⁴ "For it is as if a man, going on a journey, summoned his slaves and entrusted his property to them; ¹⁵ to one he gave five talents, to another two, to another one, to each according to his ability. Then he went away. ¹⁶ The one who had received the five talents went off at once and traded with them, and made five more talents. ¹⁷ In the same way, the one who had the two talents made two more talents. ¹⁸ But the one who had received the one talent went off and dug a hole in the ground and hid his master's money. ¹⁹ After a long time the master of those slaves came and settled accounts with them. ²⁰ Then the one who had received the five talents came forward, bringing five more talents, saying, 'Master, you handed over to me five talents; see, I have made five more talents.' ²¹ His master said to him, 'Well done, good and trustworthy slave; you have been trustworthy in a few things, I will put you in charge of many things; enter into the joy of your master.' ²² And the one with the two talents also came forward, saying, 'Master, you handed over to me two talents; see, I have made two more talents.' ²³ His master said to him, 'Well done, good and trustworthy slave; you have been trustworthy in a few things, I will put you in charge of many things; enter into the joy of your master.' ²⁴ Then the one who had received the one talent also came forward, saying, 'Master, I knew that you were a harsh man, reaping where you did not sow, and gathering where you did not scatter seed; ²⁵ so I was afraid, and I went and hid your talent in the ground. Here you have what is yours.' ²⁶ But his master replied, 'You wicked and lazy slave! You knew, did you, that I reap where I did not sow, and gather where I did not scatter? ²⁷ Then you ought to have invested my money with the bankers, and on my return I would have received what was my own with interest. ²⁸ So take the talent from him, and give it to the one with the ten talents. ²⁹ For to all those who have, more will be given, and they will have an abundance; but from those who have nothing, even what they have will be taken away. ³⁰ As for this worthless slave, throw him into the outer darkness, where there will be weeping and gnashing of teeth.'

[31] "When the Son of Man comes in his glory, and all the angels with him, then he will sit on the throne of his glory. [32] All the nations will be gathered before him, and he will separate people one from another as a shepherd separates the sheep from the goats, [33] and he will put the sheep at his right hand and the goats at the left. [34] Then the king will say to those at his right hand, 'Come, you that are blessed by my Father, inherit the kingdom prepared for you from the foundation of the world; [35] for I was hungry and you gave me food, I was thirsty and you gave me something to drink, I was a stranger and you welcomed me, [36] I was naked and you gave me clothing, I was sick and you took care of me, I was in prison and you visited me.' [37] Then the righteous will answer him, 'Lord, when was it that we saw you hungry and gave you food, or thirsty and gave you something to drink? [38] And when was it that we saw you a stranger and welcomed you, or naked and gave you clothing? [39] And when was it that we saw you sick or in prison and visited you?' [40] And the king will answer them, 'Truly I tell you, just as you did it to one of the least of these who are members of my family, you did it to me.' [41] Then he will say to those at his left hand, 'You that are accursed, depart from me into the eternal fire prepared for the devil and his angels; [42] for I was hungry and you gave me no food, I was thirsty and you gave me nothing to drink, [43] I was a stranger and you did not welcome me, naked and you did not give me clothing, sick and in prison and you did not visit me.' [44] Then they also will answer, 'Lord, when was it that we saw you hungry or thirsty or a stranger or naked or sick or in prison, and did not take care of you?' [45] Then he will answer them, 'Truly I tell you, just as you did not do it to one of the least of these, you did not do it to me.' [46] And these will go away into eternal punishment, but the righteous into eternal life."

Jesus brings his teaching about the end of the age and the coming of God's kingdom to a climax by speaking in parables. Indeed, this section of Matthew concludes with a string of four "advent parables," each one a picture of what it will be like when the kingdom of heaven finally comes, and each one addressing some problem or issue that Matthew's church was experiencing as they waited for the kingdom's advent.

The Parable of the Faithful and Wise Slave (Matthew 24:45–51)

The first of the four "advent parables" addresses the problem of the delayed kingdom, of what happens to the church when it begins to tap its foot impatiently and to have doubts that the kingdom will ever come.

In this parable, obviously, the wise path for the slave is to remain faithful to his assigned responsibilities because the master, though delayed, is sure to return eventually—which is, of course, exactly what happens. Indeed, if the slave foolishly chooses to be a slacker, he will be unpleasantly surprised when the master shows up unexpectedly (Matt. 24:50). The punishment given to such a foolish slave is described in severe terms (Matt. 24:51), characteristic of the Gospel of Matthew.

The parable is addressed to the church and has clear allegorical overtones. The delayed "master" is Christ, and the head slave represents the leadership of the church, who, like the slave, are put "in charge of his household" to see that others are given "food" (Matt. 25:45). Matthew's church would have understood that the responsibility to feed others was a duty to nourish people in all kinds of ways—to provide hospitality for the hungry, compassion for the wounded, and the sustenance of Jesus' teachings to the famished in spirit.

It is interesting to observe that the trouble begins when the head slave begins to lose a keen sense of his master's arrival, when he begins to think more about what he can do during the long and monotonous delay than he does about what the master will find when he comes back. In other words, it is the loss of advent expectation that leads to dissipation and violence. When the church stops expecting God and begins only to expect "church," this inevitably breeds discouragement, conflict, and a slackening of mission. When the church no longer anticipates God at any minute, when the church no longer expects to have its work validated by the advent of the kingdom, then it ceases to be a kingdom community and becomes a self-contained institution living only for today and competing within itself for power and status. When the church no longer saves a place at the table for the coming messiah, then it ceases to feed others and simply begins to gorge itself.

The Parable of the Ten Bridesmaids (Matthew 25:1–13)

The second "advent parable" continues the theme of the delayed kingdom. In this story about bridesmaids—some wise, some foolish—it is when the cry suddenly arises that the bridegroom is on his way that the difference between the wise and the foolish becomes critical. The lamps of the foolish bridesmaids start to fail because of lack of oil, so they try to borrow some oil from the wise maids. The wise have brought spare oil for their own lamps, but not enough to take care of everyone's lamps, so they send the foolish bridesmaids on a midnight run to the oil dealer.

The story grows sad, perhaps even tragic. While the foolish bridesmaids are off on their shopping trip, the long-awaited event finally happens: The bridegroom arrives for the wedding banquet. The wise maidens, lamps cheerfully ablaze, happily accompany him into the feast, and the door is closed behind them. When the foolish ones finally make it back to the banquet, they find themselves shut out of the festivities. They pound on the door to be admitted, but, alas, it is too late. Compounding the tragedy, when the bridegroom peers out at the forlorn latecomers, he curiously tells them he does not even recognize their faces, and the door to the banquet they were waiting for remains permanently locked.

Most scholars agree that this parable, like the previous one, is intended to be taken allegorically. That is, each major element in the parable is a symbol for something, and Matthew's readers are supposed to be able to crack the code. Some of the details are easy to decipher. The wedding banquet is a symbol of the kingdom of heaven (see Matt. 22:1–10), and the long-awaited bridegroom clearly is the expected Son of Man, Jesus Christ (see Matt. 24:30). The strange picture of the bridegroom's midnight arrival reflects the idea that the messiah will come at an unexpected time, like a thief in the night (Matt. 24:43–44; see also 1 Thess. 4:16–17). The cry of the foolish bridesmaids, "Lord, lord . . . ," and the sad response of the groom, "I do not know you . . . ," (Matt. 25:11–12), echoes the judgment of Matthew 7:21–23, where "not everyone who says to me, 'Lord, Lord,' will enter the kingdom of heaven" and Christ will turn away from evildoers with a dire, "I never knew you."

But what about the oil? What does it mean that the distinguishing characteristic of the wise bridesmaids is that they have an extra flask of oil? Some have suggested that the oil represents good works. Thus, the foolish bridesmaids are those Christians who are all fired up about Jesus but who lack the commitment to sustain the routine, and perhaps boring, effort of doing good works through the long "night" of waiting for the kingdom. The wise bridesmaids represent those Christians who keep on doing the will of God even when the kingdom is delayed. Adding support to this interpretation is the fact that ancient Jewish teachers often spoke of good works as "oil," and that Jesus, in the Sermon on the Mount, called on his followers to "let your light shine before others, so that they may see your good works" (Matt. 5:16). Without the "oil" of good works, no light can shine.

The only complication with this interpretation is that none of the bridesmaids, not even the wise ones, actually worked through the night. They *all* slept, wise and foolish (Matt. 25:5). When the parable ends by saying "keep awake," it must mean this in a metaphorical sense, because nobody, wise or foolish, stayed awake in the parable.

Perhaps a significant clue to interpreting the parable surfaces when the wise bridesmaids are described as "those who were ready" (Matt. 25:10). Ready for what? The bridegroom? No, the foolish bridesmaids were eager for the groom to arrive, too; the wise bridesmaids are distinctive not because they were ready for the groom but because they were ready for the groom's *delay*. To bring along an extra flask of oil is a signal that they were prepared for the bridegroom to come early or late. If the groom had arrived on time, if he had come when he was predicted to arrive, then all the bridesmaids—foolish as well as wise—would have cheerfully greeted him and merrily waltzed into the banquet. But, the bridegroom, like the kingdom of heaven, did not arrive promptly; he was delayed, and some two thousand years later, the kingdom is still delayed. The wise ones in the church are those who are prepared for the delay; who hold on to the faith deep into the night; who, even though they see no bridegroom coming, still serve and hope and pray and wait for the promised victory of God. Many will finally despair and turn away in discouragement, saying, "The bridegroom has left us standing at the altar, the banquet is off, there is no kingdom, life is just one cursed thing after another with no goal or end." But then in the middle of history's long night, when the world least expects it, a cry will go up, "Look! Here is the bridegroom! Here, at last, the long-expected Jesus. Come out to meet him."

The Parable of the Talents
(Matthew 25:14–30)

The third advent parable also emphasizes, in its own way, the delay of the kingdom. It is important to note that a "talent" is a rather lavish amount of money (about fifteen years' wages for a typical worker). It is perhaps unfortunate that it is called a "talent," because it tempts us to confuse this with the ordinary definition of "talent" and leads to a common misinterpretation of the parable. Routinely, this parable is taken as an encouragement to discover what gifts and talents we all have and to use them for God. Taken this way, the parable teaches that everybody has a talent; some have many, others a few, but all of us have at least one. Maybe one's talent is playing the piano, or perhaps it is the gift of hospitality or the skill of organization. Regardless of how many talents we may have, though, and whatever they may be, God wants us to use them wisely and not waste them. So goes the conventional interpretation.

There is, of course, nothing wrong with the idea that we should use our talents to glorify God, but that idea alone is too tame for this parable. The parable is not a gentle tale about what Christians do with their individual gifts and talents, as helpful as that may be, but a disturbing story about what Christians do or do not do with the *gospel* as they wait for the coming of the kingdom of heaven.

The first two slaves are called "good and trustworthy" because they set out immediately to work with the treasure entrusted to them. In the context of Matthew's Gospel, this treasure is the gospel—the teachings of Jesus—and these two "good and trustworthy" slaves (Matt. 25:21) symbolize all wise and faithful disciples who hear Jesus' words and act on them (see Matt. 7:24). The third slave, called "wicked and lazy" (Matt. 25:26), is a living embodiment of Jesus' warning that "everyone who hears these words of mine and does not act on them will be like a foolish man who built his house on sand" (Matt. 7:26).

The reason it is wise and trustworthy to act on the gospel is not simply that Jesus said so and disciples need to learn to be obedient and to follow orders. Living out the gospel truth of mercy, peace, and forgiveness is wise because the future belongs to God and those are the values of the future. The master will return, the promised kingdom is coming, and its advent will render all the false values of this age obsolete. Sometimes we look back on the anger, the harshness, the indifference toward others in our past and say, "If I had only known then what I know now, I would never have done it." One purpose of this parable is to say that we can know now what we will know in the future. What will stand at the end is the gospel and nothing else, and it is true wisdom to live out today the truth of God's future.

So, the parable is about wise and foolish disciples—those who live the gospel now and those who do not. But the parable also cuts in another direction. It is not only a story about the moral character of disciples but also a story about the moral character of God. What kind of God do we serve? Note the trembling speech of the one-talent slave: "Master, I knew that you were a harsh man . . . ; so I was afraid" (Matt. 25:24–25). Now, up to this point in the parable is there any basis whatsoever for this depiction of the master? Absolutely not. This master has entrusted his slaves with vast sums of money, not just for a night or two but for an extended period of time. Moreover, in a culture where slaves were expected to do their duty without receiving praise, pats on the back, or brass plaques (see Luke 17:7–10), astonishingly this master gives them extravagant tribute, increased authority, and perhaps even welcomes them into his home as members of the family ("enter into the joy of your master," Matt. 25:21). There is even the implication that he lets them keep the money entrusted to them along with all the profits they have made (see Matt. 25:28).

In other words, everything in this story leads us to see the master as an extraordinary man—trusting, welcoming, generous, and benevolent. That is the way the narrator of the parable presents him; that is the way the first two slaves view him—otherwise they would not have been so free to risk and act—and that is the way the master conducts himself. Clearly, the one-talent slave has badly misjudged the master, distorting the master into a tough, uncaring despot, and has foolishly acted accordingly.

When the master finds out that this mousy slave has buried the money entrusted to him and why, the master responds, "So you think I'm formidable and exacting, do you? Well, even if you think that way, you could still have invested the money in the bank and at least earned some interest." This rejoinder exposes the one-talent man even more. Even if the one-talent man missed all the trust, joy, and generosity in his master's spirit, even if he had a pinched and severe view of the master, he could still have done a little low-risk investing. The man's problem with his master, however, went deeper. He viewed his master not just as tough, but as evil. In this slave's twisted mind the master is so pernicious that there is no room whatsoever for freedom or responsible action, only paralysis. He is so afraid of this terrible master that the only choice left to him is to shove the talent back as soon as possible and have nothing more to do with this spiteful dictator. In Matthew's vocabulary, this one-talent man has an "evil eye"; all he can see is darkness, and the darkness finally engulfs him (Matt. 6:22).

The tragic news of this parable is that the one-talent man pronounces his own judgment; he gets only the master his tiny and warped vision can see. In theological terms, he gets the peevish little tyrant god he believes in. The story is not about a generous master suddenly turning cruel and punitive; it is about living with the consequences of one's own faith. If one trusts the goodness of God, one can boldly venture out with eyes wide open to the grace in life and can discover the joy of God's providence everywhere. But to be a child of the generous, gracious, and life-giving God and, nonetheless, to insist upon viewing God as oppressive, cruel, and fear provoking is to live a life that is tragically impoverished. Indeed, there is a kind of theological economy at work. For those who live in the confidence that God is trustworthy and generous, they find more and more of that generosity; but for those who run and hide under the bed from a bad, mean, and scolding God, they condemn themselves to a life spent under the bed alone, quivering in needless fear. "To all those who have, more will be given . . . but from those who have nothing, even what they have will be taken away" (Matt. 25:29).

The Parable of the Sheep and the Goats (Matthew 25:31–46)

It could be said that the whole Gospel of Matthew has been moving toward and preparing for this dramatic parable. In Matthew, Jesus is the great teacher, and this parable is his last formal act of teaching, the final point, the parting lesson, the cumulative moment in his teaching ministry. Moreover, this parable not only concludes Jesus' ministry of teaching; it also sums up the major theological themes of Matthew's Gospel by presenting a majestic picture of the triumphant Jesus reigning in glory as king and judge at the end of time.

Indeed, the parable begins as a victory hymn to Christ set in the future: "When the Son of Man comes in his glory . . ." (Matt. 25:31). The Jesus who had "nowhere to lay his head" (Matt. 8:20) is now seated on the royal throne as king. The Jesus who was accused of being an agent of Satan (Matt. 12:24) is now revealed as the holy Lord of lords. The Jesus who was rejected even by his hometown (Matt. 13:54–58) is now exalted as the judge of the whole human family. The Jesus who resisted the devil's temptation to throw himself down from the temple and let God's angels take charge of him (Matt. 4:5–7) is now elevated in glory above all earthly temples and in command of the angels.

As the camera pulls back to encompass the entire scene, we are shown all of the nations of the earth, row after row of humanity, gathered before the throne of the Son of Man. Just as a shepherd in that time sometimes would divide the larger flock, separating the sheep from the less valuable goats, so the Son of Man divides the people into the "sheep" on the right hand and the "goats" on the left.

The Son of Man pronounces judgment upon both the sheep and the goats. For the sheep, the news is good. They are given a divine blessing and are revealed as the true heirs of God's kingdom (Matt. 25:34) because they provided food, drink, hospitality, clothing, and care for the Son of Man. As for the goats, however, they are condemned "into the eternal fire" (Matt. 25:41) because they supplied none of those ministries, even though the Son of Man was hungry, thirsty, a stranger, naked, sick, and in prison.

If this were all there were to the parable—those who do good deeds are rewarded and those who do not are punished—it would be a fairly conventional morality tale, the sort of story that can be found frequently in the religious literature of many cultures. The parable takes a curious twist, though, when it becomes apparent that the sheep had no idea whatsoever that, in their compassion toward people in need, they were providing ministry to the Son of Man, and, likewise, the goats had not a clue that, in their indifference, they were in fact neglecting the Lord of all nations. Both groups are stunned and exclaim, "Lord, when was it that we saw you hungry or thirsty or a stranger or naked or sick or in prison?" (Matt. 25:44; see also 25:37–39). The surprising reply is that whenever they acted—or failed to act—compassionately "to one of the least of these who are members of my family" (Matt. 25:40), they did so to Jesus Christ.

This dramatic disclosure, that Jesus Christ is present in the world in "the least of these who are members of my family" is the focal point of this parable. The world will be judged according to whether it did or did not show hospitality to Jesus Christ, the Messiah clothed not in royal majesty but coming to the world hidden among the "least of these."

But who, exactly, are the "least of these"? Biblical scholars have produced two rival interpretations of this phrase. Some argue that "the least of these who are members of my family" ("my brothers" in Greek) refers specifically to Christians, especially to Christian missionaries who went about with no money and no possessions (Matt. 10:9–10). The case for this view is strong because, in Matthew, the term "brothers" always refers to a member of the Christian community, as does the phrase "little ones" (see Matt. 10:42; 18:6). If this is the proper interpretation of the parable, then the message is that the church is Christ's presence in the world, and the world will be judged on the basis of how it treats the Christian community and receives those sent to it on behalf of Christ. The parable becomes a narrative expression of Jesus' statement to the disciples as he was sending them out to minister in his name, "Whoever gives even a cup of cold water to one of these little ones in the name of a disciple—truly I tell you, none of these will lose their reward" (Matt. 10:42).

On the other hand, the more familiar interpretation of this parable is that "the least of these" refers to *all* human beings in need, to everyone who is poor and needy, and not just to Christian missionaries. There is evidence for this position as well. Although it is true that Jesus calls some members of the Christian community "little ones" (see, for example, Matt. 10:42; 18:6) the phrase in Greek is different from "the least of these" in the parable. Moreover, though Jesus spoke of members of the church as "brothers" (see, for example, the footnote to Matt. 18:15, 17), he refused to restrict the term "my brothers" to the church alone but taught that "whoever does the will of my Father in heaven is my brother and sister and mother" (Matt. 12:50; Meier, *Matthew*, 304). If this view of the parable is correct, the moral of the story is that the whole world will be judged—the church included—according to the compassion they showed to hungry and hurting people, whoever they may be.

So, what is the answer to the question? Does the parable of the sheep and the goats teach that the world will be judged on the basis of how it treats the church (as the Body of Christ), or does it teach that everybody, including Christians, will be judged by how they treat the poor and needy of the earth?

Recently, some students of the parables have argued persuasively that the parable, in fact, teaches both. According to this view, the phrase "the least of these who are members of my family" does, in fact, refer to the Christian community. So, the main thrust of the parable is that the peoples of the world will finally be judged on the basis of how they receive the emissaries of the gospel who come in the name of Jesus Christ. But, this is no invitation to the church to swagger with pride and authority. It is important to note that the parable calls these Christians "*the least*," not "the greatest"; they come to the world not in limousines and silk, but hungry and thirsty. They are not the power elite or the moral majority, forcing their will on the nations; they are identified with the weak of the earth and are more likely to be found in hospitals and prisons than in palaces. Indeed, the shock of this parable is that no one—not the goats and not even the sheep—recognized Christ because they assumed that the majestic, triumphant Lord of all time would surely appear as a powerful presence in history. But this is not God's way in the world. "He had no form or majesty that we should look at him. . . . He was despised and rejected by others; a man of suffering and acquainted with infirmity" (Isa. 53:2–3).

So, the Christian church is sent out to the world on a vital mission—to bear witness to the gospel of Jesus Christ. The "good news of the kingdom will be proclaimed throughout the world, as a testimony to all the nations" (Matt. 24:14). The gospel, however, is more than mere words, and the church proclaims the gospel by living in the world as Jesus lived. The disciple is to be like the teacher (Matt. 10:24); the church must become humble like a child and show hospitality to those in need (Matt. 18:1–5). In Matthew's Gospel, if you want to find Jesus, look among those who are "harassed and helpless, like sheep without a shepherd" (Matt. 9:36). The church that is faithful will be found in precisely the same place.

15. The Death of Jesus the Messiah
Matthew 26:1–27:66

The Gospel of Matthew began with "an account of the genealogy of Jesus the Messiah." There the names of Jesus' ancestors tumbled forth in the seemingly arbitrary, almost chaotic flow of the generations. How many chance occurrences are bound up in the lineage of a human being? Coincidences happen; choices are made. A young widow named Ruth decides, against all good sense, to leave the familiarity of home and to accompany her mother-in-law on a difficult journey to an unpromising life in the small village of Bethlehem. Another time, a different decision, and the family tree would have branched another way. David, walking on the roof of his house, happens to see a beautiful woman bathing, and, though she is the wife of another, he nonetheless feels the powerful lure of desire. A change in timing, a different mood, and the cadence of the generations would have been altered.

The ancestry of Jesus, like the ancestry of every human being, was the product of a thousand rolls of the dice. A glance of a man's wandering eye, a touch of a woman's hand, a choice to leave rather than remain, a decision to stay and not to go, a blowing of the wind first this way and then that, and the march of the generations moved down this path when it could have easily gone down the other. But Matthew is at pains to show that underneath the chance was a steady providence; behind the seeming arbitrariness was a firm purpose; governing the random tides of time was the One who has been a "dwelling place in all generations" (Psalm 90:1). Viewed in retrospect, the jumble of generations has a shape; the apparent haphazardness reveals an orderliness, a form molded by the hand of God who rules the ages: "So all the generations from Abraham to David are fourteen generations; and from David to the deportation to Babylon, fourteen generations; and from the deportation to Babylon to the Messiah, fourteen generations" (Matt. 1:17).

Now, the Gospel of Matthew, which began with the roll call of birth, moves to a close with the account of the Messiah's death, and the same interweaving of randomness and order marks the narrative. Politicians and religious officials respond under pressure; frightened disciples try to act brave but crumple under the strain; the trial judge vacillates between innocence and death; events cascade and collide toward a seemingly arbitrary death; yet Matthew wants the reader to feel the flow of events guided by the firm undercurrent of God's will. Jesus is no victim of whim or fate; he is firmly in charge of his life, his vocation, his mission—even his death. Despite the illusion of power on the part of the forces of evil, Jesus gives his life as a free act of sacrifice; no one takes it from him. Jesus will die, but it will not ultimately be random violence. His death will be purposeful and redemptive, for, as Joseph was told at Jesus' birth, "he will save his people from their sins" (Matt. 1:21). On the surface, this will be a tragic story, a story of how fear and rage and hatred gained control and killed an innocent man. On the surface, then, this is a story of evil with us; down deep, though, this is the same story Matthew has been telling all along, the good news of Jesus the Messiah, of Emmanuel, "God is with us" (Matt. 1:23).

THE OVERTURE TO JESUS' DEATH
Matthew 26:1–46

26:1 **When Jesus had finished saying all these things, he said to his disciples,** [2] **"You know that after two days the Passover is coming, and the Son of Man will be handed over to be crucified."**

[3] **Then the chief priests and the elders of the people gathered in the palace of the high priest, who was called Caiaphas,** [4] **and they conspired to arrest Jesus by stealth and kill him.** [5] **But they said, "Not during the festival, or there may be a riot among the people."**

[6] **Now while Jesus was at Bethany in the house of Simon the leper,** [7] **a woman came to him with an alabaster jar of very costly ointment, and she poured it on his head as he sat at the table.** [8] **But when the disciples saw it, they were angry and said, "Why this waste?** [9] **For this ointment could have been sold for a large sum, and the money given to the poor."** [10] **But Jesus, aware of this, said to them, "Why do you trouble the woman? She has performed a good service for me.** [11] **For you always have the poor with you, but you will not always have me.** [12] **By pouring this ointment on my body she has prepared me for burial.** [13] **Truly I tell you, wherever this good news is proclaimed in the whole world, what she has done will be told in remembrance of her."**

[14] **Then one of the twelve, who was called Judas Iscariot, went to the chief priests** [15] **and said, "What will you give me if I betray him to you?" They paid**

him thirty pieces of silver. [16] And from that moment he began to look for an opportunity to betray him.

[17] On the first day of Unleavened Bread the disciples came to Jesus, saying, "Where do you want us to make the preparations for you to eat the Passover?" [18] He said, "Go into the city to a certain man, and say to him, 'The Teacher says, My time is near; I will keep the Passover at your house with my disciples.'" [19] So the disciples did as Jesus had directed them, and they prepared the Passover meal.

[20] When it was evening, he took his place with the twelve; [21] and while they were eating, he said, "Truly I tell you, one of you will betray me." [22] And they became greatly distressed and began to say to him one after another, "Surely not I, Lord?" [23] He answered, "The one who has dipped his hand into the bowl with me will betray me. [24] The Son of Man goes as it is written of him, but woe to that one by whom the Son of Man is betrayed! It would have been better for that one not to have been born." [25] Judas, who betrayed him, said, "Surely not I, Rabbi?" He replied, "You have said so."

[26] While they were eating, Jesus took a loaf of bread, and after blessing it he broke it, gave it to the disciples, and said, "Take, eat; this is my body." [27] Then he took a cup, and after giving thanks he gave it to them, saying, "Drink from it, all of you; [28] for this is my blood of the covenant, which is poured out for many for the forgiveness of sins. [29] I tell you, I will never again drink of this fruit of the vine until that day when I drink it new with you in my Father's kingdom."

[30] When they had sung the hymn, they went out to the Mount of Olives.

[31] Then Jesus said to them, "You will all become deserters because of me this night; for it is written,

'I will strike the shepherd,
and the sheep of the flock will be scattered.'

[32] But after I am raised up, I will go ahead of you to Galilee." [33] Peter said to him, "Though all become deserters because of you, I will never desert you." [34] Jesus said to him, "Truly I tell you, this very night, before the cock crows, you will deny me three times." [35] Peter said to him, "Even though I must die with you, I will not deny you." And so said all the disciples.

[36] Then Jesus went with them to a place called Gethsemane; and he said to his disciples, "Sit here while I go over there and pray." [37] He took with him Peter and the two sons of Zebedee, and began to be grieved and agitated. [38] Then he said to them, "I am deeply grieved, even to death; remain here, and stay awake with me." [39] And going a little farther, he threw himself on the ground and prayed, "My Father, if it is possible, let this cup pass from me; yet not what I want but what you want." [40] Then he came to the disciples and found them sleeping; and he said to Peter, "So, could you not stay awake with me one hour? [41] Stay awake and pray that you may not come into the time of trial; the spirit indeed is willing, but the flesh is weak." [42] Again he went away for the second time and prayed, "My Father, if this

cannot pass unless I drink it, your will be done." [43] Again he came and found them sleeping, for their eyes were heavy. [44] So leaving them again, he went away and prayed for the third time, saying the same words. [45] Then he came to the disciples and said to them, "Are you still sleeping and taking your rest? See, the hour is at hand, and the Son of Man is betrayed into the hands of sinners. [46] Get up, let us be going. See, my betrayer is at hand."

Customarily, when Jesus concluded a session of teaching, Matthew signals this by saying something like "when Jesus had finished saying these things" (Matt. 7:28; 11:1; 13:53; 19:1). Here, though, he reports that "Jesus had finished saying all these things" (Matt. 26:1). The sudden appearance of the word *all* conveys that this is more than the ending of a single event of teaching; this is the final curtain on all of Jesus' formal teaching. From this time on, his ministry of instruction in the commandments of the kingdom will be carried out by his church (Matt. 28:16–20). But even though his teacher's voice here grows silent, he still has one last lesson for his disciples, the cross. He will embody there what he taught in words—faithful obedience to God, even to death (Senior, *The Passion of Jesus*, 50). Now, everything builds toward this climactic event.

A Collision of Timetables
(Matthew 26:1–5)

The tension between human grasping and the divine will is established at the very beginning of the account of Jesus' death. Jesus predicts for the fourth time that he will die (see also Matt. 16:21; 17:22–23; 20:18–19). This time, however, Jesus does more than simply announce his death; he names the date of his arrest—on Passover (Matt. 26:1–2), the Jewish festival that commemorated the exodus, God's deliverance of the Hebrew people from the cruel hand of pharaoh.

In the very next scene, however, a sharp contrast is drawn between human and divine will. The religious authorities—the chief priests and the elders—are gathered in the house of Caiaphas, who served as the high priest from A.D. 18 to 36, plotting Jesus' death, and they explicitly decide to seize Jesus on some occasion other than Passover. With all the fervent pilgrims jostling about in the city of Jerusalem, great festivals were occasions of unrest, and the religious authorities want to avoid a potentially volatile event by arresting Jesus out of the spotlight, on a quieter occasion than Passover.

So, the competing timetables are set. The divine sequence calls for the handing over of Jesus to occur on Passover; the world's scheme calls for the deed to occur on some other occasion. As the plot unfolds, the very thing the schemers decided not to do is, in fact, done. Jesus is arrested on Passover, just as he said, a sign that God's will is prevailing through all human scheming and plotting.

Thus, irony pervades the story. The religious authorities believe that they are in charge of Jesus' fate, but it is God's will that governs the course of events. They will arrest Jesus, the savior of the world, the one who gives freedom and deliverance, on Passover, the day celebrating freedom and salvation. They will conspire with the political powers to kill the true King. Indeed, Matthew's readers will remember a previous time, at the appearing of the star leading Magi from the East, when the religious leaders conspired with the political powers to produce a plot to kill Jesus. Now, the collusion is occurring again. The shadow of death fell across the birth of Jesus, and it falls again over the ending of his ministry.

Jesus Is Anointed for Burial
(Matthew 26:6–13)

As with most events in history, the death of Jesus can be interpreted in more than one way. On the surface, Jesus was a troublemaker who irritated the religious and political establishment so thoroughly that they found an expedient way to get rid of him. In their view, he stirred up the people unnecessarily, he disrupted normal business at the temple, and his teachings bordered on blasphemy. His death was but another case of a revolutionary pushing too hard, going beyond what the powers-that-be can tolerate.

However, the whole purpose of Matthew's Gospel is to render another reading of events, to enable the church to see beneath the ripples on the surface and to discern the depths, to perceive the story of Jesus not as the sad account of yet another social reformer who got in the way and was crushed when the wheel of history turned, but as a manifestation of the very life and saving mercy of God.

It is this matter of depth perception that is at stake in the account of the woman who anoints Jesus with costly ointment. On the surface, this is a very foolish thing she has done, wasting a flask of expensive perfume in a single act of extravagance, and the disciples, understandably agitated, begin to scold the woman. The ointment, they say, "could have been sold for a large sum, and the money given to the poor" (Matt. 26:9). They have a point. Had not Jesus just told a parable about the urgency of showing compassion to the poor and needy (see Matt. 25:31–46)?

At the depths, however, this woman, far from being foolish and wasteful, has acted out symbolically what Matthew hopes all of his readers will do in response to Jesus. She is the first to see what others cannot yet see, but will see in time. Up to this point in the story of Jesus, many have responded to Jesus' life; she alone has approached Jesus reverently and recognized the profound significance of his death.

The disciples do not yet understand the necessity of Jesus' death. On the three previous occasions when Jesus announced to them that he would die, they responded with resistance (Matt. 16:21–23), distress (Matt. 17:22–23), and misunderstanding (Matt. 20:17–23). This woman, however, by anointing Jesus for burial already discerns that it is by his death that Jesus is truly "Messiah" (which means "anointed"; see Matt. 1:1). Moreover, in the Old Testament, anointing is a sign of holiness (see Gen. 28:16–18), of the priesthood (see Exod. 29:7), and of royalty (1 Sam. 16:12–13; 1 Kings 1:39), and it may be that the woman's action acknowledges that Jesus' death is a holy death, a priestly death, and the death of the world's true king.

Thus, Jesus declares that her act was a "good service" (Matt. 26:10), which is far more than the mere sentiment that the woman did something nice for Jesus. Jesus means that her deed was a "good work," a proclamation of the kingdom, the kind of shining light that he spoke about in the Sermon on the Mount (see Matt. 5:14–16). She, alone at this point, has grasped what God is doing in the world and has acted accordingly, and her anointing of Jesus was a luminescent sermon-in-action, a proclamation of the saving power of Jesus' death. Therefore, she is, in her own way, the pioneer preacher, and all the preachers of the gospel who follow her will celebrate her memory by telling her story "wherever this good news is proclaimed" (Matt. 26:13). So important is her action to Matthew that hers is the only anointing story he tells (see, by contrast, the accounts in Mark 16:1 and John 19:39–40 of other anointings of Jesus at the time of death).

When Jesus tells the disciples that "you always have the poor with you, but you will not always have me" (Matt. 26:11), he is not being cynical about poverty or devaluing compassion toward the needy. Jesus does not say to the disciples, "Poor people are a distraction. You can forget them." Instead, he says, "You *always* have the poor with you." Showing mercy to the needy of the earth is an everyday occurrence for children of God's kingdom (Matt. 5:7), and being compassionate to the poor is a constant mission of the church.

The woman's action does not hinder care for the poor; to the contrary, it discloses the deep motivation for all Christian compassion. The church is charged with caring for the needy not merely because Christians are nice people who are concerned about social reform, but because Jesus died for needy humanity and the risen Christ is alive and at work among the poor. Jesus did not leave the church with a list of chores to get done before he gets back; the risen Christ is with us always (Matt. 28:20) saving the whole creation. Christians work with and for the poor because, by doing so, they join with Christ in God's own work.

Therefore, when the woman poured the precious ointment on Jesus' head, she was not draining away resources that could have been used for the poor. To the contrary, her act recognized Jesus' death, a sacrificial death, a saving death. All acts of Christian ministry grow out of this one profound act of Jesus' ministry. When the woman anointed Jesus, she proclaimed that in the death of this man was the miracle the poor need, indeed, the miracle we have all been waiting for. On the cross, Jesus joined himself to all wounded, suffering, dying humanity. On the cross, Jesus became poor. "For you know," wrote Paul, "the generous act of our Lord Jesus Christ, that though he was rich, yet for your sakes he became poor, so that by his poverty you might become rich" (2 Cor. 8:9). The woman's generous act of pouring costly ointment over Jesus was a sign of his even more generous act on the cross.

In the parable of the sheep and the goats (Matt. 25:31–46), the surprise was that those who ministered to the poor and needy were actually caring for the hidden Christ; in this story of the woman and the perfume, the surprise is that her ministry to Jesus Christ discloses the saving mercy of God for a poor and needy world.

A Disciple Becomes a Traitor
(Matthew 26:14–16)

In this story of betrayal, the tension and interplay between God's will and human will, already set in motion (see comments on Matt. 26:1–5), continues and is heightened. In the previous story, an unnamed woman anoints Jesus with a precious ointment, thereby acknowledging that his coming death is a holy event, an expression of God's will. Now, ironically, a disciple, one of Jesus' very own, rebels against God's will and becomes a pawn of human scheming.

Judas Iscariot (the name "Iscariot" may indicate that Judas was from the town of Kerioth) slips over to the chief priests and asks how much he could get to betray Jesus. He is handed "thirty pieces of silver" (Matt. 26:15), a relatively small sum of money at the time. The woman who anointed Jesus was willing to pour out a fortune to show her devotion; Judas puts his Master on sale for a pittance (Garland, *Reading Matthew*, 249).

The phrase "thirty pieces of silver" would create a sense of déjà vu for Matthew's first readers. They would remember that, in Zechariah 11: 12–13, a shepherd was given the insultingly low wage of "thirty shekels of silver," which he eventually threw in disgust into the temple treasury. Now, Judas becomes a traitor for the same paltry wage, and he, too, will eventually throw down his tainted wage in the temple (Matt. 27:5). The memory of this would prompt Matthew's readers to realize that nothing is happening here outside of God's knowledge and will, not even the amount of money Judas is paid or what he will do with it. Every little detail of this human scheming to thwart Jesus was, in fact, known by God and gathered into the saving purposes of God.

When Matthew reports that Judas "from that moment . . . began to look for an opportunity to betray him" (Matt. 26:16), he is once again underscoring the struggle between human will and God's will. "Betray," which Judas will do, is derived from the same Greek word as the phrase in Matthew 26:2, "handed over," which God will do. Matthew intends for the two uses of this word to play off against each other in order to make the theological point that although the human will thinks that it is in command and "betraying" Jesus, the deeper truth is that God is in control, freely "handing over" the Son on behalf of the world.

Jesus Observes the Passover
(Matthew 26:17–30)

Jesus' disciples begin their preparation for the Passover feast on "the first day of Unleavened Bread," which in Matthew's time was simply another way to describe the beginning of Passover. The name comes from the custom of eating only unleavened bread during the seven days following the Passover festival.

The observance of the Passover involved eating a ritual meal, and when the disciples ask Jesus where he wants them to prepare the meal (Matt. 26:17), the way Jesus answers them emphasizes two theological themes. First, there is the theme of the disciples' obedience; Jesus gives a clear command about what they are to do, and the disciples explicitly follow his directive (Matt. 26:18–19). Unlike the Gospel of Mark, where the disciples never seem quite able to rise above their blindness and lack of understanding, in Matthew the disciples, for all of their frailties and human faults, are still capable of growth, understanding, and obedience. In Matthew, the disciples are not those who merely cry out, "Lord, Lord"; they actually *do* the will of God (Matt. 7:21).

Not all of them, however, for Judas, the betrayer, is among them. Indeed, the second theological theme in Jesus' answer is the conflict between human time and God's time; between the human attempt to seize the moment for evil, as symbolized by Judas, and God's will to transform all time in mercy, as embodied in Jesus. When Jesus says, "My time is near" (Matt. 26:18), this sharply contrasts with the fact that Judas is looking not for Jesus' time but for a time of his own, an "opportune time" to betray him (Matt. 26:16). Who owns the time? Is this Jesus' time or Judas' time? Are these moments, which are leading up to the death of the Messiah, God's time or the world's? Despite appearances, the passing of time does not belong to Judas but to Jesus. This is holy time, God's time, not the betrayer's, not the world's.

That evening, as Jesus and the disciples eat the Passover meal, Jesus continues to demonstrate his command of the situation by announcing in advance how events will surely unfold: "Truly I tell you, one of you will betray me" (Matt. 26:21). Betrayal must occur, but it cannot derail God's will; indeed, it is written into the script (Matt. 26:24). But, even though treachery is inevitable, it is a tragedy for the human being who commits it, and Judas's guilty inquiry implicates himself (Matt. 26:25). "Surely not I, Rabbi?" asks Judas, his thirty pieces of silver jangling somewhere in his soul. For Judas to call Jesus "Rabbi" is a sign that his understanding of Jesus is shallow and faulty (see Matt. 23:7), and, as if to underscore this misperception, he will use the term again when he actually commits the deed of betrayal (Matt. 26:49).

Now, the two rival stories begin to unfold in their own ways, and both lead to death. The story of God's will unfolds toward the death of Jesus, an act of redemption as his "blood . . . is poured out for many for the forgiveness of sins" (Matt. 26:28). But the story of human will gone awry unfolds toward death as well, the death of Judas, the unraveling of a life caught in the tragedy of "betraying innocent blood" (Matt. 27:4). Earlier, the disciples were angry at the woman who poured perfume on Jesus' head, because they considered her act to be a "waste" (Matt. 26:8). But her extravagance was an honoring of Jesus' redemptive death. The real waste was neither her act nor Jesus' death, but Judas's death, who poured out the dregs of his guilt-ridden life in the Field of Blood (Matt. 27:8).

When the preparations had been made, Jesus and his disciples share a last meal. It is a fellowship meal, a banquet with food, drink, singing, and conversation—a Passover feast full of life (Ford, "What Happens in the Eucharist?" 369). Most scholars agree that Matthew's account of this *last* Supper (Matt. 26:26–30) was influenced by the way his church actually observed the *Lord's* Supper, the Eucharist. Matthew remembered the past in the light of the present, much as Christians today often imagine that the shepherds and the wise men all arrived at the very same time in Bethlehem to see the newborn Jesus. Why do we think this way? Because that is the way it happens in the children's pageant on Christmas Eve. Just so, the early church imagined the events of the Last Supper to be just like the Communion services they experienced in their worship. What happened that night as Jesus shared his last supper with the disciples clearly shaped how the church observes the Lord's Supper, but the process moves in the reverse direction, too. The church's worship at the Lord's Table shapes its memory of the Last Supper.

In Matthew, there is but one cup (in Luke there are two; see Luke 22:17, 20), and the ceremonies over the bread and the cup have been merged and occur as a unit in the *middle* of the meal, "while they were eating" (Matt. 26:26), instead of before and after supper (as in 1 Cor. 11:25). The probable reason is that by Matthew's time the Lord's Supper had developed into a somewhat more formal and unified liturgy, a symbolic meal something like Holy Communion in most churches today rather than an actual supper.

Part of what this means is that, when Matthew describes the Last Supper, he is also describing the theology of the Lord's Supper. Every word Jesus spoke that night, every action he performed, is an important clue to the meaning of the Eucharist:

1. *The actions.* Following the typical pattern of a Jewish ceremonial meal, Jesus takes a loaf of bread, pronounces a blessing, breaks the bread, and distributes it to the others (Matt. 26:26). For Matthew's readers, these actions recall the feeding of the multitudes (Matt. 14:19; 15:36). In the Lord's Supper, Jesus Christ once again feeds hungry people, famished in many ways, who gather around him.

2. *The blessing.* When Jesus pronounces a blessing over the bread, this is not a blessing of the bread itself, but a blessing of God who gives this and every day "our daily bread" (Matt. 6:11). When we "say grace" at mealtime, we are not blessing the food; we are praising and giving thanks to God who provides food and all else that sustains us. Moreover, we are reminded as we come to the special meal at the Lord's Table that every meal is a gift from God, every meal a breaking of bread with Jesus Christ.

3. *The words over the bread:* "Take, eat; this is my body" (Matt. 26:26). The bread represents the "body" of Jesus, that is, Jesus himself. In the Lord's Supper, Jesus Christ comes to the faithful and offers himself, his whole life, to them. And what does he give to them? The entire story of Jesus that Matthew has been telling expresses the measure of this gift. Jesus, the son of David and the son of Abraham, offers the heritage of God's covenant; Jesus the teacher offers God's wisdom and righteousness; Jesus the healer offers God's mercy and freedom; Jesus the preacher of good news offers God's promises of hope and salvation; Jesus the savior offers forgiveness of sins. "This is my body, this is myself, I give everything to you."

Not only does Jesus move toward his disciples with the offer of his life; he also commands them to move toward him with hands outstretched. "Take and eat," he tells them, inviting them to respond to his gifts of grace. To take the bread and to eat is to be joined to Jesus Christ, willingly to receive the gifts of life he provides and freely to take up his cause in the world. To take and eat the body of Jesus is to become his followers who deny themselves, take up their crosses, and follow him (Matt. 16:24), but it is also to become his faithful disciples who do mercy and seek peace and, when all is said and done, "enter into the joy" of the master (Matt. 25:21, 23).

4. *The words over the cup:* "Drink from it, all of you; for this is my blood of the covenant, which is poured out for many for the forgiveness of sins" (Matt. 26:27–28). This statement echoes three events from the Old Testament. First, when God entered into relationship, a covenant, with the people of Israel, Moses symbolized it by sprinkling the blood of an ox on all of the people. "See," he said, "the blood of the covenant that the LORD has made with you" (Exod. 24:8). Second, the prophet Isaiah spoke of a certain servant of God, one who was "despised and rejected by others, a man of suffering" who "poured out himself to death," but one who was nonetheless "wounded for our transgressions, crushed for our iniquities" (Isa. 53:3, 5, 12). And third, the prophet Jeremiah told of a time when God would make a "new covenant" with Israel, one where the law of God would be written on the hearts of the people, and God "will forgive their iniquity, and remember their sin no more" (Jer. 31:31–34).

Here at the Last Supper, Jesus invokes these three Old Testament memories to describe his own death. In the death of Jesus, God renewed the covenant with God's people. This time the sign of the covenant was not the blood of an animal, but the blood of Jesus himself. Jesus was God's true servant, despised and rejected, but who through his suffering made a new covenant with God's people by pouring out his blood "for many for the forgiveness of sins" (Matt. 26:28).

As the supper ends, Jesus tells his disciples that he will not drink another cup of wine with them until the coming of God's kingdom. With these words, Jesus is pointing over the horizon of time to God's ultimate victory, to the "marriage supper of the Lamb" (Rev. 19:9), to the great day when "many will come from east and west and will eat with Abraham and Isaac and Jacob in the kingdom of heaven" (Matt. 8:11).

But Jesus is speaking not only about the absolute end of time; he is also promising to "drink it new" (Matt. 26:29) with his disciples every time the church gathers at the Lord's Table to taste the fruits of the kingdom, when the church eats and drinks with the risen Christ, when the children of the kingdom gather to sing and pray and break bread, anticipating in hope that future day when the Son of Man will come with power and glory, when the whole human family will gather at the banquet table and the mercy of God will cover the earth like the waters of the sea.

5. *The hymn.* Jesus and the disciples conclude the meal with the singing of a hymn (Matt. 26:30). There is no way to be certain which hymn they sang, but it was probably what Jews in Jesus' day called the "Great Hallel" (which means, "Great Praise"), a medley of Psalms 114 to 118, which was traditionally sung to conclude a Passover meal. If so, as the disciples shared the cup at the close of the meal, they would have sung: "What shall I return to the LORD for all his bounty to me? I will lift up the cup of salvation and call on the name of the LORD" (Psalm 116:12–13). In these last moments before his prayer of anguish in Gethsemane, Jesus would have sung, "Not to us, O LORD, not to us, but to your name give glory" (Psalm 115:1). As Jesus and his disciples got up from the meal and went to the Mount of Olives, to the place of betrayal and arrest, they would have sung, "The stone that the builders rejected has become the chief cornerstone" (Psalm 118:22). As they plummeted toward the trial by fire, they would have sung, "It is better to take refuge in the LORD than to put confidence in mortals" (Psalm 118:8). As they moved toward the cross, they would have sung, "Precious in the sight of the LORD is the death of his faithful ones" (Psalm 116:15). And as Jesus marched toward his death, he and his disciples would have sung, "I was pushed hard, so that I was falling, but the LORD helped me. The LORD is my strength and my might; he has become my salvation. . . . Blessed is the one who comes in the name of the LORD" (Psalm 118:13–14, 26).

Jesus Foresees the Desertion of the Disciples (Matthew 26:31–35)

"Ah, holy Jesus, how hast Thou offended?" asks the ancient hymn. As Jesus departs the final meal with his disciples, he knows that the events of the rest of the night will make him offensive even to these, his closest followers. "You will all become deserters [in Greek, "be scandalized"] because of me this night," he tells them (Matt. 26:31). The biggest scandal of the Christian faith is not ministers who run off with secretaries or church treasurers who embezzle the offerings, but Jesus himself. The Son of God who submits to the violence of mere human beings and dies, the Messiah who is arrested, tried, convicted, and executed as a common criminal—this is the abiding scandal of the gospel.

The Greek term "scandalized" is also used in Jesus' interpretation of the parable of the sower to describe those who are like seed sown on rocky ground. "Such a person," Jesus said, "has no root, but endures only for a while, and when trouble or persecution arises on account of the word, that person immediately falls away [in Greek, 'is scandalized']" (Matt. 13:21). Now trouble and persecution are indeed about to arise, and the disciples, still without sufficient roots, will be scandalized and fall away.

Once again, though, Matthew develops the theme of the contrast between God's will and human will (see comments on Matt. 26:1–5 and 26:14–16). The cowardly desertion of Jesus' own disciples is a dramatic expression of the revolt of human will against God's intention, but by quoting Zechariah 13:7, Jesus announces that even this lowest, most chaotic moment in the story is enfolded within God's plan.

Indeed, both Mark and Matthew change the original text of Zechariah so that, instead of a command, "Strike the shepherd, that the sheep may be scattered," the passage is rendered as a declaration, "I will strike the shepherd, and the sheep of the flock will be scattered" (Matt. 26:31; see Mark 14:27; Zech. 13:7), which implies that God will do the striking. The theological point is not that God is inflicting violence upon God's own Son, but the deep mystery that the worst evil that the world can produce— the cowardice, defection, repudiation, and brutality of humanity against Jesus—is providentially gathered into God's merciful and saving purposes (Hare, *Matthew*, 299–300). Jesus the shepherd (see Matt. 2:6) will be struck down, and the sheep will be scattered, but, by the power of God, the shepherd will be raised up and will again gather the flock in Galilee (Matt. 26:32; see also Matt. 28:7).

Peter steps forward to protest Jesus' prediction that all of them will desert. In Matthew, Peter is the leader of the disciples, the dependable rock on which Jesus can build his church (see Matt. 16:18). "Everyone else may abandon you," asserts this solid rock, "but I will never desert you." But Jesus sees what Peter cannot, or will not, see; the storms of evil are about to strike with savage fury, and for all his bravado now, Peter, the rock, will crumble—three times—before dawn (Matt. 26:34).

Down through the ages, Christian theologians have struggled with a puzzle, a paradox, about human sin. On the one hand, human beings choose freely to sin. We are not robots with computer chips for souls, programmed to sin. On the other hand, every human being makes that choice; everyone is a sinner. As one theologian put it, humanity sins "inevitably, but responsibly."

In the story of Jesus' death, the disciples, with Peter as their spokesman, are representative of this human dilemma. When Peter vows that he will never be a deserter, he speaks out of his freedom, out of the human possibility of faith and obedience to the will of God for human life. But when Jesus responds, "Truly, you will break this very night," he speaks the sad truth of the way it goes in human life. Peter affirms God's way, but like Adam and like Eve, like Israel and like David, like the other disciples and like all human beings everywhere, he will, when the chips are down, choose another way.

Jesus' Prayer in Gethsemane
(Matthew 26:36–46)

Throughout this chapter, Matthew has drawn the sharp contrast between God's will and human will (see comments on Matt. 26:1–5; 26:14–16; and 26:31–35). Human beings have attempted to exploit events through scheming and betrayal, to seize control of history, to set their own timetable for events. But God's will has prevailed and will prevail throughout. What matters is not human plotting and betrayal, but the divine plan to "hand over" Jesus in order to save humanity. What counts is not the futile human attempts to manipulate the course of history, but the fact that this is Jesus' hour, God's time.

But, even though the distinction between the divine and human wills is clearly drawn, that does not mean that maintaining the distinction is easy or that it is simple to choose God's way. Now Jesus himself must grapple with this tension, and the struggle over his soul is profound and anguished.

Jesus goes with his disciples to a place called Gethsemane, probably a garden in a grove of olive trees (Gethsemane means "oil press"). He leaves the larger group, and taking only Peter, James, and John with him, he withdraws to a more secluded spot to pray. These are the same three disciples who accompanied Jesus onto the high mountain where he was transfigured (Matt. 17:1–8), and on that occasion, the three disciples fell on their faces in awe and fear before the glory of Jesus. Now, in Gethsemane, it will be Jesus who falls to the ground, prostrate in sorrowful humility before his Father (Matt. 26:39; Garland, *Reading Matthew*, 251).

Jesus encourages the three disciples to "stay awake," and readers of Matthew are aware that he means more than simply fighting off sleep. He is urging them to watch alertly for the coming of the kingdom. In the long night of history, when evil in the world holds sway, the children of the kingdom are watchful for the coming of God's deliverance (Matt. 24:44); even though the hour is late and the gloom is deep, they stay awake expecting salvation to arrive with a joyful shout at any minute (Matt. 25:13).

Jesus knows that his life is in peril, and he does not face the prospect with stoic resolve. He is emotional, full of sorrow and distress; like the psalmist, his "soul is cast down," and he is "deeply grieved, even to death" (Matt. 26:38; see Psalm 42:6; 43:5). Troubled, he prays for God to provide a way out, an easier road that allows his life to be spared. Jesus, who was tempted three times by Satan to compromise his identity and vocation (Matt. 4:1–11), now faces a threefold temptation from within. In the coming hours, Peter will also face temptation three times, and three times he will fail and deny Jesus. But here Jesus struggles over temptation in prayer three times, and each time he submits obediently to God's will. His intimate address to God, "My Father," and his compliant petition, "Your will be done" (Matt. 26:39, 42) are precisely what he taught his disciples to say in the Lord's Prayer (Matt. 6:10), and his unswerving obedience to God's will, his willingness to travel the hard way and to pass through the narrow gate, is a model for his followers (Matt. 7:13–14).

Jesus wants fellowship with his disciples; they prefer the sleep of avoidance. Jesus is alert to God's will; Peter, James, and John slumber through his time of anguish. While his disciples doze and falter, he leaves the place of prayer clear about his vocation and resolute in his purpose, and he gives them a wake-up call: "Get up, let us be going. See, my betrayer is at hand" (Matt. 26:46). The words "my betrayer is at hand" can also be translated "my betrayer has come near," and earlier, Jesus used the same phrase to declare that the kingdom of heaven "has come near" (Matt. 4:17). Now it is Judas, the traitor, who "has come near." Ironically, as Judas approaches to do his evil work, both betrayal and the kingdom "come near": Judas comes to perform a dark deed, but his arrival signals the beginning of the kingdom's dawn.

JESUS' ARREST, TRIAL, AND CRUCIFIXION
Matthew 26:47–27:66

26:47 While he was still speaking, Judas, one of the twelve, arrived; with him was a large crowd with swords and clubs, from the chief priests and the elders of the people. [48] Now the betrayer had given them a sign, saying, "The one I will kiss is the man; arrest him." [49] At once he came up to Jesus and said, "Greetings, Rabbi!" and kissed him. [50] Jesus said to him, "Friend, do what you are here to do." Then they came and laid hands on Jesus and arrested him. [51] Suddenly, one of those with Jesus put his hand on his sword, drew it, and struck the slave of the high priest, cutting off his ear. [52] Then Jesus said to him, "Put your sword back into its place; for all who take the sword will perish by the sword. [53] Do you think that I cannot appeal to my Father, and he will at once send me more than twelve legions of angels?

[54] But how then would the scriptures be fulfilled, which say it must happen in this way?" [55] At that hour Jesus said to the crowds, "Have you come out with swords and clubs to arrest me as though I were a bandit? Day after day I sat in the temple teaching, and you did not arrest me. [56] But all this has taken place, so that the scriptures of the prophets may be fulfilled." Then all the disciples deserted him and fled.

[57] Those who had arrested Jesus took him to Caiaphas the high priest, in whose house the scribes and the elders had gathered. [58] But Peter was following him at a distance, as far as the courtyard of the high priest; and going inside, he sat with the guards in order to see how this would end. [59] Now the chief priests and the whole council were looking for false testimony against Jesus so that they might put him to death, [60] but they found none, though many false witnesses came forward. At last two came forward [61] and said, "This fellow said, 'I am able to destroy the temple of God and to build it in three days.'" [62] The high priest stood up and said, "Have you no answer? What is it that they testify against you?" [63] But Jesus was silent. Then the high priest said to him, "I put you under oath before the living God, tell us if you are the Messiah, the Son of God." [64] Jesus said to him, "You have said so. But I tell you,

From now on you will see the Son of Man
    seated at the right hand of Power
    and coming on the clouds of heaven."

[65] Then the high priest tore his clothes and said, "He has blasphemed! Why do we still need witnesses? You have now heard his blasphemy. [66] What is your verdict?" They answered, "He deserves death." [67] Then they spat in his face and struck him; and some slapped him, [68] saying, "Prophesy to us, you Messiah! Who is it that struck you?"

[69] Now Peter was sitting outside in the courtyard. A servant-girl came to him and said, "You also were with Jesus the Galilean." [70] But he denied it before all of them, saying, "I do not know what you are talking about." [71] When he went out to the porch, another servant-girl saw him, and she said to the bystanders, "This man was with Jesus of Nazareth." [72] Again he denied it with an oath, "I do not know the man." [73] After a little while the bystanders came up and said to Peter, "Certainly you are also one of them, for your accent betrays you." [74] Then he began to curse, and he swore an oath, "I do not know the man!" At that moment the cock crowed. [75] Then Peter remembered what Jesus had said: "Before the cock crows, you will deny me three times." And he went out and wept bitterly.

27:1 When morning came, all the chief priests and the elders of the people conferred together against Jesus in order to bring about his death. [2] They bound him, led him away, and handed him over to Pilate the governor.

[3] When Judas, his betrayer, saw that Jesus was condemned, he repented and brought back the thirty pieces of silver to the chief priests and the elders. [4] He said, "I have sinned by betraying innocent blood." But they said,

"What is that to us? See to it yourself." [5] Throwing down the pieces of silver in the temple, he departed; and he went and hanged himself. [6] But the chief priests, taking the pieces of silver, said, "It is not lawful to put them into the treasury, since they are blood money." [7] After conferring together, they used them to buy the potter's field as a place to bury foreigners. [8] For this reason that field has been called the Field of Blood to this day. [9] Then was fulfilled what had been spoken through the prophet Jeremiah, "And they took the thirty pieces of silver, the price of the one on whom a price had been set, on whom some of the people of Israel had set a price, [10] and they gave them for the potter's field, as the Lord commanded me."

[11] Now Jesus stood before the governor; and the governor asked him, "Are you the King of the Jews?" Jesus said, "You say so." [12] But when he was accused by the chief priests and elders, he did not answer. [13] Then Pilate said to him, "Do you not hear how many accusations they make against you?" [14] But he gave him no answer, not even to a single charge, so that the governor was greatly amazed.

[15] Now at the festival the governor was accustomed to release a prisoner for the crowd, anyone whom they wanted. [16] At that time they had a notorious prisoner, called Jesus Barabbas. [17] So after they had gathered, Pilate said to them, "Whom do you want me to release for you, Jesus Barabbas or Jesus who is called the Messiah?" [18] For he realized that it was out of jealousy that they had handed him over. [19] While he was sitting on the judgment seat, his wife sent word to him, "Have nothing to do with that innocent man, for today I have suffered a great deal because of a dream about him." [20] Now the chief priests and the elders persuaded the crowds to ask for Barabbas and to have Jesus killed. [21] The governor again said to them, "Which of the two do you want me to release for you?" And they said, "Barabbas." [22] Pilate said to them, "Then what should I do with Jesus who is called the Messiah?" All of them said, "Let him be crucified!" [23] Then he asked, "Why, what evil has he done?" But they shouted all the more, "Let him be crucified!"

[24] So when Pilate saw that he could do nothing, but rather that a riot was beginning, he took some water and washed his hands before the crowd, saying, "I am innocent of this man's blood; see to it yourselves." [25] Then the people as a whole answered, "His blood be on us and on our children!" [26] So he released Barabbas for them; and after flogging Jesus, he handed him over to be crucified.

[27] Then the soldiers of the governor took Jesus into the governor's headquarters, and they gathered the whole cohort around him. [28] They stripped him and put a scarlet robe on him, [29] and after twisting some thorns into a crown, they put it on his head. They put a reed in his right hand and knelt before him and mocked him, saying, "Hail, King of the Jews!" [30] They spat on him, and took the reed and struck him on the head. [31] After mocking him, they stripped him of the robe and put his own clothes on him. Then they led him away to crucify him.

[32] As they went out, they came upon a man from Cyrene named Simon; they compelled this man to carry his cross. [33] And when they came to a place called Golgotha (which means Place of a Skull), [34] they offered him wine to drink, mixed with gall; but when he tasted it, he would not drink it. [35] And when they had crucified him, they divided his clothes among themselves by casting lots; [36] then they sat down there and kept watch over him. [37] Over his head they put the charge against him, which read, "This is Jesus, the King of the Jews."

[38] Then two bandits were crucified with him, one on his right and one on his left. [39] Those who passed by derided him, shaking their heads [40] and saying, "You who would destroy the temple and build it in three days, save yourself! If you are the Son of God, come down from the cross." [41] In the same way the chief priests also, along with the scribes and elders, were mocking him, saying, [42] "He saved others; he cannot save himself. He is the King of Israel; let him come down from the cross now, and we will believe in him. [43] He trusts in God; let God deliver him now, if he wants to; for he said, 'I am God's Son.'" [44] The bandits who were crucified with him also taunted him in the same way.

[45] From noon on, darkness came over the whole land until three in the afternoon. [46] And about three o'clock Jesus cried with a loud voice, "Eli, Eli, lema sabachthani?" that is, "My God, my God, why have you forsaken me?" [47] When some of the bystanders heard it, they said, "This man is calling for Elijah." [48] At once one of them ran and got a sponge, filled it with sour wine, put it on a stick, and gave it to him to drink. [49] But the others said, "Wait, let us see whether Elijah will come to save him." [50] Then Jesus cried again with a loud voice and breathed his last. [51] At that moment the curtain of the temple was torn in two, from top to bottom. The earth shook, and the rocks were split. [52] The tombs also were opened, and many bodies of the saints who had fallen asleep were raised. [53] After his resurrection they came out of the tombs and entered the holy city and appeared to many. [54] Now when the centurion and those with him, who were keeping watch over Jesus, saw the earthquake and what took place, they were terrified and said, "Truly this man was God's Son!"

[55] Many women were also there, looking on from a distance; they had followed Jesus from Galilee and had provided for him. [56] Among them were Mary Magdalene, and Mary the mother of James and Joseph, and the mother of the sons of Zebedee.

[57] When it was evening, there came a rich man from Arimathea, named Joseph, who was also a disciple of Jesus. [58] He went to Pilate and asked for the body of Jesus; then Pilate ordered it to be given to him. [59] So Joseph took the body and wrapped it in a clean linen cloth [60] and laid it in his own new tomb, which he had hewn in the rock. He then rolled a great stone to the door of the tomb and went away. [61] Mary Magdalene and the other Mary were there, sitting opposite the tomb.

[62] The next day, that is, after the day of Preparation, the chief priests and

the Pharisees gathered before Pilate [63] and said, "Sir, we remember what that impostor said while he was still alive, 'After three days I will rise again.' [64] Therefore command the tomb to be made secure until the third day; otherwise his disciples may go and steal him away, and tell the people, 'He has been raised from the dead,' and the last deception would be worse than the first." [65] Pilate said to them, "You have a guard of soldiers; go, make it as secure as you can." [66] So they went with the guard and made the tomb secure by sealing the stone.

Events move quickly now. Jesus is "handed over to be crucified" (Matt. 26:2), and the world, believing it is in command, accelerates the pace of ridding itself of the troubling Jewish Messiah.

Jesus' Arrest
(Matthew 26:47–56)

The ministry of Jesus is halted in midsentence. While Jesus was still speaking to Peter, James, and John, Judas rattles up with a large and dangerously armed mob sent by the religious authorities. Because, both literally and figuratively, this crowd would not recognize the Messiah if it saw him, a signal was prearranged. Judas stepped up to Jesus, planted a kiss on his cheek, and bubbled merrily, "Greetings, Rabbi!" With these words, the betrayer betrays himself, for "rabbi" is, in Matthew's Gospel, a negative title, a sign of shallowness and misunderstanding (see Matt. 23:7–8). Indeed, in Matthew only Judas ever addressed Jesus as "rabbi" (Matt. 26:25). Jesus responds with irony, calling Judas "friend," which, in Matthew, means something like "Buster" and is itself no term of endearment (see Matt. 20:13; 22:12). "Do what you are here to do," Jesus tells Judas (Matt. 26:50), which means, in effect, "Go ahead and play your assigned role," underscoring the theological conviction that these seemingly chaotic moments are, underneath, already known by Jesus and part of God's saving plan.

Suddenly, one of the disciples attempts to meet force with force and commits an act of violence, drawing a sword and wounding the slave of the high priest (Matt. 26:51). The Gospel of John identifies the perpetrator as Peter and specifies the victim as Maltchus (John 18:10), but the other Gospels leave the pair unnamed. This act is not an expression of valor, but another instance of grievous misunderstanding (Brown, *The Death of the Messiah*, vol. 1, 267). The disciples slept when they should have been alert (Matt. 26:40), and now at least one of them is aroused when he should have been peaceful.

Jesus orders him to put the weapon away and to stop the power play, for three reasons. First, violence is stupid, for it just escalates into even greater destruction (Matt. 26:52). Second, violence is not the way of God in the world. If God had chosen to save Jesus through a military rescue, Jesus could have simply given a whistle and a dozen angelic legions ready for combat would have appeared on the scene. But God's way is meekness and peace, not violence and warfare (Matt. 5:5, 9). Third, the scriptures call for the shepherd to be struck and the sheep to be scattered (Zech. 13:7; Matt. 26:31), not for the sheep to stand up on their hind legs and to fight back. This pathetic attempt at armed resistance is essentially an attempt to change God's script, and human beings cannot do that; "it must happen in this way" (Matt. 26:54).

But misunderstanding is not restricted to the disciples. Jesus now scolds the mob for *their* lapse in discernment. They have come after him with swords and clubs to arrest him in secret, as if he were some kind of desperado, when he has been on public display all along, teaching openly in the area of the temple (Matt. 26:55). In other words, they have confused Jesus' public ministry with private terrorism, they have misunderstood Jesus' divine authority as worldly violence, and they have mistaken the Messiah for a bandit. "But," Jesus declares, "all this has taken place, so that the scriptures of the prophets may be fulfilled" (Matt. 26:56). In other words, even with all the frenzied confusion swirling around him, events are proceeding according to the script. As if on cue, the disciples act out their designated parts in the drama. They, who once declared that they had forsaken everything to follow Jesus (Matt. 19:27), now forsake Jesus and follow their fears. As he had forecast, "all the disciples deserted him and fled" (Matt. 26:56; see Matt. 26:31).

The Jewish Interrogation of Jesus (Matthew 26:57–68)

Under arrest, Jesus is taken from Gethsemane to the house of Caiaphas, the high priest (see Matt. 26:3–5), where the Sanhedrin was convened (the Sanhedrin was an important council of priests and other leaders charged with handling internal affairs among the Jews). What takes place is a legal interrogation of Jesus that falls somewhere between a hearing and a full trial, and biblical scholars have raised a number of historical questions about this. Some argue that religious rules would have prohibited a judicial proceeding at night, especially one during Passover. Other scholars suggest that these rules are a later development in Judaism and were not in effect in Jesus' time.

In any case, observing the rules does not seem to be the point here, because, according to Matthew, the interrogators were looking for "false testimony against Jesus so that they might put him to death" (Matt. 26:59). The problem with false witnesses, however, is that they get tangled in their own lies, and the parade of willing frauds who took the stand produced no usable evidence. Finally, however, two witnesses (the minimum number needed under Jewish law) were found who spun the same tale: "This fellow said, 'I am able to destroy the temple of God and to build it in three days'" (Matt. 26:61).

The charge is a serious one. Jeremiah risked the death penalty for saying that the temple would be destroyed (Jer. 26:1–9). But is Jesus guilty of making threats to destroy the temple? In the Gospel of John, he comes close, saying to the Jews, "Destroy this temple, and in three days I will raise it up" (John 2:19). In Matthew, however, Jesus only predicts that the temple will be destroyed; he does not himself threaten to destroy it (Matt. 24:1–2). At one level, the charges are absurd. Jesus is being accused of terrorism, of being a public menace by threatening to destroy by force the center of religious life in Jerusalem. At a deeper level, though, the charges are true. Jesus is "greater than the temple" (Matt. 12:6), and his saving work on the cross will shake the very foundations of the temple establishment (Matt. 27:51).

When the high priest demands an answer to the charges, Jesus, like the servant in Isaiah, remains silent (Isa. 53:7; see Meier, *Matthew*, 332). His refusal to speak presses the high priest to a greater altitude of hysteria. "I put you under oath before the living God," he shrieks. "Tell us if you are the Messiah, the Son of God" (Matt. 26:63). Matthew's readers know that the answer to this question is yes. In fact, the high priest employs the very words that Peter used much earlier in the story to confess his faith: "You are the Messiah, the Son of the living God" (Matt. 16:16). But it will not do for Jesus to respond with a simple "yes," because the high priest is asking the question and, therefore, defining the terms. It is the high priest who dares to put the Son of God under oath; it is the high priest who invests the title "Messiah" with his own pinched meaning; it is the high priest who thinks he knows what he is talking about when he utters the name of the "living God." If Jesus says "yes," he accepts the authority of the questioner; he crosses over from his own ground to stand on the accusers' ground; he leaves the spaciousness of his own trust in God and adopts the cramped and jaded disbelief of his frazzled interrogator. Thus, Jesus instead replies, "You have said so" (Matt. 26:64), which, in effect, means, "Yes, but not on your terms." This is the way Jesus responds to all loaded questions. It is the way he answered Judas (Matt. 26:25); it will be his retort to Pilate (Matt. 27:11).

As if to underline the truth that the question is too narrow and the questioner on shaky ground, Jesus adds to his answer a blending of Psalm 110:1

and Daniel 7:13–14: "From now on you will see the Son of Man seated at the right hand of Power and coming on the clouds of heaven" (Matt. 26:64). With this word, Jesus dramatically reverses the power equation in the room. The high priest may think he is in charge, but it is Jesus, the Son of Man, who is actually positioned on the judgment seat. The high priest thinks he is the judge putting Jesus on trial for his life, but the high priest is really the defendant, and the Son of Man will ride the clouds of heaven at the end.

That was enough for the high priest. He tears his garments—a sign of rage or grief—and turns to the jury, screeching that there is no need even for witnesses, that Jesus' own blasphemous words are all the evidence required. A swift death verdict is rendered by the council, and the group vents its rage by doing what the Gentiles will later do: spitting on Jesus, hitting him, and mocking him (Matt. 26:66–67; see Matt. 27:30–31; Isa. 50:6).

Peter's Denial of Jesus
(Matthew 26:69–75)

If the interrogation of Jesus before the Sanhedrin (Matt. 26:57–68) is the picture of an innocent man falsely accused, then this story is the negative of that imprint. In Jesus' case, two witnesses were scraped up to give false testimony. Here two witnesses, both servant-girls, tell the God's truth: Peter was with Jesus. In Jesus' case, he refused to accept the deceitful oath of the accuser so that he could speak the full truth. In this story, Peter swears an oath upon himself (see Matt. 5:33–37) in order to curse and tell a lie: "I do not know the man!" (Matt. 26:72). In Jesus' case, a man who prayed three times for his bitter mission to pass, each time accepted his cup from God's hand and received his sentence of death. In this story, Peter three times pours his cup on the ground in order to stay out of trouble. Jesus was innocent; Peter was guilty, and the crowing of the rooster announced the verdict. Peter remembered then that Jesus had predicted his denial (Matt. 26:75; see 26:34), and he wept bitterly. Though he was innocent, Jesus was condemned to die. Though Peter was guilty, through the death of the innocent man, he was given forgiveness of his sins (Matt. 1:21; 26:28).

The Suicide of Judas
(Matthew 27:1–10)

Earlier in his ministry, Jesus had told his disciples that the Jewish religious authorities would condemn him to death and that they would "hand him over to the Gentiles to be mocked and flogged and crucified" (Matt. 20:18–19). And just as Jesus said, events unfold. The Sanhedrin met through the night, and by morning the verdict of death for Jesus was firm. Now, the Gentile phase of the death drama comes into play, as the Jewish authorities bind Jesus and "hand him over" (from the same Greek word as "betray") to the Roman governor, Pilate.

But before taking us into the Roman courtroom, Matthew tells the sad story of the fate of Judas. The fact that Jesus is given a death sentence shocks Judas and precipitates an astonishing about-face. Guilt-stricken, he changes his mind about what he has done; he repents, painfully aware that he has "sinned by betraying innocent blood" (Matt. 27:4). But what can he do with this change of heart? Where can one take repentance? Judas chooses to confess his sin to his partners in conspiracy, to the chief priests and the elders, but he finds no atonement there, only indifference. "What is that to us?" they shrug (Matt. 27:4). The religious leaders are not interested in any change of heart or repentance at this point. They wanted to get Jesus, not justice, and they already have what they want (Meier, *Matthew*, 338). Distraught, Judas throws his "blood money" into the temple (see comments on Matt. 26:14–16), but the coins simply clatter in the hollow emptiness; the temple speaks no word of pardon either, offers no touch of forgiveness. Trapped, guilt-ridden, convinced of his hopelessness, Judas desperately seizes the only release from his crime he can find. Slipping the noose around his neck, he jumps into the void of despair (Matt. 27:5).

The religious authorities eventually find the coins scattered around on the temple floor, and, because this "blood money" is tainted and cannot be placed in the temple treasury, they decide to use it to buy a cemetery for strangers (Matt. 27:6–10). The land probably belonged at some point to a potter and, thus, was known locally as the "potter's field" (Matt. 27:7). Because of this story, public burial grounds for the poor and indigent are often called "potter's fields."

This decision about how to use the "blood money" carries its own theological ironies. First, the picture of the religious leaders suddenly becoming ethically conscientious, not wanting to pollute the pure temple offerings, simply throws their own shameful involvement into high relief. Second, the purchase of the "potter's field" is yet another occasion when the enemies of Jesus unwittingly comply with God's plan, as evidenced by the fact that their action, like so much else in the story of Jesus, directly fulfills Old Testament prophecy (see Matthew 27:9–10, a quotation that Matthew attributes to Jeremiah but which actually is mainly a loose adaptation of Zechariah 11:12–13 with a few allusions to Jeremiah). Third, while the authorities use the "blood money" to buy a place of death for foreigners, Jesus goes to the cross to offer his blood as "a ransom for many" (Matt. 20:28), both near and far, to provide life for all the nations.

Apparently several variations of the story of Judas' death circulated in the early church (a somewhat different version appears in Acts 1:15–20). Because it involves a suicide, Matthew's account is particularly dire, and the first readers of Matthew undoubtedly felt the horror of Judas's tragic end. They knew that Judas was not alone in his treachery. Peter had denied Jesus. All the disciples had forsaken him; indeed, they knew—as we do—faithlessness and disloyalty in their own ranks and in their own hearts. The more we look at Judas, the more we see the potential for faithlessness in ourselves. Some years ago, a congregation built a small and secluded chapel for prayer and meditation, and they equipped it with twelve chairs, each inscribed with the name of one of the disciples. The chair marked "Judas" is the one most heavily worn with use.

The deepest tragedy about Judas is not that he is guiltier than others. His guilt is shared by all. The saddest truth about Judas is that he took his remorse to the place of death and not to the place of life. Like all humanity, he had innocent blood on his hands. "What does innocent blood have to do with us?" asked the religious authorities, and their answer to their own question is, "Nothing." Judas's answer was, "I have betrayed innocent blood and the stain can never be removed." But what Judas failed to hear was the answer that Jesus himself gave on the very night of his betrayal. "What does innocent blood have to do with us?" This innocent blood, he said, is "my blood of the covenant, which is poured out for many for the forgiveness of sins" (Matt. 26:28).

The Trial Before Pilate
(Matthew 27:11–26)

Pilate was the Roman governor of the province of Judea, a minor official whom history would have promptly forgotten had not the trial of all time landed in his lap. In his own day, he was a backwater bureaucrat, but now his name is known around the world because Jesus "suffered under Pontius Pilate, was crucified, dead, and buried."

Surely Pilate must have been mystified by the quarrel that spilled into his chambers as the chief priests and elders pushed a fettered young man named Jesus into his presence and began shouting charges. Jesus was a Jew, his accusers were the leaders of the Jews, and the charges also had a distinctly Jewish ring to them. Pilate, as a Gentile, would have every reason to be puzzled by what seemed to be an intramural sectarian squabble.

Aware of this, the Jewish authorities were undoubtedly at pains to make the allegations forceful to Pilate's Roman mind, and finally, they fashioned a charge that even Pilate could understand as significant. So, perceiving at last what this might have to do with him and the Roman government and why it had ended up complicating his day, Pilate rouses himself to face the accused and ask the crucial question, "Are you the King of the Jews?" (Matt. 27:11).

This is a dangerous question. Coming from Pilate, it is a purely political question and can be roughly translated as, "Are you making terrorist threats? Do you have designs on the government? Are you going to thrust yourself forward as some kind of local, ethnic king, menacing the stability of Roman rule around here?" For Jesus to say "yes" would be tantamount to treason, which was punishable by death—precisely what his accusers desire. On the other hand, Jesus cannot truthfully say "no" either. As Matthew's readers are aware, he *is* the King of the Jews (Matt. 2:2), in a way far higher and wider than Pilate's question implies. Jesus' kingship is from God, not from human beings; his kingdom is the kingdom of heaven, not some local province.

But Pilate is right to be concerned, for Jesus' heavenly kingship is not without earthly political implications. Because Jesus is Lord and Christ and King, no earthly ruler—not Herod, not Pilate—no group no matter how numerous, no despot no matter how mighty, no president no matter how wise can claim absolute authority. Those who serve Jesus as Lord and King refuse to bend the knee to any earthly lord and, therefore, they possess a threatening freedom. They cannot be bullied by potentates or intimidated by tyrants. Thus, Jesus' kingship shakes the foundations of the political world.

Jesus himself exhibits this freedom as he refuses to accommodate himself to Pilate's narrow categories, answering him in the same noncommittal way he answered Judas and Caiaphas: "You say so" (Matt. 27:11; see also 26:25; 26:64). This means, in essence, "Yes, I am King of the Jews, but I do not accept your definitions of kingship, and I do not need your permission." This reply from Jesus unleashes a furious barrage of charges from the religious leaders, but even when prompted to speak by Pilate, Jesus keeps a silent dignity (Matt. 27:14). Pilate is amazed by Jesus' silence, surely because Jesus is refusing to defend himself even in the face of a possible death penalty but also perhaps because Jesus is acting like one in command of the situation, even though he by all rights should be cowering in fear. Just as they did when Jesus was silent before the high priest (Matt. 26:63), Matthew's readers probably hear echoes of Isaiah 53:7, where the persecuted servant of God "did not open his mouth."

At this point, Matthew actually begins to shine a somewhat favorable light on Pilate. To be sure, Pilate will eventually cave in to pressure, but at this point at least he sees the situation clearly—Jesus is an innocent man who has been framed because of the jealousy of the religious leaders (Matt. 27:18)—and he attempts to get Jesus released. Employing the custom of releasing a political prisoner at Passover, Pilate gives the crowd a choice between Jesus Barabbas, a notorious criminal, or "Jesus who is called the Messiah" (Matt. 27:17). Outside of the New Testament, no historical evidence can be found for this practice of releasing criminals at Passover, but the point Matthew is making is more theological than historical. The crowds, which have followed Jesus through his ministry, who have been shepherded by Jesus and taught by Jesus and healed by Jesus and fed by Jesus, now have a decision to make. Do they want Jesus, the Messiah, the Son of God, or do they want Jesus Barabbas, public enemy number one? The irony is enhanced by the fact that "Jesus Barabbas" literally means "Jesus, son of the father."

While the crowd is mulling this choice, word comes to Pilate on the "judgment seat" (a raised platform where city magistrates sat for court in the Roman Empire) that his wife has had a troubling dream. In Matthew, dreams convey words from God (see Matt. 1:20; 2:12, 13, 19–20), and the message that Pilate's wife has received is that Jesus is innocent and that Pilate should have nothing to do with his trial. By telling about this dream, Matthew probably intends not only to underscore Jesus' innocence but also to establish some symmetry between this event and the visit of the wise men. In both cases, while his own people plot and scheme to destroy Jesus, the King of the Jews, Gentiles receive communication from God in dreams to preserve his life (Matt. 2:1–12).

Stirred up by the religious leaders, the crowds make their choice: They demand that Pilate release Barabbas and crucify Jesus the Messiah (Matt. 27:21–22). Pilate's anguished and astonished cry, "What evil has he done?" only intensifies the screams for crucifixion (Matt. 27:23). Pilate is trapped. Regardless of his personal views regarding Jesus' innocence, he has a potential riot on his hands, and he plays out the part of the weak politician under pressure. Pilate buckles and does just as the people demand, releasing Barabbas and seeing that Jesus, after being flogged, is "handed over" (from the same word in Greek as "betray") to be crucified.

In the middle of this, there is a terrible and beautiful scene. Pilate takes a bowl of water, washes his hands in view of the crowd, and declares that he is "innocent of this man's blood" (Matt. 27:24). At one level, of course, this is merely an impotent bureaucrat attempting to pass the buck. We've heard about this kind of thing before. "The woman made me eat . . . somebody else is responsible . . . I was only following orders . . . the people spoke and I heard them . . . I wasn't in charge . . . I can't be held accountable"; the refrain echoes through history. Pilate is saying to the people, "This innocent man's death cannot be charged to my account; it is on your moral bill."

At a deeper level, though, Matthew's readers will recognize that Pilate is actually performing a ritual prescribed in the Old Testament. The law states that if the body of a murder victim is found in the open countryside, then the leaders of the nearest town shall engage in a hand-washing ritual, praying as they do, "Our hands did not shed this blood, nor were we witnesses to it. Absolve, O LORD, your people Israel, whom you redeemed; do not let the guilt of innocent blood remain in the midst of your people Israel" (Deut. 21:7–8).

Perhaps, then, Matthew wants his readers to see more than a scared politician trying to keep his slate clean. Maybe we are supposed to see another story like the visit of the Gentile wise men from the East (Matt. 2:1–12). In both accounts, Gentiles symbolically fulfill the Old Testament while the leaders of the Jewish people conspire to murder their own Messiah. In this hand-washing story, the point is made emphatic, as the crowds cry out, "His blood be on us and on our children!" (Matt. 27:25).

We must be very careful here. The account of Jewish people demanding that the blood of Jesus Christ be on them and their descendants has given some misguided Christians justification to mistreat and persecute Jews throughout history. This is not what Matthew intends. Matthew's goal is not to pit "good" Gentiles versus "bad" Jews. Remember, Matthew's readers were Jewish themselves (see Introduction). Matthew's true point is first to explain to his readers, who had themselves been in conflict with their own Jewish kin over their Christian faith, how it happened that Jesus himself was rejected by his own people. Matthew also wants to open his church up to the possibility of spreading the gospel to the Gentiles around them, of looking toward the horizon of a mission to "all nations" (Matt. 28:19).

It may even be that Matthew wants his readers to hear the story of Pilate's hand-washing as an invitation to pray the prayer of Deuteronomy: "Absolve, O LORD, your people Israel, whom you redeemed; do not let the guilt of innocent blood remain in the midst of your people Israel." Even as the children of Israel scream for Jesus' blood, Matthew's readers are to remember that Jesus' blood was "poured out for many for the forgiveness of sins" (Matt. 26:28) and that Jesus, the son of David, the son of Abraham, was born to "save his people from their sins" (Matt. 1:21).

Jesus Is Mocked by Soldiers
(Matthew 27:27–31)

The Jewish crowd called for the death of their king (Matt. 27:22–23), and now it is the Gentiles' turn to scorn Jesus. Because he is King of the Jews, Jesus is the Lord and King of all peoples, and Pilate's soldiers, attempting to mock Jesus, ironically recognize this kingship. They dress up Jesus for a costume party. For a royal robe, they provide an army officer's red cape (Mark 15:17 says the robe was "purple," the color of royalty. Matthew changes this to "red," which is probably more reliable historically). For a king's crown, they place a ring of thorns on his head (most likely not to cause pain but because the thorns looked like the pictures found on Roman coins of the radiant spikes protruding from the emperor's crown). For a regal scepter, they give him a flimsy reed. Then they bow down, and no doubt holding their sides with satirical laughter, they tell the God's truth: "Hail, King of the Jews!" This Jesus *is* the King of the Jews, and he is the King of the Romans, too. This is a joke, all right, but it is not on Jesus; it is a divine joke on the powers of evil. Overruling the harsh mockery of the world is the heavenly and joyful laughter of redemption. On this day of Jesus' trial, only a few sniggering soldiers kneel in derision to call him king; on the day of God's victory, every eye will see "the Son of Man coming on the clouds of heaven with power and great glory" (Matt. 24:30), and every knee will bow and every tongue will confess that Jesus is Lord and King (Phil. 2:9–11).

Jesus Is Crucified
(Matthew 27:32–56)

In the parable of the wicked tenants (Matt. 21:33–46), the faithless stewards of the land seize the son of a vineyard owner, cast him out of the vineyard, and kill him. Now, the same fate befalls the one who told that parable, God's own Son. The soldiers take Jesus outside the "vineyard," outside of the city of Jerusalem, to a place known locally as "Place of a Skull" (from the Greek meaning "Golgotha"; from the Latin meaning "Calvaria"; thus our word "Calvary") to be crucified. Although many attempts have been made to identify this spot, the precise historical location of the crucifixion remains unknown.

Four times in Matthew's Gospel, Jesus has told his disciples that his life is moving inexorably toward this moment, toward his death at the hand of enemies (Matt. 16:21; 17:22–23; 20:17–19; 26:2). Now that the story has arrived at this fateful juncture, it seems somehow strange that Matthew gives such scant attention to the details of the crucifixion itself. In fact, Matthew describes the crucifixion obliquely, using only one Greek participle (translated as "and when they had crucified him," Matt. 27:35). Matthew seems less interested in the details of the crucifixion and more concerned with two other matters: first, how people reacted to the event, that is, to the impact of Jesus' death on the world; and second, how the crucifixion fulfilled the Old Testament scripture.

In regard to the reactions of those present at Jesus' death, Douglas Hare has observed, "Matthew's story of the execution of Jesus contains remarkably few details. No mention is made of the pounding of the nails into hands and feet, the racking pain, the desperate thirst. . . . What details are given concern not the victim but the *spectators*" (Hare, *Matthew*, 319).

Indeed, Matthew names at least three persons or groups who responded in some manner to the crucifixion of Jesus:

1. *Simon from Cyrene.* Simon is described as "a man from Cyrene" (the contemporary North African country of Libya), who was pressed into service to carry the horizontal beam of Jesus' cross (the vertical bar would already have been in place at the crucifixion site; see Matt. 27:32). In contrast to Mark 15:21, where we are told about Simon's family, Matthew gives no additional details about Simon, and he provides no motivation for his deed. It may be that Jesus, after his treatment in Pilate's headquarters, was simply unable physically to carry his own cross. Or, some have suggested that the presence of Simon, a foreigner, anticipates the mission of the church to the Gentiles. Others have surmised that Simon's being "compelled" to carry the cross of Jesus symbolizes kingdom service and true discipleship (see Matt. 5:41; 16:24). It is more likely that Matthew's church knew the detail of the story that a Cyrenian named Simon carried the cross for Jesus, and Matthew simply includes this well-known feature in his account.

2. *The taunters.* The mocking of Jesus, begun in Pilate's headquarters, continues in public around the cross. The soldiers on crucifixion detail attach a jeering sign over Jesus' head reading, "This is Jesus, the King of the Jews" (Matt. 27:37), which is, of course, ironically true.

Passersby deride Jesus, urging him scornfully to "save himself" and taunting Jesus, employing virtually the same language as that used by the devil at Jesus' temptation: "If you are the Son of God, come down from the cross. . . . He trusts in God; let God deliver him now" (Matt. 27:40–43; see Matt. 4:3, 6). In the beginning of his ministry, Jesus was tempted by the devil to take a shortcut to glory, one that avoided the cross; Jesus was tempted to relax his grip of faith and to put God to the test. Here, at the end of his ministry, the temptation is the same, "Climb down from the cross. Do not submit to the pain and suffering. If you really trust God, will not God let you off the hook? God will deliver you!"

Jesus is crucified between two "bandits" (Matt. 27:38). The usual translation "thieves" is too mild, for these two are not petty thieves but outlaws, maybe even political revolutionaries—in any case, notorious characters whose whole existence is outside the circle of respectable society. Even so, these brigands, out of tune with everybody, nevertheless join the chorus to sing out taunts against Jesus. (Matthew's theme seems to be that the whole of human society, respectable and not, derides the Messiah. He does not seem to know the story that Luke tells, that one of the two bandits turns toward Jesus in repentance; see Luke 23:39–43.)

3. *Those who keep watch and witness.* At the beginning of the crucifixion scene, the Roman soldiers are presented as mockers of Jesus, those who initiate the derision against Jesus. But, interestingly, they play another role as well. They become believers who confess that Jesus was truly "God's Son" (Matt. 27:54).

The transformation actually begins in the middle of the taunting, when the soldiers (a centurion and some of his troops) sit down at the foot of the cross and keep watch over Jesus (Matt. 27:36). Keeping watch is, of course, a very military thing to do, but it can, in a deeper theological sense be a very kingdom thing to do. Indeed, Jesus told his disciples to "keep awake" and ever to be on the watch, "for you know neither the day nor the hour" of Christ's coming (Matt. 24:42; 25:13). In fact, as these soldiers keep watch, the kingdom does happen in an anticipatory way right before their very eyes. Remarkable events occur at the moment of Jesus' death—an earthquake, the tearing of the temple curtain, the opening of tombs—signs heralding the arrival of God's kingdom (see the discussion of these events that follows). When they happen, the centurion and his companions move from being soldiers watching for trouble to disciples watching for God's wonders. "Truly this man was God's Son!" they shout (Matt. 27:54), echoing the disciples' own confession of faith (Matt. 14:33). At the foot of the cross, then, Gentiles, people from "all nations," are already becoming disciples (see Matt. 28:19).

It is not only soldiers who wait and watch; Matthew also tells his readers that "many women" watched the crucifixion from a distance (Matt. 27:55–56). Named among the group are Mary Magdalene (that is, Mary "from Magdala," a settlement on the western shore of the Sea of Galilee), whom scholars believe was the leader of a group of women who followed and supported Jesus (Matt. 27:55); Mary the mother of James and Joseph (scholars disagree about whether this was Matthew's cryptic way to describe Mary, the mother of Jesus, or whether this was another Mary who would have been known to Matthew's readers; see Matt. 13:55); and the mother of the sons of Zebedee, who was described earlier in the Gospel as asking a favor of Jesus for her sons (Matt. 20:20–23).

These women are eyewitnesses. The twelve disciples have all "deserted him and fled" (Matt. 26:56), but these women are present to bear witness. Matthew is careful to report that the two Marys are also present at Jesus' burial (Matt. 27:61) and at the tomb on Easter morning (Matt. 28:1), thus providing an unbroken chain of testimony from the cross to the tomb to the resurrection. Blessed are their eyes, for "many prophets and righteous people longed to see" what these women witnessed (Matt. 13:16–17). These women are the first who can say that the Jesus who "suffered under Pontius Pilate, was crucified, dead, and buried" was the very same Jesus who "on the third day was raised again from the dead." The church's confession of faith begins with them.

The other major theological theme of Matthew's account of the crucifixion is that what happened on Golgotha that day was a fulfillment of scripture, especially Psalms 22 and 69. The soldiers offer Jesus "wine . . . mixed with gall" (Matt. 27:34). Mark 15:23 calls this "wine mixed with myrrh," which was a narcotic to ease the pain. But Matthew turns "myrrh" into "gall" to show that this fulfilled Psalm 69:21: "They gave me poison" ("poison," in Greek, is "gall"). Jesus will not drink the poison, though (Matt. 27:34). Unlike Judas, he is not committing suicide; he is offering his life as a sacrifice. The rest of Psalm 69:21 says, "For my thirst they gave me vinegar to drink," which is also fulfilled by one of the bystanders at the crucifixion (Matt. 27:48).

Psalm 22:18 says, "They divide my clothes among themselves, and for my clothing they cast lots," and the soldiers at the foot of the cross do precisely that (Matt. 27:35). "All who see me mock at me," states Psalm 22:7, and those watching Jesus die fulfill this word by shouting their derision. Again, in Psalm 22 the taunters use not only words but also gestures; "they shake their heads" (Psalm 22:7), and so do the passersby at Golgotha (Matt. 27:39). The mockers in the psalm cry out sarcastically, "Commit your cause to the LORD; let him deliver!" (Psalm 22:8), and those at the foot of the cross follow the script faithfully. "He trusts in God," they jeer. "Let God deliver him now, if he wants to" (Matt. 27:43).

For three hours, from noon until three, darkness fell over the whole land (Matt. 27:45), as the prophet Amos had promised would happen on God's day of judgment: "On that day, says the Lord GOD, I will make the sun go down at noon, and darken the earth in broad daylight" (Amos 8:9; see also Matt. 24:29).

In other words, Matthew is making it plain that the crucifixion of Jesus is, in every detail, a fulfillment of God's saving purposes expressed in scripture. This is the place where the forces of evil give vent to their most vicious and chaotic violence, but even here—especially here—God's mercy is guiding and shaping, overruling all harm in the name of forgiveness and salvation.

Not only do the scorners quote Psalm 22; Jesus does, too, and it forms one of the most difficult to understand passages in Matthew. Just as he nears death, Jesus cries out loudly, "My God, my God, why have you forsaken me?" (Psalm 22:1; Matt. 27:46). Indeed, the people who first heard Jesus utter these words misunderstood them. When they heard Jesus say the Hebrew word for God, "Eli," they misheard this as a cry for help to Elijah (Matt. 27:46). Indeed, in popular Jewish religion, Elijah was expected to reappear just before the dawning of God's kingdom, and the crowd, assuming that Jesus was now calling in desperation for Elijah to come and rescue him, responded (probably compassionately) by holding up a sponge soaked in cheap, vinegary wine (Matt. 27:48).

But Jesus is not desperately calling for Elijah, or for God, to rescue him. To the contrary, Jesus, like the psalmist, is confessing that there will be no quick rescue, that God's salvation will not come in a way that spares him the mockery, the suffering, and the pain. There will be no Elijah swinging down from heaven brandishing a sword and cutting Jesus loose from the cross just in the nick of time. There will be no squadron of angels, no army of liberation, no last-minute surprises from Peter and the disciples waiting in the wings for their golden chance. This is not a Hollywood movie where the good guys never die; this is the story of Jesus the Messiah who must "undergo great suffering . . . and be killed" (Matt. 16:21).

So Jesus' cry "My God, my God, why have you forsaken me?" is, first, an obedient submission to death. This is the bitter cup that Jesus prayed in Gethsemane not to have to drink. His Father will not be standing at his elbow, whispering in his ear, "There, there, this is not so bad. This is not actual pain. This is not really death." No, Jesus will be left—forsaken—to the forces of evil. He will really suffer, and he will really die.

Jesus cries out because he accepts the reality of his death, but this is not a scream of despair. Jesus is not whimpering pathetically; he cries out with a loud voice, as one in command of his life and his death. Jesus is quoting a psalm of salvation, not cursing his fate. His death is not a loss of hope; it is the fulfillment of scripture. The psalmist offers his plea to God "who did not despise or abhor the affliction of the afflicted . . . but heard when I cried to him" (Psalm 22:24). Both the psalmist and Jesus trust God to save, not by magically eliminating all pain and suffering, but by working beyond human knowing in and through pain and suffering.

Finally, Jesus cries out again with a loud voice and breathes his last

(Matt. 27:50). Amazing events now occur: an earthquake rattles through the land, the curtain in the temple is torn top to bottom, tombs are opened, and saints rise from the dead. After Jesus' own resurrection, these newly raised saints appear to many in Jerusalem. Only in Matthew do we have the report of an earthquake and of risen saints roaming the streets. If something spectacular like this occurred, why is it not mentioned in the other Gospels? Indeed, one would think that the appearance of previously dead people wandering through a city like Jerusalem would have appeared in the pages of history outside of Matthew's Gospel.

Some of these concerns, at least, are addressed when we realize that Matthew is here writing not straightforward history but apocalyptic literature. The language is stretched beyond recognizable shape in order to show the theological meaning of Jesus' death. Each of these strange events symbolizes something about the kingdom of heaven established through the death of Jesus. Jesus' "loud voice" is the commanding authority of God spoken through the Son, like the sound of God at Sinai (see Exod. 19:19). The tearing of the temple curtain represents the end of the old temple system and the new access to God for all that Jesus' death makes possible. The earthquake signifies the judgment of God on the powers-that-be and the establishment of God's new rule (see, for example, Judg. 5:4–5; Psalm 68:8; Isa. 13:13; Jer. 10:10), and the saints rising from the tombs represents Ezekiel's "dry bones" coming back to life with the life-giving Spirit of God (Ezek. 37:1–14).

Jesus Is Buried
(Matthew 27:57–66)

The Old Testament law requires that any person executed for a crime by hanging on a tree should not remain on the tree all night but must be buried "that same day" (Deut. 21:22–23). As the evening comes on the day of Jesus' execution, a follower of Jesus named Joseph of Arimathea (a town northwest of Jerusalem) steps forward to take care of Jesus' burial.

Mark and Luke indicate that Joseph was a member of the Sanhedrin (Mark 15:43; Luke 23:50), and John says that Joseph, because of fear, was a secret disciple of Jesus. Matthew, however, only emphasizes that Joseph was "a rich man" (Matt. 27:57), probably to make the connection to the Old Testament prophecy that God's servant "made . . . his tomb with the rich" (Isa. 53:9).

With Pilate's permission, Joseph takes Jesus' body, wraps it in a clean burial linen, places it in his own rock tomb, and seals the opening with a large stone. One element Matthew is trying to make clear is that the body of Jesus was not somehow lost. Jesus was properly buried in a real tomb of a prominent, wealthy person, and all of this was observed by the same women who will encounter the empty tomb on Easter (Matt. 27:61; 28:1).

Matthew's church lived in constant conflict and tension with the "synagogue across the street" (see Introduction). One of the charges that Jews in Matthew's day evidently leveled against the Christians was that the disciples had stolen the body of Jesus from the tomb and then made up the whole story about the resurrection. Matthew's church had an answer to that charge, and it is found in the account of the secret meeting between Pilate and the Jewish leaders (Matt. 27:62–66).

According to the story, the religious leaders suspected in advance that the disciples would steal the body, so they go to Pilate on the day after Jesus is buried, the day "after the day of Preparation" (which is a fancy way of saying "the sabbath day," a circumlocution that keeps Matthew from having to explain why the Jewish authorities were violating the sabbath as they engage in their scheming), and ask for Jesus' tomb to be guarded around the clock for three days to prohibit body snatching on the part of the disciples (Matt. 27:62–64).

There is rich irony in the religious leaders' comment that, if the disciples "tell the people, 'He has been raised from the dead,'" that this "last deception" would be greater than Jesus' own "lie" that he would rise again after three days (Matt. 27:64). These leaders cannot tell the truth from falsehood, and they unwittingly echo Jesus' own words about them (see Matt. 12:45).

There is also irony in Pilate's order to make the tomb "as secure as you can" (Matt. 27:65). As Frederick Buechner has observed, "'As secure as you can,' the Procurator of Judea tells them. But how secure is that? . . . How do soldiers secure the world against miracle? . . . [It was] like trying to stop the wind with a machine gun" (Buechner, "The End Is Life," 295–97).

16. The Resurrection of Jesus the Messiah
Matthew 28:1–20

28:1 After the sabbath, as the first day of the week was dawning, Mary Magdalene and the other Mary went to see the tomb. ² And suddenly there was a great earthquake; for an angel of the Lord, descending from heaven, came and rolled back the stone and sat on it. ³ His appearance was like lightning, and his clothing white as snow. ⁴ For fear of him the guards shook and became like dead men. ⁵ But the angel said to the women, "Do not be afraid; I know that you are looking for Jesus who was crucified. ⁶ He is not here; for he has been raised, as he said. Come, see the place where he lay. ⁷ Then go quickly and tell his disciples, 'He has been raised from the dead, and indeed he is going ahead of you to Galilee; there you will see him.' This is my message for you." ⁸ So they left the tomb quickly with fear and great joy, and ran to tell his disciples. ⁹ Suddenly Jesus met them and said, "Greetings!" And they came to him, took hold of his feet, and worshiped him. ¹⁰ Then Jesus said to them, "Do not be afraid; go and tell my brothers to go to Galilee; there they will see me."

¹¹ While they were going, some of the guard went into the city and told the chief priests everything that had happened. ¹² After the priests had assembled with the elders, they devised a plan to give a large sum of money to the soldiers, ¹³ telling them, "You must say, 'His disciples came by night and stole him away while we were asleep.' ¹⁴ If this comes to the governor's ears, we will satisfy him and keep you out of trouble." ¹⁵ So they took the money and did as they were directed. And this story is still told among the Jews to this day.

¹⁶ Now the eleven disciples went to Galilee, to the mountain to which Jesus had directed them. ¹⁷ When they saw him, they worshiped him; but some doubted. ¹⁸ And Jesus came and said to them, "All authority in heaven and on earth has been given to me. ¹⁹ Go therefore and make disciples of all nations, baptizing them in the name of the Father and of the Son and of the Holy Spirit, ²⁰ and teaching them to obey everything that I have commanded you. And remember, I am with you always, to the end of the age."

"After the sabbath, as the first day of the week was dawning . . ." (Matt. 28:1). So Matthew begins the astonishing announcement of Easter. After midday darkness and earthquakes and sinister plots by night and the shadows of evil, at last the day was dawning, and with it a new light was shining in human history.

Appearance to the Women
at the Tomb (Matthew 28:1–10)

Mary Magdalene and the "other Mary," the same women who had been witnesses of the crucifixion and the burial of Jesus, went early on the first day of the week to see the tomb of Jesus (Matt. 28:1). What they expected to see, of course, was Jesus' grave, a monument to the sadness they felt in the soul, a confirmation of the cruel truth that the world finally beats mercy and righteousness to death.

Somewhere along the path to the cemetery, however, they left one world and entered another. Without even knowing that they had crossed the border, they left the old world, where hope is in constant danger, and might makes right, and peace has little chance, and the rich get richer, and the weak all eventually suffer under some Pontius Pilate or another, and people hatch murderous plots, and dead people stay dead, and they entered the startling and breathtaking world of resurrection and life. Jesus of Nazareth, who had been dead as a doornail on Friday afternoon, was not in his tomb that morning, and the world—theirs and ours—has been turned upside down ever since.

The call to worship on that first Easter was not a cheery "Good Morning!" but a shattering earthquake that rippled a seismic shock through history and signaled that the fault lines of human history had shifted dramatically toward grace and hope (Matt. 28:2). A blazingly brilliant angel descends from heaven to appear at the tomb, effortlessly rolling back the heavy stone and sitting on it. The angel, the earthquake, and the movement of the stone are, as we have seen before, apocalyptic symbols. The angel is really God's own presence in mediated form; the earthquake is a drum roll signaling a dramatic act of divine power; and the act of sitting down on the stone is a display of divine strength and authority, as if to say, "Well, so much for that!"

There were soldiers present at the tomb, a pathetic corporal's guard with what must surely be the unluckiest assignment in military history—making sure that Jesus stayed in the grave (see Matt. 27:62–66). It turned out to be more responsibility than they could handle, and the display of angelic lightning bolts reduces these mighty troops to a quivering mass of fear. Matthew cannot resist a small joke at their expense. They became, he reports, "like dead men" (Matt. 28:4). They are on cemetery detail, of course, to guard a dead man who was supposed to stay that way, but when their charge turns out to have become suddenly very much alive, it is they who become candidates for the grave.

The angel speaks directly to the women, "Do not be afraid" (Matt. 28:5). The angel means, naturally, not to be afraid of his astonishing and glowing presence—who wouldn't be fearful?—but he means something deeper, too. Because of the resurrection, they genuinely and profoundly do not need to be afraid of anything—not of death and not of life. Even when they endure great distress and deep anxiety and are "poor in spirit," they do not need to be afraid; the resurrection demonstrates that God keeps promises (including the promise of resurrection; Matt. 28:6), that God's mercy will prevail, and "theirs is the kingdom of heaven" (Matt. 5:3).

They came to view the sealed grave of their dead friend, but the angel beckons them to see the empty tomb, to become eyewitnesses of the great truth that "the prison room of death is empty" (Meier, *Matthew*, 362). Then he quickly sends them on their way with a mission and a message, "Tell his disciples, 'He has been raised from the dead, and indeed he is going ahead of you to Galilee; there you will see him'" (Matt. 28:7). These two women are now the human link between the great event of God and the community of faith. They are the first ones sent by God with the good news "He is risen!"; they are the first apostles of the risen Christ.

They leave the tomb with a mixture of fear and great joy, and, as such, they are the church in miniature—overcome with joy over the good news they have heard but also apprehensive as they move with this news toward a skeptical and dangerous world. The wonderful news of Easter is that Jesus is alive, and the terrible news of Easter is also that Jesus is alive, because nothing is nailed down anymore. The old joke about nothing being sure but death and taxes was at least half right; you could at least count on death. The way the world used to be, if something troubling got in the way, like a call for racial justice or a worker for peace or an advocate for mercy, the world could just kill it and it would be done with. But Jesus is alive, and righteousness, mercy, and peace cannot be dismissed with a cross or a sword. We have to decide where we stand and what we will do in this new and frightening resurrection world.

Suddenly, as the women battle to quell the fear and struggle to allow the joy to keep them moving on their mission, the risen Christ becomes present to them. Soon, in Galilee, he will promise his disciples to be with them always as they go on their mission to the nations (Matt. 28:20), and now he is true to his promise with the two women on their mission. "Do not be afraid," he says to them. "Go and tell my brothers to go to Galilee;

there they will see me" (Matt. 28:10). In the power of the resurrection, the disciples, who denied and abandoned Jesus, have been forgiven and restored to their standing as "brothers" (Matt. 12:49). In some ways, the entire mission of the church could be summed up this way: "Do not be afraid. Go and tell the world to come to me for forgiveness and reconciliation; they will see me, and I will make brothers and sisters of them all."

The Coverup
(Matthew 28:11–15)

As the women leave the tomb with their mission of truth, the guards also leave the tomb, but to become embroiled in a mission of lies. When they report to the religious authorities on the events of the morning, the officials bribe the soldiers with money, literally silver (the same form of money used to seduce Judas; see Matt. 26:14–16; 27:3–10), to swear that the disciples did some grave robbing and snatched the body of Jesus while the guards were asleep (Matt. 28:13). With a promise to make the whole mess all right with Pilate, their boss, the religious leaders send the soldiers packing. Matthew often has described the disciples of Jesus doing as Jesus told them. Now it is the soldiers who do "as they were directed" (Matt. 28:15).

The reason Matthew tells this story is probably to counter the rumor that was still around his own community that there was no truth to the resurrection story; that, in fact, the disciples just stole the body and made the whole thing up. "This story is still told among the Jews," he reports, "to this day" (Matt. 28:15). In addition to addressing the whispers, though, Matthew wants to show that the resurrection does not end opposition to God's will. As the church heads out on its mission of salvation, the world has its disciples of deceit who are just as committed to falsehood.

Appearance to the Disciples
in Galilee (Matthew 28:12–20)

The women evidently conveyed the message to the disciples, because they go to Galilee to meet Jesus, just as they were directed. The opening sentence of this account is full of import: "Now the eleven disciples went to Galilee, to the mountain to which Jesus had directed them" (Matt. 28:16). Abruptly Matthew's readers are hit with the realization that "the twelve" have become "the eleven." The treachery of Judas still hangs over the Easter community.

If the opening reference to "the eleven" carries some sadness, the closing note about "the mountain to which Jesus had directed them" conveys a surprise. What mountain does Jesus mean? In the appearances to the women outside the tomb, neither the angel nor Jesus ever mentioned a mountain in the instructions. But as soon as the reader ponders "What mountain?" the realization dawns that "the mountain to which Jesus had directed them" has more to do with theology than geography. Whatever may be said about the actual location of this mountain in Galilee, the disciples are at the mountain that has appeared time and again in the Gospel of Matthew: the mountain of revelation, the mountain of the Sermon on the Mount (Matt. 5:1), the mountain of prayer (Matt. 14:23), the mountain of feeding (Matt. 15:29), the mountain of transfiguration (Matt. 17:1). The disciples have met Jesus at a mountain where Jesus will speak new truth to them.

Before Jesus speaks, though, Matthew observes that the disciples "worshiped him; but some doubted" (Matt. 28:17). Just as the two women at the tomb were representative of the church's mixture of fear and great joy—joy over the good news of the resurrection and all that it means, and fear over the resurrection and all that it means—just so, the disciples are also the church in microcosm, worshiping and doubting, doubting and worshiping. "I believe in God, the Father almighty, creator of heaven and earth," but some days we believe more than others. "I believe in Jesus Christ, God's only Son, our Lord. . . . raised again from the dead." Moreover, "I believe in the risen Christ, who can be trusted to bring in the kingdom of mercy and peace, where every tear will be dried and death and pain will be no more"; but sometimes we wonder when and where and how. We worship, but some of us shift edgily in our pews forcing back the acid taste of doubt. This is the church. This was the church on that Easter mountain; this was Matthew's church; this is our church: fear and joy, worship and doubt.

Then Jesus speaks. The Son of Man, who only hours before chose to show his freedom from Pilate by remaining silent, now shows his authority by speaking with strength. The Son of Man, who hung in shame on the cross, derided by passersby, speaks, as he promised, "with power and great glory" (Matt. 24:30). "All authority in heaven and on earth has been given to me," he begins (Matt. 28:18). God has given to the servant all authority. The resurrection is God's validation of all that Jesus did and taught. Just as God revealed at the baptism and at the transfiguration, Jesus is God's Son with whom God is well pleased (Matt. 3:17; 17:5). God raised Jesus from the dead and has bestowed upon him all authority in heaven and on earth.

Notice that Jesus' authority is not local, but spans the heavens and the earth. Jesus was faithful to his task of being Israel's messiah, of caring for "the lost sheep of the house of Israel" (Matt. 15:24), but now, because of this faithfulness in the particular vocation, his authority is not confined to one place, one people, one nation. He is Lord of all nations, the ruler of all time and space.

When Jesus was tempted, the devil took Jesus up to a high mountain and promised him "all the kingdoms of the world and their splendor" (Matt. 4:8). It was a lie, of course; the kingdoms of the world did not belong to Satan, and they were not his to give. Now the disciples can see clearly what Jesus saw then. Now the disciples can see through the lies to the truth. Now Jesus, who remained faithful to God through the valley of the cross, stands on his own high mountain, possessing not just the glittering kingdoms of this world, which rise and fall and pass away, but all authority in heaven and on earth; all that endures in creation and beyond belongs to the risen Christ.

"Go . . . ," he tells the disciples. This is the same voice that said to Abraham, "Go from your country and your kindred and your father's house to the land that I will show you" (Gen. 12:1). This is the voice that said to Moses, "[Go,] I will send you to Pharaoh to bring my people, the Israelites, out of Egypt" (Exod. 3:10). This is the same voice that said to Isaiah in the temple, "Go and say to this people . . ." (Isa. 6:9). Now this voice, the voice of God, speaks through the risen Christ to the disciples to say, once again, "Go. . . ."

Where are they to go? Jesus sends them out to "make disciples of all nations" (Matt. 28:19). Long, long ago, when God told Abraham to "Go . . . ," God promised Abraham that "by your offspring shall all the nations of the earth gain blessing for themselves, because you have obeyed my voice" (Gen. 22:18). Now, that promise is being kept through Jesus, son of Abraham, Son of God. All the nations of the earth will be taught the gracious wisdom of the kingdom.

What are they to do when they go? First, they are to "make disciples of all nations." Notice that this is no hit-and-run evangelism. What the disciples are sent to do is not to hurl gospel leaflets into the wind or hold a rally in a stadium. They are called to the harder, less glamorous, more patient task of making disciples, of building Christian communities. A disciple is, of course, a student, and the task before the church is helping others to become good students of God's will. Jesus taught his disciples how to be "scribe[s] . . . trained for the kingdom of heaven" (Matt. 13:52), and now his disciples are to equip others with this kingdom training.

Jesus also tells his disciples to baptize the nations "in the name of the Father and of the Son and of the Holy Spirit" (Matt. 28:19). This baptismal formula is quite interesting because it is trinitarian, and evidently not all of the early Christian communities baptized in the name of the Trinity. At Pentecost, for example, Peter urged baptism only "in the name of Jesus Christ" (Acts 2:38). Where did the trinitarian formula come from on the lips of Jesus in Matthew? Most scholars think that Matthew's church had developed or adopted a "Father, Son, Holy Spirit" formula for their own baptismal liturgy, and that Matthew read back this feature of their worship into Jesus' words to the disciples.

But there is more meaning in the trinitarian formula than simply the fact that Matthew's church may have used these words in their own worship. In Matthew's time, the church had not yet worked out the sophisticated and logical doctrines of the Trinity; these were to come later in church history. For Matthew, "Father, Son, Holy Spirit" language was looser, more descriptive of the kind of intimate and loving relationships that existed among the Father, the Son, and the Spirit. Notice what happens at Jesus' own baptism (see comments on Matt. 3:13–17). There, the Spirit descends like a dove to light tenderly on Jesus, and God speaks a word of parental blessing, "This is my Son, the Beloved." This is no cold, mathematical Trinity; this is a divine *family*, full of gentleness and blessing. In baptism, we are brought into that family. To become Christian is not to be converted to an ideology; it is to be drawn into kinship with God and with all those who love God. To be baptized is to know that we are no longer slaves, but children of God (see Matt. 17:24–27).

Finally, the disciples are to teach the nations "to obey everything that I have commanded you" (Matt. 28:20). The church is to go out to the nations not as an army of occupation but as a humble tutor, teaching mercy and righteousness and forgiveness and peacemaking.

The task is staggering, and this "great commission" must have seemed ludicrous to the little band of disciples. After all, there were only eleven of them hearing these words on that mountain, and now they were being sent on a worldwide mission across perilous boundaries. These Jews would have to learn how to phrase the gospel in the thought patterns of Gentiles; these men would have to learn how to put out the welcome mat for women; these grown-ups would need to become humble like children; these Hebrew- and Aramaic-speakers would have to master the confusing polyglot of the nations.

Indeed, there was only one word that could have prevented them from collapsing in laughter or racing away in fear at the enormity of the mission, only one word that could have strengthened their resolve and sent them out to the vast and forbidding world carrying only the gospel, and that was the word Jesus spoke: "And remember, I am with you always, to the end of the age" (Matt. 28:20).

This parting, but enduring, word from the risen Christ is the heart of Matthew's whole gospel. As the church goes out with fear and joy, faith and doubt, devotion and dread to do the work of Christ, it is not promised success at every turn, a glad welcome in every heart, or even freedom from persecution and suffering. What the church is promised is that God in Christ will not abandon us but is present in the midst of the faithful—loving, encouraging, guiding, and giving hope. In the words of the old hymn:

> Though the cause of evil prosper,
> Yet 'tis truth alone is strong;
> Though her portion be the scaffold,
> And upon the throne be wrong,
> Yet that scaffold sways the future,
> And, behind the dim unknown,
> Standeth God within the shadow
> Keeping watch above His own.
>
> (James Russell Lowell,
> "Once to Every Man and Nation")

"And remember," said Jesus, "I am with you always . . ."

Works Cited

Brown, Raymond. *The Birth of the Messiah: A Commentary on the Infancy Narratives in Matthew and Luke.* Garden City, N.Y.: Doubleday, 1977.

————. *The Death of the Messiah: A Commentary on the Passion Narratives in the Four Gospels.* 2 vols. New York: Doubleday, 1994.

Bruner, Dale. *Matthew.* Vol. 1: *The Christbook, Matthew 1–12;* Vol. 2: *The Churchbook, Matthew 13–28.* Waco, Tex.: Word, 1987, 1990.

Buechner, Frederick. "The End Is Life." In *A Chorus of Witnesses: Model Sermons for Today's Preacher.* Edited by Thomas G. Long and Cornelius Plantinga Jr. Grand Rapids: Wm. B. Eerdmans Publishing Co., 1994.

————. *Wishful Thinking: A Theological ABC.* New York: Harper & Row, 1973.

Donahue, John R. *The Gospel in Parable: Metaphor, Narrative, and Theology in the Synoptic Gospels.* Philadelphia: Fortress Press, 1988.

Ford, David F. "What Happens in the Eucharist?" *Scottish Journal of Theology* 48, no. 3 (1995).

Foster, Richard J. *Celebration of Discipline: The Path to Spiritual Growth.* San Francisco: Harper & Row, 1988.

Garland, David E. *Reading Matthew.* New York: Crossroad, 1993.

Hare, Douglas R. A. *Matthew.* Interpretation. Louisville, Ky: Westminster/John Knox Press, 1993.

Luz, Ulrich. *The Theology of the Gospel of Matthew.* Cambridge, England: Cambridge University Press, 1993.

Malina, Bruce J., and Richard L. Rohrbaugh. *Social Science Commentary on the Synoptic Gospels.* Minneapolis: Fortress Press, 1992.

Meier, John P. *Matthew.* New Testament Message: A Biblical-Theological Commentary. Wilmington, Del.: Michael Glazier, 1980.

Patte, Daniel. *The Gospel According to Matthew: A Structural Commentary on Matthew's Faith*. Philadelphia: Fortress Press, 1987.

Senior, Donald. *The Passion of Jesus in Matthew*. Wilmington, Del.: Michael Glazier, 1985.

Wahlberg, Rachel Conrad. *Jesus According to a Woman*. New York: Paulist Press, 1975.

The hymn "A Mighty Fortress Is Our God" was written by Martin Luther and is found in *The Presbyterian Hynmal*, no. 260. Louisville, Ky.: Westminster/John Knox Press, 1990.

The hymn "Once to Every Man and Nation" was written by James Russell Lowell and is found in *The Hymnbook*, no. 361. Richmond, Va.: Presbyterian Church in the United States, 1955.

For Further Reading

Bainton, Roland. *Behold the Christ*. New York: Harper & Row, 1974.

Barth, Karl. *Church Dogmatics*. 4 vols. Edinburgh: T. & T. Clark, 1936–1962.

Beare, F. W. *The Gospel According to Matthew*. San Francisco: Harper & Row, 1981.

Boring, M. Eugene. *The Gospel of Matthew: Introduction, Commentary, and Reflections*, vol. 8. The New Interpreter's Bible. Nashville: Abingdon Press, 1995.

Caird, G. B. *The Language and Imagery of the Bible*. Philadelphia: Westminster Press, 1980.

Crosby, Michael. *House of Disciples: Church, Economics, and Justice in Matthew*. Maryknoll, N.Y.: Orbis Books, 1988.

Davies, Margaret. *Matthew*. Readings: A New Bible Commentary. Sheffield: JSOT Press, 1993.

Davies, W. D., and Dale C. Allison Jr. *A Critical and Exegetical Commentary on the Gospel According to St. Matthew*. 2 vols. Edinburgh: T. & T. Clark, 1988, 1991.

Dillard, Annie. *Holy the Firm*. New York: Harper & Row, 1977.

Fenton, J. C. *Saint Matthew*. The Pelican New Testament Commentaries. New York: Penguin Books, 1963.

Filson, Floyd. *A Commentary on the Gospel According to Matthew*. London: A. & C. Black, 1960.

Funk, F. X., ed. *Didascalia et Constitutiones Apostolorum*. Vol. 1. Torino: Bottega d'Erasmo, 1959.

Gundry, Robert H. *Matthew: A Commentary on His Literary and Theological Art*. Grand Rapids: Wm. B. Eerdmans Publishing Co., 1982.

Harrington, Daniel. *The Gospel of Matthew,* vol. 1. Sacra Pagina Series. Collegeville, Minn.: Liturgical Press, 1991.

Hill, David. *The Gospel of Matthew.* The New Century Bible Commentary. Grand Rapids: Wm. B. Eerdmans Publishing Co., 1972.

Kingsbury, Jack Dean. *Matthew.* Proclamation Commentaries. Philadelphia: Fortress Press, 1977.

———. *Matthew as Story.* Philadelphia: Fortress Press, 1986.

———. *Matthew: Structure, Christology, Kingdom.* Philadelphia: Fortress Press, 1975.

Lasch, Christopher. *The True and Only Heaven: Progress and Its Critics.* New York: W. W. Norton, 1991.

Luz, Ulrich. *Matthew: A Commentary,* vol. 1. Minneapolis: Augsburg Press, 1989.

Meier, John P. *The Vision of Matthew: Christ, Church, and Morality in the First Gospel.* New York: Crossroad, 1991.

Moltmann, Jürgen. *The Church in the Power of the Spirit: A Contribution to Messianic Ecclesiology.* New York: Harper & Row, 1977.

Morse, Christopher. *Not Every Spirit: A Dogmatics of Christian Disbelief.* Valley Forge, Pa.: Trinity Press International, 1994.

Overman, J. Andrew. *Matthew's Gospel and Formative Judaism: The Social World of the Matthean Community.* Minneapolis: Fortress Press, 1990.

Schweizer, Eduard. *The Good News According to Matthew.* Atlanta: John Knox Press, 1975.

Senior, Donald. *What Are They Saying about Matthew?* New York: Paulist Press, 1983.

Stanton, Graham. *A Gospel for a New People: Studies in Matthew.* Louisville, Ky: Westminster/John Knox Press, 1993.

———, ed. *The Interpretation of Matthew.* Philadelphia: Fortress Press, 1983.

Tannehill, Robert C. *The Sword of His Mouth.* Philadelphia and Missoula, Mont.: Fortress Press and Scholars Press, 1975.

Villa-Vicencio, Charles. *A Theology of Reconstruction.* Cambridge, England: Cambridge University Press, 1992.